Queen of Spies

QUEEN OF SPIES

*Daphne Park,
Britain's Cold War Spy Master*

Paddy Hayes

This edition first published in hardcover in the United States and the United Kingdom in 2016 by Overlook Duckworth, Peter Mayer Publishers, Inc.

NEW YORK
141 Wooster Street
New York, NY 10012
www.overlookpress.com
For bulk and special sales please contact sales@overlookny.com,
or to write us at the above address.

LONDON
30 Calvin Street
London E1 6NW
www.ducknet.co.uk
For bulk and special sales please contact sales@duckworth-publishers.co.uk,
or write to us at the above address.

© 2015 by Paddy Hayes

Library of Congress Cataloging-in-Publication Data
Names: Hayes, Paddy, 1946- author.
Title: Queen of spies : Daphne Park, Britain's Cold War spy master / Paddy
Hayes.
Description: New York, NY : The Overlook Press, 2016. | Includes
bibliographical references and index.
Identifiers: LCCN 2015039895 | ISBN 9781468312683 (US) | ISBN 9780715650431 (UK)
Subjects: LCSH: Park of Monmouth, Daphne Margaret Sybil Dâesirâee Park,
Baroness, 1921-2010. | Women spies--Great Britain--Biography. |
Espionage,
British--History--20th century. | Spies--Great Britain--Biography. |
Great Britain. MI6--Biography.
Classification: LCC UB271.G72 H394 2016 | DDC 327.12410092--dc23
LC record available at http://lccn.loc.gov/2015039895
A catalogue record for this book is available from the British Library

Manufactured in the United States of America

ISBN: 978-1-4683-1268-3 (US)
ISBN: 978-0-7156-5043-1 (UK)

2 4 6 8 10 9 7 5 3 1

Contents

Contents

List of Illustrations

1. Daphne Park shortly after she arrived in Britain in 1932
2. Daphne Park around the time she graduated from Somerville College in 1943
3. Daphne Park in FANY *c.* 1943
4. Sir Stewart Menzies, Chief of SIS 1939-52
5. Commander Kenneth Cohen, Chief Controller/Europe, SIS
6. Dame Professor Lisa Hall, first head of the Joint Services School for Linguistics in Cambridge
7. Sir William Goodenough Hayter, British ambassador to Moscow, 1953-57
8. Douglas DeWitt Bazata, Park's first lover
9. Bazata with Princess Grace of Monaco
10. Patrice Lumumba, first Prime Minister of the independent Congo
11. Ian Scott, British Ambassador to the Congo, with General Mobutu
12. Daphne Park and SIS colleague Hugo Herbert-Jones
13. Daphne Park in grounds of house
14. Daphne Park seated
15. John Bruce Lockhart, SIS
16. Daphne Park in Lusaka, the spy in action with customary drink in hand
17. The Grand Kremlin Palace from the roof of the British Embassy
18. Broadway Buildings (today), home of SIS from the mid-1920s to the 1960s
19. Century House ('Gloom Hall'), SIS's headquarters from 1964 to 1994
20. The joint SIS/CIA team responsible for handling Oleg Penkovsky
21. GRU Colonel Oleg Vladimirovich Penkovsky, agent HERO
22. Typical street scene in Hanoi *c.* 1980
23. Spy Station Ulaanbaatar
24. Baroness Daphne Margaret Sybil Desirée Park

This book is dedicated to the memory of
The 'Major', Commandant Paddy Keogh
(1949-2014)
'Take the Hill.'

Introduction

In the following pages you will be introduced to the life story of an extraordinary woman, the British Cold War spy Daphne Park. Her story would be outstanding in any era, but in the context of the times she lived through it is almost beyond imagining. Born into penury in 1921, Daphne Park went from living in a tin-roofed shack five hundred miles up-country from Dar-es-Salaam to becoming, in 1990, Baroness Park of Monmouth. She went from being semi-literate, studying on a plank balanced on two empty kerosene cans, to graduating from Oxford University with an honours degree and being invited back thirty-seven years later to become the Principal of her Oxford college. She went from humble wartime volunteer in 1943 to Area Controller of the Secret Intelligence Service (SIS/MI6) in 1975.

To achieve any of the three would seem like a life fulfilled, ambition satisfied. But to achieve all three speaks of ability, inner strength, determination and certainty of purpose. When so much of her life took place against the backdrop of the Cold War and of Britain's slow and often painful disengagement from Empire, it makes for a compelling story, a life well worth the telling.

This is the first biography of a Cold War SIS career officer in thirty years and one of only two or three ever published (books on the betrayers, Philby, Blake etc., excluded).[1] That is testimony, not to any lack of reader interest, but to SIS's determination to keep secret what happens within its portals. Current and former members are warned in the sternest terms of their lifetime duty in this regard. Those who ignore the rule face sanctions ranging from exclusion from the SIS 'family' at the lower end of the scale to the loss of pension rights and possible prosecution under the Official Secrets Acts at the higher end. Fortunately, for you the reader (and for me the writer) not all chose to obey that stricture. The score or so SIS officers who cooperated with me in the writing of *Queen of Spies* did so because they agreed with a former SIS Chief, who on being apprised of my intention to write Daphne's biography remarked, 'Good, Daphne deserves a decent book.' Hers is a story that the Chief felt should be told and that I and my co-operators believe can be told without causing irreparable harm to the current and future operations of Britain's intelligence services. I am deeply grateful to those who shared their experiences of Daphne and of SIS with me. You made the book possible.

Like any spy writer I relish any opportunity to reveal secrets, to bring hitherto undisclosed intelligence operations into the light of day, to identity practitioners of the dark arts of espionage, to reveal the tricks of the trade. I am also conscious that with the right to publish goes an obligation of responsibility. No serving SIS officers are personally identifiable through these pages and those former officers who are named (and who are still living) are long since retired and well out of the game. Of course another reason why any bureaucracy likes to operate in secrecy is because that way its mistakes remain 'in house' and do not become subject to public scrutiny. SIS is no different in that regard and readers will find some of what is revealed in these pages makes for uncomfortable reading.

I met Daphne Park following an interview she gave to the BBC's *Panorama* television programme as part of the intelligence agencies' process of 'coming out' (avowal) following the end of the Cold War, whereby for the first time both the Secret Intelligence Service (SIS/MI6) and the Security Service (MI5) were established by statute. I was of course well aware of Park, for she had managed, despite her devotion to secrecy, to become known within circles as an intelligence operative following her involvement in the overthrow of the Lumumba regime in the then newly independent former Belgian Congo.

Through a family friend and fellow peer (Lord Geoffrey Tordoff) I sent Daphne Park a message requesting a meeting. She replied through Tordoff agreeing to my request though stipulating that she would not discuss 'operational matters'. I was happy to go along with that, delighted with the opportunity to meet one of Britain's great spies face to face. We met in the House of Lords on one glorious summer day for afternoon tea. We did not discuss 'operational matters', but neither did we restrict our conversation to the weather and England's prospects in the Test series.

Daphne Park was every bit as interesting as I had hoped. Quite tough, I thought, uncompromising, particularly in her attitude towards the Russians, and quite vocal in decrying what she viewed as John Le Carré's skewed descriptions of life within SIS. Though, as you will read in the following pages, she was in her own SIS career to become a victim of some internecine machinations every bit as labyrinthine as anything dreamt up by Le Carré.

The main narrative focuses on Park's lifelong love affair with the secret world that commenced with her entry into the Special Operations Executive (SOE) in 1943 and lasted until her retirement from SIS thirty-six years later in 1979. Her service in London, Algiers, Vienna, Paris, Moscow, Léopoldville, Lusaka, Hanoi and Ulaanbaatar, her two love affairs, her coups, her life explored as far as the secret world will permit. The words are her own, those of friends, of admiring colleagues and of some not so admiring, of former students, of lifelong friends. She reached SIS's most senior operational rank as one of its seven Area Controllers; as one former holder of the office commented, 'We were the princes – or in Daphne's case the princesses – what we wanted we got.'

The biography also tells of her time in Somerville College as its Principal and her unhappiness while she was there, and concludes with her elevation to the House of Lords in 1990.

But this is also the story of SIS from the end of the Second World War to the end of Empire and the icy tensions of the Cold War. This parallel narrative describes how the Service enjoyed almost pariah-like status in Whitehall after the appalling intelligence debacles of the 1950s and the treachery of two of its most well regarded officers, George Blake and Kim Philby. How it set about introducing new blood and reorganising and codifying its practices as it faced its most dangerous enemy, the Soviet Union's KGB. In the words of one officer, 'Where the KGB was we were and where it was not, we needed a bloody good reason to be.' In passages that come directly from the mouths of some of its most experienced officers, it talks of how SIS cast off the old ways to become the successful, streamlined, driven 'mechanism of state' that it is today.

It is my wish that *Daphne Park, Queen of Spies* will provide you with the most intimate picture yet of how Britain's foreign intelligence service goes about its business. I hope too that you will learn something about the sort of people who spy for Britain, how they see the world, what motivates them to behave as they do. And of course I want you to learn about one spy in particular, about Daphne Park.

Paddy Hayes
Dublin

Author's Note

Acronyms

The secret world is an alphabet soup of initials that are impossible to avoid when writing about it. Throughout the text when an organisation is referred to for the first time its name is provided in full, together with a brief explanation of its purpose unless otherwise already known, thereafter by its initials. This a list of some of the terms that feature most frequently.

ACSS: Assistant Chief [of the] Secret Service (Assistant Chief of Secret Intelligence Service/SIS).

CIA: Central Intelligence Agency, the United States overseas intelligence agency, referred to in the text as either the CIA or 'the Agency'.

Clubs: London's gentlemen's clubs have long been associated with Britain's intelligence services; in fact many of the meetings this author had with former members of the Secret Intelligence Service took place in one. The four clubs most associated with SIS are Brooks's, White's, the Reform and the Travellers, while a fifth, the Special Forces Club (SFC), is home to a broader mix of (mainly) former special forces operatives, specialist police and intelligence officers from Britain and its allies. Daphne Park was a member of the SFC up to her death.

Collaborators: Intelligence services maintain a variety of relationships. Some of the most useful will be described as 'people who choose to collaborate with us'. Such collaborators are not agents in the conventional sense, and while money may well change hands collaborators do not take orders or carry out instructions in the way an agent would be expected to. In this text Minister of the Interor, Damien Kandolo and Head of the Sûreté, Victor Nendaka (Congo 1960), could best be described as collaborators (for Park and the CIA's Larry Devlin respectively) rather than registered agents, though the distinction can be thin at times.

FANY: The First Aid Nursing Yeomanry, a uniformed auxiliary service for women which provided support services for the regular armed forces. In the Second World War FANY was also used as a cover organisation for women who joined the Special Operations Executive (SOE) to be employed as radio operators, coders and decoders and in similar roles. More than forty members of FANY/SOE (of a number of different nationalities) became clandestine secret agents and were inserted into enemy territory. They were the only British servicewomen to bear arms in the Second World War.

FBI: Federal Bureau of Investigation, referred to as the FBI or 'the Bureau'.

FIAT-BIOS: Field Intelligence Agency/Technical – British Intelligence Objectives Subcommittee, the British end of an agency established by the Allied High Command in 1944 in order to ensure that when the war had ended the Allied nations would be able to make maximum use of the advanced technologies developed by Nazi Germany.

GCHQ: Government Communications Headquarters, Britain's electronic eavesdropping agency.

GRU: Main Intelligence Directorate, the Red Army's Military Intelligence arm, which was very active in overseas intelligence acquisition.

Intelligence officer: An employee of a governmental intelligence service such as the SIS, CIA or KGB, e.g. Daphne Park. Intelligence officers are the real spies (though many dislike the term because of its connotations). Most will spend about a third of their careers on overseas postings, often based in their country's embassies where they will adopt the pose of conventional diplomats. While in post they will handle the existing agents, look out for opportunities to recruit new sources and seek to identify targets for technical attack (i.e. places where they can plant listening devices and the like).

Intelligence agent (also source or asset): A person who betrays his (and they are mainly men) employer, country or cause by passing over secret information to the intelligence service of another. The terms 'betray' and 'betrayer' tend to be preferred to describe the activities of an agent, rather than value-laden words such as 'traitor' and 'treason', because what all such agents invariably do is to *betray* the organisations and countries that employ them. Some observers might consider a particular act of betrayal to be a noble one, others might consider it to be a squalid act, mostly depending on the observer's perspective.

Jedburghs (Jeds): Teams of three soldiers trained to special forces standards whose role was to parachute behind enemy lines immediately ahead of an invasion by Allied forces. Once on the ground they would coordinate and direct resistance activities by indigenous forces. The initial deployment of the Jedburghs was in support of D-Day in June 1944, though on a reduced scale from that originally envisaged.

Joint Intelligence Committee/JIC: Usually referred to as the JIC, the Joint Intelligence Committee is Britain's coordinating body for processing and analysing secret intelligence. The JIC produces the annual National Intelligence Requirements Paper (NIRP), the document that sets out Britain's intelligence priorities which are then translated into action plans by the various agencies. Its membership comprises the heads of the intelligence agencies, both civilian and military, representatives of the Foreign and Home Offices and assorted others. The JIC was originally a creature of the military, under the control of the chiefs of the imperial staff (CIGS). In 1957 it was brought under the remit of the Foreign Office, reflecting the post-war policy of civilianising the control of the principal intelligence services. In 1968 in was brought under the wing of the Cabinet Office where it remains, as part of the Joint Intelligence Organisation, now very much a creature of No 10 Downing Street.

KGB: Committee for State Security, the principal security organ of the Soviet Union and responsible for both internal and external security and intelligence collection, referred to by its personnel as 'State Security'.

MI5: The Security Service, also known as MI5, monitors threats to Britain's wellbeing from within Britain's borders, though the origin of the threat may well lie outside Britain.

Natural cover (also non-official cover/NOC, also illegals): An intelligence officer who operates outside the confines of his/her country's embassy. Such officers do not enjoy diplomat protection so if caught can face extended terms of imprisonment and even death. CIA officer Howard Imbrey, who features in this book, served as a NOC officer in the Belgian Congo before and after its independence.

SIS: The Secret Intelligence Service, also known as SIS and MI6, focuses on intelligence gathering from overseas. Where initials are used the organisation is referred to in the text as SIS. Within SIS its current and past members usually refer to it as either 'the Office' or 'the Service', depending on context, and those terms are used in the text as appropriate.

SOE: Special Operations Executive, a paramilitary organisation established on Prime Minister Winston Churchill's direct instructions in order to carry out acts of war against Nazi personnel and installations in territories occupied by Hitler's Germany.

VCSS: Vice-Chief [of the] Secret Service (Vice-Chief of the Secret Intelligence Service).

Visiting case officer (VCO): An intelligence officer who is sent to a country to carry out a specific assignment. A VCO may be used to handle a meeting with an agent in a hard-target country where the embassy-based officers are under such intensive surveillance that they cannot risk meeting the agent in person. Alternatively a VCO may be used to handle the recruitment of a potential agent thus not exposing the resident officers to the source. The late Robert Church was a successful VCO for SIS where he operated in South America. Larry Devlin, Park's CIA opposite number in Léopoldville, commenced his CIA career as an undercover VCO using as cover his employment as a travel editor with Fodor's.

Notes on Sources

These notes, indicated by arabic numbers in the text, appear at the end of the book and are included in order to support specific references and to provide further information for the interested reader on issues that are tangential to the main story.

Footnotes

Footnotes are used to provide biographical details of the key personalities featured in the text. The convention of not providing footnotes for established historical figures (former Prime Ministers etc.) is followed other than in a couple of instances where it is felt a brief biographical note would add clarity for the reader. Where former members of SIS are footnoted the reference includes – where known – details of their overseas postings and some London-based appointments. For example:

LUNN, Peter Northcote, CMG, OBE; Royal Artillery, SIS, H/VIENNA, H/BERNE, H/BERLIN, H/BONN, H/BEIRUT (1914-2011).

H/ stands for 'Head of', thus H/VIENNA indicates that the subject was head of Vienna station. The letter C/ stands for controller (the most senior operational rank in SIS) or controllerate (a controller's domain) (e.g. C/EUROPE). The letter D stands for director or directorate (e.g. D/Science & Technology). The letter 'd.' in the span of dates at the end of each entry (1943-d.) indicates that the person is deceased but that the date of death is not available; (1943-) indicates that as far as the author is aware the person is still living. In some cases these dates are unknown. A word of warning: SIS is a secret organisation so the details of appointments held by its personnel must of necessity be subject to correction and may be incomplete.

Prologue:
Moscow, April 1956

The last snows of winter still cloaked the city's jagged streetscape in a deceiving blanket of white ice crystals and the fading light also cloaked the mass of people, blurring their silhouettes, removing their separateness. But spring, though heralded, remained a reluctant bride, the biting wind whistling through the narrow Moscow street testified to that, tugging viciously at Park's clothes, turning her eyes to water. She wondered at the nature of a people who so avowedly loved their winter, praying she was one of them now, invisible, as she trudged on, shoulders hunched, her chin sunk deep into her chest but watching, always watching.

It was three hours since Park had left the embassy, grinding hours making certain she was in the clear, praying that the plan was holding. The plan! One day, when she was still settling into her role as the deep-cover officer in the Moscow station, she'd noticed something odd; it happened shortly after she'd left with Morgan, another first-timer but unlike her, a respectable diplomat. The embassy fixer, the Pole Mikhailsky, who was forever currying favour, had said that an antique shop in Stoleshnikov Pereluok near Gorky Street had some nice pieces. Despite herself she was interested and Morgan had offered to accompany her for a quick recce. Half-way there Morgan had excused himself, suddenly remembering some errand or other he had to run; the man had a head like a sieve. After a quick confab, the KGB thugs, who made no effort to disguise their presence, apparently decided to stick with following Morgan and abandoned their surveillance of her.

A few days later the same thing occurred when another colleague, Barklamb, one of the radio snoopers, left her company to go his separate way; once again the watchers wheeled off to follow him, leaving her unwatched. She decided to run a proper test, to establish if it was a pattern, predictable, exploitable. Over a few weeks she tested, careful, cautious as a cat in a city of dogs. But it looked as if she was right: each time she left the embassy accompanied by one of the men and they later split up, the watchers concentrated solely on the man, leaving her by herself, in the clear. The obvious explanation, the only one that made sense, was that the watchers assumed that the man, being a male, had to be the important one and therefore their target. Whatever the Russians knew about Morgan, they would know for certain that Barklamb did not outrank her, so this oversight had to be a gender thing; being a woman she must be 'just' a lowly clerk and not worth following in her own right. There and then she'd decided she would turn that stupid assumption to her advantage.

Now she was putting the plan into effect: no longer an exercise, it was now an operation and she was praying to the high heavens that it would work. For her decoy she had recruited the assistant air-attaché, who was sharp as a tack. The two of them had left the chancery at 10.30 and called in to the French to attend a mid-morning briefing with some visiting NATO fireman from Paris. When they left the French chancery, they separated. The attaché off on his own being tailed presumably. She'd told him not to return to the embassy until after the time of her scheduled meet with GIDEON. She'd not said anything more but he was probably canny enough to guess.

GIDEON: even the thought of meeting him made her suck in her breath, a live source inside the Soviet Union, a KGB illegal turned SIS agent; now her responsibility. Soon it would be dark but there should be just enough light cast by the meagre streetlights to make out his features. Lord, what would she do if she could not recognise him? All she had to go on was his photograph, safely back in her office; she conjured up his image, concentrating.

But she was tired, tired from the tension, tired from tramping the Moscow streets, from trailing around the giant GUM store near Red Square with its acres of empty shelves unless you counted the propaganda posters, then south to the Tretyakovsky Art Gallery, more tramping, staring glassy-eyed at the paintings, seeing nothing but straining to detect any eyes focused not on the fabulous pictures but on her. Nothing. She left the gallery taking the metro which was crammed solid with ill-tempered smelly Muscovites. She exited at Sokolniki station, all the time checking to be certain that this time the KGB hadn't altered their procedures and that they weren't sidling along behind her in the shadows, waiting to pounce.

She had used the toilets in the Tretyakovsky to change out of her topcoat, stuffing it into her carry-bag, swapping it for a heavy wadded jacket and head scarf, semi-clandestine behaviour that would be hard to explain away if she was questioned ... she prayed not, but she had to be invisible on the streets, be just another sullen Moscow housewife in shawl, winter jacket and sturdy boots, just-in-case bag in hand, heading back home to her family to make supper.

Over and over in her mind she rehearsed her lines; if questioned she had to have a valid reason for being here, something the authorities would believe. She had diplomatic protection but GIDEON didn't. At all costs she must not do anything that could betray him, cause suspicion even. The source must be protected, at any cost – how that had been hammered into her! Lord, if she did something stupid and he was blown she'd never forgive herself ...

1

From Kayuki to Clapham, 1921-32

To understand Daphne Park we must understand her origins. In 1932 the eleven-year-old was living in the Kayuki Estate in Tukuyu, five hundred miles up-country from Dar-es-Salaam in the British Protectorate of Tanganyika. Hers was the hardscrabble existence of a young girl in a dirt-poor white colonial family, as far from pink gins and *White Mischief* as Tukuyu was from Torquay. Then overnight her life changed, completely, utterly and absolutely. Park was told she was to leave the Kayuki Estate, leave Tanganyika, leave her family behind, and go to live with her two aged great-aunts (or grand-aunts) in London and attend proper school, be educated.

Daphne Park might have been only eleven, but she was smart. When the initial excitement and anticipation had subsided and she had the chance to reflect, the young girl realised that for her nothing would ever be the same. She knew too it would be a long time before she would again hug her mother or play with her younger brother David. She would miss David of course, how could it have been otherwise? Would she have gone at all if she had known that within seven years he would be dead at fourteen? She probably would have because she was tough, but his loss would score another indelible mark on her, made rawer by her failure ever to find his unmarked grave. Her father she wouldn't miss so much perhaps; he was away most of the time anyway, panning for minute specks of gold on the Lupa River which he found in equally minute quantities. Nor would she miss living in a tin-roofed shack without electric light or running water. Or filling the porcelain bath by hand, or holding on for dawn's early light to avoid having to pick her way to the privy in the dark, eyes wide-peeled for furry spiders as big as her fist.

There were things, though, that she did enjoy: the freedom, the feel of the hot African sun on her back, the comforting beat of the drums throbbing through the dark nights, the throaty cough of the prowling lioness, the love call of the hyena, the sudden, heart-stopping, cut-off screech of a terrified animal caught in the jaws of its prey. The hustle and bustle of London, the constant hum of Clapham traffic, the warning horns and clackety-clack of the trains would not compare, but they would have to do because she had made her bed and not once in the seventy-seven years that were left to her would she not lie on it. For Daphne Park there were never any second thoughts.

They said she took after her mother in all really important aspects, the dedication – in her mother's case to her daughter's wellbeing and education – the determination to see things through and above all to endure. But her father gave her gifts too: he bequeathed her his charm, his brains, his honourable ways and maybe some of that inimitable Belfast grit too.

Those first eleven years of her life both formed her and left their indelible mark on her character. Everything she later achieved can be traced back to that early upbringing in Africa. Everything measured in distance travelled from or since. Everything couched with the question: what if the letter to her mother had never been written?

How Daphne's father, John Alexander Park,[i] came to be panning for gold in East Africa is as short a story as it is sad. When he had obtained his degree from Queen's he left Belfast as the nineteenth century gradually gave way to the twentieth. He had a few pounds of his parents' money in his pocket, but he wasn't so much seeking his fortune as warmer and drier climes. John Park did not have a farming background nor, as it was to turn out, had he a particular head for business. Had he stayed in Belfast he would probably have followed his father into Queen's and perhaps been appointed to a Chair. But his tuberculosis saw to that, so warmer climes it had to be, his parents paying for the passage to Beira in Mozambique. When he first arrived in Africa he quickly ran through their seed money. He then tried a number of jobs, including working underground in a mine (not something that made much sense for a TB sufferer, his daughter was to remark acerbically seventy-five years later when she recounted the story) before making the long trek to Nyasaland where he rented a tobacco plantation. TB or not, when the First World War broke out John Park answered duty's call and enlisted in the Nyasaland Frontier Force, being wounded in the quite bloody four-year campaign in German East Africa. It was in 1918, while recovering from his wounds, that he and Daphne's mother, Doreen,[ii] met.

In fact it was Daphne's grandmother (Anne)[iii] he was due to meet, through a pen-friendship established to pass the time while he was convalescing. We don't know why, but Anne brought along her daughter, Doreen, to that initial meeting, a daughter who was nineteen and beautiful and who won John Park's heart. Whether the mother had been prospecting on her own account or on her daughter's we don't know either; there is some suggestion that Anne was widowed by that time. Within six months Doreen and John had married, despite John being forty-four to his bride's nineteen, not as unusual then as now. After the wedding, the pair returned to John Park's rented tobacco farm. Three years

i PARK, John Alexander (1876-1952).
ii PARK, *née* Cresswell-George, Doreen Gwyneth (1899-1982).
iii CRESSWELL-GEORGE, *née* Hammon, Temperance Emma Anne (1870-d.).

later, in July 1921, he and his pregnant wife set sail for England for her to give birth to their first child, christened Daphne Sybil Margaret Désirée. D.S.M.D. Park had arrived in this world.

They spent nine months in Britain; time enough for John Park to show off his beautiful bride and baby daughter to his mother in Belfast, his father having passed away, and for Doreen to do likewise to her extended family in Wales. On 13 April 1922, mother, father and baby Daphne embarked on the *SS Goorkha* bound for Beira in Portuguese Mozambique.[1] It was time for the family to return home.

When they arrived at the farm about a month later they were in for a terrible shock. Park's business partner, a defrocked Portuguese priest about whom he had earlier been warned (a warning he had foolishly ignored), had made off with all he could from the partnership, not only that but the bumper tobacco crop was ruined and the insurance premiums were unpaid. Everything John Park had striven for was gone. He was ruined, but being an honourable man he used what little money he had left to pay off those he owed before giving thought to his own situation. Doreen Park's brother (Daphne's uncle) Estcourt Vernon Herbert Cresswell-George[i] had heard rumours about gold being found in the Lupa River, close to the town of Mbeya in nearby Tanganyika (German East Africa no longer, thanks to the wartime efforts of John and his comrades). He had gone there and John and Doreen Park decided to follow him.[2] They would be joined by hundreds more, mainly British naturally, all desperate for a chance to stake their claim and make their fortune, including, in time, Doreen Park's other brother, James Richard Cresswell-George.[ii] All would head for the Lupa, on foot, on bicycles, motor bikes and even donkeys. Most would barely scrape a living. Doreen Park would be the first European woman to live there, raising baby Daphne in a mud hut without running water, inside sanitation or electric light. And, given that a gold rush was taking place, it was a pretty insalubrious place to be raising a young baby. Doreen's brother James seemed to have been particularly affected, complaining continually about the licentious, alcohol-fuelled behaviour of the prospectors, and eventually returning to live in England in disgust where he would continue his campaign of disapproval.[3] After three years Doreen Park became pregnant again and she and the young Daphne returned to England where she gave birth to Daphne's younger brother, David, a sickly child.[iii]

When the enlarged family returned to the Lupa, Doreen Park put her foot down and demanded something better and more permanent in which to rear

i CRESSWELL-GEORGE, Estcourt Vernon Herbert; later Lieutenant Colonel, King's African Rifles (1902-1981).

ii CRESSWELL-GEORGE, James Richard (1898-d.).

iii PARK, David John Cresswell (1925-1939).

her brood. It was agreed that the mother and two children would move to the highlands, where Doreen would lease a small coffee *vihamba* (farm) that she would work. With great excitement the family moved into their new home in the Kayuki Estate in the townland of Tukuyu, in one of the three main coffee growing areas of Tanganyika. It was quite isolated – a ten-day round journey on foot from where her father had his claim, and a day's walk to the nearest fellow Briton, probably her uncle Estcourt. That said, the family's new home was an improvement. It was built from proper mud-bricks with a corrugated-iron roof and had proper headroom, though the drumming sound of the rain on the roof during the wet season was deafening. It still had no electricity, no running water and no inside sanitation, but it did have a porcelain bath, even if it had to be filled by hand. Smoky kerosene lamps provided the only source of light after darkness had fallen, but the hut did boast a nice rubberoid floor covering, something that separated it from those of the natives.

Daphne's next seven years were spent on the farm, and it is probably fair to say that if 'the son is father to the man' then, then in this case at least, 'the daughter was mother to the woman'. How her mother Doreen coped with it all one can only imagine. Bereft of adult company for most of the year, she had to fill the role of both parents, rearing her two children single-handedly. On top of that she had to cook the supplies (a couple of weeks at a time) for her husband and his native labourers *and* manage her own coffee plot with its essential cash crop. She would have had some help, probably a native maid working for little more than food and board and a couple of labourers for the farm. Apart from that she was on her own without even a radio or gramophone to help pass the time. In later life she was described as being 'quite hard' and with little of her daughter's charm; small wonder.[4] For Daphne life meant growing up without any friends, her main stimulation being the books sent by her grandfather's family living back home in Britain and the correspondence course run from Dar-es-Salaam by the Anglican church.

That was to be her saviour. The colonial population of Tanganyika was small and thinly spread and without the critical mass to afford any structured educational facilities. When George Chambers[i] took up his post as the first Anglican archbishop of Tanganyika, he was determined to address that issue and so established a correspondence school. In time it became the Arusha School, which exists to this day.[5] The school was administered by his daughter Mary. Lessons were sent from Dar-es-Salaam to its far-flung pupils by a combination of lorry and train. In Daphne's case the distance was about five hundred miles, with the last part delivered by a runner who had to ford a river to complete the delivery. Sometimes lessons arrived wet if the runner was careless while fording. Park and

i CHAMBERS, George Alexander (1877-1963).

her brother did their prescribed exercises and submitted their homework using the same means.

It is not hard to imagine the sense of utter astonishment that Daphne must have experienced when out of the blue her mother received a letter from Mary Chambers saying that her daughter was far too clever to complete her schooling in this 'remote village in an outpost of the Empire'. What was needed was for her to be sent to a proper school, one in England ideally, since there was as yet none suitable in Tanganyika. Astonishment must have turned to barely dared-for hope as her mother wrote to her aunts[i] (Daphne's great-aunts), two of whom were now living in London, and asked if it would be possible for her daughter to go to live with them and attend school.

Waiting for the response must have been almost unbearable for the young girl. Would, after all, the opportunity be snatched away from her? And then that most magic, unforgettable of days as she read with trembling hands how her great-aunts, Mary Elizabeth and Emily Clara, would be *delighted* to *welcome* their great-niece Daphne to London, furthermore that a fine school, quite convenient to where they lived, would be pleased to enrol her as a pupil.

Though it must have broken her heart, Doreen Park decided to put her daughter's welfare ahead of her own, and she wasn't the first mother to do that. But her decision was more layered even than that; very many women (as well as men) were not then in favour of education for girls, seeing it as unnecessary and wasteful. Such education as many girls did receive was focused on 'the three Rs', reading, writing and arithmetic, with the privileged few being tutored in social skills, etiquette, and perhaps a foreign language, most often French. Proper education was the preserve of those who would later require it for navigating the grown-up worlds of diplomacy and commerce and public life; young gentlemen, in other words.

But Doreen Park was not of that ilk; she wanted her Daphne to have what she herself had not. She wrote back to say she accepted the offer and would send Daphne off to live in London. With that unselfish gesture she altered her daughter's life prospects beyond measure. And while Daphne must have been on the verge of ecstasy over her change of fortune, that change would not be without its consequences. Her departure from Kayuki Estate would disrupt that most intimate of bonds, the one between mother and daughter. This rupture she would take into adult life, Daphne being described to the author as a 'dutiful' daughter – and dutiful she was in abundance – but not necessarily as a loving one.[6] The immediate concern was financial: the money for the journey had to be found, and that meant jewellery pawned, savings emptied. Daphne, it was

---

i Mary Elizabeth Jane TREMBETH, *née* George; Mary Anne Josephine DUINS-COOKE, *née* George, Emily Clara Josephine GEORGE, all of Trefynwy, Monmouthshire, Wales (dates unknown) (source: https://histfam.familysearch.org//getperson.php?personID=176702&tree=Welsh).

decided, would sail to Southampton from Dar-es-Salaam. Family friends who were making the same journey would keep an eye on her while on board.

The first part of the journey was to Dar (as the city was called). The only way was to cadge a lift on the metalled road that led the five hundred miles to the city. It was quite well travelled so hitching the lift would not present a problem, particularly for a young colonial. Getting to the road was difficult, though, the distance being about thirty miles. There was no means of transport, so walking it was the only practical solution; this would take three days, but there was nothing for it. One of the more reliable native labourers would have been detailed to act as her guide, carry her case and generally look out for her.

Early in 1932 Daphne Park left her home in Kayuki Estate for the last time, leaving behind her parents, her young brother David and her young cousin Michael,[i] the firstborn of what would in time become her African-based family,[7] with whom she would remain connected for the rest of her life. After three days she reached the nearest road, tired but triumphant. Soon she was picked up by a trader who was heading to Dar to replenish his supplies. The journey to the coast was without incident other than an encounter with her first locust swarm. It was unlike anything she had ever experienced, even dreamed of. They wound the windows up as tightly as they could and stuffed the air vents with rags, but still the insects got in to the cabin, into her clothes, her hair, everywhere. Then, almost like a mirage out of the distance, came her first sight of the metropolis. She had of course seen illustrations of the city and of places further afield, but nothing could have prepared her for the real thing. The tall buildings; the streets crammed with people, everyone seemingly in a great rush; the traffic – cars, lorries, horse-drawn carts and pushcarts – the noise must have been frightening. The trader dropped her off close to the hotel where her parents' friends were booked in, awaiting the departure of the steamer.

An hour later she was learning how to flush a toilet, switch on a light and turn off a tap. Two days later she stood on the rail of her ship watching the coastline of Africa slide from sight over the purple horizon. London must have seemed a long way away and so, increasingly, must Kayuki.[8]

i CRESSWELL-GEORGE, Michael Croft (born 13 August 1930 in Tukuyu).

2

Born now bred, 1932-43

On arrival in England in 1932, the young Daphne moved in with her great-aunts in Clapham. One (Mary Elizabeth Trembeth) was married with children; the other, whose engagement had been broken (probably Emily Clara Josephine), played the role of companion, a job for which she was neither trained nor suited.[1] They do not appear to have had much money at all, not a new situation for the young girl. As Daphne Helsby (*née* Whittle) a school-friend of the time later recalled:

> Her poverty was only too evident in her school dress. While the rest of us were smart in our neatly-pleated outfits, made of good woollen stuff, Daphne wore a gymslip which must have seen many owners, was a faded mauve and worn so thin that it would not hold a pleat and fell in shapeless folds. Her personality was such, however, that we soon ceased to notice.[2]

Britain in the 1930s was a world where order prevailed and people knew their place. Where the King was still the King and Empire reigned supreme with almost a quarter of the globe still coloured pink on the maps that adorned every schoolroom wall. Little of the wealth generated by the Empire may have 'trickled down' into the pockets of ordinary men and women, but the mere fact of its existence contributed to a palpable sense of pride and place. To be British was best, everyone knew that, but to be English (*whisper it*) was best of all. And Park, that child of Empire,[3] was English to her core, born in England and now about to be raised and educated in that most English of environments.

But to fit in she would need to acquire four very different sets of learning and life skills. The first was how to live in an urban society. She wasn't quite Kim the jungle boy but she wasn't that far off him either. Even getting to and from school through this strange landscape would take some learning, as would the task of familiarising herself with the extraordinary (to her) urban architecture of one of the world's great cities. She needed too to figure out how 'proper' school worked with its endless rules and its lessons that were far more structured than she was used to. And she needed to figure out how friendships were made, establish her place in the social pecking order and not stand out (though that was difficult). And finally there were puberty and periods and sanitary towels, all without a mother's guiding hand, or a pal's, for the young Daphne made no close friends while in Rosa Bassett. It is understandable perhaps; most of us learn how to make friends in kindergarten, but Daphne Park was friendless for the first eleven years of her life. And though generally well-liked in school, as Daphne Helsby said, 'Daphne had no close friends, she came to us as an adult among suburban teenage girls. How could we possibly understand such an intellect, conditioned by such a background?'[4] Park referred to this lack herself later in her life:

> I was reading one of those books about girls in boarding school and I suddenly realised I had no close friends and perhaps I ought.[5]

So she set about making friends, and she started by making them laugh. She wasn't the first to choose that means of ingratiating herself with her fellows nor would she be the last (not that she was ever the court jester). But given what she later became it is illustrative of her thought process.

For Daphne Park knew that the chance she'd been given was so out of this world that nothing, should be, could be, would be allowed to come between. Not many eleven-year-olds have that sense of awareness of their circumstance that Daphne Park had. She took the bit between her teeth and she galloped. And she loved her time in Rosa Bassett; it was everything she must have dreamt of:

> I loved school. I loved the whole experience of being there ... I went to a very good state girls' school – the Rosa Bassett School, in South London – where we all really thought we could conquer the world. It never occurred to us that we couldn't do what we wanted with our lives – that we couldn't go where we wanted in the world.[6]

She earned a scholarship to France in her final school year, spending three months in Paris living with a French family,[7] a perfect precursor to reading French in Oxford. Entry to the university came by virtue of the results in her final state examinations, scoring 100% in history, leading the chief inspector of exams to ask to meet 'this extraordinary pupil'. These results qualified Park both for two further scholarships; a state scholarship and a Surrey County Council's County Major scholarship to Oxford University. Given her finances, both were needed if she was going to be able to take up the offer.

With the two scholarships worth £75 under her arm, in 1939 she went up to Somerville College in Oxford to read French. Somerville was one of a few colleges in Oxford open to women; the university was still only slowly coming to terms with the idea of women graduates. Park continued to dress in her hand-me-downs, something that did not stop her becoming both the secretary and the president of the Oxford University Liberal Club and only the second woman ever to address the Oxford Union. She described this honour at the time as being 'primarily due to the wartime shortage of men'. Granted men were in short supply, but it was obviously more than that. She also admitted to enjoying a few 'chaste affairs' during her undergraduate days.

An interesting insight into the young Park's personality is provided by a fellow undergraduate in an account of an event that took place shortly before her graduation in 1943:

> A number of undergraduates volunteered to take part in a mock blitz organised by the City Council to test Oxford's preparedness for an emergency. The Principal was subsequently congratulated by the Town Clerk on the histrionic ability of one Somervillian 'whose realistic impersonation of a hysterical foreigner deprived of house and sense and all coherent speech had shown up some weak spots in the city organisation'. The undergraduate in question was later identified as a modern linguist in her final year, Daphne Park.[8]

In the spring of 1943, with her Final Honour School approaching, Park realised it was time to decide on her future. The obvious course for an ambitious girl was to accept the offer of a place as an administrative entrant (fast track) in either the Treasury or the Foreign Office. The wartime shortage of men meant that there were openings in both that would not normally have been available without very stiff competition. But they held little appeal for Park and her particular friends so were, in Park's words, 'turned down with great contempt'.[9] That left the women's armed services, the WRNS, ATS and WAAF (Women's Royal Naval Service; Auxiliary Territorial Service; Women's Auxiliary Air Force). One had, apparently, to crawl on one's knees to gain entry to the WRNS (and Park was never one to crawl), while the recruiters to the other two services stressed the safe nature of the work ('education officer'), so that ruled them out.[10] Daphne Park wanted adventure and she reckoned that if war offered one thing it was that possibility. Lots of middle-class schoolgirls probably experienced faint stirrings of rebellion faced with the prospect of lives seemingly laid out on the straightest of tracks. However, the combination of Kayuki, Rosa Bassett and Somerville had created in Daphne Park someone who wasn't ready to conform, not if she could help it anyway. By August 1943 Park knew she had to make her mind up or have it made up for her. Call-up for single women had been in effect since December 1941. Her university exemption was over; if by September she had not enrolled in a war occupation she would be allocated one, and the chances that it would be adventurous and exciting were slim to none. There was also the issue of earning some money; enjoyable as Oxford had been, her student days were done, her scholarship funds depleted.

One day Park headed up town to meet two friends from Somerville who, like her, were still unsure of what to do with themselves. The three had just met at the foot of Oxford Street and were heading off to the Women's War Work Enquiries building[11] when they ran into a former Somervillian and fellow linguist, Mary Monk,[12] who had graduated in the year ahead of them. She was wearing a uniform that none of the three recognised. They asked her what she was doing.

'Oh something frightfully boring at Whitehall, carding my dear,' she said, but in a smug sort of way that made the three think that maybe it wasn't quite as boring as she was making out.[13] They pressed her further and learned that in fact she was working for an organisation called the First Aid Nursing Yeomanry, known to all as FANY. Park had heard of FANY but did not know much about it. In wartime Britain all that anyone knew about anything even faintly to do with the fighting was what the authorities decreed they should know. In fact the Yeomanry had its origins during the Boer War but had come into its own in the First World War, providing nursing aides to work immediately behind the Front.

When the Second World War broke out in 1939 the women's branch of the army, the Auxiliary Territorial Force (ATS), engineered a takeover and FANY became subsumed into it, its members becoming drivers and the like, and crewing anti-aircraft guns. But a small rump rejected the idea and insisted on remaining independent. They sent for the Gamwell sisters, Marian and Hope,[i] FANY stalwarts who had served the organisation with distinction in the First World War. The sisters were a sturdy pair who had driven ambulances through the midst of German artillery bombardments, tended to wounded soldiers and generally displayed exemplary quantities of courage, patriotism, grit and determination. After the First World War ended the two, figuring their chances of becoming married were past, had their hair shorn and thereafter dressed in khaki for the rest of their lives. They then left Britain to live in Africa where they grew coffee on a plantation in Abercorn in Northern Rhodesia (now Mbala in Zambia). They heeded the call, returned to England and set about revitalising their branch of the organisation which became known briefly as Free FANY, partly because its members were all volunteers (and so initially unpaid) and partly because it was not subservient to the ATS. As it happened FANY was one of the very few wartime organisations that offered a route to adventure for women.[14]

All this was as yet unknown to the three potentials; all they could agree on was that it was the sort of organisation where well brought up young ladies, who wanted to while away the war doing something faintly useful (such as chauffeuring a General around), joined for the duration. But *something* about the way Mary Monks had spoken told Park it was worth exploring. Not for the last time she followed her nose, and so the three decided to make for FANY headquarters in Wilton Place near Hyde Park Corner in Knightsbridge.

When they arrived at the headquarters building and announced themselves they found their welcome as warm as hour-old soup. It seemed that FANY had not been holding its breath for the imminent arrival of the three young Oxford graduates, who despite their excellent qualifications could not drive a car, something that was in demand in Free FANY as well as in its subsumed sister organ-

---

i GAMWELL, Colonel Antonia Marian, OBE (1891-1977) and her sister Hope (1893-1974); both First Aid Nursing Yeomanry.

isation. Drivers apart, this FANY was not currently recruiting, the well-spoken young receptionist told them, other than for particular but unspecified roles. Again something told Park to persist. She insisted on speaking to someone 'in authority'. Surprisingly, her persistence paid off. Interviews were hurriedly arranged for the three. In Park's case the interviewer seemed interested in her East African background (FANY was operational there) and in her competence in French. The fact that her uncle, Estcourt Cresswell-George, had by this time abandoned the Lupa and was commanding a battalion of the King's African Rifles (KAR) in Burma, may have helped.[15] She was told she would be called back for a second interview, but her two friends were not and exited for pastures unknown. After the second interview and following a routine security check by the Security Service (MI5), Park was told she was being accepted into FANY.

The standard practice was for new FANY volunteers to attend a two-week orientation and suitability course in Overthorpe Hall, near Banbury, under the stewardship of the rather intimidating Mary Martin.[i] The new recruits were taken through their paces, learned the basics of drill, and were lectured on first aid, military organisation, the history of the organisation, military communications and similar skills. At the end of the course they were assessed for their overall suitability and, if graded satisfactorily, assigned to a unit. Having passed this first hurdle, Park expressed an interest in coding and was sent on a specialist introductory course in the coding training centre across the street from FANY headquarters, where she would have been billeted.

At its heart coding is about mathematics, not that the trainees were expected to grasp the detail of that. In fact the level of instruction was fairly basic with the emphasis on following set procedures, the importance of accuracy; routine, in other words. That said, everything learned in the classroom had to be memorised; taking any form of written note was forbidden for security reasons. There were daily exercises in coding and de-coding messages of increasing length, which Park found quite interesting if not terribly challenging. There was considerable emphasis on the importance of attention to detail; this was not work for the flibbertigibbet.

Close to the final day the class was introduced to the concept of unreadable messages, the so-called 'indecipherables'. These, they were told, were messages sent in circumstances where the senders were operating in very tense situations and so very often made mistakes in their coding. The effect was to make their messages unreadable, initially at least, and so various techniques had been developed to turn them into readable text. This was essential, the class was told, for the messages to be understood and acted upon if needs be, but also to avoid them having to be resent with a resulting increase in danger for the senders.

i MARTIN, Mary Evelyn; First Aid Nursing Yeomanry (1919-1978).

What the class was not told was the nature of the tense situations these senders might be in, nor who they might be; servicemen of some sort, they assumed. The fortnight passed almost as quickly as had the two weeks in Overthorpe, and Park and her colleagues were told to prepare for the final exam that would determine their suitability to be fully trained as coders.

The first question on the exam paper was one about the use of codes in wartime and required a simple and straightforward answer of no more than a dozen or so words. But that wouldn't do for Park. Her mind seemingly still in its Oxford mode, she embarked on a detailed essay quoting Pythagoras *et al.* as if she was still in Somerville. When she finished her answer she discovered that she had not left anywhere near enough time to address the practical test which was the one that was critical to passing. The next morning Park was summoned by the Commandant and told that she had failed the exam and was the first to do so, *ever*. Since she had failed the exam she could not progress further. The only road open to her was to work as an orderly, a polite term for a waitress, pending a final decision about her future. The option of resigning was available as FANYs were volunteers, but resigning was unlikely to have had any appeal for Park. She wasn't a quitter so an orderly she became, serving in the HQ canteen.

This was her first real setback since she had arrived in England. Park's entire mindset, and one she was to follow throughout her life, was to grab hold of every opportunity offered and to cling on if needs be for dear life while figuring how to exploit it to the full. And yet here she had slammed shut the door on her pursuit of adventure because she had allowed herself to become distracted by the answer to an 'interesting' question and had not followed the instructions on the exam paper, thus failing an exam that girls with half her brains had sailed through.

A few evenings later her misery was compounded when, in the middle of a dinner for a great hero, whose name and deeds the mere waiting staff were not permitted to know, she slipped and the dozen or so dinner plates that she was extracting from the dumb-waiter fell to the floor with the most enormous crash, reducing every one of them to smithereens. She had now reached her nadir, unsuitable even for the job of waiting on tables. The next morning she was summoned to the personnel office where she fully expected to be dismissed.

'A Mr Marks wants to see you,' the personnel officer said, 'why I do not know, he is quite a young man but terribly important. You are to go to this address,' she said, handing Park a folded sheet of paper, 'you are expected this morning, off you go now.' As Park stood to go she had one final thing to say.

'Goodbye, Volunteer Park, I suspect we shall not be seeing you again.'

She was correct, though she didn't know it, but then neither did Daphne Park, for the failed waitress was headed for Bingham's unit and no one *ever* came back from there.

3

SOE 1 – Bingham's unit, 1943-44

It was a brisk twenty-minute walk from Wilton Terrace to the Baker Street address Park had been given. She must have wondered what was in store – hardly an offer of another waitressing job; she'd burnt that particular bridge (without any regrets). If she assumed anything it was probably that some boring clerical position had been dredged up that someone thought she *might* be capable of doing. But for the Daphne Parks of this world hope springs eternal, so she presented herself at the entrance to Norgeby House in the hope that fate might be ready to do her a good turn. There was nothing about the building that offered her any clue as to what might take place inside, other than a small brass plate inscribed with the words 'Inter-Services Research Bureau'.

After presenting herself at reception she was told to wait until Mr Marks was ready to see her. The wait was a short one and within a few minutes an armed escort – now that was interesting – was accompanying her to her destination. Mr Marks turned out to be a young man about her own age occupying a large office filled with a horrible fug of smoke bellowing from the pipe clenched between his teeth.

> [Marks] loved drama and he was sitting at his desk, quite a large room, and when I went in and stood before him he took no notice of me and went on reading. And I looked at what he was reading and I saw it was upside down so I thought that's interesting and I waited a minute or two, he still took no notice of me, so I sat down, picked something up and started reading it upside down myself. And he looked up, burst into roars of laughter and said 'Oh well you know, let's talk now,' and obviously I'd done the right thing and so he instantly made me an instructor on the principle, which is a very sound one, that as I'd made every mistake in the book I was going to be able to know when other people made mistakes, which was very true.[1]

In that extraordinary way that she had, Park had fallen on her feet, not once but twice. First, because even though it had not been explained to her during her course, she (in common with her classmates) was being evaluated for her suitability to work as a coder for the Special Operations Executive (SOE). SOE was a secret organisation established on Churchill's orders and directed to wage underground war against the Nazis in the occupied countries. Her second piece of good fortune was that her idiosyncratic exam answer to the question on the nature of coding had been sent – to amuse – by her Commandant to Leo Marks.[i]

i MARKS, Leopold Samuel ('Leo'); SOE (1920-2001).

At the age of twenty-two Marks had been put in charge of ensuring the security of SOE's wireless communications to and from the thousands of agents it deployed behind enemy lines. His job was to devise codes (he invented the famous WOK – Worked-Out-Keys – forerunner of the onetime pads. The WOK reduced the time needed for agents in the field to code and decode their messages *and* significantly reduced the error rate). His job was to make SOE's messages undecipherable to anyone (specifically the Germans) not in possession of the correct decoding 'key'. He was extraordinarily talented, innovative, persistent, questioning, irreverent and no respecter of either rank or precedent; exactly the qualities needed for the job he did for SOE. Marks was constantly on the lookout for that special something in his 'girls', the coders and decoders (separate talents required) of SOE's communications department.[2] Most candidates he rejected, to the intense frustration of his spotter/recruiters; others, like Park, came in through a variety of backdoor means. It was an example of what recruiters today might refer to as 'thinking outside the box'. Within minutes Park found herself standing in front of Staff Commander Bingham,[i] head of FANY personnel in SOE. She was a clever, polished woman whose FANY rank was equivalent to that of an army Lieutenant Colonel.

Phyllis Bingham's story provides another example of the seemingly haphazard way so much of Britain's war effort came into being. Her initial involvement was through her wealthy American husband. He organised a small shipment of arms, a couple of suitcases worth, to be sent from the United States to SOE in Britain. This was before America had entered the war and was more a very welcome token of support rather than any serious attempt to arm the nascent organisation. Next, one day early in 1940, Major General Colin Gubbins[ii] telephoned Marian Gamwell's office in FANY HQ to see if she could send him a couple of FANY 'girls' for some unspecified work. Bingham was acting as Gamwell's temporary confidential secretary so it was she who took the call. The two recognised each other; they had been peacetime neighbours. They met and Gubbins explained that he was going to need to recruit on a regular basis but because of the secret nature of the work SOE did he needed to do so discreetly. Bingham suggested that FANY act as his private recruitment agency. Suitable 'girls' would be recruited into FANY which would act as their cover employer though they would in fact be on SOE's roster. Thus the secretive 'Bingham's unit' was established in SOE headquarters from which a girl 'once posted, never returned'.

Bingham explained that this part of FANY was a voluntary organisation but that the War Office had agreed that Volunteers (Park's rank) would be paid

i BINGHAM, Phyllis; First Aid Nursing Yeomanry. The 'founder of the feast' in many respects, Bingham was eventually forced out of FANY, mainly for not conforming to its conventions.

ii GUBBINS, Major General Sir Colin McVean, MC, DSO, KCMG; Royal Field Artillery, Director of SOE 1943-46 (1896-1976).

eleven shillings and nine pence a week plus rations and accommodation. The news about pay and rations would have been well received; Park's scholarship fund must have been well depleted and she was probably penniless.

Bingham took Park through the do's and don't's, emphasising the need to behave in a ladylike fashion at all times if she was not to incur the wrath of Colonel Gamwell. Initially at least FANY recruits were drawn from the solid middle classes (though that did change in time) and were expected to uphold the staunch values associated with their kind. Their uniforms reflected this, they were fashioned from barathea, the same fabric that was used in officers' uniforms and tailored in Lillywhites or Simpsons. They had the choice of white or khaki shirt and green tie, topped off with either a peaked cap or a dress bonnet with a badge on a red flash. The overall effect was further improved by the addition of a smart leather belt.[3] It compared favourably with the shapeless serge uniforms issued to the women rank and file in the other services. Small wonder then that Park and her pals had not recognised the uniform when they encountered Mary Monks in Oxford Street.

Park was told she was forbidden, on pain of instant dismissal, from using the words Special Operations Executive or even SOE outside the building. If she had to refer to it she should use its cover name, the Inter-Services Research Bureau (ISRB), or better still use the term 'the organisation', though as she was to discover most of those in it referred to it as 'the racket', much to the disapproval of the higher-ups. Secrecy was paramount. This was not just in regard to the content of the coded messages, which was understandable; after all the messages were, by definition, secret. The secrecy went beyond that. She must not reveal to *anyone* anything about the nature of the work she did. She was told, in the most serious tones imaginable, that if asked she should describe herself as a simple FANY doing the most 'boring' and 'dull' jobs imaginable and promptly change the subject if the questioner persisted. Park's conversation with Mary Monks must have come to mind as this was explained.

The secrecy was understandable, given SOE's role in conducting sabotage missions against German forces in the countries under Nazi occupation. The missions were carried out by secret agents, trained in Britain and then inserted (usually by parachute) back into their operational territory. There they worked with the local resistance forces, coordinating attacks with supplies of arms and explosives sent from Britain, again usually dropped in by parachute. Agents were provided with portable wireless telegraph (W/T) (radio) sets which they used for their communications with SOE headquarters. Secure and effective two-way communications were the lifeblood of the operation; without them the entire operation would have shrivelled and died. Park's job as a coding instructor would be teaching trainee SOE agents in the practicalities of coding and decoding those vital messages which were transmitted in Morse code. Just as she turned twenty-one, Daphne Park had entered the 'secret world' and it would be thirty-six years before she would leave it for the final time.

SOE was organised along territorial lines, with separate sections for each country in which it operated. The trainee agents were taught their skills in a variety of dedicated training schools – paramilitary and endurance training in Arasaig in Scotland for example, parachute training in Ringway Airport in Manchester, radio operator training in Fawley Court near Henley, and so on. When the trainees' core and specialised training was completed they were sent to 'finishing schools', many of which were located in large houses dotted around Beaulieu in the New Forest, requisitioned by SOE from their reluctant millionaire owners for the duration. Most were well hidden from public view, connected by hidden pathways and narrow winding roads, patrolled round the clock by armed field security. There the agents would be prepared, safe from prying eyes, for insertion into their operational territory. Great care was taken to ensure that trainee agents from one country section did not encounter agents from a different one. This was to avoid cross contamination in the event of an agent being captured and tortured. There were two sections within SOE devoted specifically to operations on French soil; RF (République Française) section and section F (for France). RF tended to be the preserve of French nationals (though not exclusively). F was mainly made up of those who had connections with the country and who spoke the language fluently but were not its natives. Park worked mostly with French agents in the RF (Gaullist) section, but she also trained Czech and Polish agents. RF was headquartered in Dorset Square in London, but in common with the other country sections in SOE made use of the various specialist training centres and of its agent 'finishing school' in Beaulieu. Park speaks of being there.[4]

Agent training was conducted very much with D-Day in mind, for once the long-heralded invasion of Europe eventually did occur the work undertaken by the two French sections would alter radically. Once the Allied forces had actually landed, the SOE-organised *résistants* would be unleashed on the Germans. Prior to that, attacks on German personnel had been scaled back due to the ferocity of German reprisals against the civilian population, with sabotage of war-related facilities being instead the principal focus. After D-Day there would be no further holdback and, as a consequence, civilians would pay a heavy price – but then so would the Germans.

In modern parlance Park seems to have been a sort of trouble-shooter for Marks, to be used as best suited him (and without much heed for her convenience). In his book, *Between Silk and Cynaide*, Marks refers to a 'FANY instructress' (probably Park) providing last-minute training in codes to the extraordinarily brave Tommy

Yeo-Thomas,[i] an RF agent, immediately before he was to be dropped into France where he was a 'known face' to the Germans.[5] While her principal focus was to do with instructing RF agents in their codes she also spent some time with the Polish country section of SOE. On one occasion she recalls being dispatched by Marks, with only hours' notice, to Scotland to train Polish resisters.[6] These are likely to have been members of Cichociemni mission, based in Inverlochy Castle in Scotland. She also speaks of knowing 'Perks' (Colonel H.B. Perkins[ii]) 'well';[7] he was the head of the Polish country section in SOE (E/UP), suggesting that her involvement with E/UP went beyond just the one training session.

Training real secret agents who were only weeks away from being parachuted behind enemy lines was a privilege and was seen as such by Park and by most of the instructing staff in SOE. For her in particular it was a total eye-opener and the fact that their number included women, girls really, must have had an extraordinary impact on her, confirming her in her view that no door should be closed simply because of gender.

The Commandant in Beaulieu during Park's brief time there was a Lieutenant Colonel Spooner,[iii] a man with a fundamentally different view from Park's regarding the role of women in war. Reportedly with the reddest hair and the bleakest blue eyes imaginable, Spooner was the sort of man who relished being described as 'not suffering fools gladly' and took evident pleasure in not mincing his words. He used to greet every agent training intake with the words, 'The average time an agent survives in France is three months; my job is to extend that.'[8] And while no one could disagree with the sentiment, the mode of expression caused more than one agent to swallow hard. SOE practice was *not* to emphasise the likely fate of agents who were captured. Most knew well enough anyway; having them dwell on it risked unnerving them. Adding to the sense of woe was Spooner's edict forbidding trainees from drinking in the evening, something that was permitted in the other training schools and which most felt provided a much needed escape valve.[9]

Of more direct relevance to Park was Spooner's opposition in principle to the use of women in warfare on the grounds that such use contravened the Geneva Convention and in the event of their capture the women would not have its protection. Overall his attitude to the women trainees was pretty negative and this may well have extended to female 'instructresses' like Park. Spooner was based in a house called The Rings, the admin centre for the dozen or so large houses devoted to SOE activities in the New Forest. The set-up was principally male with ad hoc

i YEO-THOMAS, Wing Commander Forest Frederick Edward ('Tommy'), GC, MC and Bar; RAF, SOE (Agent SHELLEY), also known as the White Rabbit (1902-1964).

ii PERKINS, Lieutenant Colonel Harold B.; Merchant Marine, SOE, SIS, later H/ROME, H/ISTANBUL (1902-1964).

iii SPOONER, Lieutenant Colonel Frank Vivian; 30th Lancers, SOE, Jedburghs (1895-1968).

arrangements for the few female admin and instructing staff. Women attached to The Rings shared a cottage in the woods whose occupants included a former ATS officer called Dorothy Wicken.[i] It is likely that Park bunked in there while she was in Beaulieu, mixed gender accommodation being rare in the Forces at that time.

Wicken was personal secretary to Spooner at that point. The other member of the household was a seventeen-year-old typist, Ann Keenlyside, of beguiling appearance but no great secretarial experience, an acceptable combination it seemed. For Park, life in Beaulieu would have made an interesting change from London. There were pubs to visit and occasional dances in the Domus, the former lay brothers' refectory in Beaulieu Abbey. Keenlyside, who had embarked on an affair with a married RAF officer-instructor, her first, was far from being the only one consorting with someone she oughtn't. Perhaps that atmosphere was helped by the pervasive sense of comradeship, the feeling of participating in something that was vital to the war effort, with the added thrill of being privy to national secrets totally unknown to the common populace.

While codes and communications security were Park's main areas, the ethos of Beaulieu was that everyone mucked in and helped out where they could. Members of the support staff were detailed, on occasion, to go to a nearby town like Bournemouth and to observe and follow a trainee agent whose description and approximate location they would be given. The agent would be told to be on the lookout for the surveillance and to see if he or she could identify it and then shake it off without being too obvious. But the instructing staff often assigned two watchers. One, the decoy, would make themselves obvious and allow themselves to be shaken off, while the second, often female, would be the real watcher. Not many of the staff members assigned to this work were reported to have enjoyed looking at a trainee's face the next morning at the de-briefing while they detailed every move he or she had made the day before in the naive belief that they had lost their tail. Nor to watch while Dorothy Wicken, who the previous evening had been a sultry temptress in some low dive, detailed exactly what some hapless trainee had revealed about himself, so blowing his cover story wide open. For in addition to her secretarial duties Wicken was one of Beaulieu's *agents provacateurs*.[10] She had the job of approaching trainees in bars around Southampton or Bournemouth, where they had been sent on some ruse or other, and using her feminine wiles to persuade them to break their cover stories. Tough love, perhaps, but as was emphasised time without number, the instructors were training their students to stay out of the hands of the Gestapo. The Germans were up to those sorts of tricks and more.[11] In later life Park used maintain that the 'quiet courage' of her trainees impressed her deeply and served as a model for her own behaviour when operational herself in her SIS career after the war.

i WICKEN, Dorothy; ATS, FANY/SOE (1905-d.).

In January 1944 it was all change, for Park, just a few months after she had commenced working as an instructor, was to be transferred yet again. This time she was headed to Military Establishment/65 (ME/65) with promotion to the rank of sergeant. Her secret war had, if anything, just got more secret.

ME/65 was SOE's code name for the vast sepulchral edifice known as Milton Hall, in Cambridgeshire, about three miles outside Peterborough. The Hall was home to the 8th Earl Fitzwilliam, who by this stage must have been getting used to giving up his ancestral home every time Britain went to war, though to sugar the pill the Earl and his family were accommodated elsewhere on the estate and the land continued to be farmed. ME/65 was the base for the Jedburgh mission. The mission, a joint British and US set-up, was high profile, signed off personally by General Dwight Eisenhower, the Supreme Allied Commander (and later US President).

The Jedburgh teams (Jeds), specially selected and highly trained combatants, would parachute behind enemy lines in groups of three ahead of large-scale assaults by conventional forces. Once on the ground they were to bring a degree of military coordination to the often haphazard and disorganised activities of indigenous resistance groups. In essence the 'law of the lever' would apply. The three-man teams would use their skills to 'lever' the resistance groups, which cumulatively might number many tens of thousands, into at least quasi-efficient fighting groups. The Jeds would remain in constant radio contact with Allied headquarters and so would be able deploy the *résistants* in support of Allied ground force operations where and when needed. The initial deployment would be in support of D-Day, the Normandy invasion. Lieutenant Colonel Spooner, whom Park would have known (or at least have been aware of) from Beaulieu, was camp Commandant. Spooner's deputy Commandant was an American, a US Marine Corps Major called Fuller.[i] Their job was to get the Jedburgh mission off the ground. It was both a prestigious appointment and a difficult one. In many respects the two were pathfinders, the Jeds being the direct precursor of the modern special forces. Indeed the training curriculum devised by Spooner and Fuller became the basis for the one developed later for the United States Army Special Forces.[12]

Park, like Spooner and Fuller, was a member of the 'permanent party'; a complement of about two hundred officers and men of whom about forty were army instructors in addition to the FANY complement. They would soon be joined by the students, the two hundred and eighty or so young men who had volunteered to take part in the operation, the actual Jeds in other words. To say Park was

i FULLER, (later) Brigadier General Horace ('Hod') W.; USMC, OSS, Jedburghs, CIA (1908-1989).

delighted would be a huge understatement. To have the chance to play a more direct part in the invasion of Europe was both a privilege and a joy.

Her promotion to sergeant went with the position and was not necessarily because of any perceived ability. According to Ron Brierley,[i] a Jedburgh trained by Park, it was decided that those British W/T operators who were not already of sergeant rank would be promoted to sergeant. No one said why exactly but the rumour (as heard by Brierley) was so they would enjoy parity with the Americans, all of whose W/T operators were sergeants. Army logic dictated that since the Other Ranks (OR) trainees were now sergeants the 50% of the instructing staff who were OR should also be sergeants. So a sergeant-instructress she would be at the head of a team of four FANY instructors responsible for instructing the Jeds in the use of their codes, a critically important part of their operational readiness. Park and her team were billeted off site, travelling to the camp every day.

She had just a couple of days to orient herself and get used to her sergeant's stripes when the Jeds arrived, fresh from a few weeks commando training in Scotland. They were an exuberant bunch, full of vim and vigour, talking nineteen to the dozen, all volunteers, all ready to take on the Nazis in whatever form was required. Just breathing the same air as them must have been a joy. The Americans were superb physical specimens, big men in the main, from an outfit which few had never heard of, called the Office of Strategic Services (OSS), the sabotage and intelligence organisation that was forerunner to the CIA. Some had fought in the Pacific but many, in Park's words, '... were green young men who'd done their jumps at Fort Benning and absolutely nothing else and they were very, very green.'[13]

The French, who were not yet up to strength, were experienced fighters in the main and were attached to the Free French Bureau Central de Renseignements et d'Action (BCRA).[14] The British were a mixed bunch, some were fairly inexperienced but many were from the Long Range Desert Group which operated to special forces standards, and there was a sprinkling of escaped POWs.[15] However, no one *ever* referred to those organisations by name. If someone asked, they would cite the name of their parent units; if that someone pressed they would get a very cold stare indeed and maybe a box on the jaw to go with it. Once they had dumped their kit in their assigned accommodation, one of the Nissen huts – prefabricated, circular-roofed steel huts – erected on the lawn, the Jeds were ordered to assemble for their welcome speech from Spooner. The speech was akin to what one imagined an overly pukka commanding officer might have given to a bunch of newly arrived junior officers in the Indian Army. Forewarned, Park may have been expecting something like that, but it was clear

---

i BRIERLEY, Sergeant Ronald, MM, OBE; Royal Tank Regiment, Royal Armoured Corps, Jedburghs, Force 136 (1921-2005).

from the Jeds' reaction that they were both surprised and disappointed. They were used to their commanders exhorting them into battle, not to them speaking of the importance of discipline and of comporting themselves like proper soldiers. It was not the best of starts.

The first thing the Jeds had to do was to form themselves into their three-man teams. It was decided that this was best done by the Jeds themselves, subject to sign-off by the brass. It was described as akin to a courtship; chatting, moving on, stopping to chat with someone else, arrangements slowly coalescing. Encounter, engagement, marriage (and occasional divorce), the process of selecting those on whom you would be depending for your life is best unhurried.

While this was proceeding Park began to hear the first rebellious mutterings about Spooner. He was insisting that the Jeds parade at dawn and go through the standard army parade-ground disciplinary routines. The Jeds didn't mind rising at six, but they wanted to use the time productively, not on parade ground bull. One French officer described Spooner as 'having a sense of formal discipline, maybe narrowly minded'.[16] A British Jed, Captain Stanley Cannicott, described the occasion when Spooner attempted to call the formation to attention:

> The dutiful Brits sprang to attention, the French raised their eyes and their hands and said, 'we do not understand,' the Americans looked the other way and I will not print what they actually said.[17]

Another British officer, Captain John Montague,[i] decided to test Spooner's resolve. Montague began bellyaching about the endless physical jerks. Spooner met him head-on, put him on report and dispatched him to see Gubbins in London to be disciplined. Montague assumed he would be in for the chop but Gubbins just told him to behave himself in future and sent him back.[18] Someone better able to read the signs might have seen Gubbins' action as a gentle suggestion to loosen the reins a little, but Spooner wasn't that man. He carried on regardless, encouraged apparently by his RSM (Regimental Sergeant Major). Park began to grow restless. As an instructor she had been 'bigoted',[19] i.e. added to the BIGOT list[20] of people who were made privy to the date of the D-Day landings. She (in common with the other instructing staff) would have needed to know this in order to design the training regimen for the Jeds and ensure they were ready by a given date. She began to grow increasingly concerned that the Jeds would not be ready in time:

> ... the man who was in charge was a man called Colonel Spooner who was an ex-Indian Army Colonel I think, and who was very, very orthodox. Had no notion of

i MONTAGUE, Captain John Cook; Royal Tank Regiment, Royal Armoured Corps, Jed-burghs, Force 136 (1913-1995).

paramilitary operations, had no notion how to deal with that kind of person and spent a great deal of his time cancelling night operations which we really needed, practice you know operations, in favour of parading people and inspecting their buttons – I'm exaggerating a little bit but that was his general style – and everyone got extremely frustrated and restless. [21]

Most people in Park's situation would probably have been inclined to ignore Spooner, or leave it to someone more established to do something about it. Park was after all a total novice with less than six months' service. On top of that she was a female auxiliary in a unit only tangentially attached to what was very much a man's army. But Park wasn't most people. One day she was summoned to London by Leo Marks for a progress report. Park told Marks that in her opinion the operation was being put at risk by Spooner's approach. Marks told her it was her duty to make a report.

> So he [Marks] said to me, 'Well you know it's your duty to make a written report about this,' so I said 'All right,' and I sat down and made a written report. And he said, 'And it will have to go to Brigadier Mockler-Ferryman,'[i] who was my Signals Brigadier, 'and it will have to go to SHAFE [Supreme Headquarters Allied Forces Europe] ... and Lord Louis [Mountbatten] and all that lot you know,' and so he said, 'I'll get my secretary to type it, it'll go off tomorrow.'[22]

Off the letter went, and Park, ever conscious of doing the right thing, duly placed a copy of the letter in Spooner's pigeonhole on her return to Milton Hall. Spooner reacted predictably. The following morning she was paraded in front of all the instructing staff, where he treated her to a diatribe of abuse such as she had never experienced. During the torrent of invective, Park, who had been standing, decided to sit down. When roared at by the RSM to stand to attention, she refused on the grounds that the manner in which Spooner was addressing her was inappropriate for an officer and she would remain seated until he did. At that she was dismissed and issued with a one-way travel warrant to London. Her time with the Jeds in Milton Hall had come to an end.[23]

When Park arrived back in FANY headquarters it was to a very cold reception. Spooner wrote to FANY accusing her of 'having disgraced the Corps'. It was assumed that this meant that she had been sleeping around with her trainees. A court of inquiry was held. Park could not, however, offer a detailed defence. The entire Jedburgh operation was Top Secret and she was not permitted to breathe a word about it to anyone who was not cleared to know, and the FANY orderly office (administration) was most definitely not inside the ring of secrecy. So all she could do was to repeat, 'Well I'm sorry but I can't say anything about it at

i MOCKLER-FERRYMAN, Brigadier Eric E., CB, CBE, MC; Royal Artillery, SOE (1896-1978).

all, but what you are saying is not true.' She denied that she had been sleeping around and told the court she was a virgin and could prove it. Her defence did not cut any ice and her sergeant's stripes, of which she was hugely proud, were cut 'Dreyfus style' from her uniform. She was now officially in disgrace. This was without doubt the lowest point of Daphne Park's young life.

4

SOE 2 – *Coup de foudre*, 1944

Now reduced to the rank of Volunteer, Park went back to Marks, who being the non-conformist he was (deliberately remaining a civilian member of SOE throughout the war, never 'joining up' so never being subject to military discipline[1]) promptly put her back to instructing RF agents in their codes. Given that he was more than partly responsible for the situation in which she found herself that was probably the least he could have done, but he did it, that was the point, and she was grateful. And while she loved training her agents she missed the Jeds dreadfully, she had been so proud of her association with them. After about three weeks had passed Park was sent for by General Gubbins, Director of SOE. She probably thought she was going to be given her discharge papers, but what he said surprised her.

> 'You've been having a hard time, haven't you?' and I said, 'Yes I have.' 'Well,' he said, 'I think I owe it to you to tell you what's happened.' 'Uh,' he said, 'as a result of what you said ... a certain amount of restiveness had reached us, there's been a court of enquiry, the CO has been removed and several of the instructors have been removed and they have been sent a new CO.'[2]

Park was astounded but delighted. However Gubbins told her that he could not restore her to the strength of Milton Hall. That would fly in the face of all military discipline. The correct procedure for her to have followed would have been to lodge her complaint through the chain of command (something that is close to religion in its observance in military organisations), in other words hand her complaint (about Spooner) to her commanding officer, Spooner. The fact that in so doing the complaint would have been stifled at birth was not the point, the chain must be followed. So Park would remain instructing her RF trainee agents. Gubbins did say, though, that she would be appointed a briefing officer and so could attend the final briefings that the Jeds would receive immediately prior to going into action. Finally he told her that he could not, alas, restore her sergeant's stripes, that matter was purely one for FANY.[3]

There was more to the affair that Gubbins let on to Park. For a start, the chances that a complaint from a junior FANY NCO would result in the transferring-out of a special forces camp commandant three months before his troops were due to go into action on D-Day were about as likely as her being offered the job of commandant herself. It makes for a good story, but it does not square with reality. Britain in 1944 was not Britain in 2015. For a start, the role of women in society was totally different. Women were the 'weaker sex', a subjugated gender, subservient to men socially and legally and nowhere more so than in the armed services of a country at war. It is inconceivable that a complaint of that nature would have or could have been acted on in the way that it supposedly played out. In fact Park didn't create a problem for Gubbins, she solved one. Reading between the lines in US accounts[4] (and some British ones[5]) of the Jedburghs' training time in Milton Hall, it is clear that it was the *Americans* who were far from happy with Spooner. And with the Americans unhappy there was only one way the affair was going to end. Gubbins himself referred to it, albeit obliquely, when he spoke to Park of 'a certain amount of restiveness' having reached the upper echelons of SOE (see above). If Park hadn't lodged her *billet doux* when she did the Americans would in all likelihood have demanded Spooner's removal, thus provoking a confrontation if not quite a crisis. As it was they made it clear they favoured replacing him with a US officer. They settled instead for the appointment of the more easygoing and affable Lieutenant Colonel Richard Musgrave.[i] He had been responsible for the US contingent in Milton Hall and so was a known quantity. The Americans did extract a price; they insisted on overall control of the Jeds being passed to the new Special Forces HQ (SFHQ) in London, a joint UK/US set-up. It was further agreed that all radio communications between London and the deployed Jeds were to be handled in Poundon, which was a new US-commanded receiving station, and not by SOE in Grendon as originally planned.[6] This was a significant concession; as SOE well knew whoever controls communications, controls the operation. The Americans were flexing their muscles, the senior partner no longer prepared to defer to some assumed expertise of the British in these matters. Under this new thinking there was no room for a stiff-backed martinet of the Indian Army variety. He had to go and Park provided the perfect alibi.

There was another strike in SOE against Spooner. While still Commandant in Beaulieu 'that bastard Spooner'[7] had taken against a trainee W/T agent called Noor Inayat Khan[ii] during her final training.[8] Spooner put in a damning report stating that she should not be sent to France as an agent/WT operator on grounds of her lack of mental toughness.[9] Not only had he put in the report, he had sent a copy of his adverse findings to the most senior officer, Gubbins, in order to spike Colonel Buckmaster's[iii] (head of section F) guns completely.

i MUSGRAVE, Lieutenant Colonel George Richard ('Dick'); Royal Artillery, Jedburghs (1909-1959).

ii KHAN, Noor Inayat, GC; Women's Auxiliary Air Force/FANY/SOE (Agent MADELEINE) (1914-1944).

iii BUCKMASTER, Colonel Maurice James, OBE; HM Forces, SOE, head of Section F (1902-1992).

But Buckmaster was desperate for W/T operators; one of his most important networks was without one. So he had responded by having Leo Marks conduct a 'special test' of Khan's coding ability which she 'passed' with flying colours and so was cleared to go operational.[10] She had parachuted into France, undertaking heroic work, but had been captured within four months. Her current whereabouts were unknown but they feared (correctly) for her life. Buckmaster was very much the type of man to hold grudges. It is not improbable therefore that the Noor Khan episode fed in to his decision to support the removal of Spooner from Milton Hall.

That wasn't the only significant aspect to the affair. Spooner's implication about Daphne Park's romancing had been accurate, to some degree at least. Spooner was no dummy, just a little premature. Daphne Park may not *at that point* have slept with one of her charges but she was definitely involved with one. Her claim to be a virgin might have been true or might have been a bluff, as was her remark to her interviewer:

I was in love with the whole 300 [Jeds] but that's where it stopped.[11]

Park may well have been in love with all three hundred, but she was head over heels in love with one in particular, a US Jed called Douglas Bazata.[i] In retrospect he was exactly the sort of man she was likely to fall for (many girls did) and probably the sort she shouldn't have. Douglas DeWitt Bazata was an unusual man in every sense. There are some people of whom it is said they were 'born in the wrong century', but Douglas Bazata was born in the right one and at the right time. He was meant for war. His physique, his bearing, his entire demeanour was that of a warrior, as hard as iron, as brave as a lion with a head of fiery red hair and a temper to go with it. He was a qualified sharpshooter – he scored thirty-five consecutive bulls-eyes during officer-candidate training in Fort Benning, a Marine record. He was also a former Marine boxing champion from his service there before the war; he'd left in 1937 but rejoined in 1942 and was commissioned in as a captain.

Despite his oft-broken nose he was attractive, lean and lanky. He was also charismatic, irreverent and a charmer, managing to get away with addressing all colonels as 'Sugar'.[12] He certainly charmed Daphne Park; she fell for him, hook, line and sinker.[13] Of course he was married at the time, but she wasn't to know that until later, much later. We do not know for certain if the affair was ever fully consummated: Park told the historian Steven Kippax, after the war, that on one occasion at least she had avoided intercourse with Bazata by feigning a

i BAZATA, Major Douglas DeWitt, DSC; USMC, OSS/Jedburghs, CIA (1911-1999). Later special advisor on counterterrorism to the US Secretary of the Navy, Dr John Lehman (Reagan administration).

bout of diarrhoea,[14] but fall passionately in love she did. The affair, of course, consummated or otherwise, was rudely interrupted by her dismissal from Milton Hall and that was not about to be reversed.

Meanwhile back in Milton Hall the new CO, Lieutenant Colonel Musgrave, was soon in place, Spooner having taken up duty as overall head of SOE training schools where he could do less harm, presumably.[15] Musgrave seemed a straightforward type; there were rumours that before the war he'd been a big game hunter and to look at him one could imagine that all right. He had solid combat experience, having fought in Somaliland[16] in 1941 under Orde Wingate.[i]

In fairness to Spooner, he was not simply a desk wallah. He had served on the Western Front in 1914/15 in the British Expeditionary Force. He had been a second lieutenant in the 30th Lancers (an Indian Army regiment). And while the 30th was not a particularly distinguished regiment – it had never been awarded battle honours, for example – its losses, particularly among the officers, had been severe. Whether commanding 'native troops' was the best preparation for supervising the training and deployment of such an individualistic group as the Jeds is questionable. Three hundred or so exceptionally able, highly trained young fighters of three separate nationalities, cooped up and pumped up as they waited for the 'off'. As an added complication, whereas in the average combat unit the CO would lead his men into battle, sharing the danger with them and in part deriving his authority from that, in Milton Hall when the Jeds sallied forth into battle the CO stayed behind, the job being more about administration than traditional leading from the front. Everyone agreed that the Jedburghs constituted a high risk op and needed strong leadership. Most would probably have agreed that the command was a tough assignment and that Spooner had a difficult job. Another term for special forces is elite forces and the Jeds were an elite with all that that implies. Notwithstanding that, Spooner had been a poor choice and it was this realisation rather than Park's complaint (though she lit the fuse) that led to his removal.

As D-Day approached Eisenhower had a rethink about the best means of utilising the Jeds. The original plan had been to parachute the ninety or so teams into France on the eve of D-Day. Once on the ground they would make contact with their pre-allocated resistance groups and organise them to cause mayhem behind German lines as the invasion took place, focusing on disrupting German efforts to move supplies of men and materials to the invasion zone. But a new imperative had arisen, and that was the need to maintain the ruse that the D-Day landings in Normandy were a feint and that the 'real' invasion would follow days later in

i WINGATE, Major General Orde Charles, DSO and Two Bars (1903-1944). Wingate was the creator of the Chindits, airborne deep penetration forces who operated behind enemy lines in the Far East in the Second World War.

the Pas de Calais, the location favoured by Hitler. That deception, if it worked, would mean the Germans delaying the deployment of their fearsome Panzer regiments which Hitler was maintaining in reserve, to be deployed only on the personal order of the Führer. This, if successful, would give the invasion forces the vital time needed to build their bridgehead and establish a secure foothold. Eisenhower reasoned that the deployment of the uniformed Jeds in strength in Normandy would risk tipping his hand to the enemy. So it was decided that only eight out of the over ninety Jed teams available would participate in the days immediately surrounding D-Day. Park took part in a number of their briefings, as promised by Gubbins. Needless to say the remaining Jeds in Milton Hall were outraged when they saw that the invasion was taking place without their participation. All (including Douglas Bazata) were eventually deployed in the months that followed.

But Park's engagement with the Jeds was not over. Back in the first week of May fifteen teams (six more joined later) under Major Hod Fuller, the Deputy Commandant, had been shipped out of Milton Hall. Fuller stood down from his command post in order to participate as a Jed, as did a dozen or so members of the instructing staff. They were given only twenty-four hours notice and were told to pack everything as they would not be returning to Milton Hall. No one had any idea of where they were headed; the rumour mill went wild, though somewhere hot like Algiers was the favourite guess (correctly). Three of the fifteen teams had been dropped into France in support of D-Day, the remaining twelve were scheduled to take part in the support operation for the second seaborne invasion of France, Operation DRAGOON, scheduled for 15 August. But with DRAGOON fast approaching the Jeds were mouldering away in a mosquito-infested camp in Algiers, unable to get any aircraft allocated to them. The demand for places on aircraft always outstripped supply; there were daily allocation meetings, but the Jeds did not have anyone present at those meetings to fight their corner. As they saw it they were in danger of missing out on the fighting altogether. But these were resourceful men. Two of them, Lucien Conein[i] and Osborne Grenfell,[ii] smuggled their way onto an American general's flight to London, determined to do something about their plight. They went and saw Gubbins, putting their case to him as forcefully as they could. Park described the encounter thus:

> 'Sir,' [Conein said], 'we're not getting anywhere, can we come back and jump from here like the rest, you know, there we are eating our hearts out and we haven't a hope of getting an aircraft. We've got to have a briefing officer of our own who can

i CONEIN, Lieutenant Colonel Lucien Emile; OSS, Jedburghs, CIA, DEA (1919-1998).
ii GRENFELL, Major Osborne Pascoe; Royal Tank Regiment, RAC, Jedburghs, mentioned in dispatches (1911-1971).

fight our corner.' And he [Gubbins] said, 'I simply haven't any, everybody's flat out, it's impossible. Very sorry but you know that's it, that's how it is.'[17]

But the two men refused to admit defeat; they sought out Park, whom they would have known from Milton Hall. They decided over lunch that Park would make the ideal briefing officer in Algiers if they could swing it. They said nothing of this to her but returned to Gubbins and made their pitch.

'We've found our briefing officer,' and he said 'Who?' and they said, 'Daffers, Daphne Park.' Mind you I was a volunteer by that time, I mean I had no rank whatever of any kind. And General Gubbins looked at them and he said, 'But she isn't even commissioned, she wouldn't have a hope.' 'Well,' they said, 'Surely you can do something about that,' and he said, 'But you know could she really do it?' 'Yes,' they said, 'She could because we'd tell her what we wanted and she'd fight for us, we know she'd do that, there wouldn't be a problem and what do you lose by it, you know why not try.'[18]

Gubbins, obviously conscious of the wrong done to Park over the Spooner affair and naturally keen to see his men go into action, agreed to approach Colonel Gamwell and see if she could see her way, not only of reinstating Park in FANY's good books, but promoting her to officer rank, an essential if she was to perform the role of briefing officer in Algiers. Gubbins duly met with Gamwell and asked her to consider the situation, stressing that he needed Park at once for essential war work. Whether he told her the truth about the Spooner business we do not know. Gamwell was aware of the work that SOE undertook and the role of the almost two thousand FANYs who were serving in it in a variety of support roles in war theatres in Europe, the Middle East and Far East. In fact most of SOE's female agents were commissioned into FANY in the forlorn hope that, in the event of their capture by the Germans, their 'uniformed status' might afford them some protection. Each such potential agent was interviewed personally, in her London flat, by Gamwell prior to being admitted into FANY and thence into SOE. In a post-war interview Gamwell made it clear that she had no role in selecting the agents; that task was for others 'more qualified' than she. But her admiration for them and by implication for the work that Park would be doing was profound.[19]

So being General Gubbins he thought about it and he went and saw Gamwell ... and told her I suppose, the story. He said he needed me immediately but he needed me commissioned, couldn't do the job without. And she said well one, she'd want to see me and two, she'd have to think about it. So she talked to the orderly room who of course only knew me as this wicked girl who'd destroyed the reputation of the FANYs, and she said well this is an operational thing I can't talk to you about but it necessitates making her ... giving her a commission. So they all were fairly furious about that naturally, and they said well at least Gamwell you will have to make her promise never to do the same sort of thing again.[20]

So Park was summoned to Wilton Place without being made aware in the slightest of what was in store; she probably assumed it was to be admonished yet again. When she arrived she was escorted to Colonel Gamwell's office. Gamwell told her that she was being recommended for promotion to the bottom rung of officer rank, what in FANY was called a cadet-ensign, prior to going operational. There was, however, a 'however'. She had committed a 'serious breach of discipline' by going outside the chain of command in the Spooner affair and so her promotion was conditional on her agreeing to conform in future.[21] Daphne Park wouldn't have been Daphne Park if she'd agreed to that. She told Gamwell that on the contrary should a similar situation arise again she would absolutely *not* conform and would in fact do the same.[22] Gamwell responded that if Park had answered otherwise she wouldn't have promoted her.[23] Coincidentally, the Gamwells' farm in Africa (in Abercorn in Northern Rhodesia) was only about two hundred miles from Park's home in Kayuki Estate. Perhaps it was something in that African air that ensured that those very formidable women held each other in such high regard.

Gamwell told Park she was being transferred on promotion to SOE Massingham to act as briefing and dispatch officer for the Jed teams who would be dropped into Southern France as part of the second invasion.[24] The drumbeat of war was coming ever closer; Daphne Park was back in the game.

SOE 3 – Daffers goes to war, 1944

There are two villages called Massingham in England, Great Massingham and Little Massingham, located in each other's shadow in Norfolk. During the war 'the greater' was home to a Bomber Command airfield (RAF Massingham) flying missions against targets in Nazi Germany's industrial heartland of the Ruhr. Presumably it was in order better to confuse the enemy that SOE chose to call its secret North African operational headquarters Massingham *aka* AMF *aka* Inter-Services Signals Unit 6 (ISSU6) *aka* the Special Projects Operations Centre (SPOC). This 'Massingham' was in reality a requisitioned resort located at Cap Matifou beside the village of Guyotville, some fifteen miles from Algiers in the French colony of Algeria. It was from there that operations in the Mediterranean theatre were directed and it was to there that Park flew a week ahead of the planned invasion of Southern France.

Park must have been delighted; delighted with her reprieve, delighted to be back with the Jeds, with advancement to commissioned rank, with the change of scenery, but delighted, most of all, with her new responsibilities. She would be a briefing officer, the person responsible for ensuring that any Jed teams under her direction would go on their mission fully briefed, prepared and equipped. Hers would be the last friendly face the Jeds would see before take-off, the first they would see when they returned, if they did.[1] She hurried to Special Forces HQ where she collected her maps and briefing papers for each of the eighteen teams left to be deployed from Algiers, stuffing them into her large rucksack. Then, bearing a passport signed in person by Anthony Eden, the Foreign Secretary, she left England on 7/8 August[2] for Gibraltar.

> Flying out was funny because ... I had to take out an enormous kit bag full of maps for the ... for the various operations and papers of various kinds. The result was [not being] ... able to take anything for myself, I think I just had a change of uniform and that was about it. But I went on an aircraft from [RAF] Lyneham, which was otherwise full of officers of flying rank you know, Air Marshals and things. And I was the only woman and I was the dizzy rank of ensign but as far as they were concerned, you know, I was there. They were all mystified by me and they all thought I was somebody else's PA ... and ... they kept saying to me now me dear, um, you mustn't be surprised if we ... if the plane jinxes a bit. And I would say no sir, thank you very much, I won't be surprised. But all the way they still kept looking at me and thinking who did I belong to; nobody knew, nobody knew why I was there and it was ... it was a very funny journey.[3]

When she arrived safely in Gibraltar, Park changed aircraft for the final leg of her journey to Maison Blanche airfield outside Algiers. The main Massingham base was in the former Club des Pins, a large colonial retreat favoured by French millionaire settlers, the Pieds Noirs, keen to escape from the torrid summer heat of Algiers. Following TORCH, the successful amphibious invasion of North Africa in 1942, SOE had requisitioned the club for use as its local ops base. It looked far from a colonial retreat as she was driven past accordions of barbed wire, guard huts and towers manned by tough, alert-looking Spahi[4] sentries. Accommodation was a combination of Nissen huts, tents and the original holiday villas that were dotted around the site. Most of the thirty or so FANYs shared a couple of these large villas. The accommodation was a peculiar combination of the quasi-luxurious and the Spartan – there were cooling marble floors and enormous bathrooms but no hot water on tap. Not the most delightful prospect given that the temperature was hovering around 80°F/27°C, but preferable perhaps to the winter with temperatures as low as 43°/6°, for the camp offered no heating either.

But there was of course the sea: the club boasted an expansive beach (the site of the main TORCH landings), and during their free time the camp's inhabitants were able to indulge themselves and keep fresh. At night some of the girls apparently took to swimming in the nude, leading inevitably to 'romantic' encounters with the men with one or two pregnant girls being repatriated back to Britain every so often. According to some the French '*armée féminine*' behaved with even more abandon, but perhaps that was just wishful thinking.

Her first call would have been to the base CO, the aristocratic, well-connected and highly regarded Lieutenant Colonel Dodds-Parker.[i] Dodds-Parker was a busy man and Massingham was a busy place. The invasion of southern France would have been occupying every minute of his time, with some hundreds of agents under his command all vying with each other for the means to get into action, but he was also supporting substantial operations in other theatres, Italy and Greece in particular. Park would have joined in the fray, focusing on her own objectives: establishing the precise arrangements for the allocation of aircraft, when the decision-taking meetings were held, the running order, how priorities were set, the likely availability of aircraft and so on, the meat and bones of how things were run.

With her information in hand Park then went to meet the Jeds' superior, the kilted Major 'Bing' Crosby.[ii] He had taken over command of the Jed detachment from Major Fuller, who had been inserted into the Ardèche leading Team

i DODDS-PARKER, (later) Colonel Sir Douglas; Grenadier Guards, SOE, later a Conservative MP and Foreign Office minister responsible for SIS during the Suez crisis (1909-2006).
ii CROSBY, (later) Lieutenant Colonel M.G.M., OBE, MC; Gordon Highlanders, SOE, Jedburghs, Force 136 (1911-1993).

BUGATTI. Park knew Crosby from Milton Hall where he had been on the instructing staff but had left to go operational. Both loud and sound, he was a total adventurer though very focused on the job in hand. Crosby would have told her that she was barely in time, for the invasion of Southern France was imminent. The US 7th Army under General Patch had commenced embarkation and hundreds of ships and landing craft were steaming through the Med. While DRAGOON was not on the same massive scale as OVERLORD, it was still a huge operation and was scheduled to hit the beaches near Marseilles on Tuesday 15 August 1944, a few days after she arrived. Eighteen Jed teams were to be dropped in to support the invasion and its aftermath; her job was to see them off safely and in good order. OVERLORD, the main invasion, was proceeding to plan, pretty much, but the enemy was far from defeated. A decent lodgement area had been established in Normandy and the Allies had seen off the counterattacks by the enemy panzers – a success that was due in no small measure to the actions of SOE agents, some Jeds and other Special Forces and the *Maquis* themselves. The chances of the Allies being pushed back into the ocean were fast receding. However, there had been no instances of mass surrenders by the Germans or any of the other signs of a disintegrating army, far from it, in fact. The enemy was still well armed, equipped and motivated. This was resulting in casualty levels at the very limit of what the Allies could sustain.

Eisenhower knew he needed to break out from the coastal area and press inland. The landing of the 7th Army on the southern coast would coincide with an almighty push by all the Allied forces on the ground. Park's Jed teams were needed to organise *Maquis* attacks on the enemy aggressively and in numbers once this four-army push began.

Park knew she had little time to prepare. Her next job was to go to Camp W to meet her Jeds, begin the briefing process and establish a workable plan to get them off the ground, into the air and on their way to war. She must have received a heroine's welcome; in modern parlance she'd 'made the cut', been appointed their briefing officer, and was now their route into action. RAF Blida, the mission take-off point, was next on her list. Blida was about twenty-five miles from the camp and was home to RAF 624 Squadron and, more recently, USAAF 885 Squadron. The base had been established to fly Joes[5] and their supplies into the southern part of Occupied Europe. The RAF flew Halifax Mark2 Specials heavy bombers, the USAAF similarly adapted B24s, both stripped of everything that was surplus to requirements. They flew through the night for three to four hours to their destination, doing their best to skirt around known anti-aircraft batteries and night-fighter bases. They used the light from the full moon to find their pinpoint location, perhaps a small field referred to as the drop zone (DZ) into which the human cargo and the war matériel would be dropped by parachute. The field would be lit by signal fires in an agreed formation. Once the DZ was located and confirmed they would make their drop, flying at only a few hundred feet above the ground. On most nights they would make two, sometimes three separate drops before turning around for the lengthy journey back to base, hoping once more to avoid concentrations of enemy fighters or the ever-present flak. The work took guts and exceptional endurance. Crew losses were considerable.

The first team to be dropped in direct support of DRAGOON was Team EPHEDRINE; the team went in on the night of 12/13 August just a few days after she arrived. The landing zone was quite close to where the DRAGOON landings were scheduled to take place; they would be in the thick of it from the moment the team landed. EPHEDRINE was led by Lieutenant Lawrence 'Larry' Swank. The detailed briefing completed, Park's next task was to give Swank a tiny piece of microfilm which had to be read using a powerful magnifying glass. It contained a number of French phrases with a code word beside each. When Swank wanted to organise a drop of matériel he was to send a radio message to London with the coordinates of the DZ. The message would include a code word taken from the microfilm for verification purposes. Each evening they were to listen to the BBC 19.15 news broadcast in French. At the end of the news a series of seemingly meaningless *messages personnels* would be read, most of which were in fact important, being secret messages to SOE agents and resistance groups. When Swank heard the phrase that corresponded to his selected code word he would know to expect a supply drop that night. It was simple and relatively foolproof. Later called a One-Way Voice-Link (OWVL) it became a method favoured in the Cold War for communications from head office to agents in the field.

Park took them through the detail of their mission and operational procedures for the final time (and probably ran them through their codes as well). It was very different to the classroom rehearsals in Milton Hall: no jokes, no witty asides, just intense and constant focus. Any questions they had she would have answered as best she could, but the overwhelming feeling among them would be one of relief that at last they were going to war. The Jeds were like that, often more interested in the fact of action than in the detail. At around 18.30 the briefings would have been completed and the final countdown began. The aircraft was scheduled to take-off after 20.00. Flying time to each drop zone would be between three and four hours, undertaken in night conditions, dawn not breaking until well after 05.00.

The navigator for the flight presented himself and confirmed the details of the drop zone, DZ ASSURANCE, in the Alpes de Haute Provence of France. Only the navigator among the crew would know the exact coordinates, the pilot would be told only enough to know approximately where they were heading in order for him to calculate fuel usage, check weather forecasts and plan for any hazards such as nearby mountains. The pilot was next to introduce himself and take them through the flight plan. Their journey would allow them to skirt Menorca making landfall to the west of Toulouse and on to the DZ. He explained that releasing the containers and packages over the right spot was the responsibility of the navigator/bombardier and he would do so at two hundred and fifty feet on the first run over the DZ. It would be the dispatcher who would be responsible for hooking the team up the static lines and giving them the 'Go' signal. He would do so on the second run at seven hundred feet, at approximately 120 mph. First would come the red light ('Ready') followed by green and the command 'Go, Go, Go'. The three would exit through the 'Joehole' in the floor, the commander first, followed by the radio operator, the second-in-command completing the drop.

Next was a security check. A security officer went through every piece of clothing, wallets, pocket books and pockets themselves to make sure that no one was carrying anything that might represent a security breach or assist the enemy in any way. That check was also to prevent someone carrying perfume or nylons or silk knickers for their girlfriends. The French were notorious for bringing their welcome home with them. The search completed, the team was brought to the dressing hut.

They were already wearing their holstered Colt automatics, so the first weapons handed them were their M1 carbines, smelling faintly of gun oil. Park would have allowed the three men to set the pace, she would have noticed how unhurriedly they did everything; how carefully they handled the loaded magazines, checking each to make sure the rounds had been inserted correctly (essential to avoid the weapon jamming) before stashing them in their ammo pouches. They followed the same procedure with the pistol magazines, pressing down hard against the springs to check their tension (weak springs can also lead to weapons jamming). Next she handed each a compass, morphine syrette, torch, field bandage, first aid kit and binoculars, a 1/50,000 scale map of the landing area and a 1/150,000 Michelin road map of their area of operations, checking each one off the list. She pointed them towards a side table stacked with filled water bottles, bags of rations and survival kits, similar to those issued to the aircrews.

The next to last item she gave them was the other essential of guerrilla warfare – banknotes – making the standard little joke about not running off with them. The purpose was serious enough: if people were going to throw in their lot with the Resistance their families would still have to eat and needed to be provided for. Each of them took the money belt stuffed with 100,000 francs and 50 US dollars, for which 'they would be held strictly accountable' (the francs were forged so little account was paid to them afterwards). Their rucksacks and the two Jed-sets (B2 radios) were packed in the dark green supply canisters that would be dropped with them. The final items to be donned were their parachute smocks and helmets. They would need them; at seven hundred feet, the fall would take about fifteen seconds with the parachute deploying fully only a few seconds before they crashed to the earth. As Sergeant Ron Brierley (who made two drops into France and who had been trained by Park) told this author, 'the only way to make a parachute landing is either drunk or unconscious'.[6]

Park's next duty was her most difficult. The Jeds had already been issued with amphetamines which would enable them to operate without sleep or rest for up to seventy-two hours. Now it was time for the L (for lethal) pills, theirs to use if they chose to in the event of facing torture after capture. Once they chomped on the glass ampoule the bitter-tasting potassium cyanide solution would be released. Death would follow *almost* immediately. Taking a deep breath she held out the pills in their protective brown rubber covering, keeping her eyes focused on the pills, watching them settle in her palm, waiting in silence for each to decide whether or not to take one.

She conducted a final visual check, making sure their stilettos were secure in their scabbards, their holsters strapped and taped shut. She was a bit like a mother fussing over her charges, but she probably noticed too that the distancing process had begun. Swank and his men would have been cutting themselves off from anything but each other, sitting in a tight group speaking in low tones, occasionally referring to a map or gesturing to make a point. Park was watching men about to go to war, girding their loins to face the enemy, commencing that bonding process that is unique to combat. They knew what lay ahead, that no quarter would be given, this was to the death. Of this aspect she was not a part; quietly she left them to their thoughts. The clock ticked on, and sooner than anyone expected it was time to go. She entered the room where Swank and his team were waiting, pale-faced but otherwise impassive.

We can only guess at the words spoken by Daphne Park that night as she addressed those men who were about to embark for France. She was, in effect, there at their instigation, she knew that. She would have made it clear that she was passing on the orders of their commanders, stressing the critical importance of the task facing them, the need to provide leadership and inspiration for the members of the French Resistance, the *Maquis*. She would have been aware how privileged she was to be addressing them, just twenty-three years old, barely a year in SOE, delivering the final exhortation to men on the eve of going into combat.

She would have told them that the *maquisards* were brave, but they were not organised militarily. For them to confront the enemy effectively they needed arms and equipment, some of which the Jeds would bring with them; more would be supplied later. The *maquisards* also needed leadership which the teams had to provide as well. The *maquisards* were free men; they were not subject to

Allied discipline, but they needed to be led into battle in an organised fashion. Any delay could be fatal to Allied plans. Park would have told them not to depend on others to achieve this task. Not to wait for reinforcements. Not to delay; just attack, attack, attack ...

Then it was time to go. They were driven across the tarmac where about a dozen aircraft, painted a sinister matt black, were readying for take-off. When they reached their B24 they clambered out of the Jeep, their equipment making movement difficult. At about 20.30[7] on the night of 12 August the B24 carrying Team EPHEDRINE took off from RAF Blida en route to France, the throaty roar of its engines deafening in the otherwise silent night. Park watched it bank to avoid the towering Atlas Mountains and stayed watching until its silhouette disappeared into the darkness. Four long hours later a wireless signal was received to say that her first team had been successfully inserted into France and was on the ground. Then she went to bed.

The next week was among the most hectic of her life as she helped complete the insertion of eighteen teams of Jeds into France. Sleeping was almost impossible as they raced from the base to Camp W to Blida and back again. Crosby, who suffered terribly from his ankles, was excused parachuting, instead he went in with in a Dakota via Corsica on 8 August (Team GRAHAM). Crosby's aircraft actually landed in a field in France, discharged its passengers and took off again with a fresh load in a faster turnaround than even Ryanair can manage. Lucien Conein (Team MARK) went in on the night of 16/17 August; one can easily imagine him giving Park a special smile as he boarded his aircraft. Osborne Grenfell (Team SCION) likewise; his was the final team to go, on the night of 29/30 August.

But the Allied push was working. When the Germans reneged on the 1940 Armistice and occupied Vichy France, among their first acts was to disband the standing Vichy French Army. The discharged former soldiers were told that they were subject to a form of conscription under the Service de Travail Obligatoire/ STO (Obligatory Work Service Law). This meant going to work in German factories as *Zwangsarbeiter* (forced labour) to fill the gaps created by call-ups of German workers. This had little appeal for the French on any number of grounds and so many tens of thousands took to the hills and became available to the *Maquis*. Of course France being France it was never going to be that simple. Many *maquisards* had concentrated mainly on keeping out of German hands for the previous two or three years and were content to continue with that strategy, preferring to engage in occasional skirmishes and then scurry back to their rural fastnesses. Others were interested in looting opportunities and general brigandry, still others in raising political war chests and laying the groundwork for the governance of post-war France, while as many again were classed as *sédentaires*, men who had yet to declare officially but were 'on hand'. And into that went the

Jeds: to many it seemed that the fighting element was the simpler, getting the French to cooperate and actually do something was the difficult bit. But these diplomat/soldiers had been well picked for their brains as well as their brawn, and by the time of DRAGOON there were hundreds of thousands of *résistants* engaged in fighting the Nazis.

This second invasion added to the incipient sense of panic then seeping through the German lines. The Nazis were already taking a pounding from three massive army groups; those of Montgomery, Bradley and Patton. Now Patch's 7th Army joined the fray. The four Allied armies attacked the Germans with a ferocity unprecedented at that stage of the war. Barrage after barrage of artillery rounds rained down on the German lines as tank-led assaults constantly probed and prodded for any weaknesses which were ruthlessly exploited. From the air, Typhoons, Mosquitoes and Mustangs strafed and bombed around the clock while right in the Germans' midst armies of *résistants*, many coordinated by SAS, Commandos, OSS Organised Groups and Jeds, attacked at will. Hundreds of thousands of German soldiers were killed, wounded and captured. And in the face of the onslaught they caved in. The previously impregnable Wehrmacht turned tail and made a dash for the illusory sanctuary of the Siegfried Line.[8] It was Blitzkrieg in reverse. On 25 August Paris was liberated. Now the Fatherland itself could be put to the sword.

The defeat of the Germans in France and the continuing progress in Italy meant that the SOE base in Massingham was soon too far distant from the fighting. In September it was closed, its functions being parcelled out elsewhere. RAF 624 Squadron and USAAF 885 Squadron were stood down soon afterwards. The Americans had been fortunate and hadn't lost any aircrew, but twenty RAF airmen sacrificed their lives in DRAGOON and its aftermath.

Park, however, was still the blackest of black sheep as far as the orderly office (administrative staff) in FANY was concerned, so she was left kicking her heels in Massingham, and none too happily.

I of course was one, an anomaly and two, deeply unpopular with all the other FANYs. And when it came – this is something I must say I never ever got over really – when it came to the time when everybody decamped to France, you know after it was all over and they had a triumphant procession up to Paris drinking all the way, I was left behind, I wasn't allowed to be any part of this at all. And of course my Jedburghs were in ... on the ground and there was nobody to say it would be nice if she went too. So I sat in Massingham for about a month eating my heart out and wanting to do things and not being able to do anything and then they kindly sent me back by sea in charge of a convoy of FANYs who were being returned empty so to speak, because they also either were not needed or hadn't behaved terribly well.[9]

On the voyage back to England Park's convoy was attacked by a German submarine and one of the ships was sunk. When she finally arrived Leo Marks still had work for her to do. She was assigned to the SAARF (Special Allied Airborne Reconnaissance Force), an operation organised on broadly similar lines to the Jeds (i.e. teams of three men) who were being readied to rescue Allied POWs whose life might be at risk either from deliberate action by retreating Nazi forces, or from malnutrition due to the collapse of the German war machine, or from some lunatic last stand by Hitler. The plan was to send teams of medical and support staff armed with appropriate supplies into Germany. Some would go in by air, others would follow the land armies. The operation was based in Virginia Water in Surrey in the Wentworth Golf Club. When that operation was cancelled Park volunteered for the Far East, for what was called Force 136, but the atom bombs on Hiroshima and Nagasaki put a halt to that particular gallop, to Park's great chagrin:

> Yes, it was infuriating, it's a dreadful thing to say but it was infuriating. And of course my Jedburghs had all gone there, which was another point as far as I was concerned, I would have liked to go with them.[10]

There was still work to be done: returning teams to be debriefed, reports to be written and answers to be sought, after-action reports to be filed, inquiries to be conducted. In all about seventeen Jeds had been killed in action in France. Two of the Massingham teams briefed by Park lost members: Larry Swank[i] died in an exchange of accidental fire within days of being dropped, while Tony Mellows[ii] died in a POW camp from wounds received in combat.

For Daphne Park it had been, in her own words, 'an interesting war'. Her rank when she finished was that of Commander, an almost unheard of rank in the Yeomanry. She had scaled the heights in Massingham and plumbed the depths in Milton Hall, but through it all to her own self she had remained true. She volunteered to be sent to the Far East – but the bombs put a stop to that. She volunteered to be dropped into France as an SOE agent, but she was too late, and more to the point she knew too much, too much about codes and had seen too many faces. The pettiness of FANY rankled, of course, the spiteful denial of her right to participate in the Paris jamboree being just one more example. Perhaps that was the reason why 'her Jeds' organised the SOE armourer to make for her a tiny – but fully functioning – pearl-handled pistol as a token of their regard for their warrior princess.

---

i SWANK, Lieutenant Lawrence Edwin ('Larry'); OSS, Jedburghs (1921-1944).

ii MELLOWS, Captain Thomas Anthony ('Tony'); 27th Lancers, RAC, Jedburghs (1920-1944).

She had mixed views about Marks, the direct cause of her falling into disgrace in FANY. While she felt that the decision to write the letter of complaint about Spooner was the right one, nonetheless she felt she had been manipulated by Marks because (and this was the part that really rankled) she thought he was acting from a sense of 'devilment' (to use an Irishism) rather than from any sincere concern.

> ... and of course he was a curious mixture of good and ill because if he [Marks] hadn't been so overjoyed at the idea of putting a bomb under the ... under SHAFE [Supreme Headquarters Allied Forces Europe] and the military by making me write my report, I wouldn't have written it and if I hadn't written it in fact it would have been a bad thing, it was a good thing that I did it and it had the results that they moved somebody not suitable for the job and put in somebody highly suitable for the job. So in the end he turned out to be right but I wouldn't put £100 on the fact that that was his intention. I mean I think his intention just was to put a little bomb under the soldiers and show them what idiots they were. And I'm not sure that he was thinking deeply about, you know, the real needs of the ... of the ... of the Jedburghs.[11]

She found the secrecy a little bit irksome, not about the detail, of course – she was far too aware of the need for absolute operational secrecy, most particularly after she was made privy to BIGOT. It was more the pretence that she was not really making a serious contribution:

> Because that was one of the things about the war that people don't understand about the FANYs I think ... that they were always written off by everybody, people said oh well you know she has a wonderful time driving Generals and you know moving in high life and every FANY had to pretend that's what they were doing. You weren't ever allowed to say you were doing something worthwhile.
> I can remember my great-aunts who were my guardians in England and who were tremendously patriotic were amazed, they couldn't understand me, they said, 'Darling why aren't you in the Wrens or something?' and I would say, 'Well you know it's ... its quite fun and it's not too bad in London.' And then I would go to Scotland or somewhere and they would say, 'Where were you?' and I would say 'Oh well you know great fun, jaunted up to Scotland and back.' And you know that's how you had to be, you had to pretend you were doing something either intensely boring or intensely frivolous. The one thing you weren't allowed to do was say I'm doing something jolly important and valuable.[12]

So effective were FANY in maintaining this attitude that after the war their contribution was little recognised, its members not being granted the Defence Medal, which, according to Park, even Churchill's garden girls (wartime secretaries in Number 10 Downing Street) were to receive. That rankled with her.[13] Of course the discretion aspect was excellent training for her later life in the Secret Intelligence Service.

Park had one last piece of business to attend to, making contact with her lover, Captain Douglas DeWitt Bazata. After a death-defying series of adventures in France the wounded soldier eventually made it back to Britain and was sent to Hatherop Castle where he and Hod Fuller were to train teams of Danish Jeds. We don't know what took place between him and Park but we do know the outcome. Maybe it was then that Bazata told her that he was a married man, having married a Diana Chirieleison in 1943, shortly before embarking for the UK.[14] There was no future for Park in his life, he said, their romance, such as it was, was dead. Something died in Daphne Park that day too, and it would be many, many years before the flame of love was once more lit in her heart. And it was on that sad note that Daphne Park's war drew to its close.

Vienna role, 1946-48

Park finished her war still a member of SOE and listed on the electoral roll as resident in Horse Guards in Whitehall, one of the cover addresses used by SOE in official employee documentation.[1] We don't know what her long-term aspirations were, but if they included staying on in SOE that wasn't to be. In January 1946 Clement Attlee's post-war Labour government adjudicated on the continuing internecine war between Colin Gubbins, Director of SOE, and the Chief of the SIS, Sir Stewart Menzies.[i] Menzies triumphed, with Attlee decreeing that SOE would be shut down, those of its functions for which a continuing role was foreseen being subsumed into SIS. The process was to take about a year.

So Park's twenty-one-month career on secondment to SOE was at an end. Now would come the difficult bit, how to manage the transformation from wartime employment to a civilian job. While she was employed by FANY, the Yeomanry would have offered very little future and in any event not one that would have appealed. So that was one route closed off. All that she would have been certain of was that she was enamoured of the secret world and was determined to make her career behind its secret walls. Because for Daphne Park the war had changed everything: it had opened doors hitherto not only closed but invisible to all but a tiny fraction of the population. She knew she had to find a way in before those doors were shut in her face.

So, true to type, she got in touch with anyone who knew someone who might be able to do something or, if not, suggest someone elsewhere who could. As the reality of peace stared people in the face anyone with any sort of strings was pulling them as vigorously as they could. Park had one advantage over many: she was inside the 'ring of secrecy', not inside the innermost ring perhaps, but far enough inside for people to take her into their confidence. And as she sniffed the Whitehall breeze she noted that the Diplomatic Service had lifted its ban on recruiting woman diplomats. That change in employment made her sit up and take notice.

As late as 1934 the Inter-Departmental Committee on the Admission of Women into the Diplomatic and Consular Services (known as the Schuster Committee) had concluded that the bar on entry to women should remain. And remain it did.[2] A loose alliance of women's organisations had forced the issue onto the political agenda, where it encountered a campaign of opposition of

---

i MENZIES, Major General Sir Stewart Graham, KCB, KCMG, DSO, MC; Grenadier Guards, SIS, Chief 1939-52 (1890-1968).

military precision, orchestrated by the Foreign Office, that, had its ferocity been applied to the German advance through the Low Countries in 1940, might have seen off Hitler in record time. The Foreign Office viewed the advent of women diplomats in much the same way as, fifty years later, Royal Navy traditionalists viewed the thought of women serving alongside men on Her Majesty's ships, i.e. not so much with distaste as with absolute abhorrence. The presence of these women in His Majesty's embassies threatened to destroy the cosy, well-ordered world of the overseas missions, with the ambassador in the role of *paterfamilias*, his wife, the ambassadress, as his most loyal and dutiful consort, and the rest of the embassy 'family' playing their assigned roles according to rank and position. This was how it was, how it had been for centuries and how it should remain. This, despite women having been admitted into the professional ranks of the Home Civil Service for some considerable time without that world (apparently) coming to an end.

However, in 1946, as a result of a promise extracted in wartime, the ban was ended, though with conditions. The first was that no more than 10% of entrants to the Diplomatic Service's Administrative Branch (officer class) in any one year could be women (lest the men be submerged in a sea of female flesh). Another was that women would be obliged to resign on marriage. That last stuck in the craw but – sufficient unto the day – the battle to break down the final barrier could be left for another time. The Foreign Office marked the change by admitting just one Administrative (A) Branch woman entrant, a Miss Monica Milne,[i] in the autumn of 1946; three more would follow within the year.[3] Another part of the grapevine told Park that SIS was recruiting in order to be able to fulfil its expanded post-war role. She figured that since the Diplomatic and Consular Service (now united) provided cover occupations for SIS officers on overseas postings there was no particular reason why women might not be admitted into SIS. In fact to her surprise she also learned that the SIS had at least two and possibly more women already on its rolls. Both were in operational jobs, though she knew that that might well be put down to the exigencies of war.

She decided to put her name up for entry. On the surface she made a credible candidate. She was bright, articulate to the point of forcefulness and fluent in French, then an essential qualification for entry to the Diplomatic Service (and by extension into SIS). Her wartime experience should also have helped, but to her surprise and immense chagrin she was turned down. SIS told her that the decision at the time was to do with her wartime service. As an instructor she had been exposed to members of the French Resistance, and many of the *résistants* were 'communist sympathisers'.[4] She had also been exposed to many Czech and Polish agents, most of whom had returned to their countries when the war

i MILNE, Monica May; Foreign Office (1918-d.).

ended, many being arrested and imprisoned. In intelligence jargon, she had been 'burnt'. That may have been the real reason or equally it may not. Experience of working with *résistants* did not stop SIS recruiting Ernst van Maurik,[i] 'Terry' O'Bryan Tear[ii] and Tony Brooks[iii] in its post-war intake, and plenty more besides.[5]

Her gender and her SOE pedigree would not have helped her cause, and were probably the real reasons for her rejection; in more modern parlance, 'her face didn't fit'. More than three decades would pass before the Service routinely recruited women into the Intelligence Branch, though occasionally it opened the door and would allow one to slip through. This was of little comfort to Park: all she would have been certain of was that the end was nigh in FANY and she had better do something 'toot sweet' if she wasn't going to be summarily demobbed and told to find a job teaching in a girls' school or learning shorthand/typing in Denson's (a secretarial college in Queensgate). So she upped the pace, which was her way, her *modus operandi*: never to accept the first rejection, nor even the second and certainly not the third. She would not learn typing, she would not become a teacher, she would not conform. The increased pressure worked, someone did indeed have a word with someone else and Park was offered a job in FIAT-BIOS (Field Intelligence Agency/Technical – British Intelligence Objectives Sub-committee). That someone was Captain Ian Garrow,[iv] a colleague of Airey Neave's[v] in MI9 and a wartime hero in his own right. Garrow was a co-founder of the PAT Line, an escape route for British military personnel stranded in France

A recommendation from Garrow carried considerable weight, and soon Park found herself en route to Germany where she would handle liaison between FIAT-BIOS and the French army of occupation which was headquartered in Baden Baden. By the time Park arrived in Frankfurt, the location of FIAT-BIOS's headquarters, the powers-that-be had changed their minds and instead dispatched a navy officer ('a splendid old buffer'[6]) to Baden Baden to fulfil the liaison role. Park was offered the consolation of an admin job as PA to the commanding officer, in her words, 'an incurable drunk'.[7] To Daphne Park being a PA offered no consolation whatever; if she was determined on one thing it was that the woman who had dispatched the bravest of the brave on their perilous missions to Occupied France was not going to commence her post-war career as someone's personal assistant.

i Van MAURIK, Ernst, OBE; HM Forces, SOE, SIS, H/MOSCOW, BERLIN, H/BUENOS AIRES, H/COPENHAGEN, H/RIO (1916-2012).

ii O'BRYAN TEAR, Captain Hubert ('Terry') OBE; HM Forces, SOE, Jedburghs, SIS, H/MOSCOW, H/STOCKHOLM, H/MANILA, ADEN, SINGAPORE, H/BAHRAIN, H/BERNE (1918-1993).

iii BROOKS, Anthony ('Tony'), MC, DSO; SOE, SIS, H/SOFIA, turned down H/HANOI, CYPRUS, PARIS, GENEVA (1922-2007).

iv GARROW, Captain Ian Grant, DSO; Highland Light Infantry, MI9 (1908-1976).

v NEAVE, Airey Middleton Sheffield, DSO, OBE, MC, TD (1916-1979).

And I said well one I don't type and do shorthand and two I don't drive and three I don't want to be a PA and I've never been one and I don't intend to start.[8]

A stand-off ensued, broken by the return to England of her mother Doreen whom Park had not seen since she left Kayuki Estate in 1932. Park was granted three weeks' leave to go to London to see her mother. Doreen Park returned to Britain alone shortly before Christmas 1946 and went back to Africa in the New Year. Her husband John was still alive but suffering from blackwater fever and not well enough to travel.

When Daphne Park returned to Frankfurt in the New Year a replacement PA (a FANY originally recommended for the PA role by Park) had been assigned to the job and was getting on famously with the 'incurable drunk', who had presumably transferred his affections to her. That was another reason why Park had so objected to the position originally – being a PA was bad enough but being a PA *and* the subject of unwanted amorous advances from her boss would have been way too much. The CO, now pleased as punch with his PA, suffered a fit of remorse and decided to make it up to Park. As the chief of staff of FIAT-BIOS said to her over breakfast one morning:

> 'The old man feels frightfully guilty, he feels that you have been done out of a very important job, he feels bad about it, so he's thought of something for you.' So I said, 'God only what,' and he said, 'Well he's just been down in Vienna staying with his old chum, who was the AOC and he's going to open an office of FIAT-BIOS in Vienna and you're going to open it, you're going to run it,' and I said, 'What will I do?' 'Oh,' he said, 'it'll be fine,' he said, 'you'll have a major who is an expert in rockets and a air force officer who is an expert in something else, you'll have three major advisors who can interview with the people you are going to find hiding out in ... in universities and so forth and you'll have twenty drivers for all the people who come out to interview them and you'll have an office and you'll be attached to the Air Force and your nominal boss will be Robin Speight. But in fact you'll be your own boss.'[9]

Commander Park, who didn't speak a word of German, didn't have a military background, couldn't read a blueprint or any form of technical diagram, would run the FIAT-BIOS operation in Vienna. Early in 1947 she commenced work in the city. Her mission was to acquire German scientific and technical secrets. The secrets might be in scientists' minds, or be contained in reports, research papers, devices, weapons and/or the factories/laboratories associated with their development and manufacture. Her raw material consisted of thousands of pages of monthly and annual progress reports duly submitted by the methodical German scientists to their command during the war. Her personnel were almost exclusively military officers on assignment plus some secretarial and support staff. The original decision, made in 1944, to establish FIAT-BIOS resulted from the post D-Day realisation by the Western military of just how far behind the Germans they were. At the outbreak of war the prevailing attitude in both London and Washington could be summed up as a combination of 'there's little that Johnny Foreigner can teach us' and 'if we're not able to build a machine to do something it is because such a machine simply cannot be built'.

This proved wrong on both counts, and by the end of the war it was acknowledged that the Third Reich was up to a generation ahead in practically every area of core military science, with the exception of radar and the atom bomb and a few other random areas (such as the proximity fuse). And despite the massive Allied onslaught, the output of German war matériel remained largely unaffected by the bombing. Not only was Germany developing equipment that was far superior to its Allied equivalent (if the Allies even had an equivalent), it was able to deploy the results in potentially decisive quantities: ballistic missiles, fighter jets, tanks, torpedoes, infrared aiming and detection systems, anti-tank rocket launchers, synthetic fuel, synthetic rubber and so on. The Germans came tantalisingly close to developing not just one but a plethora of secret weapons with the potential, if not quite to turn the war decisively in their favour, then to extend it considerably.

And, as is so often the way, when the generals did come round to a new way of thinking they began to pursue the Nazis' *wunder* technology with the same degree of effort and enthusiasm formerly exhibited in dismissing its significance. In the modern jargon, seizing German scientific secrets became the only game in town, a vicious four-ball struggle between London, Paris, Moscow and Washington. Soon all pretence of working together was thrown aside other than an agreement between Britain and the US that at all costs the Russians must be prevented from gaining the upper hand, particularly in the atomic weapons sphere – something that became increasingly hard to maintain since over two-thirds of Germany's industrial capacity was inside the part of Germany occupied by the Russians.

So by the time Park joined FIAT-BIOS it was more a collection of competing interests than an organisation united by a common purpose. It was nominally headed by a British officer, Lieutenant Colonel R.J. Maunsell,[i] an experienced intelligence officer. Maunsell's second-in-command was an American, Colonel Ralph Osborne.[ii] The contribution for which Maunsell is principally remembered today (possibly unfairly but understandable if he was 'an incurable drunk') was adding the 'T' (as in Technical) to the phonetically unsympathetic FIA, turning it into the more pronunciation-friendly FIAT. What was driving the inter-country rivalry was not any great desire by the military to line the pockets

i MAUNSELL, (later) Brigadier R.J., CBE; Royal Tank Regiment, Security Intelligence Middle East (SIME), FIAT (1903-d.).

ii OSBORNE, (later) Brigadier General Ralph M.; US Army, FIAT (1903-1991).

of their country's industrialists,[10] but rather a realisation that the end of the Second World War was more a hiatus than a culmination. That it also marked the beginning of another and potentially far greater conflict, one between the Soviet Union of Josef Stalin and the Western Allies, and that it was up to each to ensure it was not left behind in the arms race that was sure to erupt.

The electoral roll for the years 1947 and 1948 shows Park's place of residence as 31A Wilton Place, FANY headquarters; it would appear to be an address of convenience while she was on secondment in Vienna.

Park's job was easier to describe than to accomplish: to locate eminent German/Austrian scientific brains resident in that country. Despite Austria being declared the first official 'victim' of Nazi tyranny, both races were regarded as being equally 'German' (i.e. culpable) by most Allied officials. Park was to establish the potential value of any scientist she came across and then nab the best of them for Britain. She was to ensure, as far as possible, that none of the candidates had been 'ardent' Nazis and that none had conducted medical experiments on concentration camp inmates in furtherance of war-related objectives. In fact FIAT had a role in coordinating the prosecution of those creatures.[11] Other than that she had free rein.

Despite Britain's largely inchoate and less than successful initial campaign to grab Germany's secrets, by early 1947 the British had a reasonable idea of the likely whereabouts of Nazi Germany's principal scientific brains, referred to as 'dragons'.[12] So Park would have had a target list of sorts assembled by the American's Joint Intelligence Objectives Agency (JIOA).[13] She would also have had a copy of *Who's Who in Nazi Germany*, a directory listing a couple of thousand of the Third Reich's most notable personalities, covering the military, SS, Nazi party and also leading industrialists and scientists.[14] But knowing was not the same as having, and in actually securing the services of German scientists Britain was far behind the others.

The Americans, for example, driven by their air force, had secured the services of over a hundred key German guided missile experts. It hadn't taken the USAF long to figure out the strategic implications of placing an atomic bomb onto the nosecone of the German V2 ballistic missile. Nor to figure the edge an atom-tipped missile development program would give the Air Force over its Army and Navy rivals in the fight for Congressional budget dollars. The Americans (and later the British) quickly got over any scruples they had with regard to the Nazi past of their new recruits, while neither the Russians nor the French ever evinced any in the first place.

SIS unwittingly played a key role in assisting the Americans assembly of Nazi Germany's top rocket brains. Desperate to boost the progress of their scientific research, the Nazis recalled their formerly discarded intellectuals to put them to work developing *wunder* weapons. First, though, they needed to ensure their political and ideological reliability. An engineer/scientist called Werner Osenberg who headed the Military Research Association was given the task of determining which scientists were 'Nazi-enough' to be entrusted with this task of vital importance to the Reich and its Nazi leadership. The list of scientists, predictably called the Osenberg list, was circulated and a copy fell into the hands of SIS some months before the end of the war. In the spirit of the times SIS forwarded the names to the Americans who used it to identify the cream of the Nazi crop, those scientists who were to be captured, interrogated and offered jobs. Not surprisingly Wernher von Braun, Nazi Germany's premier rocket scientist, became the top priority.[15] Persuasion (it certainly worked with von Braun whose negotiating skills were on a par with those of a modern football agent) was the preferred recruitment method with each of the four powers, including Russia, offering lucrative personal employment contracts, residence permits for families and generous tobacco allowances. However all were prepared to use a degree of coercion if needs be. The Soviets were quite happy to take that to the point of a gun with mass seizure being used on occasion. Britain preferred to invite them to come and visit Britain and then intern them until they revealed what they knew.[16]

It's fair to assume that even as she hunted her scientists Park was still trying to forge her longer-term career, for it was obvious that FIAT-BIOS too was going to go the way of SOE and be wound up within a couple of years or so. She was not spoiled for choice. The wartime job offers in the Treasury and the Foreign Office, which she had discarded with youthful disdain, were no longer open. SOE was well into the process of being wound down. FANY itself held little appeal and in any event had already demobbed the bulk of its wartime personnel. That left SIS and MI5. Park wouldn't have known very much about SIS, which was of course what it wanted, but enough to know that it sounded 'interesting'. Her work in SAARF in Virginia Water may have brought her into contact with SIS. Someone must have told her what SIS did and how to be put in contact with the organisation. Despite her disappointment at her initial rejection she hadn't completely given up on SIS, though she probably knew that overturning a decision once made is far more difficult that getting one's way in the first instance. There was of course the matter of her gender. Since 1942 SIS had employed at least one woman in an operational role, Doreen Milne,[i] who served in Tangier during the Second World War and in Geneva immediately after. That could be taken as a sign that the Service did not appear to have an official position on the matter so was, in theory at least, open to the idea of employing a woman in an operational role. That said, everything she heard suggested it might be devilishly difficult to get in.

i MILNE, Doreen Margaret; SIS, TANGIER, GENEVA, ROME, H/MOSCOW (1916-2004).

However, in that regard at least SIS seemed a bit more advanced in its thinking than its sister service, MI5, which appeared to be populated in the main by former colonial policemen. The Security Service had dismissed its sole wartime woman intelligence officer, Jane Archer,[i] in 1940.[17] Archer had been shown the door because she criticised a spectacularly incompetent superior.[18] It is unlikely that is would have warmed Park to a career in the Security Service. Then she had a piece of good fortune. She came across someone of potential value to Britain and who was prepared to cooperate.

According to Gordon Corera's previously cited interview,[19] Park was approached and asked if she could arrange to smuggle a Red Army major out of Vienna. The major was being transferred back to the Soviet Union and did not want to go there, perhaps fearing he might be liquidated. Park apparently approached George Young,[ii] then H/VIENNA (head of the SIS station in Vienna). Young was interested but, reportedly, hadn't the resources available to hand to carry out the task, so he asked Park to use her own military contacts to do it instead. Young then put in a word for her and SIS reconsidered its original refusal. There is an alternative version, that Park offered the opportunity to SIS for it to exploit rather than attempt to hold on to it herself, and that she approached George Young with that in mind. She could have had a couple of reasons for going about it this way. For a start FIAT-BIOS did not appear to have the resources or capability to mount a clandestine extraction operation, so there was a risk of screwing it up. But there may have been another, far more salient reason. Park hadn't given up on her ambition to get into SIS, far from it. So she offered Young a 'cash for glory' deal: in return for her handover of the Russian major (she uses the term 'defector' in her interview with Martyn Cox) he would persuade SIS in London to re-think its rejection of her candidature. Park didn't give a damn about not getting the kudos as long as he delivered on his side.

Either way, she was spot-on in her choice. The tall, red-haired, flamboyant Young was ambitious, energetic and a risk-taker, just what Park needed. He was also an intellectual dynamo who had joined SIS during the war where he had done well and had even been 'mentioned in dispatches', no small honour. He resigned in 1945 to return to his pre-war occupation as a journalist but rejoined SIS in 1947 and was posted to Vienna. In 'The Final Testimony of George Kennedy Young', a document written in the third person but attributed to George Young, the former spy writes in detail about his SIS career. The testimony includes a summary of his activities as H/VIENNA in 1947 and contains an oblique reference to some of the SOE people he worked with in Vienna later becoming 'stars in SIS'.[20]

i ARCHER, Kathleen ('Jane'), *née* Sissmore; MI5, SIS (1900-1982).

ii YOUNG, George Kennedy, CMG, OBE, CB; King's Own Scottish Borderers, SIS, H/VIENNA, CYPRUS, D/R (Requirements), Vice-Chief 1958-61 (1911-1990).

Later that year, in the summer of 1948, Park received a letter from a body called the Coordination Staff in London inviting her to apply for entry into 'government service involving periods of service abroad'. She had to include with her application the sum of £3 in postage stamps, in order, it said, 'to discourage frivolous applications for employment in government service'.[21] The one thing we can be certain of is that there was nothing the least bit frivolous about Park's application, though she did admit later that she was so nervous that she left her handbag behind her after her interview. That was not to count against her, and in August 1948 Daphne Park was welcomed into the SIS. She is the only woman known to have joined that summer.

7

A world changing, 1947-48

The Secret Intelligence Service that Daphne Park was joining was far removed from its modern counterpart, further even than the sixty or so years that separate them might suggest. The Second World War was well over and the wartime influx of brains and talent had by 1947 become an outpouring. The Service was in danger of drifting back to its pre-war mediocrity, a mediocrity that had seen it ill-prepared for the outbreak of hostilities. Within six months of the start of the Second World War SIS had no agent networks of substance left standing in Germany or indeed throughout most of Occupied Europe. Its principal central European networks had been betrayed when two incompetent (even by the then SIS standards) officers, Payne-Best and Stevens, allowed themselves to be lured to the border between the Netherlands and Germany by Gestapo intelligence agents. The agents bundled the two hapless officers into a couple of cars and then dashed across the frontier and into the Reich.[i]

The embarrassment resulting from the capture of two senior officers was made worse by SIS's pre-war policy for operations in hard-target countries to be controlled from an adjoining one. Thus intelligence-gathering inside Nazi Germany was handled from the SIS station in The Hague, run by the two men. The pair weren't made of the sternest material and soon told the Nazis all they knew, so blowing whatever chance SIS had of extracting some decent intelligence from Nazi Germany. As the great betrayer Kim Philby[ii] put it (more or less truthfully for once), 'when the war broke out SIS had not a single agent between the Balkans and the Channel'. On top of that, the few agents it had left had no means of communicating any intelligence back or receiving instructions in return, as no plans had been laid for wartime communications between head office and its agents in mainland Europe. There were no hidden radios, no *poste restante* addresses in neutral countries, no couriers or border-crossers. All that was left was a scattering of mainly venal agents without either the means or motivation to do SIS's work.

What saved SIS from the ignominy it probably deserved was its role in securing the top secret German Enigma coding machines which led to the ULTRA (as in 'of *ultra* importance') signals intelligence breakthrough. Possession of the machines meant that tens of thousands of top-secret German wartime communications

i PAYNE-BEST, Captain Sigismund (1885-1978) and STEVENS, Major Richard Henry (1893-1967); the pair spent the war in concentration camps but survived.
ii PHILBY, Harold Adrian ('Kim'); SIS (KGB) (1912-1988).

could be either fully or partially decoded, giving the Allies a priceless tactical and strategic advantage in practically every theatre of the war. However, had the Germans realised that their codes were broken they would have altered them at once and the advantage would have been lost completely. This gave rise to the classic intelligence quandary: how, on the one hand to exploit (take advantage of) the intelligence gained, while on the other ensuring that the source was not compromised. That task was given to Stewart Menzies – circulate the intelligence, he was instructed, but at all costs keep the source secret. And he succeeded: the Germans never realised that the Allied High Command was privy to the content of the messages of all of its three services, Wehrmacht, Kriegsmarine and Luftwaffe. The codes were far from being an open book and massive effort had to be expended to make them readable (and even then many were not, or at least not soon enough to be operationally useful). Still, it was an extraordinary trove and its management was very much down to Menzies' handing and the protocols put in place by him. Empowered by this success, within a year of the war's end, Menzies had seen off the 'SOE upstarts' who in fairness had enjoyed a pretty good war but not quite good enough to prevent their abolition. So the saboteurs, many of whom were quite keen to turn their attention to the burgeoning Soviet empire, were out of a job. As a sop a few of SOE's more robust were taken on by SIS and a special section was established with the avowed purpose of providing SIS with an SOE-style paramilitary capability. That suited it quite well, not because SIS wanted to blow up bridges and rail lines – it never saw that as its purpose – but because it wanted to be able to overthrow governments it didn't like and paramilitary skills come in handy for that.

But the Service Park entered wasn't all bad; *some* of the worst aspects of its pre-war environment had been attended to; it had beefed up its training regimen and reorganised its field operations, though recruitment remained haphazard.

Menzies realised that the pre-war system for controlling its operations was well past its 'use-by' date. In the 1920s SIS practice had been to dispatch its officers to their allotted geographical region and more or less let them get on with it. This was understandable, distances were long and communications far too slow to allow any form of hands-on control. It did however lead to its officers interpreting their instructions as they saw fit and acting accordingly, often with undesirable or at best unpredictable consequences. In the 1930s this very loose 'system' had been replaced by posting officers to diplomatic missions as 'passport control officers', a department being established for that purpose for both cover and revenue-generating purposes. The revenue-generating part worked, but as a cover for an intelligence officer it stank. Soon every intelligence service worth its salt knew that to identify the local SIS representatives all it need do was look up the roster for the British passport control office.

In fairness, the new arrangement did aid command and control, not least because Broadway could avail itself of the established diplomatic communications network of diplomatic bags, king's messengers and telegraphs. That did not, however, mean that SIS operations became better aligned with government policy, rather that it was just better able to do things its own way. In the words of one former officer, 'the Chief steered his own ship, without any undue reference to Whitehall and what it might consider desirable or appropriate'.[1] This naturally gave rise to a somewhat jaundiced view of its operations among the mandarins. For that reason most heads-of-mission refused point blank to have anything to do with the local SIS officer, nor did the Diplomatic Service particularly encourage them to do so.

The ambassadors felt that they and their staffs were quite well-qualified to report on conditions based on their conversations with their host governments and their officials. And indeed if someone wanted to burgle safes for the blueprints of some secret weapon that was fine with them, but there was no justification for housing such fellows in an embassy, and to be truthful many of SIS's finest were a pretty rum lot. So while formally attached to embassies, the passport control offices (and officers) were located in buildings apart from the embassy chancery. An exception was made for service (military) attachés, since they were gentlemen and though dull fellows in the main, could be relied upon to behave. Now Menzies decided to phase out that paper-thin cover entirely. The position of passport control officer would remain but its holders would be just that, conventional officials in the employ of the Consular Service. SIS officers were to be listed on the embassy roster as first, second or third secretaries or even as counsellors (but that came much later), according to seniority. They would enjoy the perks of embassy life but would not enjoy being within their ambassadors' ambit of control, leading to forms of Mexican stand-off in many cases, with resultant mutual detestation.

From a purely technical standpoint, though, communications were much improved. The Diplomatic Wireless Service (DWS) was set up immediately after the war in order to provide reliable and secure radio communication between London and its overseas missions. The first transmitters were on Signal Hill in the village of Gawcott in Buckinghamshire. SIS was able to piggyback on that and for the first time exercise some effective command and control over its overseas-based officers. At this time SIS also set up its own transmitters for sending messages to its agents. The best known station was known as 'The Lincolnshire Poacher' (from its interval signal/signature tune). It was co-located in Gawcott, remaining there for many years after the DWS moved to Hanslope Park.[2] The SIS operation was a 'numbers station' with a voice reading out series of numbers, in five-letter groups, which were (and still are) in reality encrypted messages meant for agents overseas.[3]

To cap it all SIS personnel were now semi-established civil servants, subject to the norms of the Inland Revenue with regulated pay and conditions, a personnel department, promotion boards and even pensions. There were aspects of their remuneration that needed attending to, but the time when they had to supplement a meagre wage by stealing money that was due to be paid to their agents and sources was over. SIS had entered the twentieth century, albeit when it had a little over half its course to run.

Of course the post-war Service was of its time and for Britain that time was dominated by the end of Empire. The Indian Independence Act of 1947 created the independent Dominions of India and Pakistan. The 'Jewel in the Crown' was no more. The farseeing saw this as an irreversible process, marking the end of an empire 'on which the sun never set'. But farseeing people were as thin on the ground then as they are today and for the bulk of Britons the Empire was still there to stay if for no other reason than they believed that was how their subjects wanted matters to remain. Or to put it more accurately, because they *wanted* to believe that was how their subjects wanted matters to remain. So for most Britons this remained the era of the 'white man's burden', with a solemn duty to rule over those less fortunate than they. However, this grew increasingly difficult to sustain. Indian independence did indeed mark the beginning of the end. The following two decades would be a time of enormous change as the Empire, which had been the centrepiece of people's upbringing, first shrank, then practically disappeared before their eyes.

The process was not altogether peaceful, with a number of wars of liberation of which the Mau Mau campaign in Kenya was probably the most bloody, but there were armed wars of liberation in Ghana, Aden and Cyprus, a form of proxy independence war in Malaysia, and an attempted takeover of Borneo by the Indonesians. For Park, a child of Empire, the process was deeply unsettling. Her imperial credentials, even bloodline, were 'Empire' through and through. Her expectant mother had made the pilgrimage back to Britain, not once but twice ensuring that both Park and her brother were born in their motherland. Her paternal grandfather (born in Monmouth) was a colonial police officer who had fought the Boers. Her maternal grandfather was a Protestant Belfast academic. And of course her father had 'done his bit' in the Great War and had been wounded, a badge of courage if ever there was one. For her and her generation all of the certainties, the knowledge of Britain's pre-eminent place in the world, were gone – and this despite beating the Germans and winning the war.

But if 1947 marked the end of Empire, then 1948 marked some beginnings. One was the start of mass immigration from these soon-to-be-former colonies. In that year the *Empire Windrush* had docked in Tilbury carrying 448 passengers from Jamaica who had answered British government appeals to come to Britain for a new life and to assist in the post-war reconstruction of the country. Within a few short years white, homogeneous Britain was on the irreversible path to multi-culturalism. But not the SIS, which remained as white as the driven snow. Its officers were almost exclusively white, male 'chaps'. The pre-war practice of eschewing university graduates ('not to be trusted'[4]) in favour of military officers or colonial policemen was slowly being abandoned in favour of recruits from the 'great universities' of Oxford and Cambridge.[5] Most were recruited through the recommendation of a small group of trusted dons or tutors, or on being demobbed on completion of their wartime service in the Forces. Some transferred in from the shrinking colonial police[i] (though increasingly rarely, that now being more the preserve of MI5).

Even so 1948 did mark the year when the Service made a determined effort to embark on the road toward creating the civilianised service that it is today, when its natural orientation would be to the Foreign Office in King Charles Street rather than to Sandhurst and the Regiments of Guards in Wellington Barracks. The 'old' (pre-war) Service could have been characterised as a cosy 'hankie up the sleeve' sort of place, in that SIS brains weren't over-valued, foppishness was frowned upon, and book learning had its place but not a sizable one. Patriotism was taken for granted, as was one's loyalty to one's friends and one's class. To the gentlemen of SIS it made absolutely no sense to think that one of their own could possibly turn against his own. In fact loyalty, whether to country or to colleagues, was the standard against which a man's character was measured. What was cherished was a spirit of adventure, of derring-do, of plot and counter-plot, of 'bashing on regardless' when faced with adversity. The old SIS mentality was part Baden-Powell, part Bulldog Drummond (Park's fictional favourite), mixed in with the gentlemen's clubs of St James's and the playing fields of Eton.

While the post-war Service still contained many of the elements of the old, it began to realise that a more hard-nosed attitude was required. The Service was in the front line in the war to preserve Britain's place in a very turbulent and dangerous world, and that was going to require steel and savvy. SIS had to learn how to recruit and run agents in the most hostile environments; in that it was greatly assisted by SOE's wartime experience. It had to learn too that the new post-war world was far more interdependent and interlinked than had been the case previously. Just how interlinked it was, was made very clear to the British Prime Minister Anthony Eden in 1956. His decision to invade Suez saw his country's currency being mortally threatened from a city three and a half thousand miles to the West (Washington DC) and its population being threatened with atomic annihilation from a city one and a half thousand miles

i For example, CRAIG, Richard ('Dick'), OBE, MC, CPM; Colonial Police (Palestine/Malaya), SIS (1921-2000) .

to the East (Moscow), and all in the space of a couple of weeks. This wasn't the way things had been, certainly not for old SIS hands.

Naturally it wasn't all new. SIS continued to befriend the 'ins and the outs' (those in power and those out of power – for one never knew). Where necessary it toppled leaders or their governments and installed new ones in their place as it had done for decades as it simultaneously combated insurgents and subverted *their* aims. SIS was also learning that, unlike the old days, when the enemy was many hundreds, if not thousands, of miles over *there*, with these 'damn' communists one could never be too careful. The consequent need for absolute secrecy about its affairs was instilled in every new recruit from the moment they joined. The habit became so ingrained that the vast majority would respect it to the end of their lives.[6] Very quickly recruits learned they had joined not so much an organisation as a praetorian guard, or set of janissaries perhaps, with all the attendant risks that that entails. As one former officer put it:

> The service was divided between those who saw membership of it as imposing special responsibilities and those who saw themselves as special through belonging to it. I tried hard to encourage the former attitude.[7]

What was not in doubt was the emphasis on loyalty, respect and tradition, on putting the needs of the Service before self, for SIS demanded much but in turn could give much back. Not everyone who joined bonded with their fellows. Most who didn't accepted the inevitable, either leaving of their own accord or when quietly asked to. But some stayed, when it would perhaps have been better for all concerned if they had heeded their instincts and departed for pastures new. One who could swear fealty was Daphne Park. Into the Service came the twenty-seven-year-old on a junior officer's starting salary of £400 per annum, determined that neither her gender, nor her former SOE status, nor anything else would prevent her from enjoying the career on which she was set.

That said, Park would have been forgiven for wondering what was in store for her as she left her new home in No. 381 London Road, Ewell in Epsom, and presented herself that first morning at the Broadway Buildings head office of SIS in St James's. Ewell (North Cheam) was a pleasant place to live, part of the prosperous suburbs, and she would continue living there for the next three years. It compared well with Broadway Buildings which, according to Kim Philby's account, 'was a dingy eight-storey rabbit warren with its wooden-partitioned offices that were akin to hutches, crammed with dusty files and fitted with opaque frosted glass internal windows and all served by a creaking lift operated by an equally creaking retainer'.[8] What standard Philby was using to judge the offices is not clear; certainly Broadway would have compared well with Soviet government offices of that era.

It can't have been made too easy for Park. While not quite so hidebound as the Foreign Office, SIS was still an organisation whose middle and top echelons were bound together by a shared wartime experience and resultant male camaraderie. The role a man played in the war dominated other men's view of him and nowhere more so than in an organisation such as SIS. Was a chap's chest 'bare of campaign medals'? Did he serve in a frontline combat unit? Had he been wounded? Decorated? Someone who had seen out the war in the Educational Corps was not going to attract much admiration, not just three years after the guns had fallen silent. That same judgement would not have applied to Park; she was after all a mere woman and so not expected to have risked her life on the battlefield. Her service in FANY/SOE helped, of course. It wasn't the same as combat but she had worn uniform and that counted for something. More to the point perhaps, Park's time in SOE meant that she was used to the company of men and of servicemen specifically, though one thing that was made abundantly clear to her was that she had to cut off all contact with her wartime pals in FANY/SOE, other than those who had been accepted into SIS.[9] Dealing with men on an equal footing was not a new experience; it was not something that she found intimidating. However, more than a few of the men she had to deal with had an air of assumed superiority and were not prepared to accept her as their equal.

To describe SIS as chauvinistic is perhaps misleading; in the Britain of 1948 every organisation of substance was almost by definition chauvinistic. Throughout society women were defined as the weaker sex, engaged almost exclusively in support or auxiliary roles in every walk of life. Women were secretaries not managers, nurses not doctors, bus conductors (clippies) not drivers, canteen workers not factory hands. Those few women who had broken through and were enjoying real careers were expected to abandon them on marriage so that people would not look pityingly on their husbands as 'poor fellows who could not control their wives'. And for this they were expected to be grateful, or at least to feign gratitude.[10] The 'heady' days of wartime Britain when the doors of opportunity were thrown open to women were fast disappearing. The Nazis may have been well beaten but it was their adopted slogan *Kinder, Küche, Kirche* (Children, Kitchen, Church) that now seemed once again the order of the day.

Standard office attire for the men was a bowler hat (though only in London), a dark grey suit and stiff collar. For women, plain frocks to the mid-calf were the norm. The work day commenced at 10 a.m. in order, it was said, to allow time for the overnight telegrams – which determined much of the day's business – to be deciphered and circulated. Fitting in included observing the social norms; in SIS that meant one addressed one's colleagues by their given names rather than by their surnames, considered quite *avant-garde* given that use of surnames was the Foreign Office way, which in turn was thought to be far more collegial than the standard for the Home Civil Service, which was 'Mr' or 'Sir'. Park also learned 'never to knock on a senior officer's door: open the damn thing and go straight in, and withdraw only if plainly inconvenient. One would not knock, a vulgar habit, in a friend's house, would one?'[11] At lunchtime every day there would be a row of chauffeur-driven limousines lined up outside Broadway ready to take their owners to lunch in their clubs in St James's.[12]

Women, apart from the rare exception such as Park, were restricted to secretarial duties. Most secretaries were the well brought up daughters of senior SIS personnel or else of generals, admirals and the occasional bishop. They were educated in private schools in the Home Counties and in finishing schools in France or Switzerland in place of going to university. They were in effect already vetted and had discretion bred into them from birth. Many were accommodated (until they got their own flats) in the hostel SIS maintained in Cromwell Road under the supervision of a fierce dragon-lady, waiting for the day when they might catch the eye of a keen young officer in the Intelligence Branch.[13]

Dick White,[i] who was to be appointed Chief in 1956, and so would be Park's ultimate boss for almost one third of her service in SIS, summed up his attitude to women in SIS thus:

Our secretaries need only two things; good legs and a good upbringing.[14]

For her part Daphne Park did not consider herself to be a feminist, not that the term had the same salience then as it has today. But feminist or not, she was determined to get her due.[15] She wasn't in SIS to type letters while she snared a husband. So she decided just to get on with it. She had her own not so secret weapon, a personality that included an infectious sense of humour that, when she chose to, could be used to envelop people almost irresistibly. People who had not met her in decades still speak of her in glowing terms, as 'someone who once met was never forgotten'.[16] Not indeed that she was entirely without friends in the Service. She had an extensive network of connections of her own, former SOE hands who formed a 'firm within the Firm' and who looked out for each other, to some degree at least, until wartime loyalties gradually faded to be replaced by newer shared experiences.

Of course not everyone was an admirer. Someone as forthright as Park was going to make enemies, and she did. Others, while affecting to like her, would question other aspects of her personality: her obdurate nature, her Margaret Thatcher-like love for the simple solution over the more complex, her tendency to exclude those with whom she disagreed or whom she did not rate, but all that was to come later. For now she had a job to do, a career to build.

---

i WHITE, Sir Dick Goldsmith, KCMG, KBE; Director of MI5 1953-56, Chief of SIS 1956-68, Co-ordinator for Intelligence and Security 1968-73 (1906-1993).

8

Into the lion's den, 1948-51

When Park joined SIS Sir Stewart Menzies, its wartime Chief, was still in place. To those few in Whitehall who actually knew of him he was CSS (Chief of Secret Service) or just C. Within SIS he was referred to either as C or Chief, though the more senior dared to refer to him as the 'August Presence', if only behind his back. For reasons of secrecy he signed his letters to overseas stations with any three consecutive letters of the alphabet. Communications within Whitehall he signed with a plain C. All were written in green ink on SIS's traditional deep-blue plain notepaper; which is perhaps not so exotic as it might seem, given that the Foreign Office custom of the time was for the Secretary of State alone in the office (and ambassadors while abroad) to write their letters in red ink, the better for them to stand out (or so it was said).

In some respects C's role was as much if not more to do with handling relations with Whitehall and the Service's customers than exercising executive direction over his Controllers, SIS's highest operational rank. It was more a case of first among equals than 'Hail to the Chief'. The Controllers, and in particular those who were far distant from London, had significant autonomy, reigning over their individual fiefdoms much like princelings of the Roman Catholic Church and equally protective of their privileges. Menzies did have the trappings of office. He had the use of a private house in Queen Anne's Gate, a privilege still enjoyed by the head of the Service though whether at the same address we cannot say. He occupied a well appointed office on the fourth floor of Broadway with Chippendale furniture and plush red carpets. Entry to his office was through his PA's. Here the formidable Miss Kathleen Pettigrew, a much feared fixture in the Service (she and Menzies were lovers), held sway, assisted by two junior secretaries. A red/green signal-light system was used to indicate when it was permitted to proceed from her room to his.

The executive floor was quite unlike the rest of the building, where the staff worked in 'gloomy rooms where the floors were covered in worn lino, quite dangerous in places, where walls were a mucky grey/white/cream and the rooms were lit with bare light bulbs; only senior personnel were allowed to have desk lamps'.[1] Reporting to C were two deputies; General Sir John Sinclair,[i] the Vice-Chief in charge of Production, i.e. the acquisition of intelligence, and a half-rung

i SINCLAIR, Sir John Alexander, KCMG, CB, OBE; RASC, SIS, Chief 1953-56 (1897-1977).

below him the Assistant Chief, Air Commodore Jack Easton[i] who was in charge of Requirements, the department that set the intelligence-collection priorities. Production was organised on geographical lines, each country or region being given a numerical designation: P1, P2, etc. Requirements on the other hand was organised on functional grounds: R1 (political intelligence), R2 (air force intelligence) and so on. It was referred to as the 'circulating' department and was the link between the Service and its external customers. The next in line was SIS's Director of Finance and Administration and senior personnel officer, Major General J.C. Haydon.[ii] Domination of SIS's senior ranks by the military brass was almost total, which was exactly how they liked it. But Whitehall didn't, not at all.

SIS was designed to operate on a 'pull' as opposed to a 'push' system. The intelligence was supposedly 'pulled' from SIS to meet the demands of its customers – the Joint Intelligence Committee, the armed services, Whitehall departments, etc. – rather than 'pushed' at them at the whim or discretion of the Service. In that way SIS would always be subservient to the needs of its customers. That at least was the theory. Customers would complete an 'MI6 Special Question' form to let Requirements know what it was they needed. This might be in specific terms ('the Soviets are about to deploy a new tank, we need to know about its armour') or in more general ones ('the state of readiness of the Soviet armed forces in Germany') or very occasionally personal ('we really should do something about this chap Nasser'). Requirements would forward each request to the P section it considered best placed to acquire the intelligence or carry out the task. When the intelligence was secured, if it was, Requirements would circulate it to the customer with a source-note indicating in general terms the source of the intelligence, how reliable the *original provider* (source) thought it was and in turn how reliable the source was considered to be by his SIS handler ('reliable' – 'generally reliable' – 'believed to be reliable' – 'as yet untested'[2]), together with a request for feedback as to its usefulness/accuracy. SIS's customers had learned that it was wise to be both demanding and sceptical. SIS's pre-war reputation for obtaining reliable, timely intelligence was abysmal.

Menzies, ever the Whitehall warrior, was nothing if not wily. He had realised as early as 1945 that the post-war world would settle down into 'Germany slowly becoming our ally while Russia becomes our enemy'. In that opinion he was not alone; the more virulently anti-communist of his officers, men such as George Young, went so far as to see the Second World War as principally an interruption in their war against the Bolsheviks. Young was not without cause in this view: in official papers *circa* 1919 the Service was quite often referred to as

i EASTON, Air Commodore Sir John ('Jack'), CBE; RAF, SIS, Vice-Chief 1956-58 (1908-1990).

ii HAYDON, Major General Joseph C., CB, DSO, CBE; Irish Guards, Commandos, SIS (1899-1970).

the Anti-Bolshevik Secret Service.[3] Others thought that an over-concentration of resources on the Soviet threat at the expense of others perhaps more pertinent to Britain's future interests was dangerous, as one put it:

> It was typical of that generation to take down the target board inscribed Nazi Germany and put up one showing Red Sovs. I thought that too simplistic. 30% of the Service's effort was directed to the SovBloc target during the Cold War and it achieved very little apart from the safe reception of defectors, and seemed not to understand how little it achieved.[4]

This was to be an ongoing debate, not resolved until the Soviet threat removed itself. Park would have numbered herself among the hawks, those who believed that the Soviet threat could not be over-estimated and required whatever resources were available. In fact her abhorrence of the Russians did not dissipate significantly even after the collapse of the Soviet Union. She remained a resolute foe of things Russian for many years afterwards, indeed right up to the end of her life.[5]

Menzies was canny enough too to realise that the Service could not take on the Soviets on their own: the combined resources of both Britain and America would be required. To this end he threw open the doors of head office to a foreigner for the first time in its history, inviting the nascent CIA to dispatch one of its senior officers (William Harding Jackson[i]) to London to act as liaison, thus laying the groundwork for the close relationship between the CIA and SIS.[6] The Americans accepted the invitation, though what Jackson thought of Menzies' Miss Pettigrew being permitted to keep a parakeet (at least according to Menzies' biographer Anthony Cave Brown) in her office is not recorded. Perhaps it was a case of as long as the 'damn bird didn't talk it didn't matter'. Menzies had also completed a major review of SIS's organisational structure to reflect the belief that Nazism was dead and the Soviets were the only meaningful threat.[7] The review led to the short-lived experiment of three Chief Controllers being introduced: CC/Europe, CC/Mediterranean and CC/Pacific. Each assumed responsibility for the production of intelligence within their broad geographical areas. Operations in 'denied areas' i.e. within the Soviet Union and East European satellites (SovBloc) and those in the United States and Canada were handled separately by the equal-in-rank Controller/Production Research. The Chief Controllers now ranked with the Assistant Chief but reported (nominally) to the Vice-Chief.

Daphne Park was not a terribly vain person, but she was not above 'burnishing the legend' occasionally, just a little. So when she later told the former Deputy Chief of SIS, Gerry Warner,[ii] that 'she did not receive any operational training on

i JACKSON, William Harding; Deputy Director CIA 1950-51 (1901-1971).
ii WARNER, Sir Gerald, KCMG; SIS, H/WARSAW, C/MIDDLE EAST, Deputy Chief and later Co-ordinator for Intelligence and Security (1931-) .

joining SIS',[8] implying that she had to sally forth with only her wits to protect her, that was strictly true but only because her first job was not an operational one and there was therefore no requirement for her to be sent on the standard six-month General Tradecraft Course. In a sense SIS had given with one hand and taken back with another, in that it permitted her to join the Service but not the part she most earnestly desired, the Intelligence Branch. The Intelligence Branch (IB) was, and remains, at the heart of SIS. Its members were its Knights Templar, its soldiers-of-the-line. IB personnel manned (and they were mainly men) the overseas stations. It was they who toppled governments, bribed politicians, ran the agents and acquired the secret intelligence on which the Service depended for its daily bread. Behind the IB was the General Service which was in a support role, the rear-echelon in military parlance. Very important, couldn't be done without, etc., but far, far from the sharp end, and no medals to be won while serving there.

And so Park was sent on a three-day course on report-writing, because writing reports was to be her role. This is unlikely to have enthralled her, but it was a case of one step at a time. She was in and for now that was all that mattered.[9] After nine months mouldering away writing reports, she got her next break. She was appointed as a staff officer to Commander Kenneth Cohen,[i] one of the three newly appointed Chief Controllers.

The general consensus in Whitehall during this period was that war between the Soviet Union and the NATO countries was almost inevitable. And given the huge superiority in numbers of the Soviet ground forces it was assumed that in all probability they would overrun NATO defences, initially at least. This was particularly so given the large number of assumed sympathisers, fifth columnists in Second World War parlance, in the various national communist parties who could be expected to support a Soviet invasion. It was decided that a stay-behind organisation should be established which would have access to radios and arms and explosives in the event of their country being occupied by Soviet forces. Memories of being totally cut off from what few agents it had left on the continent after the Nazis overran most of Europe were still fresh in SIS minds. Most countries in Western Europe participated in the operation, which became known as GLADIO, though it went through a number of different codenames and manifestations. Park's initial role was as 'stay behind officer' for Andrew King's[ii] Eastern Area Controllerate, comprising Austria, Switzerland and Germany.[10] She coordinated the stay-behind activities of the SIS stations in those countries and would have worked closely with King.

i COHEN, Commander Kenneth Herman Salaman, CB, CMG; Royal Navy, SIS, CC/ EUROPE 1948-53 (1900-1984).

ii KING, Charles Andrew Buchanan, MBE, CMG; SIS, ZURICH, H/VIENNA, HONG KONG (1915-2002).

Her timing, as ever, was impeccable. Cohen had just been told by Peter Lunn,[i] George Young's successor in Vienna, that he had figured out a way to build a tunnel under the streets of the city that could be used to tap into all telephone and telegraph communications between the Soviet High Commission in the Imperial Hotel and the Soviet Central Commandant in the Epstein Palace, and between those two locations and the Kremlin. Lunn's source was an established SIS asset working for the Austrian Telephone & Telegraph administration (AT&T). As an added bonus Lunn expected to be able to listen in to communications between Moscow and Belgrade and Budapest on account of Vienna being the original telecommunications hub of the Austro-Hungarian Empire, laid down between 1890 and 1910.[11] The tunnel was a politically highly sensitive operation, being conducted without Foreign Office approval, though Lunn had told his ambassador, Caccia,[ii] and then sworn him to secrecy.[12] Cohen would have wanted a close eye kept on it. Given Park's intimate knowledge of the city, it is likely he used her for that. For her it was a plum appointment; while still not operational, it brought her that bit closer to that side.

Tunnelling without being detected was not going to be without its difficulties, as Park well knew; she'd spent two years in the city so knew exactly what problems Lunn would face. It would involve excavating in the midst of a city where 'every street had a thousand eyes'. To be able to pull this off undetected was going to take some doing, but the intelligence 'product' would be of inestimable value. And Lunn did pull it off. An underground control and recording centre, called 'Old Smoky' because of its poisonous atmosphere, was established underneath a shop selling Scots tartan and Harris tweed. Here banks of recorders recorded all voice and signal traffic passing though the monitored cables. The centre was concealed behind packing crates and guarded around the clock by Intelligence Corps soldiers armed with Sten guns. The most elaborate arrangements were entered into in order to avoid giving away any signs of what was going on. Eventually three such centres were built which succeeded in monitoring Soviet traffic in and out of Vienna until both Soviet and Western forces left Austria in 1955.

Cohen was an established SIS figure who had come in through the parallel pre-war Z Organisation. His empire, which covered all of Western Europe, was divided into three areas, each with its own Area Controller. Controller/Northern Area (Harry Carr[iii]) was responsible for Scandinavia and Denmark; Controller/ Eastern Area (Andrew King) covered Germany, Switzerland and Austria; while

i LUNN, Peter Northcote, CMG, OBE; Royal Artillery, SIS, H/VIENNA, H/BERNE, H/BERLIN, H/BONN, H/BEIRUT (1914-2011).

ii CACCIA, Baron Harold Anthony, GCMG, GCVO, GCStJ; diplomat (1905-1990).

iii CARR, Harry Lambton, CMG, MVO; Royal Artillery, North Russian Expeditionary Force, SIS, C/Northern Area 1944-54 (1899-1981).

Controller/Western Area (Simon Gallienne) looked after operations in France, Italy, the Iberian Peninsula and North Africa.[13]

Park settled in quickly to her new role. By coincidence Cohen had run the SUSSEX infiltration operation during the war which, given Park's experience of the Jeds, meant that the two had common ground from the outset.[14] (Cohen's son, Colin, intimated to this author that his father may have been instrumental in 'rehabilitating' Park in SIS eyes after her time in SOE and was thus at least partly responsible for her being accepted into the Service.) Between that and her personality, she soon made a firm friend of her boss for whom she had (in her own words) 'very similar feeling for him as the fictional James Bond had for M', describing Cohen 'as a very great, great man'.[15] It was a friendship that was to last for the rest of his life. Even after Cohen's death his wife, Mary, spoke with gratitude of the great support she received from Park after he died in 1984.[16]

While the Vienna tunnel was important, Cohen's immediate priority was whether Stalin intended solving 'the problem of Berlin' by tactics such as the Berlin Blockade or by more direct military means. John Bruce Lockhart,[i] head of station in Bad Salzuflen (with a hundred and twenty officers at his disposal) was straining every muscle in his efforts to determine the first signs of any such military attack. Between them his officers were running about four hundred agents in East Germany. Most, however, were fairly low-level spotters and the like; higher-level agents with access to policy were practically non-existent, as this remark by Bruce Lockhart indicates:

> We have all but given up on trying to run agents inside the Soviet Union, we are getting nowhere. We have no SIGINT, no POWs to debrief, no aerial reconnaissance.[17]

Just how poor their intelligence was came out months after this remark when the Soviet Union exploded its first atomic bomb. This was five years ahead of the SIS estimate. The man responsible for the acquisition of atomic intelligence in SIS was Commander Eric Welsh,[ii] described by Young as

> ... a complete charlatan ... who for a number of years had bluffed the different departments over his hush-hush work. Welsh's qualifications for his job were somewhat slender. He had been in the MI6 wartime Norwegian section at the time of the Commando raid on the heavy-water plant, but had no specialist knowledge of nuclear weaponry. However he did his best to impress the Atomic Energy Authority that his work for 'C' was too delicate to be revealed, while his MI6 colleagues were told that this applied to his AEA liaison: if need be his

---

i BRUCE LOCKHART, John, CMG, OBE; Seaforth Highlanders, SIS, H/PARIS, H/BAD SALZUFLEN (Germany), H/WASHINGTON, D/MIDDLE EAST & AFRICA, Vice-Chief (1914-1995).

ii WELSH, Commander Eric; Royal Navy, SIS (1897-d.).

confidential exchanges with the Americans were invoked as a further excuse. In fact MI6 intelligence on Soviet nuclear development was practically nil.[18]

The political shockwaves in Western capitals were nearly as severe as those on the site of the explosion itself in Kazakhstan, and in fairness to Welsh the CIA had estimated that it would be four more years (1953) before the Soviets would be able to explode the atom bomb.

It was noteworthy that the blast was confirmed though technical means ('spying without spies') rather than traditional espionage. Even though the Soviet atomic explosion was not expected for some years yet, both the RAF and the USAF operated regular flights close to Soviet air space designed to detect the minute radioactive particles that would be released by such an event. In September 1949 the first traces were identified by the Americans and later confirmed by special RAF flights. The love affair with technology as an intelligence tool had begun.[19]

Espionage of the more traditional kind ('spying with spies') was the suspected source of the leak which enabled the Soviets to explode the bomb a couple of years earlier than they might otherwise have done. Espionage also enabled the Russians to discover that the Americans and British had learned about the blast.[20] Their source was an agent in the British embassy in Moscow.[21]

In 1949 SIS was still preoccupied with the possibility of uncoupling the Soviet satellites from under Stalin's thumb.[22] Even before SIS reopened the Moscow station in 1948, it had set up shop in Prague, Warsaw, Sofia and Vienna, cities where it had stations from the 1920s. Many of the wartime SOE networks in Eastern Europe were still in place, to some degree at least, and were utilised in a variety of failed operations aimed at preventing the countries from coming completely under Soviet domination. However Stalin was determined to have what he called his 'string of pearls' in place. That meant having at least one country as a buffer between Germany and Russia. He reasoned that if Germany was once more going to invade the Soviet Union he would ensure that they would have to go through the buffer country first, which would be well garrisoned with Soviet troops, thus giving him time to mount a proper defence of the Motherland. One BARBAROSSA in a lifetime was enough for anyone.

So, brooking no opposition, the Soviets imposed their will on East Germany, Poland, Czechoslovakia, Hungary, Romania and Bulgaria. Austria, which the Russians regarded as being indistinguishable from Germany, they were prepared to negotiate over because Hungary stood between it and home soil. In each 'string of pearls' country all opposition was stifled, whether by assassination, imprisonment, torture and intimidation did not matter, what did was that the people needed to understand that this was their new reality and resistance would be futile. Both the CIA and SIS tried to hinder this process, Operation

ROLLBACK being the best known attempt. SIS heads of stations contacted the remnants of the SOE wartime networks and attempted to use them to foment political opposition. Little was achieved other than most members being arrested and executed by the NKVD (KGB).

Latvia, Lithuania and Estonia on the one hand and Albania and the Ukraine on the other were seen as different, as special cases; these were the 'touch-paper' countries. All that was required, it was reasoned, was for small armed groups of nationals from those countries to be inserted back into their homelands and the fuse of freedom would be lit, leading to the people rising up spontaneously against their oppressors. Well meaning possibly, but pure fantasy. Working in concert the CIA and SIS put operations in place to turn this dream into a reality. All were doomed to fail from the outset. Both agencies underestimated the iron grip that the local security forces had on the populations and the absolute ruthlessness with which any opposition would be put down. Both agencies were also unaware that the officer coordinating their activities (Kim Philby) was a Soviet spy who was passing over to his Soviet controllers details of every agent insertion. As the teams of agents landed, either off small boats or by parachute, they found 'welcoming parties' awaiting their arrival. Not only were the captured agents executed, so were their extended families, up to forty at a time.

The CIA and SIS officers running these operations (who included Harold Perkins, whom Park knew from their time together in SOE) appeared to be 'omelettes and eggs' types that refused to see the deaths as anything but the expected casualties of this sort of operation; the possibility that their plans might have been betrayed was unthinkable. It seemed that all the learning that was supposed to have been obtained from SOE's appalling handling of the betrayal of its Dutch networks in the Second World War (about which SIS had brayed the loudest) had come to nought when it came to its own back yard.

The SIS and CIA officers involved in the infiltration operations seemed to feel that with so many deceased agents 'invested' they had no choice but to carry on, and in fairness they did not have the benefit of hindsight. Agent running is a down and dirty business and the consequence of their lack of insight was that hundreds of SIS and CIA trained agents were sent to their deaths unnecessarily before the realisation slowly dawned that things might be seriously amiss.

Park was a lowly staff officer so bore no responsibility for those dreadful debacles. Her superior Kenneth Cohen must have accepted a share of the responsibility. He was organisationally responsible as CC/E and was enthusiastic in his support for the Albanian operation (VALUABLE). But though Park was not responsible she knew what it was like to parachute into hostile territory, knew what these betrayed agents must have felt as they realised the enormity of the betrayal. Soon she was to experience at first hand the reality of clandestine behaviour. Park was about to go from staff to operational.

The Western Area Controllerate (C/WA) was one of three that reported to Park's boss Cohen as CC/Europe. Western Area encompassed the Iberian Peninsula, Italy and France. Spain and Portugal were under the control of the two staunchly anti-communist dictatorships of Franco and Salazar. Italy and France were the problem children. The Italian communist party (PCI) and its French equivalent (PCF) were both powerful enough to take control, democratically or otherwise, of their countries, with serious consequences for Western Europe. Both the British and US governments decided that this was not something that would be allowed to happen, certainly not without a fight. The Paris embassy had a resident SIS station, opened after the war by John Bruce Lockhart. While the French, in theory at least, welcomed its presence on their soil, they were nonetheless wary of what the Paris station might get up to and regularly demanded reassurances about its good intentions. The ambassadors tended to want to go along with the view that SIS should really do no more than liaise with the appropriate French service.

Simon Gallienne, the C/WA, was prepared to go along with this to some degree but not wholly, because France represented a particular problem for SIS. It felt that an internal communist-led coup was likely to occur ahead of any Soviet invasion. It decided that GLADIO in France would be focused on the internal enemy rather than on the external. In a note to Cohen at the time Gallienne wrote:

> Apart from attacking the enemies of France on French soil no accusation could be levelled against the station that it is in any way pursuing activities inimical to the French state.[23]

The natural members of these French stay-behind organisations were members of the non-communist wartime Resistance movement. These were people whose courage was already demonstrated and who were already trained and experienced in armed resistance. SIS decided to step up its internal monitoring of the political situation, Cohen making it clear in an internal SIS memo that he had made it plain to his French counterparts that:

> I am not prepared to rely entirely on their estimates of Communist activity in France and that I make a practice of pursuing direct enquiries into these matters.[24]

What Cohen did not say was that the activities went further than monitoring and included a plan, BLUEPLAN (later *Rose des Vents*), which would enable anti-communist elements to be ready to counter any communist-led coup d'état. Established initially in Brittany, it soon spread with Resistance cells and arms caches, paid for by Washington and London, throughout the country. Park, who spoke fluent French, was assigned to this activity and with that assignment came entry into the prized Intelligence Branch.[25] The woman who in 1946 had been refused entry into SIS on the grounds that 'her face was known to members of the French Resistance who might include among their number members of the communist party' was now ordered to approach those same members and organise them into an anti-communist brigade with access to buried arms caches. Whether or not she saw the irony of this did not matter, Park was delighted and went about her work with a will. Years later she told her friend Jean Sackur[i] how thrilled and pleased she was with the posting.

> Up to then I felt I was on the fringes of SIS and was very unhappy. Then all of a sudden I was in. Of course meeting all those members of the Resistance and working with them was such an honour.[26]

Park's time with the RF section in SOE now paid enormous dividends. 'Madame Daphne' was a known and trusted figure. She had trained these people, been with them right up to the moment they parachuted into France and into mortal danger. The success of their missions, their lives even, had depended on her and the codes she taught. So she could leverage those wartime connections to their maximum, and she did. If some form of roadblock needed surmounting, if she or a colleague needed an introduction to a key influencer or to have someone to vouch for them, it all could be arranged. Park's real career as an intelligence officer had begun.

---

i SACKUR, Jean, *née* La Fontaine, anthropologist.

9

Moscow bound, 1951-54

SIS knew that the life it offered was not for everyone, so its newly appointed officers were obliged to complete a three-year probationary period before permanency was granted. Park's was up at the end of July 1951. She was now a member of the Intelligence Branch and so qualified for a regular operational posting overseas. Breaking into the IB constituted an extraordinary achievement for her, indeed for any woman at that time. Ginger Rogers, the movie dancing partner of Fred Astaire, was once said to remark that 'she had to do everything that Fred did but she had to do it backwards and in high heels'. For a woman in SIS to be considered a man's equal, to be seen as being capable of holding down an operational post, she had to do it in high heels, backwards *and* while blindfolded. Park's close relationship with Cohen had probably stood her in good stead, but she'd had to the heavy lifting herself, prove herself not once but twice; first just to get in the door of Broadway, second to get right in, and now to get into the holy of holies, SovBloc, the department of SIS dedicated to operations against the Soviet Union and its principal intelligence organs, the KGB (Committee for State Security) and the GRU (Main Intelligence Directorate/Military Intelligence).

At the time most SIS stations had a complement of two intelligence branch officers, one of whom would be the designated head of station. They would be backed up by a secretary and sometimes by a clerk/general gofer. Smaller stations would have only one officer and might even share a secretary with a larger station in an adjoining country. Of course regional control centres such as Singapore, Amman and Cairo (later substituted by Beirut) had more staff. In a hostile operating environment, and Moscow met that definition comfortably, one of the two would be the designated 'deep cover officer' while the other would be under standard cover. Neither would be declared to the Soviets as being an intelligence officer, unlike the situation in a friendly state where the more senior would be 'declared' to the host government and the duties would include liaison with its intelligence services.

Deep cover officers would try to remain pretty deep; they would not, for example, attend meetings in other embassies with intelligence officers from the CIA or from other NATO countries. Instead they would act in every way possible like 'respectable' (SIS's preferred term) diplomats in order to gain as much operational freedom as possible. Among embassy personnel only the ambassador would be made aware of the deep cover officer's true role; others might guess.[1]

SIS gave a good bit of thought to the selection process and liked one at least of the officers to have a respectable look about them. One way of achieving that was to select early career-stage officers who were less likely to have come to the attention of the Soviets. It was that slot that Park was angling for. In this, as in so much, luck was on her side; she had avoided Philby. If she had been known to have been identified by him she would probably have been ruled out on those grounds alone. But the betrayer had been posted to Ankara in 1947 before she joined and from there had been transferred directly to Washington as SIS representative in 1949. He had visited Broadway a few times, once to attend a course lasting two or three weeks, but they are not known to have met. When he returned to Britain in 1951 it was under a cloud of suspicion and he could do little further harm. Another point in her favour was the SIS practice of further diverting suspicion by deploying women in key operational roles behind the Iron Curtain. One such was Miss J.M. 'Jill' Sheppard[2] who had served in the deep cover role in Moscow a couple of years before Park. Sometime later SIS sent a Miss Ruth Chaplin (1963-64)[3] and a Miss Margaret Milne (1964-65)[4] to Moscow, also in fully operational roles.

So for the first and possibly only time in her career Daphne Park found her gender an advantage, or at least not a disadvantage: not only was SIS taking advantage of its reputation for not deploying women operationally, it was also playing to Soviet prejudices. KGB practice at the time was to use women only as 'swallows' (sexual bait) and decoys, and human nature being what it is the KGB assumed that if that was how they did things it was how everybody did things. Park's next task would have meant attending at Personnel Branch, then located in Petty France (a street near Westminster) to hear about her future. She was told not only that had she passed her probationary period but that she was to be nominated for one of the two slots coming due in the Moscow station. However the Foreign Office was far from convinced about the desirability of having SIS officers serve in embassies under the pretence of being 'regular' diplomats. The Foreign Office argued that it would become immediately obvious to the host governments that the SIS officer was a sham. Park was not impressed:

> They [the Foreign Office] were convinced that we were – how can I put it – such total hicks that we couldn't possibly be diplomats and they said they couldn't possibly give us diplomatic cover. We'd have to be forever and a day Passport Control Officers. Well there is a limit to the number of those you can have in any embassy.[5]

On the contrary, as far as SIS was concerned the era of the passport control officer as cover was well past its use-by date. As a cover it was paper-thin and it offered no access to potentially interesting people who might be recruited. SIS wanted its officers to be able to mix in the circles diplomats move in and cultivate as appropriate.

> So my brilliant master fielded about twelve of us and we all did the exam. I was the only woman, because there were very few women in the office in those days and we were all Cambridge and Oxford graduates so could do it standing on our heads and we did and we proved we were quite as bright as they needed us to be.[6]

Eventually a compromise was reached. SIS agreed that its officers would, in effect, do two jobs. They would perform their SIS role but they would simultaneously carry out their assigned regular diplomatic work in accordance with whatever slot they occupied. So, if one was posted, for example, as a visa officer, he or she would be expected to issue the visas, complete the paperwork and so on.

> That's the beauty of the Service; you did a good job as a diplomat and an even better one as an intelligence officer.[7]

Park was delighted with the news of her posting but she knew she would not actually take up the position until 1954 because much preparatory work needed to be done. Haydon would have told her she would need some sort of 'respectable' diplomatic track record to pass Russian scrutiny. However the Foreign Office had one more trick up its sleeve. It determined that Park would be posted to UKDEL NATO (British diplomatic mission to NATO), which was then still headquartered in France, in Fontainebleau outside Paris. She would be the press attaché to the head of mission, Frederick Hoyer Millar.[i]

> They [the Foreign Office] next thought of jobs that couldn't conceivably be done. Mine was I was appointed press attaché to Sir Derick Hoyer Millar, the head of the UK delegation to NATO in Paris. But I never met a single member of the press. I never had an office anywhere near Derick Hoyer Millar and my entire claim to my title was that it was in the diplomatic book.[8]

In his memorial address following her death, Gerry Warner, a former Deputy Chief of SIS, acknowledged Park's contribution in this area:

> Certainly she convinced the Ambassador in Moscow that she was a great asset and not an embarrassment. Thereafter our presence in Embassies, even in the Soviet Bloc, was readily accepted, and we who followed her had a much easier time.[9]

Warner's tribute was well spoken and well deserved.

---

i MILLAR, Sir Frederick R. Hoyer ('Derick'), GCMG, CVO; diplomat (1900-1989).

Nominally at least, her Paris position was a 'straight' post and perhaps it was as well it was largely nominal for she had much work to do. She needed to learn Russian, which she would do by attending a year-long intensive course in the Joint Services School of Linguistics (JSSL) in Cambridge under the cover of taking a diploma in Russian in Newnham College. When she completed her course she would go and live with an émigré Russian family in Paris for six months, conversing only in Russian and French. During the day she would receive additional one-to-one tuition in Russian from professors in the Sorbonne. She would also, at last, get to attend the six-month General Operations and Tradecraft Course, held in Palace Street in London and in Fort Monkton in Hampshire.[10] The revised post-war course was set up and run by a former SOE colleague, Lieutenant Colonel John Munn;[i] the first Commandant of SOE Beaulieu (and briefly and unsuccessfully Commandant of SOE Massingham). Roland Carter[ii] was to be the other station officer (MOS/1), joining a couple of months after her, in January; he was junior to Park having joined SIS in 1953. Like Park, Carter was later made ambassador to Ulaanbaatar.

Though it is unlikely that Park would have been aware of it, her former lover Douglas DeWitt Bazata was just then attracting the negative attention of the CIA. According to a report filed in November that year (1951) by Lucien Conein,[11] a fellow former Jed and now a CIA officer, Bazata was living with the winemakers, Baron and Baroness von Mumm, in what remained of Schloss Johannisberg in West Germany.[12] By this stage Bazata had divorced his first wife and remarried. Though without any 'visible means of support' (according to the CIA report), he was 'associating with State Department employees and the higher stratum of society in Germany' and 'travelling in France, Belgium, Switzerland, Spain and Germany'. In fact he was living in a *ménage à trois* with Baron Mumm and his wife. He had long left OSS and 'appeared to be at odds with the CIA'. He would greet any former colleagues he encountered with accusations that they must be members of the CIA and exhort those in his company to be careful of what they said because this stranger from America was a spy. Since many of the former OSS colleagues were in fact spies, this practice was causing some annoyance. Consideration was given to what could best be done about it. In fairness, none of the suggested remedies was extreme or suggested that violent means be employed. Park was probably well off without him, but whether she would have seen it that way is another matter entirely.

---

i MUNN, Lieutenant Colonel James Walter ('John'), OBE; Royal Artillery, SOE, SIS (1908-d.).

ii CARTER, Roland; HM Forces, SIS, MOSCOW, BERLIN, HELSINKI, H/ULAAN-BAATAR, KUALA LUMPUR, H/PRETORIA (1924-).

In 1950, as Britain emerged slowly and painfully from the war (rationing had still not been totally abandoned), the country was introduced to the first of the long-running series of 'sex and spy' sagas that were to engulf it for the following decade and a half and that would impact hugely on the first half of Park's career, a period during which the spectre of betrayal was rarely absent. The first arrest was probably the least 'glamorous' (at least from the media's perspective). It was of Klaus Fuchs,[i] a nuclear physicist central to the British development of atomic weapons. Initially Fuchs had worked in the UK but moved to the US where he worked directly on the 'Manhattan Project' (code name for the development of the atom bomb) in Los Alamos in New Mexico. A convinced communist, Fuchs passed on everything he knew to his Soviet contacts. He was sentenced to fourteen years' imprisonment following his ninety-minute trial, at which he pleaded guilty. Three months later another nuclear physicist, a naturalised Briton called Bruno Pontecorvo,[ii] did a midnight flit from Rome to Moscow with his wife and family.[13] The combination of Fuchs and Pontecorvo's betrayals played into the prevailing view among many in Washington of a decadent, dissolute Britain in the throes of post-Empire decay, unwilling or unable to recognise that a new era had dawned. Things were not to get any better soon. In May the following year (1951), two Foreign Office diplomats, Guy Burgess and Donald Maclean, fled to Moscow. Following receipt of intelligence from the Americans (the source was Soviet cables intercepted during the war but just then decrypted), MI5 had decided to question Maclean about passing information to the Soviets over a period of about twelve years under the codename HOMER. Afraid that Maclean would crack under pressure, Kim Philby, who had been working for the Soviets for about the same length of time, warned him and told him to get out. Guy Burgess, his comrade in arms, decided to flee with him. When the news of their defection broke it created a media firestorm. It had everything that Fleet Street loved: louche 'shirt-lifting' toffs up to their necks in debauchery, drunkenness and deceit. It seemed that those whose position in life enabled them to enjoy 'the days of *la douceur de vivre*' (the sweetness of life)[14] and on whom life had bestowed so much of its bounty had been the first to spit in their country's face.

Within informed circles (a *very* tight circle) suspicion at once fell on Philby. Desperate to avoid a major political scandal, Menzies sought to play down the evidence against him, describing it as circumstantial and speculative. The Americans weren't having any of that. They demanded his immediate recall from Washington (where as H/WASHINGTON he was SIS liaison with the CIA) on pain of withdrawing all intelligence cooperation if SIS failed to comply. Menzies was left with no choice but to summon Philby back to London. Within the upper

---

i FUCHS, Emil Julius Klaus (1911-1988).
ii PONTECORVO, Bruno (1913-1993).

echelons of SIS, when the initial shock had subsided, opinion was very much in Philby's favour. The majority simply refused to countenance the idea that he was a traitor; there was after all no precedent for a betrayal so foul. However Dick White, then deputy-head of MI5, who interviewed Philby a number of times, had no doubt that the man was an arrant betrayer. Easton (far brighter than Sinclair) was also certain Philby was bad; Menzies appears to have been clinging onto a forlorn hope almost to the end and was reportedly 'crushed' when the spy's betrayal was later proved beyond all doubt.

For now, though, the betrayer had covered his tracks well; admissible evidence was practically non-existent. Like a practised serial killer he had learned how to operate without leaving any telltale traces. Such evidence as there was appeared to be circumstantial, coming mainly from the early days before he had perfected his craft (as is often the way with serial killers too). His main problem was that *someone* had tipped off Burgess and Maclean and he was the most obvious suspect, what the press began calling the Third Man (to be followed by a Fourth and a Fifth). As any defence lawyer will testify, one of the most effective means of casting doubt on the prosecution's case in a serious criminal trial is to be able to point a convincing finger at someone *other* than the accused for the jury to mull over. But for Philby there was no someone else, at least no one obvious. So a compromise was reached: nothing would be said in public, and Philby would be allowed tender his resignation from SIS. The issue of a pension would be determined pending the outcome of the continuing investigations.

The Service was wounded. Whitehall was once more viewing SIS with questioning eyes; some were beginning to wonder aloud if the damn penny was worth the candle at all and speaking about the benefits of a merger of the two agencies, MI5 and SIS, a prospect viewed in SIS as worse than death itself. But, though wounded, SIS was still delusional. Philby had been, and for most of them was still one of their own. Westminster School and Trinity College, Cambridge, the chap had had a good war, was a 'natural', a possible future Chief, drank too much of course and a bit of a womaniser, but a betrayer? *God forbid.* For if Philby could not be trusted, who could? Doubts were set aside; Philby was deemed sound.

While this was happening Park's mother and father returned to Britain, leaving behind them their deceased son David, who had died in 1939 at the age of fourteen. John Park's prospecting efforts had paid off at last, though he had found deposits of mica rather than gold. This, however, was still enough for him to sell up, move to England and buy a house in London into which the extended Park family moved (Park's grandmother had returned earlier, in 1939). Sadly he was not to enjoy his new life for very long, dying just three months later at the age of seventy-six.[15]

When Park departed on her long journey via Helsinki to Moscow in November 1954, she left behind a Service still struggling to come to terms with Philby's betrayal. Philby was still living in London, still free, to the continuing annoyance of the Americans who thought his freedom was more to do with a lack of will on the part of the British than any lack of courtroom evidence. The betrayer had however secured his first scalp; Menzies had been forced out as Chief. Many in Whitehall thought he had overstayed his welcome anyway. William Hayter, a senior Foreign Office official who was head of the (Secret) Services Liaison Department and who coincidentally was to be Park's ambassador while she was in Moscow, said in 1949 that the approach of Menzies' sixtieth birthday the following year offered 'an appropriate moment for making the change'.[16] But Menzies was allowed to remain in place more because a lack of enthusiasm for any obvious successor than regard for his continuing tenure. In 1952 he was replaced, as previously arranged, by the Vice-Chief Sinclair with the Assistant Chief Easton moving up a slot, on the promise that the top job would be his when 'Buggins's' (Sinclair's) turn had ended.

Sinclair's appointment was far from being universally welcomed, Hayter saying he thought him 'rigid and unimaginative and I think a Secret Service run by him would be wonderfully organised but never find anything out'.[17] Sinclair justified Hayter's damning analysis. This is what Sinclair had to say about Philby in 1955, four years after White had first told him that he was convinced that Philby was a Soviet agent:

> It is entirely contrary to the English tradition for a man to have to prove his innocence even when the prosecution is in possession of hard facts. In a case where the prosecution has nothing but suspicion to go upon there is even less reason for him, even if he were able to do so, to prove his innocence.[18]

This noble attitude, admirable if bonkers, was steadfastly maintained throughout his tenure and had the effect of compounding the damage tenfold when the undisputed truth finally emerged. But Philby wasn't the only betrayer SIS had in its ranks. For just as two scientists had defected to the Soviet cause and two diplomats had followed suit; so too was the Service betrayed, not by one but by two of its own. George Blake (*né* George Behar) who had joined SIS during the war on a HO (hostilities only) basis, was the second of SIS's great betrayers. Blake had been made permanent in 1947 and sent to Cambridge to learn Russian under Professor Lisa Hill (on the same course that Park was to attend a few years later). He was then been sent to Korea under diplomatic cover where he was captured by the North Koreans when they took Seoul.

While in captivity Blake volunteered his services to the Russians, and when he was released in 1953 he began spying for them. His initial post-release appointment was to the Russian section where he was able to pull the MI5 file on his first KGB case officer (General Nikolai Rodin[i]) and provide him with a copy. Shortly afterwards Blake was posted to Y section in Carlton Gardens where he was responsible for the translation and transcription of the tapes from the Vienna tunnel operation. It is unlikely that he was in a position to betray Park up to that point; she was in Paris when Blake returned to duty and so they were unlikely to have encountered each other. More to the point, the Service had successfully introduced compartmentalisation. Officers attached to one section were under orders not to discuss that section's business with colleagues from other sections unless strictly required for operational reasons, and by and large that was adhered to. But Blake was able to betray the Vienna tunnel bugging, though the KGB waited a full year before even alerting the Soviet military to the possibility that the conversations of their soldiers were being monitored by Western intelligence. Even then they were careful to avoid saying anything that could point to Blake's existence. Nor did they take any overt action to counter it, for the same reason, and it remained in place and operational until both Soviets and Allied occupation forces left Austria in 1955.[19]

Park was going to Moscow right in the middle of SIS's darkest period: twenty-one years, from 1940 to 1961, when SIS operations directed against the Soviet Union were comprehensively and enthusiastically betrayed. But of course Blake's betrayal was then still unknown. When Park entered the chancery on the banks of the Moskva River for the first time it was not with Philby that she was concerned (and certainly not Blake) but how she would make a decent fist of the job she was given, because making a decent fist of it she most definitely intended to do.

For most of her tenure in Moscow Park's London Director was Harold 'Shergy' Shergold.[ii] She had, she was told, three main intelligence priorities. The first was Soviet 'Intentions intelligence'. Park was expected to be on the alert for anything that might indicate an altered state of readiness among Soviet forces. This was the Holy Grail and would remain so until developments in satellite technology provided an alternative and more reliable means. Shergold would have told her that while radar was a wonderful invention it would only provide a four-minute warning of an atom bomb attack from the Russians, perhaps even less if the attack came from low-flying Tupolev bombers screaming in across the North Sea from Murmansk. That reality dominated everything. Four minutes for SIS to advise the Prime Minister and the Chief of the Imperial General Staff (CIGS)[20] on whether or not to launch V-bombers from Scrampton. The Service simply had to provide an earlier warning. That was its *raison d'être*, Shergold told her,

i RODIN, General Nicolai B. (pseudonym Korovin); KGB, *Rezident* in London 1956-61, later head of Department 13 (assassinations).
ii SHERGOLD, Harold ('Shergy'); SIS, BAD SALZUFLEN, C/SOVBLOC (1916-2000).

to provide the Prime Minister and the defence chiefs with time to arm Britain's defences and strike back.

She was handed two lists prepared by JIC (the Joint Intelligence Committee) and told to familiarise herself with them. The first, the Red List, set out the things JIC believed the Russians were most likely to do immediately prior to an all-out attack. The second, the Amber List, contained a further fifty or so actions that they might be expected to undertake in times of increased tension, potentially leading to an attack. Everyone involved – SIS, the armed services, the listeners in Cheltenham – was on a constant watch for indicators. The RAF, she learnt, was flying forward air patrols to the very edge of Soviet airspace, at great risk. Submarines were lurking off the Soviet coasts, so close that their snouts were almost resting on the beaches, there to monitor the movement of Soviet submarines and surface ships from their ports. Troopers from the Special Air Service (SAS) were infiltrating East Germany up to a hundred miles beyond the border, monitoring the movement of Soviet tanks and troops. Agents equipped with wireless transmitters, many controlled from Bad Salzuflen, were located within eyesight or earshot of scores of Soviet airfields, army bases and known force-assembly areas. Park was told that in the station safe in Moscow she would find a special list of things to look out for in the city if war is threatened. Study it, she was told, and pray to God she'd never get the instruction to commence active monitoring.

The station's second priority was to assist the regular diplomatic staff and the ambassador in particular in its Kremlin-watching. The ignorance about the most basic aspects of how the Soviet power structure operated was profound. With Stalin now mercifully gone to his eternal rest there was a realisation that if any sort of progress was to be achieved between East and West then the West was going to have to understand how the levers of power were actually exercised and who was doing the heavy pulling. The third priority was to fill in as many blanks as possible about practically any and every aspect of Soviet military and civilian life. She was to get hold of any official publication that fell into her hands, such as telephone directories, which were regarded as state secrets. She was to attend as many industrial fairs, exhibitions and conferences as she could gain entry into, ideally in the guise of a Soviet citizen. And there were the operational angles. It wasn't likely she would be able to recruit any new sources. Contact between Soviet citizens and foreigners was actively discouraged other than as part of official duties, and these were closely monitored. But there were a small number of ongoing intelligence operations that would need to be supported.

One thing was for certain, Daphne Park thought as she entered the chancery building: she would not be bored. Little did she realise just how not bored she would be.

10

Moscow 1 – Either silence or prison, 1954

Before Park left London one of goals she set herself was to establish a good rapport with her ambassador, William Hayter.[i] This was not as easy as it might appear. For a start the ban on the entry of women into the Diplomatic Service had only been lifted eight years previously and there would have been no more than a tiny handful of women holding down overseas posts in embassies, ten or so if that. And of course the removal of a formal ban did not necessarily mean that the underlying prejudices had been ameliorated to any significant degree. Hayter wasn't the worst in that regard, nor was the head of chancery, Patrick O'Regan,[ii] so her path was eased somewhat. O'Regan was ex-SOE; he was dropped into France from Massingham on 7 August 1944, so he and Park had missed each other by hours. The two would have had much in common, though despite his SOE background O'Regan had plumped for the respectable side of the Foreign Office and became a regular diplomat.[1]

The second hurdle was that relations between SIS heads of station and their ambassadors tended to occupy the spectrum from the lukewarm to the downright hostile. The fact was that SIS station heads enjoyed a reputation within the Diplomatic Service of being a 'bloody bolshie' lot; to be 'bolshie' was the ultimate sin and it would take a long time for that reputation to be erased (to the extent that it has, for to some extent it lingers still). An embassy was a little like a ship: all hands on deck, everyone pulling their weight and pulling together. However, SIS officers, while nominally diplomats, were hewn from a different rock. They preferred to steer their own course, often selecting the 'road less travelled' as the route to their destination. Station heads would often report back to Broadway without any consultation with their ambassadors, not infrequently scoring points by disagreeing with the embassy's reporting and without giving the embassy the opportunity to comment.[2]

This was not behaviour likely to foster warm relations between station and ambassador, not least because an embassy operates on the medieval principle of *cuius regio, eius religio* (whose realm, his religion) with little tolerance for sedition. Park knew that in order to win over Hayter she would have to prove herself a reliable and trustworthy partner, and that it would not be made easy.

i HAYTER, Sir William Goodenough, KCMG; diplomat, later Warden of New College, Oxford (1906-1995).

ii O'REGAN, Captain P.V.W.R., MC and Bar; Intelligence Corps, SOE, diplomat (1920-1961).

At forty-six Hayter was young for the Moscow post, but he was seen as a highflier, energetic and enthusiastic and enjoying a stellar career. He had served on the secretariat for TERMINAL, the post-war Potsdam Conference attended by Stalin, Truman and Churchill, and was afterwards appointed to the Foreign Office's influential policy-formulating Russia Committee. Later still he chaired the Joint Intelligence Committee and made the running in handling the fallout from the abortive defection of GRU Colonel J.D. Tassoev (agent CAPULET) in 1948, just as Park was joining the Service. He knew the intelligence scene better than most in Whitehall and had never been slow in voicing his opinions about it.

As far as London was concerned, Stalin's death was seen as an opportunity to build a less confrontational relationship with the Soviets, and it wanted someone in Moscow who might be able to contribute to that process.

The total head count in the Moscow embassy ran to about eighty or so staff in total, of this number about twenty could be considered accredited diplomats with immunity. The rest were support personnel such as typists and stenographers, cipher clerks, radio operators from the Diplomatic Wireless Service, porters and guards. Both the chancery and the ambassador's living quarters were contained in the one building on Sofia Wharf which was within glaring distance of the Kremlin, on the other side of the Moskva River. Built originally for a wealthy sugar merchant, it was a hodgepodge of different styles. The main reception rooms, accessed by an immense Gothic staircase, were on the first floor. They included a 'Louis Quinze' dining room with painted ceiling and walls lined with red silk, dominated by a painting of George V, who bore a striking resemblance to his cousin, the last Tsar, something that required prompt explanations to Russian guests. There was also an 'Empire' ballroom and a 'Renaissance' smoking room. The ambassador's private quarters were also on the first floor; there were some staff quarters in the main building, but most lived in flats beside the building or in adjacent streets. Park lived on Sadovaya Street, a ten-minute walk away.

In the embassy roof-space, sealed off from general access and connected to an array of aerials on the embassy roof, was specialised electronic listening equipment imported under diplomatic seal. Staff from GCHQ, attached to the embassy, used it to listen in on Russian air force and army communications in the Moscow district and to beam directional microphones at the windows of the Kremlin across the river. The ground floor was the chancery proper (working quarters), while the basement was given over to stores and living quarters for the locally-based servants. That area, it was universally agreed, was to be avoided where possible: it was quite appalling.

Hayter, who had been in post for little over a year when Park arrived, would have told her to have few illusions about the task facing them. During his previous term in Moscow as 3rd secretary from 1934 to 1937 he had experienced

Soviet life at its worst. This was the height of the Great Terror, the time when the Soviet populace lived in abject fear of the midnight knock on the door from the secret police. When they answered they would be torn from the arms of their loved ones and in all probability never seen again, except perhaps as an almost unrecognisable shadow of themselves in a photograph from an orchestrated treason trial. This was the time when Stalin's final pre-war purge was reaching its height with hundreds of thousands of unexplained disappearances. For Soviet citizens, of whatever rank, life was simply terrifying, and even though Hayter's status as a diplomat afforded him protection, with Stalin one could never really be certain. The atmosphere since Stalin's death was much improved; the man had been such an awful tyrant that even those closest to him were demanding an easing of the terror.

From Hayter's perspective what he needed most from Park, apart from her behaving herself, was help in understanding how the levers of power actually worked in that society. How was power exercised? The Communist Party was obviously pivotal but what was its relationship to government? Was it similar to that of the Conservative or Labour parties at home? And how was power and authority divided between the Supreme Soviet, the Council of Ministers, the Presidium, the Politburo? In 1953, the year before she arrived, a delegation from the British Labour Party was passing through Moscow on its way to China. Embassy protocol was to organise for such groups to meet their equivalents in the host country. Since the delegation was led by Clement Attlee, leader of the Opposition, Foreign Office protocol demanded that the leader of the Opposition in Moscow, if such a position existed, should be invited. They cast around and eventually someone suggested that a man called Khrushchev seemed the nearest thing. Khrushchev appeared to have no official position other than as a leading Secretary of the Communist Party, but in any case an invitation was issued. To everyone's amazement, the reply to the invitation said that those attending would include Malenkov, Molotov, Vishinski, Shvernik and a few others as well as Khrushchev: this was everyone of significance in the entire Soviet leadership, they knew that much. Hayter was amazed; London was amazed; the Prime Minister, Winston Churchill, demanded a personal report. The day came, they all turned up and while nothing of any great significance was said, just to spend that much time in their company and observe the interaction between them was illuminating. They later learnt that Khrushchev, far from being the leader of the Opposition, was probably the most important person in the room; he had been practically ignored by his hosts because he was seen by them as a nonentity. That was going to have to change.[3]

The dinner signalled some thaw in the relationship, at diplomatic level at least. Over the previous three years there had been only two occasions when *any Russian* had entered the embassy to dine. Now Russian dinner guests became a frequent occurrence, though all invitations still had to go through official channels. Direct contact was prohibited, with militiamen at the embassy gates barring entrance to anyone other than holders of officially approved invitations and members of the indigenous (Russian) staff. Interestingly, the embassy never knew until the principal actually turned up whether or not he would be accompanied by his wife, making catering for dinners exceptionally tricky. And when all were seated, genuine dialogue was stilted, as Hayter described:

> Conversations were like *Pravda* leading articles on one side and *The Times* leading articles on the other; well-grooved long-playing records went round and round.[4]

But this felt infinitely preferable to what had gone before. However, while Soviet officials might attend a dinner *en masse* they rigidly – and given the circumstances sensibly – avoided any attempt at follow-up meetings. Speeches were safer than conversations, delegations preferable to individual meetings, making cultivation of potential sources impossible.

Hayter also observed that while Moscow as a city might be dull, as a diplomatic outpost it now had status. He told Park more than once how the calibre of diplomatic representation had improved since his first tour. Then the Soviet Union wallowed in its isolation: a backward place, speaking an incomprehensible language and ruled over by a savage tyrant; in summary a country where nothing of any great consequence occurred. A blinkered view, perhaps, but it had still prevailed. Highfliers used not have Moscow on their dance cards – London, Berlin, Paris and Rome for sure, and maybe Washington, topped the list. Not so now. The Soviet Union maintained the second largest standing army in the world and occupied a clutch of countries in Western Europe. Most frighteningly of all, it could project its power, possessing the means to obliterate practically any city of its choosing in at least half of the world, and that included any in the United Kingdom. So Moscow mattered. Distinguished visitors of every hue poured in: India's Pandit Nehru, West Germany's Konrad Adenauer, Yugoslavia's Tito and Iran's despotic ruler, the Shah of Persia. Being there was good for Hayter, good too for Park.

The other thing Park was learning was that life in Moscow was about as much fun as a dry Wales village on a wet October Sunday. There was almost a complete absence of anything to *do*. Once the rather frantic Christmas festivities ended, life assumed what would be its normal pattern. That meant work from Monday to Saturday and parties at weekends, for there was a simple lack of anything else to do. There were only a couple of restaurants worth eating in, places such as the Central House of Writers Restaurant which could serve up a half decent meal, or Praga in the Arbat. But both were expensive.

Bars were scarce, drab and dirty and closed early even at weekends. One of the very few exceptions was the bar in the airport in Vnukovo, which stayed open until well after midnight. It wasn't unknown for those desperate for a companionable drink to get the bus out there. There were no nightclubs or dance halls, no places where the young could let off steam and meet members of the opposite sex; such entertainments, staples of Western society, did not fit in with the Soviet ideal. There was a sort of 'jet set', Moscow-style, the young sons and daughters of the elite (senior Party officials) who read black-market copies of *Vogue,* smoked Western cigarettes, listened to banned jazz records and generally misbehaved in a minor sort of way.[5] There were also the Soviet equivalent of Teddy Boys, the *stilyagi,* young zoot-suiters, hooligans mainly, who hung out and got up to a bit of mischief.[6] But these were tiny groups and not ordinarily accessible to Moscow diplomats. Prostitution did exist but on a tiny scale, certainly when compared to the West. This was partly as a result of official action but had a lot to do with the housing shortage: there was simply nowhere for the women to bring their clients (and for most of the year it was far too cold to be doing it out of doors). Some resorted to completing the transaction in the back seat of a roaming taxi, but that had its drawbacks. Homosexuality officially did not exist, but there was a sexual underground which catered for both heterosexual and homosexual tastes. The authorities tolerated this even though the idea ran completely counter to every instinct of their puritanical ideology. It was seen as a necessary safety-valve and useful as a honey-pot to trap unwary foreigners who could afterwards be blackmailed. So the general embassy consensus was that that scene was best avoided.

There were some big stores, Moscow's GUM being the best known, but the shelves were as bare as a newborn's bottom. No Moscow housewife left her home without her 'just-in-case' bag in her hand, 'just-in-case' she came across anything in a shop she could buy for her family's supper, with luck chancing upon something that would then be out of stock again in a flash. And the theatre, which would have been Park's choice, was duller than a widower's wardrobe. Stalinism and even the faintest form of independent self-expression did not go together, so the Russian theatre had ossified, as indeed had pretty much anything associated with the arts. The directors and actors were neutered; the companies reduced to putting on the same productions of the same plays, often with the same actors playing the same roles as they had in 1937 when Hayter had been there before.[7] Such cinemas as there were showed appalling films laden with propaganda. And to cap it all, the audiences smelled. Certainly seen through the eyes of the embassy personnel the average Muscovite was unwashed, unkempt, undernourished, quarrelsome and tetchy. Not their fault perhaps, but that was hardly the point.[8]

Embassy staff could go ice-skating and often did; the embassy had a tennis court which was flooded in winter and served as their very own rink, and that could be fun. And the Moscow Circus was justifiably famous, though for most the novelty soon wore off. Hayter, to be fair, attempted to compensate. His wife Iris – the ambassadress – was charged with organising almost daily entertainments: quizzes, charades, talent shows and occasional full plays and musicals by 'the Moscow Embassy Players'.

And, of course, in winter it was not only dismal but cold – cold and dark. This made Moscow a tough station, reason enough for posts there, even for relatively junior staff, to attract a hardship allowance of £1,000 a year (the equivalent to about £20,000 in 2015 money), without the deduction of any tax. That sort of money would burn a hole in anyone's pocket, so people did what people in that situation always do – they partied. Most were small affairs (the tiny flats did not facilitate large gatherings), many impromptu with music provided by gramophones and booze obtained from the embassy commissariat. At least the single people stationed in Moscow entertained themselves with parties and celebrations, whereas the married couples stayed in their flats, as miserable as their surroundings, playing whist or canasta and dreaming of their next trip home and the new kitchen they'd buy with their accumulated savings.[9] Of course, as Park never grew tired of emphasising, the wise – whether married or single – only partied with their fellows; any friendly approach from a presentable (a cause for suspicion in itself) young Russian was best viewed as a provocation, succumbing to which would lead inevitably to a nasty career-ending encounter with the secret police and a one-way ticket home.

Embassy personnel were in effect prisoners in full view, free to leave the embassy and walk about but not to converse or engage with the local citizens. Even to attempt such would have sentenced the unlucky locals to a camp in Siberia.[10] '*Ili schweigen ili gefängnis*' was how one German-speaking Russian (using a mixture of Russian and German) put it in a rare moment of candour.[11] All they could do was stare and be stared at in turn, a form of mutual zoo with the secret police in the role of keeper. The dreadful isolation combined with the alcohol-fuelled partying invariably led to romantic entanglements. Affairs with colleagues were not uncommon, nor were affairs with opposite numbers in other missions, the Americans and French, natural allies, predominating.

Ordinary friendships also blossomed. Colleagues spent far more time in each other's company than would be the case in most missions. Park and John Deverill,[i] the assistant air attaché, became lifelong friends. She also became very friendly with the former SOE officer, Patrick O'Regan, a friendship that lasted until cut short by O'Regan's premature death *en poste* in Paris in 1961. However she successfully avoided romantic liaisons, perhaps because she was still getting over Bazata, but also because of her naturally cautious attitude.

i DEVERILL, Wing Commander John; RAF (1922-).

CX/MOSCOW[12] was a small operation consisting of Park, her colleague Roland Carter, and a couple of station secretaries. In order to disguise their real occupation from the locally employed staff, Park and Carter's desks were in the Russian secretariat, the section of the embassy that devoted itself to studying as much overt material on the Soviet Union as it could acquire.[13]

When Park got down to work her starting points were those open and semi-open sources engaging in what the KGB counterintelligence services called 'dry' operations, which they had little choice but to tolerate. Radio Moscow was listened to, naturally, but the official monitoring was done in London by the BBC in its monitoring centre in Caversham Park in Berkshire. At the time the BBC was seen as being within the 'ring of secrecy', with specially vetted staff and access to secret Foreign Office analyses. In turn it briefed the Foreign Office on the contents of Soviet broadcasts.

Newspapers were monitored by a joint US-UK press monitoring unit based in the American embassy. There were the obligatory official 'voices' like *Pravda* (the voice of the Communist Party), *Izvestia* (the voice of the Soviet government), *Red Star* (the voice of the army) and *Trud* (the voice of the trade unions), and the many hundreds of locally produced newspapers. These could be surprisingly rich sources of information; not top secret material but information about the arrivals and departures of military units in their locality, warnings about impending manoeuvres, and so on. Of particular value was information coming from different newspapers that built into a composite picture from which conclusions might be drawn. If newspapers in several different regions reported a lower than expected harvest, for example, that could be an early pointer towards a lower harvest nationally, something of significant political impact. Many Muscovites had local newspapers sent to them by relatives in the country so the monitoring unit had an operation going to take advantage of that route to get copies for themselves. There were too many to be read with the limited resources available between the two embassies, so a press reading and translation centre was established by the CIA and SIS in the grounds of Caversham, giving gainful employment to scores of linguists.[14]

Technical journals and periodicals could be interesting, but those in the public or semi-public domain were subject to such censorship that their contents were anodyne; the interesting ones were treated as secret state documents. Another useful information source was encyclopaedias, of which there were many. The principal one was the *Great Soviet Encyclopaedia*, a subscription service which was updated on a regular basis; practically every household in the country took it. Shortly before Park arrived the embassy received a circular from its editors enclosing an article on the Bering Sea, which they said should be inserted in place of the entry on Laventiy Beria,[i] the recently executed head of the secret

---

i BERIA, Laventiy Pavlovich; head of the Soviet Union's state security apparatus under Stalin (1899-1953).

police. The original entry was to be removed, it instructed, 'using a sharp blade'. This instruction arrived *ahead* of any announcement of his fate.[15]

A hugely popular work was *The Book of Tasty & Healthy Food* (*Kniga o Vkusnoi i Zdorovoi Pishe*, usually shortened to the *Kniga*) which was produced by the USSR Ministry of Food and supposedly written by people's commissar Anastas Ivanovich Mikoyan. A new edition was published every year. As with almost everything in the USSR, it contained much commentary and admonishment, often useful clues to official thinking. Popular too was the magazine *Soviet Woman*, though its contents were predictably 'safe', as the following extract – advice to mothers of teenage girls – might suggest:

> High heels have an adverse effect on the development of young girls during this period. They bring the centre of gravity forward and backward, which may affect the form of the pelvis and the position of the uterus.[16]

All was grist to the intelligence mill, however, and would be handed to the Russian secretariat for initial reading and analysis.

For their part the Russians never let up in their attempts to penetrate the embassy. This wasn't yet the time of 'peaceful coexistence' or 'detente', and while relations between the Soviet Union and Britain were less chilly than under Stalin this did not extend to the respective intelligence services, nor does it now. The siege was led by the Second Department of the KGB's Second Chief Directorate (2B[17]), led by Ivan Markelov. According to Victor Cherkashin,[i] the KGB was running a number of low-level agents in the embassy at that time, 'secretaries and drivers'. The cipher office, consular and administrative sections and security guards were Markelov's particular targets.[18]

In addition to whatever agents the KGB had inside the embassy, it co-opted the locally-provided administrative and support staff, KGB-vetted Russian nationals in the main, to look out for its interests. Shortly before Park's arrival SIS had received intelligence from the Americans about some new resonance microphones the Russians had developed which did not require a local power source (battery or electrical connection) to operate, making ineffective many of the devices available for identifying such plants. It wasn't just the British embassy of course; practically every diplomatic mission in Moscow was a target for KGB bugging, much as most missions in Washington and London are apparently subject to routine electronic surveillance by the NSA/GCHQ today. So all-pervasive was this electronic penetration that, lacking a safe-speech room, UK embassy personnel were forced to conduct sensitive conversations by exchanging paper notes (later burnt) or while walking around the embassy grounds.

i CHERKASHIN, Colonel Victor Ivanovich, KGB (1932-).

The electronic monitoring was backed up by intensive surveillance of such embassy personnel as were either suspected or had been positively identified as being intelligence officers. The KGB's Seventh Department was responsible for this, having about fifty watchers and three follow cars devoted specifically to monitoring the British mission. Provocations of all sorts were commonplace, and Park would have been well-warned about them. A failed honey-trap attempt had even been made on Winifred Van Maurik,[i] the wife of the first post-war station head (Ernst Van Maurik).[19]

This was the nitty-gritty of intelligence and counterintelligence work, known, with good reason, as *'operativnaya igri'* (operational games), at which the Russians excelled. Their moves were planned in cramped offices in the Lubyanka by men in ill-fitting suits, as the KGB tried to devise ever more ingenious ways of penetrating the embassy, compromising its personnel and stealing its secrets, while at the same time attempting to inhibit any intelligence-gathering activities by Park and her colleagues. In even more cramped conditions and constantly fearful of being overheard, Park and her tiny cadre of somewhat better dressed fellows planned how to carry out their own tasks unhindered.

i Van MAURIK, Winifred Emery Ritchie, *née* Hay (1921-1984).

11

Moscow 2 – The squirrel and his nuts, 1955

Intelligence services love their secret lore, war stories, jargon, mottos, terms like 'cabbages & kings' – to describe the process of sifting through page after page of documents or endless transcripts of deciphered transmissions in search of the one tiny nugget (the king) that might lie therein. Another favoured SIS expression is 'The farmer is not concerned about whether or not the squirrel gathers its nuts but you better believe that the squirrel is.' This captures one of SIS's core operating philosophies: steal the opposition's secrets from under its nose because the enemy does not recognise the value of what is being stolen. Park used to joke with one of her colleagues about how she got hold of the most useful 'stuff' in the Soviet Union from right under the noses of the Russians.

One example was during her regular trips to provincial cities in Russia. The trips required official permission from the Burobin, the department that provided services for diplomats and resident foreign correspondents – a sort of Intourist for non-tourists. Apart from keeping her eyes open generally, she took to making the acquaintance of journalists working on the local newspapers. She would chat away in that seemingly innocuous way she had, in her émigré-taught Russian, charming the socks off them. The 'take' was significant but invisible to the KGB watchers and so she got away with it. Over time she built up a surprisingly intimate picture of everyday Soviet life, the shortages, the regulations, the permits required for this and that.[1]

Park took any opportunity to gather information, no matter how seemingly insignificant. For example, she made a practice of accompanying her servant (a Communist Party member and watcher) to the local market when the servant was finished work for the day. Out on the street both knew they were safe from the ever-present listening devices. Park would use the short trip to ask her about life in Moscow. Sometimes, according to Park, the maid would answer and other times she would not, but it all helped to build a picture. One day the maid was in a particularly bad mood, complaining about a new arrival in her already overcrowded apartment with its communal kitchen. When Park asked about the circumstances the maid told her the new arrival, a woman, had just been released early from a camp (gulag). 'What was she in for in the first place?' asked Park. The answer chilled. The woman had been in a queue and started grumbling about the shortages. Everyone within hearing distance in the queue had to decide whether or not to report her. Those who did not risked being sent

97

to the camps themselves because the woman could well have been a *provocateur* and would have reported those who had not denounced her. So she was reported and sentenced.[2]

One officer who was posted to Moscow shortly after Park spoke of attending public meetings designed to keep Soviet citizens abreast of developments. The meetings would be advertised on posters in Metro stations and the like. He would dress up like a Muscovite, slip in unnoticed, and sit up against the wall so that he could surreptitiously take notes. One meeting he attended was a talk given by a Communist Party senior official on a tour he had conducted of communist parties in all the major Latin American countries. The official was extremely frank about how disappointed he was with their organisational state, finances and membership. This information was passed on to an appreciative CIA.[3]

The same officer used to specialise in stealing telephone directories whenever he had the opportunity. Directories were considered state secrets and their circulation was tightly controlled. Park went one better and succeeded in getting hold of a copy of the national rail timetable. Timetables were even more secret and were restricted to the *nomenklatura* (mandarin class); ordinary citizens had to make do with consulting boards in stations or asking an official.[4] The particular value of the timetables was the ability of experts to use them to calculate the carrying capacity of the rail network.[5] But Park went beyond even that. One of her responsibilities was to act as the station's 'book-buyer'. Before she left London she was given lists of thousands of books (the lists were provided by the Bodleian Library, GCHQ and the British Museum) that she was to attempt to acquire and ship back to Britain.[6] Books were a source of potentially highly interesting information. They were also one of the limited number of commodities in which there was some sort of permitted unofficial trade. Books could be purchased in state bookshops, of course, but also on bookstalls and from other unofficial outlets.

The constant search for 'interesting' books may be what brought Park into contact with a variety of people who might best be described as being on the fringes of Soviet society, people of alternative viewpoints to the extent that any such were tolerated. While buying the books was part of her remit, making contact with semi-underground types was manifestly not. It is quite possible that it was her work that opened up the communication channel to Boris Pasternak and enabled SIS, a year later and after she had returned to Britain, to obtain a filmed copy of the original manuscript of Pasternak's epic *Dr Zhivago*. By then the Moscow station was under the command of Freddie Love[i] with Alan Urwick[ii] in the role of deep cover officer. It may have been Love who passed it on to the

---

i LOVE, Frederick Raymond ('Freddie'); SIS, ISTANBUL, H/MOSCOW, HONG KONG, SINGAPORE, H/HONG KONG (1926-d.).

ii URWICK, Sir Alan Bedford, KCVO, CMG; HM Forces, SIS, BERLIN, MOSCOW, diplomat, Sergeant-at-Arms/House of Commons (1930-).

CIA, who in turn arranged for it to be printed in its original Russian and distributed clandestinely in the Soviet Union.[7] This activity brought Park to the notice of the KGB and surveillance on her was increased. It also came to the notice of the Office that this newly trained officer, on her first serious operational posting, in Moscow of all places, was flouting the rules. The Office was not best pleased.[8]

Another escapade also attracted the notice of the KGB. Park and the assistant military attaché, John Deverill, received official permission to visit Kalinin (renamed Tver in 1990), a medieval town about a hundred miles north of Moscow at the confluence of the Volga and Tvertsa Rivers. In fact for hundreds of years it had been called Tver but was changed in Stalin's time to Kalinin in honour of the Bolshevik hero, Mikhail Kalinin. Kryuchkovo Soviet Air Force base was close to the town. Deverill's people were keen to know what its precise role might be and whether it was a home to units of the Soviet Long Range Air Force (its equivalent of Bomber Command), *ergo* his interest. Park went along because that was the rule; officials were never to travel on their own outside Moscow and anyway her Russian was better and two pairs of eyes were always better than one.

When the day arrived they took the train from Leningradsky station. Their escort remained behind in the station – standard practice. When they arrived in Kalinin a few hours later they wandered around for a bit, getting their bearings, wondering if arrangements had been made with the local KGB office to resume the surveillance, but it appeared none had and they weren't being observed. They were walking down a street when they came upon what looked like an interesting building – interesting in that the dozen or so ground floor windows were barred. As they passed the entrance they glanced in. There was no one around but in the gloom they could make out a bank of telephones. Beside the phones were instructions telling people how to use them to denounce their neighbours. Citizens were to pick up the handset, wait for an official and then dictate their denunciation, remembering to provide full details of the guilty party. Park and Deverill stared at one another: telephones were unknown in ordinary Soviet households, so the solution was to provide a bank of phones to allow people to drop in and inform on their fellows. It must be the local KGB office, they decided. It seemed that while the KGB hadn't found them, they had found it.

There was no one guarding the entrance so they stepped in for a closer look. Immediately to their left were stairs leading upwards. Hearts beginning to race, they headed up. On the next floor was a long corridor lined with doors to various offices, perhaps half-a-dozen on each side. On each was a sign presumably denoting who or what was inside. Deverill whipped out his notebook and started to scribble down the details. They split up, he taking one side, Park the other, working their way down the length of the corridor, scribbling as they did and ignoring the sounds of voices and movement from behind the doors. As was bound to happen, just as they reached the end of the corridor a door opened and through it stepped a woman. When she saw them she stopped and stared, obviously unsure of their status, then stepped back into the room and slammed the door shut.

They knew they had to make a run for it. As they made it onto the street they could hear raised voices behind them in the building. They then headed back towards the main square and what they hoped would be the anonymity of crowds. The trouble with that plan was that there weren't any crowds, not to speak of. They had no choice but to keep moving. In Kalinin it seemed all roads led to the rivers and soon enough they found ourselves at a river bank: the Volga probably, it was wide enough for sure, but it could have been the Tvertsa. They decided to track along it, not with any plan in mind, but movement was better than being stationary. They had gone a few hundred yards when they heard a shout behind them. They had been spotted. A uniformed figure at the head of a small group was pointing towards them from the town, gesticulating. They looked at each other.

'Only chance is to swim,' Deverill said. 'Can you?'

Already he was unbuttoning his trousers. Park stepped out of her skirt; this was no time for maidenly modesty. She stuffed her outer clothes into her attaché case; Deverill did the same. Then they plunged into the river. They were fortunate for the river had warmed up, somewhat, but the shock of the cold nearly made her heart stop. Inside a couple of minutes they were floating around a bend in the river and out of sight of the police and militia. Soon they were back on land, on the far bank, where they crawled out and collapsed, exhausted and panting. After a while they dried out and dressed themselves again. They walked for two hours, crossing the river again but by a bridge this time, before they saw the spires in the distance. They would be in time for the train, just. Five minutes later they were seated in a carriage watching Kalinin slide slowly past. And soon they were busy working out what to tell Hayter when they got back to Moscow.[9] Of course it wouldn't have taken the KGB very long to establish Park and Deverill's identities. It would have meant another check-mark on her file, another reason to think of her as an 'operator' and not 'just' a clerk, in other words someone worth keeping an eye on.

One of the more important continuing projects was maintaining discreet contact with UK visitors to the Soviet Union, who were referred to as legal-travellers. Up to the deployment of image-recording satellites in the mid 1960s, operations such as legal-travellers played a significant part in gathering intelligence from inside Russia. The travellers were businessmen, scientists, tourists or – more rarely – relatives visiting relatives and prepared to act as unofficial information-gatherers.

When the section in London learnt of someone's plans to travel to the Soviet Union discreet inquiries would be made as to their reliability and suitability.

Those who passed the vetting process might be asked if they would be prepared to undertake some voluntary tasks 'of a confidential nature' in the 'national interest'. Most agreed. Some were quite excited by the prospect, but they were warned against involving themselves in espionage. They were only to undertake the task given; that might be making specified purchases or arranging their journeys, or on occasion diverting from their official route, to places where they might be able to observe or surreptitiously photograph an installation of particular interest. Sometimes photographs were taken through the windows of lower-flying turbo-prop passenger aircraft whose flight paths took them over sites in which SIS had an interest. But that required care – taking clandestine photos in the confines of an aircraft cabin was tricky and often needed an accomplice. Alerted to the practice by George Blake, the Soviets took to placing British and American travellers, and diplomats in particular, in seats beside the wings in order to prevent them seeing what they shouldn't.

Many legal-travellers would call into the embassy on arrival in Moscow on some pretext where they would be briefed by Park or her colleague. Quite a few called back when they had performed their task and handed over any exposed film or purchases. Park or Carter would arrange for whatever it was to be sent back to Britain in the diplomatic bag. That route avoided the risk of it being discovered in one of the many stringent checks on departing visitors and the brouhaha that would arise if a British citizen was found to be in possession of material linked to espionage. While the British programme did enjoy some success, it wasn't helped in later years by the betrayer, George Blake, being made aware of it.

The CIA also ran a legal-traveller programme. In scale it was many times bigger that the British one. Furthermore it was not compromised by a betrayer (other than in principle) and as a consequence produced a sheaf of extremely useful intelligence.[10] Over time the legal-traveller programmes were expanded to include travellers from third countries who might attract even less suspicion and therefore surveillance and grew to include attempts to 'befriend' Soviet nationals with a view towards eventually recruiting them as sources.

There were of course the 'wet' (as in 'intelligence', not 'assassination') operations that the KGB did not tolerate at all and made every effort to counter. One of the rare successful Moscow 'wet' operations of that time was the Yo-Yo Project, a joint CIA/SIS operation in which Park would have been intensively involved. It commenced life earlier in the decade when the CIA and SIS jointly issued a watch order to their Soviet operations to be on the lookout for signs that the Soviets were developing a surface-to-air (SAM) anti-bomber missile ring surrounding Moscow.

Late in 1953 an observant military attaché, Park's colleague John Deverill, had noticed some unusual road construction on the outskirts of the city. Service attachés are selected for their curiosity and he was no exception. He produced a remarkably accurate sketch of what he saw, which ended up in CIA headquarters in Washington where the experts pored over it. The sketch showed three parallel roads about a mile long connected by other roads about half a mile long, forming a herringbone pattern. There was not sufficient evidence to reveal the purpose of the network but enough to make people curious. It was agreed that a watch should be kept and any developments noted. SIS was brought into the picture at that stage.[11] As construction progressed so did attempts by attachés in both embassies and by Park's predecessors, Terry O'Bryan-Tear and Jill Sheppard, to figure out exactly what was happening. Both sides contributed photographs and sketches as the opportunity presented. But they had to be careful, for if the Soviets suspected anything they might take precautions such as erecting screening to prevent further inspection. Worse still, they might assume that the system was compromised and start building something elsewhere.

The analysts were busy working things out, and they were starting to put forward some ideas. They started with the location. When it comes to determining the purpose of any new construction analysts *always* start with the location: buildings are built where they are built for a reason, often a compelling one. The analysts asked themselves (1) what would make the most sense to be built right there? And (2) what might require three one-mile long roads? The Americans became convinced that the position of the site, twenty-five to thirty miles from the centre of Moscow, and the presence of two large metal disks, pointed towards it being part of a radar-controlled anti-aircraft missile battery, a potentially serious development. SIS's best guess, from one of their experts back in Britain, was that the two wheels/disks, which were about a foot apart, suggested part of a machine for crushing rocks, something of no great significance at all.[12]

If the SIS expert was correct there would be only one or two locations (each with a nearby source of rocks). If the Americans were correct then there should in all probability be a ring of them encircling the city. One anti-aircraft missile battery does not defend a city. So the experts drew a circle around Moscow starting from the known location and asked if between the two countries they could spot any other sites on or around that circle and (just to be on the safe side) if any stone quarries existed near the original site. The project had advanced to the point where it required a name. Yo-Yo was selected from to the disks' resemblance to the eponymous toy.[13] Everybody then got to work, starting to the left and right of the known site but quickly extending their search. It wasn't an easy task; the circumference of the circle was close on two hundred miles long. Organising a methodical search of a circle that long and doing so without attracting any untoward attention was bound to be difficult.

Park participated with her usual enthusiasm, going on train journeys, bus rides, car journeys or anything that would enable her to intersect physically or visually with that notional circle. The sites were big, three miles long at least, and while efforts at concealment might be expected they would still need to be accessible by road for the delivery of construction materials and for general access and egress, so they were potentially identifiable. The plan worked. Park (and the various attachés who were similarly engaged) noted 'suspicious' construction activity in a number of locations and pretty soon were able to plot the likely points of intersection on the notional circle, making finding the others more a simpler task. Matters appeared to be advancing, buildings resembling barracks and hardstands (parking for heavy vehicles), ventilation shafts and so on were being added to the installations. One installation was under the flight path of aircraft travelling from Vnukovo Airport in Moscow to Leningrad, enabling covert photographs to be taken from inside the aircraft's passenger cabin. The site was reasonably adjacent to the closed city of Zelenograd, the centre of much Soviet weapons research, something that might or might not be significant. Further examination of the disks and the associated equipment showed without any doubt they were a form of radar dish. They consisted of two truncated equilateral triangles in a Star of David pattern; so much for the SIS expert's suggestion that it might be a rock-crushing machine.[14]

By this time the CIA had appointed its first resident case officer in Moscow. His name was Edward Ellis-Smith, Agency pseudonym 'Little Guy'.[i] His appointment arose from the Agency's securing a source in the Red Army's military intelligence service, the GRU. The source's name was Pyotr Popov, one of what became known as 'the three P's',[ii] three senior military intelligence officers who spied for the CIA over a period of years during the Cold War. All were eventually discovered and executed. At the time of his recruitment Popov – the first to be recruited and the first live CIA source inside the Soviet Union – was based in Vienna, then still under military occupation by the four wartime Allied armies (Britain, France, USA and Soviet Union). When the occupation ended in 1955 and the forces were withdrawn, Popov was transferred back to Moscow. At that time the CIA had no Moscow presence and so did not have the ability to maintain contact with their agent. In a panic the Agency tried desperately to remedy that situation. Its solution was to send Ellis-Smith who had some familiarity with the city, having previously served there as an assistant military attaché. The CIA chose not to tell the US ambassador, Chip Bohlen,[iii] that it was placing an officer on his staff, pretending instead that Ellis-Smith had resigned from the CIA and then been employed by the State Department as a security officer.[15] That piece of subterfuge was to turn out to be a bad mistake.

i ELLIS-SMITH, Edward; CIA (1921-1982).
ii POPOV, Colonel Pyotr (d. 1960); PENKOVSKY, Colonel Oleg (d. 1963); POLYAKOV, General Dmitri (d. 1988).
iii BOHLEN, Charles Eustis ('Chip'); diplomat (1904-1974).

The standard method of communicating with an agent in a hostile operating environment, such as Moscow, was to use a 'dead drop' rather than meeting face-to-face with the attendant risk of the assignation being spotted by counter-intelligence officers. In a dead drop a site was picked where messages between the agent and his case officer could be deposited by one for the other to be retrieved when the recipient had satisfied himself that he was free from surveillance. The site would usually be somewhere that the agent could have a plausible explanation for being, such as a public park on his route to and from work, ideally in a remote corner that would be difficult for surveillance officers to monitor without being spotted. Sites for dead drops were many and varied and great care was taken in their selection. However for this method to work effectively, messages needed to be exchanged about the time or location of the next exchange or a special request, and so on. This required Popov to leave brief notes for Ellis-Smith, which he wrote in Cyrillic text that Ellis-Smith could not read. This resulted in communications being lost between the CIA and Popov for the duration of what turned out to be a brief posting to Moscow.[16]

Despite his presence in the embassy, the breakthrough in the Yo-Yo project, when it came, seems to have had nothing to do with Ellis-Smith or the CIA directly. All we know for certain is that CIA analysts in Washington were handed a 'packet of photographs' which had somehow come into the possession of the Agency. The officially released account of the Yo-Yo operation[17] does not disclose the source for the photographs but it does not seem to have been through any CIA operation. Popov has been discounted as the provider since, as already noted, Ellis-Smith's inability to read Cyrillic meant that the Agency was not able to establish contact with Popov during his relatively brief period in Moscow before he was posted back to Schwerin in East Germany, when communications were re-established. If it wasn't the CIA then the most likely source was a 'friendly' intelligence service, possibly SIS, but there is no evidence to identify the specific service other than an acknowledgement by the Agency of British assistance on another aspect of the operation:

> A month later, about the beginning of December [1954], British observers riding on a train southeast of Moscow noticed a fenced area with a microwave antenna on a pole at one end. In the center of the enclosure there was an earth bunker with one open end facing the pole. There they saw a 'double rotating disk array,' each disk, they judged, about ten feet in diameter and making about 120 revolutions per minute. (CIA Report)[18]

Wherever the photographs came from, this was a significant coup. If it was a British source then Park would have been his case-officer for the duration of her posting. The photographs were taken in daylight and from different angles, providing a comprehensive view of the installation, a considerable bonus given that the site was under twenty-four-hour guard, and strongly suggestive of an inside contact rather than some opportunistic US or British military attaché peering over a fence and snapping away. The intelligence suggested that there were two concentric rings of radar sites, an outer and an inner, not one as previously thought. The purpose of the spinning disks (the Yo-Yos) was now clear. In the case of the outer ring, fifty miles from Moscow centre, one (radar) disk would track incoming bombers, while the second disk would guide the air defence fighters. These would be the first to respond, engaging the bombers probably with barrage (unguided) air-to-air rockets. The bombers that survived the fighter screen would be picked up by the inner ring's radar, thirty miles out. One disk would be used to track the bomber while the second would guide the missile to its target. The implications for US and UK bomber strategy were immense, raising the spectre of 'the bombers *not* getting through'. Apparently the project had been initiated in 1950 when Stalin made a late-night phone call to the senior engineer in charge of a particular aspect of Soviet guided-missile development. He was to drop everything and make the defence of Moscow the top priority. The engineer immediately put together a team of Russian scientists assisted by a number of German 'dragons' (prisoner-scientists).

Stalin excelled in these crash projects, possessing the power and the will to mobilise massive resources focused on one key outcome. 'Everything for the Front' had been his rallying cry when Russia was attacked by Hitler in the Second World War. He had repeated it to push through the development of Russia's atom bomb in 1949, fearing immediate nuclear annihilation. Now he did so again, determined to protect his country's capital city (and possibly his own skin). He appointed Sergei Laurentevich Beria (son of the secret police chief) as the project's second-in-command, in effect its chief procurement officer. That gave Stalin (through Beria senior) full control and also enabled him to ensure that the project was given access to all the necessary resources. And it worked. Naturally when Stalin died and Beria was executed his son was promptly removed, but progress was still considerable. In 1957 the CIA produced a map of the installations (see p. 107), most of which were almost fully built.

The project was at a very advanced stage, with deployment expected sometime the following year, 1956. The capacity was estimated to be around 2,500 missiles, prototypes of which had been tested in Kapustin Yar, a Soviet missile launch and development site located near Volgograd. The Yo-Yo installations were a cause of deep concern to the Americans. While most scientists believed enough bombers would get through and would inflict enormous damage on the city, the presence of a couple of thousand anti-aircraft missiles guided by sophisticated radar made that much less of a certainty. Yo-Yo worried the British government for the same reason. With Yo-Yo deployed Britain's much vaunted V-bombers would be relatively speaking sitting ducks, in effect neutralising Britain's nuclear deterrent.

In 1953 British military chiefs had requested permission for an over-flight of Kapustin Yar to determine the progress of the anti-missile testing located ground there. The request was referred all the way up to the Prime Minister, Churchill, who gave the okay for a surveillance flight using an RAF Canberra fitted with the latest American aerial camera. The aircraft would take off from a field in West Germany and fly 1,500 miles over Poland, Belarus, the Ukraine and Russia itself to its target.

The operation proceeded and as feared the Canberra was picked up by Soviet air defences. A terrifying game of cat and mouse followed, as the Canberra weaved in and out of the clouds, banking this way and that, hoping its high flying ceiling of 60,000 feet would be enough to protect it from Soviet air defence fighters and anti-aircraft missiles. The Russian Mig interceptors flew to the top of their operational ceiling, then fired their air-to-air barrage (unguided) rockets from almost vertical nose-up positions before banking away, their jet engines unable to cope with the thin air. They scored some proximity hits and started to inflict damage. The Canberra was forced to turn tail and headed for the Caspian Sea following the course of the Volga River, pursued all the way. The plane got away by the skin of its teeth, the aircraft reportedly having more holes in it than a colander when it landed in Iran. The mission was semi-successful, producing some usable images.[19]

When all of the intelligence on Yo-Yo was reviewed, it became clear to analysts that the decision to build almost sixty anti-bomber missile sites simultaneously meant that someone very high up in the Soviet leadership must have given the go-ahead. For a development on that scale the 'someone high-up' could only have been Stalin. The Americans were saying that something must have prompted Stalin to act. They thought that that something was one more secret leaked by Philby, the secret of TROJAN,[20] the US Air Force plan to obliterate fifty named Russian cities in the event of war between the Soviet Union and America. Philby had been privy to the detail of US war planning so had had access to TROJAN. The resultant intelligence leak, the Americans argued, must have led to Stalin's decision to accelerate the development of the Yo-Yo missile sites. It was clear that the Philby affair still rankled with Washington; understandably the CIA wasn't about to let it go, not with the SIS Chief, Sinclair, still in a state of absolute denial about his once star officer. This open wound did not bode well for the immediate future of SIS/CIA cooperation. For Park in Moscow, however, how the Philby affair would play out was not her main concern. For a start she was not privy to the detail, and in any event it would have been a distraction. Park, ever the hands-on spy, was absolutely determined to obtain any intelligence that would help build a better intelligence picture back in Britain. And she was about to get the chance to do just that, as she was asked to run SIS's first ever live source inside the Soviet Union.

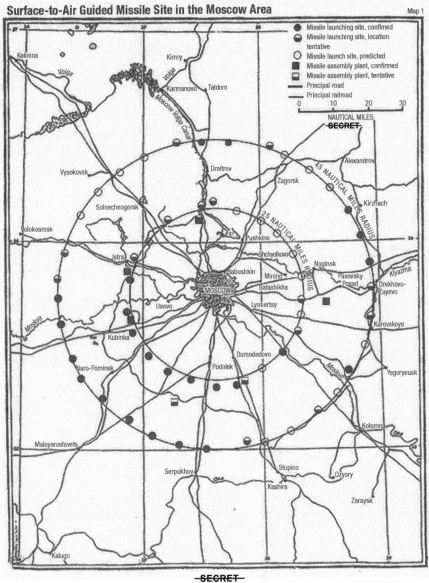

(Courtesy of CIA Archives)

Moscow 3 – The strange affair of Yevgeni Brik, 1956

By 1955 West Berlin rather than Helsinki had became the operational centre from where Russian-directed espionage was controlled, though Helsinki would remain a critical operating post. During the summer of that year George Young – who was now Director of Requirements – held a series of conferences in West Berlin where the intelligence priorities for Soviet Russia were re-set.[1] Obtaining reliable political information from inside the Kremlin became the first priority, in order to be able to determine the intentions of the Soviet leadership both militarily and politically. The second priority was the acquisition of scientific/technical intelligence intended to keep abreast of Soviet armaments development. War intentions intelligence was the third.[2]

The announcement in September that year that the Soviets were about to sell significant quantities of modern weaponry ($86 million worth of munitions in return for 100,000 tons of Egyptian cotton) to Egypt's President Nasser, in defiance of existing conventions, was exactly the sort of intelligence (in advance) that SIS's Whitehall customers were demanding from Young and that SIS (and for that matter the CIA) was failing to provide. The armaments, to be 'officially' supplied by Czechoslovakia, would radically alter the military balance in the region and play into the decision by the Israelis to invade Egypt the following year in the infamous Suez affair. The West was well aware that talks were ongoing, but SIS consistently told Whitehall that Nasser was posturing and would not sign any agreement. CIA ignorance was more understandable. Egypt was acknowledged as being within Britain's sphere of influence and the convention at the time was to depend on allies for intelligence from countries in such situations. SIS should have done better, but according to Hugh Bicheno it totally (and fatally) underestimated the Egyptians;[3] this despite Cairo having a substantial station in its own right and also being the current regional headquarters for SIS. But the Service misread the situation completely, not for the first time.

Young, by far the most dynamic among the SIS middle management, was determined to change that. In fact soon he would take up the position of Controller/Middle East & Africa (C/ME&A) and so could attend to it at first hand. (Interestingly it was at those conferences that Young circulated his famous *cri de coeur* on the nobility of the espionage profession, duly passed on to his Soviet masters by Blake.)[4]

In May of the following year (1956) Park was to find herself summoned to West Berlin for reasons other than simply attending conferences. A priority message from Broadway instructed her to make arrangements to travel to West Berlin post haste and to give, as her reason, a troublesome tooth that needed urgent attention. No other explanation was provided, nor was any needed. She made the arrangements. Ten days later she was in Berlin, staying in conditions of great secrecy in the home of Foreign Office official Oliver Wright,[i] then on a diplomatic posting as political advisor to the British Control Commission in the city. She was under instructions not to leave the house other than to meet her dentist's appointment, the cover reason for her visit.[5] Even at that stage Wright was seen as a highflier in the Foreign Office and, as was her wont, Park was not one to let slip the opportunity to create another friend or make a point.

> He [Oliver Wright] and I sat up and talked. This was just three months after the 20th Congress [of the Soviet Communist Party, held in February 1956] at which Khrushchev had spilt the beans on Stalin. And we had written about twelve dispatches from Moscow on all aspects of the conference and I had written three of them ... and Oliver said to me 'Fascinating, but the two I liked best were ...' and they were two of mine. And I said proudly, 'Those were mine.' He looked at me and said, 'What do you mean? Your lot don't do anything like that.' So I said, 'Certainly I do, I do a full job in the chancery as well.' He said, 'You wrote those dispatches?' I said, 'Yes, I did.' So there was a pause and he said, 'I suppose you tried for the [Foreign] Office and couldn't get in?' And I said, 'I am doing my first choice, I don't mind being a diplomat as well, I can take that in my stride ... but I always wanted to be an intelligence officer.' And he said, 'Well in ten years' time I shall be a minister and you shall probably still be a second secretary.' And I said, 'Yes probably, but of the two of us I shall have more power, more responsibility and more satisfaction, you wait.'[6]

Power always interested Daphne Park.

The following day Park was briefed personally by her Director (probably Shergold) in Wright's house, rather than in London Block, the centre of British administration in the city, home also to SIS Berlin station with its hundred members of staff, where her presence might have been noticed. After the barest minimum of niceties he got right down to it. The Service, he said, had a potential source in Moscow and she was to be given the opportunity to handle him. The source was Yevgeni Vladimirovich Brik. Brik was a KGB illegal, originally from Kiev in the Ukraine, who had been sent to Canada by Moscow Centre in 1951. Aware that border controls between Canada and the US were lax to the point of invisibility, the KGB plan was to use Canada as a staging post for the infiltration of its illegals into the United States, the 'Principal Adversary', Britain being

---

i WRIGHT, Sir J. Oliver, GCMG, GCVO, DSC; Royal Navy, diplomat (1921-2007).

reduced by this time to the status of 'Principal Ally'. The illegals (officers working under assumed identities) were to be used to handle US-based KGB agents such as the 'atom spies'. After two years training Brik was dispatched to Canada using two false identities,[7] the standard KGB insertion methodology at the time. The first he used to gain entry to the country, abandoned immediately after to be replaced by the second, which would serve as his long-term operational name. Once ensconced in the country he settled down in the low-rent Verdun suburb of Montreal under the guise of a professional photographer.

As it turned out, Brik was not a good choice. He had a serious drinking problem probably exacerbated by his clandestine life, and was lonely for his Russian wife. She had remained behind in Russia, as was the norm. Shortly after arrival in Canada he began an affair with the wife of a Canadian soldier and (predictably) after a period he confessed his true role to her. She persuaded him to go to the police. They turned him over to the Royal Canadian Mounted Police (RCMP) Security Service who decided to run him as a 'double' codenamed GIDEON. Brik's life as a 'double' lasted for two years. His every move was monitored more closely than a laboratory mouse as the RCMP determined to learn everything possible about KGB operations in Canada. The monitoring led to the uncovering of several KGB sources but it was hard-earned: Brik 'the double' was at least as much trouble to his Canadian handlers as Brik 'the illegal' had been to his Soviet ones.

Then Brik was recalled to Moscow. This was supposedly to attend a pre-arranged debriefing and to spend some time with his wife. Despite his concerns that he might have been compromised, Brik's hubris encouraged him to go ahead with the visit, convinced he could outwit the KGB's interrogators. His RCMP controllers weren't so sure, but the opportunity to obtain a fuller picture of KGB operations from inside Russia swayed them. However the Canadians were not set up to handle Brik while he was in Moscow, so they turned to SIS who had been briefed on Brik from the beginning. SIS had, in theory at least, the capacity to run an agent in the Russian capital and was happy to take over. The possibility of a source inside the Moscow KGB, if only for a few months, was hugely attractive. Ignorance of the inner workings of the Soviet security apparatus was profound. The Service also wanted anything it could get about the whereabouts and activities of the two defectors, Burgess and Maclean, who had yet to surface after almost four years. SIS was also desperate for anything that might point conclusively to the guilt or otherwise of Kim Philby.

Leslie Mitchell,[i] then H/WASHINGTON, was dispatched to Ottawa to brief Brik and take him through the various operational procedures. According to

---

i MITCHELL, Major Leslie Herbert, CBE; HM Forces, SIS, OSLO, COPENHAGEN, H/TEHRAN, H/WASHINGTON, H/BONN.

Harold Shergold, Mitchell had his work cut out. Brik was at times over-emotional, irrational and arrogant, behaviour that was not uncharacteristic of agents and of double-agents in particular. Mitchell, however, was an old hand and he persevered. He drilled into Brik the need to memorise the location of a rendezvous point for his *treff* (meeting between a case officer and an agent) with his Moscow-based SIS case officer (Park) and a two-word *parole* (recognition signal). He was provided with the locations of a couple of 'dead drops' for 'comms' purposes. In the event that he had to make a dash for it, he was provided with the location of a hide containing a short-wave radio, fake passports, internal travel permits, money, maps of the border area between Russia and Norway and a silenced pistol.[8] No one appears to have been particularly optimistic about his chances of making it across the border, but it was something. Park's task, Shergold said, was to establish contact with Brik and satisfy herself he was not under KGB control. If she suspected that to be the case she was to abort, otherwise she was to put the regular contact arrangements in place. This was a judgment call that was hers alone to make. The prize was attractive but the embarrassment that would follow if an accredited UK diplomat was caught in clandestine contact with a Soviet official had to be avoided. Apart from anything else it would justify the Foreign Office's original reluctance to sanction the reestablishment of Moscow station and could lead to the ban on operations within Soviet borders being reimposed. The next day, at her Director's insistence, Park attended the dentist. 'In this city you never know who's watching you,' he said, 'always best to be sure.' Then, with her jaw still hurting, she returned to Moscow to meet her agent.

The meeting with Yevgeni Brik, Park's first operational *treff*, did not go as planned, though not through any lack of preparation by Park. She approached the meeting with the thoroughness that would mark her career. Her first priority was to ensure that she was not under KGB surveillance when the two met. Case officers use the term 'to dry-clean' to describe the process through which they ensure they are not being watched when they meet an agent. Typically they will spend two to four hours checking for the presence of hostile surveillance, longer if they are the nervous type. Park's plan was to take advantage of a weakness she had discovered in the KGB's surveillance procedures.

One day, when she was still settling into her role, she had noticed something odd; it happened shortly after she'd left the chancery with a colleague on some routine business. Half-way there the colleague had excused himself, remembering some errand or other he had to run. After a quick 'confab', the KGB followers, who made no effort to disguise their presence, apparently decided to stick with following the (male) colleague and abandoned their surveillance of Park. Ten days later the same thing occurred when another male colleague left her company to go his separate way; once again the watchers wheeled off to follow him leaving her unwatched. She decided to run a proper test, to establish if it was a real pattern and thus predictable, exploitable. Over a few weeks she tested. But it seemed to be so – each time she left the embassy accompanied by one of her male colleagues and they later split up, the watchers concentrated solely on the man, leaving her by herself, in the clear. The only explanation that made sense was that the watchers (all men) assumed that the man, being a man, had to be the important one and therefore their target. She must be just a lowly female, probably just a clerk and not as worth following in her own right. KGB practice at the time was to use women only as 'swallows' (sexual bait) and decoys. It was an easy mistake for the KGB watchers to make, to assume that the British SIS would have the same attitude to its female employees as did the Soviets. (In the Intelligence business it is known as 'transferred imaginings' – the practice of ascribing to the subjects of intelligence assessments the same behavioural characteristics as the person preparing the assessment.) Park decided she would turn that chauvinistic assumption to her advantage.[9] The planned *treff* with Brik would give her the opportunity.

On the day of the *treff* with Brik she left the chancery well ahead of the scheduled time of the meeting, accompanied by one of her male colleagues. At a pre-arranged time he left her company. As predicted, the surveillance team wheeled off leaving her unwatched. She spent another couple of hours making absolutely certain she was in the clear before heading for the rendezvous. Finally as she walked down the street, her heart racing, she saw a man approaching who looked like Brik. She waited to make sure she had identified him correctly; the two had never met so all she had was his picture, now safely ensconced in the office safe. It was Brik, but there was a problem – two in fact. The first was that he was accompanied (by a tough-looking woman) when the arrangements called for him to be on his own. The second was that the visual recognition signal was wrong.[10]

Park had a big problem and only seconds to decide whether to continue with the meeting or to abort. She decided to abort, reasoning that meeting protocols are there for a purpose and are designed to be followed to the letter. Any deviation should be seen as an attempt by a blown agent, under enemy control, to alert his handlers to his situation. Park returned to the chancery and sent a coded signal to Broadway describing the outcome. In London, SIS assumed that Brik had been rumbled and was under KGB control and that Park had done extremely well to spot the attempted deception and act as she had.

According to the Mitrokhin Archive,[11] the situation was not quite what it seemed. Yevgeni Brik had been betrayed all right. A heavily indebted driver in the RCMP Security Service, a Corporal James Morrison, who had once been given the job of driving Brik from the Security Service offices to his home, contacted the Ottawa KGB legal residency and gave them Brik's name in return for a payment of $5,000. While initially suspicious that Morrison might be a prov-ocation, the KGB decided to investigate. Soon they became convinced that in all probability Brik had been turned by the Canadians. Aware that their spy was due to return to Moscow for a pre-arranged period of R&R, the KGB decided to bide their time and wait until he was back on home soil, where he could be interrogated at leisure. Unaware of his impending fate, Brik set out for home via Paris and Helsinki, monitored all the way by KGB shadows.

Immediately on arrival in Moscow in August 1955 Brik was arrested. Again according to the archive he confessed after considerable 'pressure' and 'told all'. He gave his interrogators details of the arrangements of his *treff* with his SIS Moscow controller but was instructed not to make contact. He was permitted to live in his flat with his wife in order to maintain the illusion that he was not under KGB control. The flat was bugged and he was recorded trying to persuade his wife to flee the country with him; wisely (as it turned out) she refused. The KGB then ordered Brik to send a message to SIS that he was ready to resume contact at a pre-agreed rendezvous. According to the KGB file on Brik he was not permitted to attend the rendezvous but Park did, enabling the KGB to iden-tify her as an operational SIS officer in Moscow.

It is difficult to reconcile Park's account with that of the KGB as reported in the Mitrokhin Archive. (Mitrokhin claims that 'Brik was not allowed to meet any member of the SIS station in the Moscow embassy for fear that he would blurt out what had happened to him, but was instructed to arrange a rendezvous which he did not keep'.) Perhaps Park made a mistake and mistook someone else for Brik: a perfectly innocent man out for an afternoon's shopping with his wife, maybe. Park had little direct field experience prior to being posted to Moscow. She wasn't a total neophyte; while her wartime work in SOE was tutoring in codes and ciphers, and wasn't field work as such, she would have spent considerable time in the company of the agents and some of their training regimen would have rubbed off on her. And she had spent a couple of years working in Vienna with FIAT which would have required some familiarity with basic tradecraft at least. But, and it is a significant 'but', she was handling her first ever live *treff* in the toughest operating environment in the world. That meant performing well beyond her operational experience and to the very limits of her capabilities, and it could be that she got it wrong.

Perhaps the archive record is slightly inaccurate and Brik was allowed to be present at the rendezvous (in order to flush out the SIS operative) but not to make contact. This would suggest that Brik had after all held something back and in the end honoured his arrangement with SIS and warned them that he was under control. But that's a stretch. Former RCMP Security Service officer, Dan Mulvenna, says that in his view Mitrokhin got it wrong:

... as part of a KGB 'Operational Game' to ensnare SIS, GIDEON was subsequently pressed to fly a prearranged emergency signal for a 'meet', as per the joint RCMP/SIS emergency exfiltration plan, which by the way both Services regarded as being probably unrealistic, to which Daphne responded. As Daphne reported, and told me personally many years later when I spoke with her in the UK, when she arrived at the rendezvous site she immediately picked up on KGB surveillance. And when GIDEON arrived at the rendezvous, arm in arm with a rather burly Russian woman, certainly not his [common-law] 'wife', Daphne further observed that his 'signal' [which was not a shopping bag] was not correct. She aborted the meet thereby avoiding a possible ambush arrest. But of course her 'cover' was now blown.[12]

This author agrees with Mulvenna that the most likely explanation is that the KGB engaged in some more of their '*operativnaya igra*' (operational games) in order to flush out Park (or whomever). It is likely therefore that they decided to seize the opportunity and deployed a decoy, possibly a lookalike, whom Park mistook for Brik. We shall probably never know which for certain (though SIS does). What is known is that in place of the automatic sentence of death handed out for treachery Brik received a sentence of fifteen years. Such a sentence of imprisonment was in itself unusual, as the absolute norm under Soviet rule for betrayal by a serving intelligence officer was death. Civilians, such as scientists, might on occasion be allowed off with a hefty prison sentence, but for those in the Great Game, betrayal was treason, treason was punishable by death, and death was invariably the result.

Were allowances made for Brik's cooperation in this operational game? The KGB file on Brik indicated that he had cooperated in such a manner, so that might well have been the case. It is impossible at this time to say with any certainty what if any were the reasons for the comparative clemency. And it was comparative – fifteen years in the special camp, Perm-35, was no picnic. Better that, though, than a bullet in the back of the head. It would be interesting to know what Park really thought about her abortive encounter with the 'man with the shopping bag in the wrong hand' all those years later when Brik told his tale. Her cover as a 'clean-skin' diplomat was blown, at least from the autumn of 1955 until she left Moscow the following year. She never alluded to that in her reminiscences though she did recount the tale of the KGB being fooled into following 'the male' on several occasions, it forming part of her mystique.

In the mid-1980s, thirty years after the missed *treff* in Moscow, Yevgeni Brik, now released from the Gulag and seeing the communist world collapsing all around him, made his way to Riga in Latvia where he telephoned an official in the British consulate and gave him his two-word recognition codeword, held precious for all those years. The SIS station head in the consulate contacted London, unsure whether he was dealing with a hoax or the real thing. There wasn't anybody left in the Service from that time who'd been involved operationally with GIDEON, but there were plenty of retirees, including Park, who remembered it well. They now knew that their putative spy had not been sentenced to death as they had assumed, but to a term in the Gulag.

They consulted the archives and their memories and confirmed the authenticity of the parole. A meeting was arranged to confirm that Brik was indeed their man. The spy, codename GIDEON, long thought dead was in fact alive. The Canadian government retrieved details of KEYSTONE from the archives and were encouraged to step in on the basis that Brik had in fact been their spy. With some assistance from SIS the Canadians smuggled Brik out of the Soviet Union and resettled him in Canada under a false identity. However the turncoat spy never settled down to enjoy his late retirement. His imprisonment had left him far too damaged for that, and he remained bitter and paranoid to the end.

Mulvenna's account differs slightly from the above, but not in its fundamentals.

GIDEON's cooperation with the KGB in this attempted 'Operational Game' probably saved his life. Many years later, after he had been released from prison and after the subsequent collapse of the Soviet Union, GIDEON surreptitiously established contact with the former RCMP Security Service [now CSIS]. He was subsequently quietly exfiltrated from Russia. He was thoroughly debriefed, provided with a new cover identity and lifetime compensation and re-settled in Canada, where he lived out the remainder of his life. He died several years ago. He never appeared in public and never made any public comments.[13]

13

Moscow 4 – *Annus horribilis*, 1956

There are at two views among former SIS hands about which particular event made 1956 the single most important year in SIS's post-war history. Concerning the year itself, however, there is a surprising degree of unanimity. For some (including many who were yet to join the Service), 1956 was the commencement of SIS's slow but definitive journey to becoming a much more professional, more accountable intelligence service. It is peculiar, though, that for years within the organisation it was known, not as the 'year of discovery' or 'year of renaissance', but as the 'year of horrors'. In fairness, the 'horrors' were pretty horrible, but they needed to be if they were going to be able to bring about such a wholesale alteration in attitude and practice. The events themselves were of two kinds, those that were intelligence driven (but with ramifications), such as the 'Crabb Affair', and those that were geo-political in nature but where SIS played a significant role, such as the invasion of the Suez Canal, or where it failed to do so, as in the Hungarian Uprising.

For most of 1956 Park remained stationed in Moscow, so she saw the events unfold through that particular prism. She was still a relatively junior officer, not yet a 'major player' but far from a bystander. The Kremlin's opaque machinations would be pivotal to how events played out. Furthermore before the year was over she would be asked to undertake the most critical operation of her career to date, to determine whether the Soviet Union was preparing to go to war with Britain. However, as 1956 dawned in a cold, grey and cheerless Moscow, all that was yet to come.

The first event was no more than a footnote to history, a bleak press conference, though it was barely that, being attended by just two Soviet reporters and two from Britain. At the conference the renegade Foreign Office officials, Guy Burgess and Donald Maclean, appeared for the first time since their flight from Britain five years previously. What they said added little to the existing understanding and was designed perhaps to draw attention away from their comrade in arms, Kim Philby, the betrayer-in-chief. It is ironic that the modern use of the term 'The Establishment' came into being when the journalist Henry Fairlie[i] penned an article in *The Spectator* magazine in 1955 in which he spoke of

---

i FAIRLIE, Henry Jones; journalist and author (1924-1990).

'The Establishment' coming together to shield two of their own, Messrs Burgess and Maclean.[1]

The next revelation was pure SIS business. It was confirmation that the 'fight against Soviet occupation' by the 'partisans' in Estonia, Latvia and Lithuania, by the 'nationalists' in the Ukraine, by the 'freedom fighters' in Albania, was no more than a ball of smoke. All had been betrayed by combinations of treachery, incompetence and double-dealing. Some campaigns had in fact been the creation of the KGB, while others had been infiltrated by it and effectively turned, on similar lines to the double-cross operations of the Second World War. This was a huge blow. Whitehall had been made promises that SIS simply had not kept. And these were major intelligence/paramilitary operations costing millions of (mainly US) dollars, running over the best part of a decade with the loss of hundreds of agents' lives. The agents had been parachuted into the operational territories on flights from Cyprus, or landed on the Baltic coast from motor torpedo boats based in Kiel, or infiltrated across land borders. For all the good they did SIS and the CIA might as well have parcelled them up and posted them direct to the Lubyanka.[2] As one CIA officer later put it: 'The only thing these drops achieved was to confirm the laws of gravity.'[3]

Harry Carr was SIS's Controller/Northern Area and a 'big beast' in SIS terms. Yet under his watch all Northern Area's special operations had been effectively controlled from Moscow for an entire decade (1944-54).[4] He was quietly transferred to Copenhagen, out of harm's way. Naturally the failure did not stop the award to him of a MVO (Member of the Royal Victorian Order) in 1957 to go alongside his earlier CMG (Companion of the Order of St Michael and St George). That was 'old' SIS, protecting its own, looking after itself at all costs, never admitting failure. As it happened, as part of her original briefing Park had been told to beef up attempts by the radio communications staff in the embassy to contact the partisans but hadn't been successful; now she knew why. But even though SIS remained silent the event did not pass unnoticed in Whitehall.

Park's notification of the first of the seminal events of that year, what became known as the 'Crabb Affair', came in April when the bell on the teletype pinged to announce the arrival of an enciphered telegram from the Moscow desk in Broadway. Its contents were stark: a sensitive intelligence operation, mounted on home soil, had been compromised. Worse, much worse, the story was breaking in the newspapers. She was warned to expect considerable flak and to report on the fallout in Moscow.

For an organisation used to cloaking its failures in a comforting shroud of secrecy this was bad news. It seemed that a former Royal Navy frogman had disappeared while attempting to examine the hull of a Soviet cruiser moored in Portsmouth harbour. But not just any cruiser – the vessel, the *Ordzhonikidze*, was being used to ferry Nikita Khrushchev and Nikolai Bulganin on their official visit to Britain. Of course Park was aware of that aspect; she had been intimately involved in the preparations for the visit. This was the first time the Soviet leadership had come to Britain since the foundation of the communist state. The invitation had been issued at Ambassador Hayter's instigation and its acceptance was a key gain in his attempt to 'reset' Anglo-Soviet relations in the wake of Stalin's death. Official Britain was going to pull out all the stops to make the visit a success, to show the world that the country still counted and that its Prime Minister was a statesman to be reckoned with.

All this seemed to pass SIS by. In its 'job jar' was a Priority One requirement from the Admiralty for intelligence about the underwater noise characteristics of Russian warships. This had significant implications for the operation of acoustic torpedoes and anti-ship mines. So SIS consulted with the Naval Intelligence Division of the Admiralty and it was agreed between them that an operation would be mounted against the *Ordzhonikidze*; the operation was given the codename CLARET. SIS's London station (BIN), then being run by highflier Nicholas Elliott,[i] was given the job. Had the vessel been making a routine 'fly the flag' visit then CLARET would probably have gone off without too much trouble and if it hadn't, it would have been no more than mildly embarrassing. Similar operations by both sides against the others' warships were routine. But mounting an operation against a vessel bearing its country's leaders was of a different order of risk entirely.

To this day no one is certain about exactly what happened, or to put it more accurately, those who do know are not saying. The scenario that best fits with the publicly ascertainable facts is that security on board the *Ordzhonikidze* had been heightened due to its VIP passengers, though they weren't actually on board that night, they were staying in Claridge's.[5] There may also have been a general awareness that some form of intelligence operation might be launched against the vessel or indeed quite a specific one. In his book, *A Spy Among Friends*, author Ben Macintyre speculates on the possibility that Elliott may have told his friend and colleague, Kim Philby, about the planned operation and that it was Philby who tipped off the Soviets.

Either way, an alert sentry spotted the diver, a decorated former Navy frogman called Lionel 'Buster' Crabb,[ii] approaching the vessel underwater and sounded the alarm. Concerned that the vessel could be under threat of attack, armed divers were sent down to confront the intruder. In the ensuing struggle Crabb was killed.

i ELLIOTT, John Nicholas Rede; Intelligence Corps, SIS, CAIRO, ISTANBUL, H/BERNE, H/VIENNA, H/VIENNA, C/UK, H/BEIRUT, H/TEL AVIV, C/EUROPE, D/R (Requirements) (1916-1994).

ii CRABB, Lionel Kenneth Phillip ('Buster') Crabb, OBE, GM; Royal Navy (1909-presumed dead 1956).

When Crabb failed to return on time from his dive a search was launched. It failed to locate him and panic ensued in Broadway.[6] Had he drowned? Had he been captured? Was he at this moment spilling the beans, being readied for a triumphant Soviet press conference?

If there was panic in Broadway, then in Whitehall there was utter confusion. The Admiralty and SIS kept quiet, leaving the government completely in the dark for all of two weeks. Eventually the Admiralty issued a statement to the effect that a diver had been lost on a mission further up the coast. No one was fooled, least of all the Russians who issued a ringing condemnation.[7]

The affair exposed to Whitehall's appalled stare the fundamental weaknesses of SIS. For a start the Service never looked at the context of the visit, nor did it carry out any proper risk/reward analysis of the operation. Next it made a complete hash of the operational planning. By rights Elliott, as the officer ultimately responsible, should have stood back and ordered that the task be handed over to the Special Boat Squadron (SBS) which had the necessary expertise. Instead he permitted the cobbling together of a slapdash, 'kiss-my-arse' type operation which predictably blew up in his face.

He started by recruiting Crabb, an out-of-condition Second World War veteran, to do the dive. Then he walked away from the operation, handing it over to a subordinate who in turn passed it on to someone even more junior. Meanwhile the Navy press-ganged one of its officers to act as the operations controller while the on-the-ground controller, a Bernard Smith, lurked in the shadows on the quayside like a character from *The Third Man*.[8] Smith's concept of operational security too was quaint. The pair could have stayed in Fort Monkton, the SIS training base in nearby Gosport. Failing that, standard procedure would have been for the pair to register in their hotel in false names and pay in cash. Not, as they did, checking in under their true names, though Smith's was at first assumed to be a pseudonym. Worse still, Smith allowed Crabb to pay a social call on the evening before the operation (at which he unwisely drank heavily), providing further evidence of his presence in the area. When the alarm was raised Portsmouth Police were contacted and told to get to the hotel *pronto* and destroy the incriminating evidence, i.e. the hotel register. But they were too late; the cat was out of the bag, the register, with its pages torn out, only adding to the furore. For the newspapers had got wind of it (probably from the police) and started asking questions, deciding to ignore the 'D Notice' system then in operation.

Finally, when it was found out, instead of owning up, SIS tried to conceal the truth for *two weeks*, so compounding Whitehall's original embarrassment and chagrin.

When Park heard the news in Moscow she was horrified. The effort that had been put into the visit had been enormous, the embassy having been consumed by it for months. Later Khrushchev made it clear to Hayter that he wasn't personally affronted by the affair, his attitude being 'it was just business'. But the damage to SIS was done.

In Whitehall Sinclair (C) mounted a stern defence. He claimed that SIS had in fact sought permission from the Foreign Office advisor to the Service and when he did not object assumed it had the go ahead. This was true up to a point, but the advisor (Sir Michael Williams) was distracted by his father's death earlier in the day and did not refer the plan up the chain for approval. However it did not address the other issues and was too little too late. The Service had committed the gravest sin of all; it had embarrassed its Prime Minister. Eden took his revenge. Sinclair's retirement was brought forward and instead of Jack Easton stepping up to the job of Chief it was given to Dick White, then head of MI5.[9]

This was a calculated act of humiliation, of displeasure expressed. But as far as most of the Service was concerned it went right over their heads. To a man (and they were all men) the senior strata took the view that Whitehall might as well have appointed Ivan Serov of the KGB as *this bloody secret policeman*. Only a few of the more discerning saw it for what it was – a not so thinly veiled warning that unless the Service got its house in order, the next step would be the merging of the two agencies. And who better to supervise that than a Chief of SIS who had also been head of MI5?

Sinclair protested vociferously. He detested White, blaming him for 'mislabelling' Philby as a traitor. But in vain, Eden was adamant.

There was other fallout from the affair. The first operational deployment of the revolutionary U2 high-altitude surveillance aircraft to RAF Lakenheath in Suffolk, using the cover of a USAF weather research squadron, was cancelled. Eden requested the deployment be delayed, but rather than delay the Americans redeployed to West Germany instead. Part of the 'rent' payable by the USAF would have been the right to nominate an agreed number of flights for UK-determined missions. Given Eden's issues in the Middle East, that would have been useful.[10]

Matters weren't about to get better anytime soon. The following August the entire SIS station in Cairo was rolled-up by Egyptian Intelligence and thirty of its agents arrested. The timing could not have been worse. Relations between the Egyptian leader, Gamal Nasser, and Britain were worsening by the hour. Nasser was an Arab nationalist who just a month previously had taken control of the Suez Canal without as much as an advance whisper reaching the ears of SIS. The canal mattered to Britain, both prestige-wise and strategically. It took weeks off the sea journey from Europe to Africa, was an umbilical cord between Britain and its Empire, and allowed whoever controlled it to exercise great influence on the region. It was also a matter of huge national pride to Egypt, a massive foreign exchange earner, and of course control of it now gave Egypt, not Britain, access to its levers of power.

At the precise moment when the Service (and Whitehall) needed a functioning intelligence operation on the ground, they hadn't got one. SIS had made the fatal mistake of underestimating the Egyptians, seeing them as a bunch of 'fuzzy-heads' incapable of mounting effective counterintelligence operations.[11]

In September, John Coates,[i] the scheduled replacement as H/MOSCOW, arrived in the city. His arrival was welcome; Park had been shorthanded since Carter, her number two, had left the station the previous February, posted to Germany. The political temperature was heating up and she could do with his presence.

What was raising the temperature was what came to be described by some as the 'brain fever' of the Prime Minister, Anthony Eden. Eden had come to see Nasser as the personification of evil, the 'Muslim Mussolini'. He decided that his response to Nasser's nationalisation of the canal would be to invade Egypt and install a new, more pliable, administration, one that would restore British control of its 'asset'.

Sir Anthony Nutting,[ii] a Foreign Office minister at the time, recalled receiving a telephone call from Eden:

The telephone rang and a voice down the other end said: 'It's me.' I didn't quite realise who 'me' was for a moment. However, he gave the show away very quickly by starting to scream at me. 'What is all this poppycock you've sent me about isolating Nasser and neutralising Nasser? Why can't you get it into your head I want the man destroyed?' I said, 'OK. You get rid of Nasser, what are you going to put in his place?' 'I don't want anybody,' he said. I said, 'Well, there'll be anarchy and chaos in Egypt.' 'I don't care if there's anarchy and chaos in Egypt. Let there be anarchy and chaos in Egypt. I just want to get rid of Nasser.'[12]

In conjunction with France and Israel (each of which had its own motivations) Eden put together a military plan to achieve this. In all of this Eden was encouraged, quite vociferously, by a cabal of right-wing Tory MPs known as the 'Suez group' (led by Duncan Sandys and Julian Amery), who were in cahoots with a cabal of senior SIS officers (led by George Young), who in turn were allied to a cabal of senior military officers (led by the CIGS General Templer), while the proprietors of the *Times, Express* and *Daily Mail* (Viscount Astor and Lords Beaverbrook and Rothermere) roared them on.

A weakened SIS's main contribution to the operation was a number of wild schemes to assassinate Nasser (at Eden's insistence). These ranged from poisoned coffee and chocolates to the introduction of nerve gas through the ventilation

i COATES, John Gordon, DSO; Intelligence Corps, SOE, SIS, HAGUE, VIENNA, H/MOSCOW, H/HELSINKI (1918-2006).

ii NUTTING, Sir Harold Anthony; diplomat and politician, resigned over the Suez affair (1920-1999).

system in Nasser's palace (which would have led to countless deaths), and an exploding razor.

As all of this was coming to a head, in Budapest 100,000 students suddenly rebelled against Soviet rule, backed by about 15,000 workers. The rebellion had its genesis in Khrushchev's 'secret' speech to the 20th Party Congress a few months earlier which appeared to open up the possibility of some deviation from pure Soviet orthodoxy. This was aided by some relatively minor CIA activities and a steady stream of irresponsibly encouraging messages broadcast by Radio Free Europe and Radio Liberty in Munich.[13] From the Soviet perspective Budapest was a serious cause for concern. It was the second revolt in three years against Soviet rule in the East European satellites. The first, the Workers Uprising in East Berlin, had been crushed by Soviet tanks. Western governments had limited their response to ringing denunciations of 'Soviet tyranny'. Khrushchev needed to figure out (and figure out quickly) if the West's response to Budapest would be the same. He didn't have to worry as far as Britain was concerned. There was no room in Eden's brain for a second, simultaneous crisis, so he dismissed it from his consideration. White, still new to the job, did try; he dispatched John Bruce Lockhart to the city to report on the situation. The ambassador, Leslie 'Bunny' Fry, told Bruce Lockhart that the Russians would not allow Hungary to leave the socialist 'fold' and would intervene militarily if it came to the push. Britain, said Fry, needed to develop a policy to take account of that.[14] He could have saved his breath to cool his porridge.

For Park in Moscow the situation was deeply frustrating. Her problem was that she simply had no *sources* in Moscow capable of supplying actionable (or even insightful) intelligence on Soviet intentions. All she had available were newspaper reports, statements carried by TASS, the Soviet news agency, and diplomatic tittle-tattle which was totally circular with everyone rehashing and recycling the same miserable titbits. She and Hayter (separately as ambassador) did what they could to inform London but it was slim pickings.

But even if she had been possessed of solid intelligence, London wouldn't have been in the mood to listen. Suez was all that mattered; intelligence supporting the planned invasion was given excessive prominence; contrary intelligence was suppressed, derided or otherwise ignored. This was facilitated by an extraordinarily tight ring of secrecy on the war planning imposed by the Prime Minister. Swathes of senior civil servants, cabinet ministers and generals were kept outside the circle of knowledge in a demonstration, since repeated, that when a Prime Minister is intent on war he (or she) can be devilishly difficult to halt.

In the Kremlin, Khrushchev fulminated. It wasn't just the Hungarians and the East Germans, the Poles too were restless. Only months earlier the Soviet leadership had faced down a challenge from Warsaw (the Polish Spring) without having to send in the troops. Now here was another satellite attempting to cast off the shackles. The Soviet leader feared (probably correctly) that if one satellite went they would all go. More than anything Khrushchev was worried about the reaction of the Americans. The Soviets were aware that the CIA had a number of operations in train with the general aim of fomenting unrest in Eastern Europe. Radio Free Europe and Radio Liberty had upped their rhetoric, broadcasting calls for liberation of the 'oppressed peoples of Eastern Europe' virtually around the clock. The Russians didn't know if Eisenhower had it in mind to escalate this to war in certain circumstances. (In fact he hadn't.)

The Russian leadership wavered; reluctantly it ordered the withdrawal of Soviet forces from the Budapest region. The Hungarian rebels sensed victory. Then two things happened, the Hungarians upped their demands, making it obvious that the intention was for Hungary to abandon Soviet hegemony altogether.[15] Next the air forces of Britain and France commenced bombing raids on Egyptian military facilities protecting the canal, an obvious precursor to an invasion; this despite Britain having told Eisenhower in the most solemn terms that they would not initiate military action against Egypt.

All at once the game had changed. Khrushchev now saw a way out. He erupted in 'righteous anger' at the 'appalling actions' of the 'Anglo-French warmongers', saying that Russia would support their Arab friends who 'had been able to pull the British lion by its tail'. Next he dispatched his steely sidekick, General Ivan Serov,[i] to Budapest with orders that he and the ambassador, Andropov,[ii] should use the appearance of negotiating a Soviet withdrawal to apprehend the rebel leaders while the Red Army organised itself for an all-out assault. On 5 November the assault commenced with no holds barred, the same day that British and French paratroopers landed on Suez. Further emboldened, Khrushchev threatened to dispatch aid to the Egyptians in the form of a Red Army expeditionary force or even, if further provoked, to launch his rockets against Britain. There were now two major conflagrations taking place, one in Budapest, the other in Suez. While neither was linked by causation or by direct participants, both were very definitely linked by Cold War politics, something of which Eisenhower was only too well aware.

Isolated in Moscow, Park could only watch and wonder. Trying to pump her CIA opposite number, Ellis-Smith, even if he was prepared to talk, was no longer an option. A couple of months earlier he had fallen for his (KGB) maid, the beautiful 'Valya'. The KGB had figured Ellis-Smith as a 'possible' from the word

i SEROV, Ivan Alexandrovich, Chairman KGB 1954-58, Director GRU 1958-62 (1905-1990).
ii ANDROPOV, Yuri Vladimirovich; Chairman KGB 1967-82, General Secretary Communist Party of the Soviet Union 1982-84 (1914-1984).

go and had even given him a target code name; *Rhzhiy* (REDHEAD). Then the KGB reeled in the line and showed Ellis-Smith the compromising photos taken using an automatic camera concealed in the lovely Valya's handbag. The KGB demanded his cooperation. First of all he deliberated, then confessed all to his ambassador Bohlen, surprising the Agency who expected its officer to man-up, keep quiet and take his medicine. Bohlen, learning for the first time that the Agency was represented in his embassy roster, was outraged by the CIA's deception and Ellis-Smith's stupidity. So he sent him home, leaving the embassy without any CIA presence.[16] Bohlen later claimed that no less than twelve embassy employees had admitted to him that the KGB had attempted to blackmail them using photographs secretly taken during sex with KGB plants. If twelve admitted to it, one wonders how many others did not.[17]

What happened next, or perhaps what did not happen, makes for one of the most puzzling stories about Daphne Park's SIS career. The episode commenced with a top secret 'decipher-yourself' telegram, sent from the Moscow desk in Broadway to Moscow station on or around 5 November. The telegram stated that the codes used for diplomatic communications between the foreign ministry in Cairo and its embassies abroad had been broken in a joint MI5/GCHQ operation (an 'infinity' bug was installed in a telephone in the London embassy's cipher room). The operation was part of a comprehensive ongoing programme to bug diplomatic communications in the city, one that continues to this day. Like most such activities it was multi-faceted; this included placing vans fitted with sophisticated listening equipment in close proximity to embassy buildings where electronic pulses emanating from communications equipment could be detected and their contents read (a more up-to-date version of stealing used typewriter ribbons). Similarly RAF ferret aircraft were used to fly over specific buildings and detect emissions from overhead while the London station in Vauxhall Bridge Road (codenamed BIN) housed a massive telephone intercept station that eavesdropped on all phone calls going in and out of targeted diplomatic missions.

It was one particular deciphered signal that was the cause of the panic telegram to Park in Moscow, because Whitehall was worried, seriously worried. The signal stated that the Soviets had begun to mobilise military aircraft preparatory to becoming involved directly in the Suez crisis on the Egyptian side.[18] Broadway told Park that if the Soviets intervened directly in Egypt, as they were threatening, then war between the Soviet Union and Britain would be the most probable outcome. When the telegram arrived the ambassador, Hayter, was hosting a function in the embassy ballroom. After she deciphered it, Park went up to him and requested 'the pleasure' of the next dance. Covered by the music she told him about the news from London. She said of the episode afterwards:

Oh, it was on the dance floor – I thought we shouldn't be overheard there and I could keep a good hold of him.[19]

So far, so straightforward, but then it becomes anything but. Park told two separate sources that she was instructed by Broadway to see if she could detect any signs of Soviet military war preparations. If the Soviets intended interfering militarily they would need more than aircraft; they would require ships as well. An expeditionary force large enough to intervene in Egypt (where there were now *three* invading armies on the ground, British, French and Israeli) would create chaos on the road networks leading to the embarkation ports. Park told the producers of the *Panorama* television programme (but not on air) in which she appeared that she and the military attaché had travelled as far south as they could to see if they could detect any signs of war preparations or transport movements heading in or around the Black Sea ports of Odessa and Sevastopol in the Crimea. This is quoted in spy-author Steven Dorril's book *MI6: Fifty Years of Special Operations*[20] and confirmed in person to this author by Dorril.[21] Her claim is *separately* quoted in Peter Hennessy's book *The Prime Minister*.[22] This author was unable to contact Peter Hennessy to verify with him directly the circumstances of his quoted conversation with Park. However, and this is a significant caveat, John Deverill, who was a service attaché in Moscow at that time and who was Park's regular travelling companion on their jaunts around the Soviet Union, told this author that such a trip never happened, not with him certainly and as far as he was aware not with any of the other service attachés either.[23] Deverill expressed himself as certain that such a mission could not have taken place without him becoming aware of it, either then or later. None of the SIS sources this author spoke to have been able to either confirm or deny it, other than one who later served in Moscow and who told this author that 'when Daphne came back from her posting in Moscow, her reputation was made'.

There is no doubt that London was seriously concerned about the threat of Soviet intervention; that is something that is well established historically. And asking the station in Moscow to see if it could verify whether war preparations were being made would not have been an unusual step. That was how things were done at that time. In 1983 KGB officers stationed in London and Washington were instructed to do something similar when Moscow feared a surprise nuclear attack from the West. That activity, which was in deadly earnest, was codenamed Operation RYAN (an acronym in Russian for nuclear attack). Later in that decade British security sources told this author that the Prime Minister Margaret Thatcher summoned a meeting of COBRA when the British military, mistakenly, read movements of Soviet ground forces as preparations for war. In fact they were being mobilised to assist in the harvest and the alert was soon stood down.[24]

Monitoring war signs in the Soviet capital would have been possible, to some extent at least. Embassy personnel could have been told to drive past a prepared list of key government/military installations in the city to see if there were any signs of increased activity, night-time working, beefed-up security and similar indicators. The radio monitors in the embassy roof-space would, in any event, have been put on round-the-clock watch and told to set their dials to the frequencies that the Russian military and political leadership were known to use in times of war. While much of the traffic would be enciphered and not readable, the mere fact of increases in volume or the use of reserved channels and frequencies would be pointers enough.

Going on a totally clandestine trip to the likely embarkation ports in the Crimea was of a different order of magnitude altogether. However, desperate times demand desperate measures. London was crying out for confirmation or otherwise of Soviet war preparations, and given that the Americans were most definitely not playing ball London had precious few resources that it could bring to bear directly. RAF Canberra reconnaissance aircraft could make only the most fleeting of reconnaissance missions if they were to avoid being shot down. The U2 aircraft was in service but this was an American resource and in the circumstances not available. Of course, as everyone in Whitehall knew, if it wasn't for the botched job on the *Ordzhonikidze* the deployment of the U2 would have gone ahead in Lakenheath as originally proposed and there might have been an opportunity to pressurise the Americans into organising some over-flights using them. But because of SIS's bungling the Americans were using them themselves for God only knew what (to monitor the joint UK-French invasion force, as it happened, and they were also watching for any signs of Russian mobilisation).

For her mission to bear fruit Park would have had to get close enough to the embarkation ports to eyeball the evidence. Signs she would have been looking out for would have included arbitrary road closures by military police to give priority to military traffic, the creation of security zones close to the embarkation ports with roadblocks and identity checks, and a noticeable increase in general military activity as headquarters and logistics companies are established. That was the problem: internal travel within the Soviet Union was strictly controlled; Soviet citizens required travel passports to travel outside the region where they lived. Rail inspectors routinely demanded these permits as well as travel tickets. That said, this was precisely the sort of operation that SIS loved, for once the Service could actually do *something*, demonstrate that it had a real function and purpose. And in Daphne Park it had someone with the necessary chutzpah to take it on and bring the bacon home. The first decision would have been to decide under what identity the two would travel. As diplomats Park and the attaché were subject to stringent movement controls and required specific permission from the foreign ministry to travel more than twenty-five miles outside Moscow. In the circumstances there was little chance of that. So the decision would probably have been to travel as civilians, perhaps as a pair of British tourists off to spend some time in a Black Sea resort.

Providing a pair of British passports would not have been a problem as a stock of blanks was kept in the embassy for (mainly) legitimate purposes. They would have required the necessary Soviet entry stamps and visas. As part of its contingency planning the Moscow station had familiarised itself with the detail of travel requirements within Russia and had the capability to reproduce the various forms and stamps. This plan had come into use just twelve months previously when, as part of his escape kit, the station had provided their agent Yevgeni Brik with the necessary blank travel permits to get to the border with Norway. This expertise was a legacy of SOE's wartime activities when it acquired the ability to reproduce speedily and accurately the endless iterations in the mass of official documentation required by citizens in the subjugated countries. Working through the night they would have put together their legend, forged hotel reservations in the destination ports, Intourist itinerary, travel permits, and learned off the details of their new identities, planning the journey (most likely by rail) in detail. They had the benefit of having their purloined railway timetable, stolen earlier by Park.

The journey was close to one thousand miles, taking over twenty-four hours by train. They were not going to be able to withstand a detailed scrutiny by counterintelligence officers, but they didn't need to be able to. They weren't facing Gestapo-level checks in wartime Europe, their papers just had to be able to pass the scrutiny of ticket inspectors, who while an officious lot weren't trained to look out for forgeries. So did they go on their mission, leaving the embassy separately, losing their surveillance, before meeting up again in Kurskaja station for their journey to Sevastopol? While they had diplomatic immunity the consequences of being discovered meant failing in their mission and God only knew what else.

The answers to these questions are locked deep in the vaults of SIS and the Cabinet Office and, based on previous experience, that is where they will remain, well hidden from the eyes of scholars, authors and historians. In the absence of SIS confirmation we are forced into the realm of speculation. This author believes that Daphne Park was speaking the truth when she told the *Panorama* producers and Peter Hennessy about her mission. While anyone can be tempted to embroider a little and gild the lily on occasion, to think that a person like Park would totally fabricate such an account and then tell it to an author of Peter Hennessy's standing simply does not add up. She would have known that it would appear in his book, a book that would be read, *inter alia*, by people in Whitehall and the Service who would have known it was a lie if it had been. Her own self-respect alone would have prevented her from following that course. John Deverill is obviously speaking the truth as he knows it, of that there is no doubt. So either the mission took place in such secrecy that he was not informed or his recollection, at this remove, is faulty.

We do know that for seventy-two hours Whitehall shivered before word came from the Turkish authorities that the Russians had not requested passage for a naval armada through the Bosporus, the essential precursor for the engagement of Soviet forces in the Middle East. The Americans resumed communications and told London that Khrushchev's threat of military intervention in Suez was 'a bluff'. Politically matters soon came to a head. Eisenhower, the American President, whose anger knew no bounds at what he regarded as a combination of British insolence, imperialism and deceit, took a series of what would be deciding steps. He instructed the US Federal Reserve to start selling British pounds, driving down the value of sterling, and at the same time he blocked the International Monetary Fund from offering any support. His ambassador to the United Nations went to the Security Council with a demand to impose immediate and severe sanctions if the French and British did not immediately withdraw. Eisenhower also ordered American oil companies not to make up the shortfall in Britain caused by the just-imposed Middle East oil embargo. In the face of this Eden collapsed both physically and psychologically, a broken figure. British and French forces were ordered to withdraw and were gone within weeks.

Park's view of the Budapest/Suez affair was that Budapest represented an opportunity slowly to uncouple Russian control over its East European satellites, a key objective of all the Western powers. Invading Egypt sacrificed that and did enormous reputational damage to Britain, both in the Middle East and beyond. Suez grievously damaged its relations with the US government, its military and intelligence agencies. Khrushchev scored a victory of sorts but at significant cost to the reputation of the Soviet Union. Eden's career was destroyed, as was his health. He resigned two months later and Harold Macmillan, who as the hawkish foreign secretary should have shouldered much more of the blame, took over as Prime Minister.

SIS did not carry the can for Suez, but it did not emerge with its reputation enhanced. The unprecedented scale of the catastrophe, the national humiliation that resulted, reverberated throughout Whitehall, and SIS could not but be tainted. Its agent networks had been rolled up by the Egyptians, thus denying it the intelligence so badly needed. Its predictions were shown to be totally off the mark: 'no nationalisation of the canal'; 'no Russian move against the students in Budapest'; 'no US intervention'.

Mildly in its favour was that White, despite his reservations, had instructed the Service to do everything it could to support the invasion once it got under way, thus demonstrating his loyalty. He lacked the confidence and was perhaps too new in the job to make his reservations about the enterprise count. Young, on the other hand, politically the better connected of the two (he was privy to the invasion details, while his boss, White, was excluded), remained unrepentant saying, 'We should have gone on in and taken Nasser's scalp.'[25]

At the end of November Park returned to Britain, her stint in Moscow done. Neither she nor Hayter enjoyed their final weeks. Relations with the Soviets were icy, with practically all contact cut off. Hayter was not invited to pay his ambassadorial farewell call on the Soviet leadership, a slap in the face for a man who had set out with such high hopes. The ambassador had considered resignation while in Moscow but stayed in post from loyalty. Though promoted to the number two slot in the Foreign Office on returning to Britain, he remained disillusioned. A year later he had left the Foreign Office for the post of Warden of New College, Oxford.[26]

Park's time in Moscow had gone well. The Brik affair had gone against her but he had been 'blown' before he left Canada so her ability to influence matters in any event was limited. She had collected most of her two thousand books and snaffled her train timetable. She had swum the Volga to escape her KGB pursuers, cultivated her ambassador, run her legal-travellers, monitored the construction of the Yo-Yo missile ring, gathered her 'nuts' and generally kept SIS's end up. Whether or not she went to the Crimea, as an SIS officer said, 'by the time she came home from Moscow her reputation was made'.[27]

She would return to a Service that knew it had to change. White had not had the best of starts. The mandarins had made their displeasure clear and notice would be taken. But for White and SIS things would not get better just yet. The Service was about to enter the darkest night of its soul since its foundation. It would be some time yet before it once more emerged into the sunlight.

From SovBloc to sun-block, 1957-59

When Park returned to Broadway from Moscow in January 1957 she found a Service still reeling from the aftermath of Suez. White, the new Chief, had had a baptism of fire and was busy assembling a small team of close advisors to help him move SIS to where he, and Whitehall, believed it badly needed to go. The team was led by his personal assistant, John Briance,[i] a tough former colonial police officer who had seen service in Palestine and was also a veteran of the Mossadeqh affair.[1] Though Park would have been aware that the Service had a new Chief, his appointment would have had little direct day-to-day impact on her. SIS was at that time very hierarchical with the bosses mixing only rarely with their minions.

It wasn't as though White hadn't enough on his mind in any event. His immediate priority was to alter the focus of SIS from political 'operations' towards conventional intelligence gathering. He did not see SIS as being in the business of removing governments of a politically unattractive persuasion. And he most certainly did not see Britain as some form of moral policeman obliged to topple tyrants in whatever guise they might be found. In short, he wanted no more cowboy operations of any sort; no more Crabbs, no more Suezes. This brought him into direct conflict with his robber barons, sometimes referred to as the 'inter-war greats', who ran their areas as personal fiefdoms and for whom the 'Great Game' was still the only game. White was determined on change but didn't consider that he was powerful enough just yet to take on the barons directly. Instead he started by attacking the layer beneath them. Old stalwarts like Harold 'Harry' Carr, Harold 'Gibbie' Gibson,[ii] Wilfred 'Biffy' Dunderdale[iii] and others were eased out[2] (Dunderdale being given the sinecure of consul-general in Chicago). Easton had been appointed Deputy Chief partly as a sop for not being given the promised job of Chief and partly to ease White's entry. However he was not considered to be much of an asset and so was marked for early removal (being given the sinecure of consul-general in Detroit). Briance, the architect

---

i BRIANCE, John Albert, CMG; Palestine Police Force, SIS, TEHRAN, CAIRO, H/WASHINGTON, SINGAPORE (1915-1989).

ii GIBSON, Major Harold ('Gibbie') Charles Lehrs, CMG; SIS, H/BUCHAREST, H/RIGA, H/PRAGUE, H/ISTANBUL, H/BERLIN, H/ROME (1895-1960).

iii DUNDERDALE, Commander Wilfred ('Biffy') Albert; SIS, H/PARIS, C/SPECIAL LIAISON (1899-1990).

of the cuts, would be rewarded for his knife-wielding skills by being given the H/WASHINGTON slot the following year. Ten years later he would return to White's side to complete the knife-work.

There were those who thought White did not go far enough (there always are in these situations), but White was cautious, sometimes to the point of timidity. So while the barons' time was running out it would be a full decade before the last of them had finally exited the building. It was a long time for him to tolerate people for whom he had such little regard. All of this was above Park's pay-grade and she wasn't more than tangentially aware of it. To most junior staff White was a far distant figure known only as the Chief or by his code name 'C'. Any members of staff (other than the most senior) who might have had occasion to share the lift with him would not have known they were in the presence of the Chief, nor would White have known who they were. The Chief entered the Broadway head office building by a secure walkway from his flat. He then took the lift to the fourth floor where the security officer was waiting to escort him to his office. Once ensconced therein he remained *in situ* until lunch or it was time to go home. He would see two of his department heads, one from Production and one from Requirements, every day in rotation over the week. Only very exceptionally would more junior officers be invited inside the green baize door. On occasion he invited returning officers, whose reports interested him, to come to his office and speak about their experience at first hand.[3] It is possible, given the importance of Moscow, that Park too may have been invited up to see White, though given his attitude to women expressed in a conversation with a colleague ('they're different to us, they've got no balls'[4]), perhaps it is unlikely.

Overall the practice among senior managers of keeping themselves to themselves was, in part, the style of the times. Directors' dining rooms, management-only canteens were the norm. The era of accessibility, of management-by-walking-about (MBWA) which stressed the importance of corporate managers being visible to their 'troops', was yet to arrive. But it was more to do with mystique; built into the culture of both MI5 and SIS was the perceived need to maintain an air of mystery, both internally and externally. Both were secret services and secret is as secret does. MI5 officers, for example, were taught that in their dealings with police Special Branches they must never show surprise at any information provided to them. A simple 'I see, how interesting' was all that was required by way of response, the all-knowing facade to be maintained at all costs. White, a taciturn individual in any event, was a product of that and he believed in it.

So Park and her colleagues worked away in their cubbyholes in conditions which were quite primitive, far more so than could be justified even by the standard of the times. The lighting was abysmal but desk lamps were permitted only for senior staff. The linoleum was torn and chipped and represented a serious safety hazard, while the lift (through a fault) stopped only at the fourth and seventh floors, all others having to be accessed by the stairs. But of all of this White chose to be blissfully unaware. For someone whose role was Intelligence he displayed precious little when it came to the working conditions of his own staff. However, working conditions apart, change was coming and it wasn't just White and his coterie of supporters who were demanding it. A divide, some might say chasm, was beginning to open up between the new breed of post-war recruited officers and the old inter-war hands.[5] Park was part of that debate. Here is what one colleague from that period said about it:

> The culture took a long time to change, the idea of 'doing operations' as a mark of virility (and apart from Daphne the intelligence branch was almost entirely male: regular recruitment of females to it did not begin until about 1980) as opposed to 'undertaking appropriate and mutually agreed operations', persisted in some quarters, and even among some senior officers, for a very long time. Some of the war-time recruits never changed their attitude and continued to cause occasional embarrassment. Some of these people were also of a markedly lower standard than the post-war recruits but still had twenty years or so of their careers to run. When posted abroad they did not easily earn (or even seek to earn) the respect of their FCO [Foreign and Commonwealth Office] colleagues.[6]

The new breed considered themselves to be altogether brighter (typically they had Firsts). They would claim to hold a more sophisticated world view than the old guard, for example they thought that the Service's focus (they described it as an obsession) on SovBloc did not accurately reflect what should have been its priorities and the allocation of resources.[7] Worse of all they considered the 'oldies' to be boozers and bunglers, amateurs and shamateurs, unsuited to the demands of the modern era. To them the Crabb episode illustrated precisely why there should be no place for them, thus their criticism of White's failure to clean out the stables in their entirety. As the new brooms saw it, operations were developed and carried out without reference to Whitehall or any attempt to consult with the affected departments, or to weigh up whether the penny was worth the candle. Undertaking operations had become an end in itself, a sign of their virility in what was a very virile environment. In fact to many of the robber barons the very idea of seeking Foreign Office approval for an operation was anathema.[8] For decades they had been judges in their own cause, not even sharing the detail of their riskier escapades with the Chief. To be asked to consult, worse still get permission from some Foreign Office desk-wallah was intolerable. But ask they would have to. By the end of the decade (1960) a Foreign Office under-secretary had been brought in to take over the Service's administration and finances and a Foreign Office officer of counsellor rank had been installed in Head Office as Foreign Office Adviser to the Chief.[9]

Park was neither of one side nor the other, though manifestly she would have been against anything 'cowboy' in nature. She had joined after the war but had been in the secret world since 1943, had worn khaki, had some longevity, so some connection with the old. She was academically bright but not exceptionally so, with a 2.1 rather than a First. She believed absolutely that SovBloc should be the Service's main priority and never deviated much from that. She was close to and admired many of the old guard. George Young was one to whom she had reason to be grateful. She did share many of his analyses, though not of the Middle East – she was dead set against Suez for example, though being in Moscow at the time probably influenced that.[10] Park was never a fence-sitter but neither would she come down on one side or the other for the sake of expediency, so she largely kept her own counsel.

Operationally Park would spend the next couple of years in D/P4, SovBloc operations as the Production Officer (P Officer) for the four SIS stations in West Germany. This meant lots of shuttling back and forth between London and West Berlin, Bonn, Hamburg and Bad Salzuflen, head office for West Germany. Naturally one of the people Park knew well was the second great SIS betrayer, George Blake.[i] Blake was handsome, outgoing, engaging. He enjoyed mini-celebrity status within SIS because of his 'ordeal' in Korea, and his company was sought after. When his betrayal was later revealed Park was devastated, wondering, as did every officer, what she had said that had ended up being reported to East Germany. Had she been indiscreet? Said something she ought not to have? It was a lesson well learned and not just by Park.

Park's affection for George Young was understandable, because not only had he eased her way into the Service but it was an initiative by him that would ultimately result in her being posted to Africa. In 1956, when he was still Controller/Middle East & Africa, Young dispatched a thirty-three-year-old officer, Frank Steele,[ii] on a tour of Britain's key diplomatic missions and colonial outposts in Africa, with instructions to report back on the intelligence situation on the ground. Young must take the credit therefore for discovering that an entire continent existed and that what was going to happen on that continent would impact significantly on Britain's interests. This was Young at his best. Up to that point, as far as SIS was concerned, Africa meant Egypt. The rest, the colonies, were MI5's concern to the extent that they were anyone's. But already Eritrea, Gold Coast (Ghana) and Sudan had seized the opportunity to break free from their colonial masters. An armed campaign (the Mau Mau Uprising) was under way in Kenya which, while being contained, was inevitably going to lead to independence. For the rest of the colonies, it was really only a question of time before they too were

---

i BLAKE, George, *né* Behar; SOE, SIS (KGB) (1922-).

ii STEELE, Frank Fenwick, OBE; SIS, BASRA, AMMAN, TRIPOLI, BEIRUT, H/AMMAN, H/NAIROBI, seconded to Northern Ireland Office, D/MIDDLE EAST (1923-1997).

granted their sovereignty. And it was not just from Britain; France, Belgium and Portugal also had colonies that were either already scheduled to gain their independence or were likely to. Certainly somebody in SIS needed to be thinking about the implications; they could bet that Moscow was.

Steele was a good choice of emissary. He was intelligent, adventurous and open-minded. After he joined SIS in 1951 he was posted to Basra in Iraq where he became a close friend and travelling companion of the great explorer Wilfred Thesiger[i] who had served in both SOE and SAS in the war. Steele had spent a year in Uganda in 1950 as a colonial civil servant prior to joining SIS and had had also served in Libya. By the then standards of SIS, that made him something of an expert on the continent. Today Steele is probably best remembered for the back-channel to the Provisional IRA that he and fellow SIS officer, Michael Oatley, established in the early 1970s. But Steele's African odyssey laid the groundwork for the eventual establishment of a network of SIS stations on the continent.

The reason for the delay was the 1946 Attlee Doctrine. The Doctrine had its origins in a 1931 agreement between SIS and MI5 that specified each organisation's sphere of operations. MI5 would be responsible for 'domestic' security. Crucially, that would include the colonies. SIS would restrict its activities to 'foreign' countries, former colonies excluded. When India became independent in 1947 the 1931 agreement was challenged by SIS. The then Prime Minister, Clement Attlee, decreed (though never in writing which further complicated matters) that SIS was not to operate in Britain's *current* or *former* colonies without the prior consent of MI5. Current and former colonies would be classed as 'domestic' and thus the preserve of the Security Service.

MI5 appointed security liaison officers (SLOs) who were 'declared' (i.e. made known to) the host security and intelligence services. The SLOs' strategy was to maintain close relations (as far as they could) with the emerging nation's internal security apparatus but not to run agents or engage in covert operations, both of which were seen as being outside their remit and as 'unfriendly' acts. And since all SIS did, more or less, was to run agents and engage in covert operations, it perceived MI5's absence from the field as confirmation of its worst opinions about its sister agency. As SIS saw it, which does not make it true, MI5 was more interested in ensuring that SIS stayed out of its patch than it was in gathering intelligence, running operations and generally making itself useful. Unfortunately for SIS, the MI5 approach had the support of the Commonwealth Relations Office (CRO) led in its attitude by a feisty assistant-secretary called Cyril Grove Costley-White.[ii] The wheelchair-bound Costley-White, in SIS eyes at least, seemed to see it as his sacred duty to maintain the purity of the new

---

i THESIGER, Major Sir Wilfred Patrick, CBE, DSO, *aka* 'Mubarak bin London' ('the blessed one from London'); SOE, SAS (1910-2003).

ii COSTLEY-WHITE, Cyril Grove, CMG; Commonwealth Relations Office (1913-1979).

commonwealth and prevent the freebooters of SIS from plotting and suborning their way to its destruction. In some respects SIS had itself to blame for this; its reputation among the Whitehall mandarins remained abysmal. Not, of course, that the Service saw it that way; its view of the CRO was practically unprintable, as the following might indicate:

> It [CRO] was staffed largely by people who were unable to get into the Foreign Office and whose undemanding work abroad was to be nice to Canadians, Australians, New Zealanders and the inhabitants of one or two other bits and pieces in the Caribbean. CRO people tended to believe that the Empire had been a rather shameful chapter of history which was best quickly forgotten, that the Colonial Service was staffed by oppressors who must certainly be resented by those over whom they ruled, and that the sooner the latter could be welcomed into the brotherhood of the Commonwealth the better. It now gleefully foresaw vast expansion of its territorial responsibility and immediately began to build walls around it. (In the intelligence sphere MI5 joyfully did the same.) It had an inferiority complex vis-à-vis the Foreign Office. It rejected the Colonial Service as generally beyond the pale. Its brightest luminary, Sir David Hunt,[i] invented a theory, which he set out in his despatch on leaving his post as the first High Commissioner to an independent Uganda saying, patronisingly, 'these colonial chaps tell you stories about tribal divisions which may be expected to cause trouble, and they may have been right in their time, but when one flag comes down and another goes up a nation changes, it becomes a nation, and all these fault-lines, which have been present during the period of British rule, disappear'. No sooner was the ink dry on this document and his pompous Excellency comfortably on leave, than the aforesaid fault-lines showed themselves in the starkest way as Amin's troops set fire to the Kabaka's palace and the citizens of Kampala stood dumb-struck in the streets.[11]

In keeping with this presumed attitude Costley-White steadfastly refused to provide cover for SIS officers posted to CRO outposts. At one point SIS was forced to establish a station in a neighbouring country, in which it had no particular interest, in order to be able to carry out operations in Nigeria. The head of station was permitted, by the CRO, to visit Nigeria during daylight but not to stay overnight.

> At the end of my tour I reported the likelihood of civil war in Nigeria and recommended establishing stations in Lagos, Kaduna and Enugu. On my return I was summoned by 'C', Sir Dick White, who said to me, 'I have read your report and your recommendations and I accept that you are right about what is happening and about what we should do to prepare for it. I wanted to tell you that, but also that there is no possibility that the Commonwealth Relations Office will allow me to do what you suggest.'[12]

---

i HUNT, Sir David Wathen Stather, KCMG, OBE; diplomat, later winner of BBC *Master-mind* (1913-1998).

But support for SIS expansionism was thin on the ground. The various high commissioners, consuls-general and governors-general that Steele met on his African odyssey made it clear that SIS would not be welcome in their territories with lots of 'over my dead body' talk. And not just in former British territories: when Steele inquired of the British consul-general in the Belgian Congo how he viewed the future he was assured that the Belgian Congo would remain Belgian for 'fifteen years at least' and that if SIS did need to know anything they could simply ask the Belgians. But that sort of thinking was being (very slowly) consigned to the dustbin. George Young was determined that SIS would be represented in the emerging post-colonial Africa and he had the clout to insist. Despite the Suez debacle White, who was probably afraid of Young, had made him his Deputy Chief after Easton's forced departure in 1958. Young's appointment was probably one of the worst decisions of White's tenure and one he came to regret bitterly. What he realised too late was that while Young was undoubtedly a genius he was also slightly mad and, rather like George III, he was getting madder by the day.

John Bruce Lockhart, a robber baron if ever there was one, who had been a wartime recruit into SIS and who had run SIS operations in post-war Germany with some flair and energy, was offered D/P2 (Middle East & Africa) as a solace for being passed over for the Deputy Chief's job. Bruce Lockhart shared the Service's frustration and used to return from meetings with Costley-White wanting to lynch him and his CRO chum, Morris James. Sometimes loopholes could be found; for example when Nigeria was waiting for independence it came under the control of the Colonial Office, which unlike the CRO was prepared to be accommodating when it came to providing cover for SIS posts.[13] But the issue was far bigger than just finding slots for SIS officers. As Bruce Lockhart was to complain some months later in a report to Prime Minister Macmillan:

> British interests in Africa are the responsibility of no less than three independent Ministries in London with often different and sometimes even conflicting policies and philosophies about Africa.[14]

So a meeting to discuss an issue affecting (say) Congo, Southern Rhodesia and Nigeria would need to be attended by representatives from the Foreign Office (responsible for the Congo), CRO (responsible for Southern Rhodesia) and the Colonial Office (responsible for Nigeria). Each, as Bruce Lockhart said, with its own minister, each with its own individual approach and none particularly cognisant of the close inter-relationship existing between events in neighbouring countries.

Once it had been determined that SIS representation in Africa required boosting and that Park should be assigned to the continent, the original plan was to send her to Guinea. The country had recently been granted its independence from France and had swung sharply to the left politically. However when her name was mooted the local consul-general pointed out that since Guinea was largely Muslim, the effectiveness of a woman in the role of SIS station head would be severely curtailed.[15] Of possibly greater significance was that when the entry ban on women was lifted it was agreed at the 1945 Gowers Committee (which recommended the end of the ban) that women would not be posted to Muslim countries in *representational* roles, i.e. they could be posted as secretaries and typists but not as diplomats.[16] This was something that took many years to alter and was a cause of serious disadvantage to the career opportunities of women diplomats, denying them entry into the 'camel corps', the route to the top for many SIS and Foreign and Commonwealth Office (FCO) highfliers.

So attention then turned to the Congo, seemingly next on the list for independence. In January 1959 a violent riot in Léopoldville, capital of the Belgian Congo, took place when police banned a gathering of the Alliance de Ba-Kongo (ABAKO), a tribal cultural society cum political party with widespread support in the capital. The excuse for banning the meeting was that it coincided with a major football match. Three days of rioting ensued. Fifty Africans died, two hundred and fifty were wounded, and, most ominous of all in Belgian eyes, fifty Europeans were injured. Afraid that the local (native) population might be about to embark on a colonial war, there was a complete *volte-face* in Belgian thinking. What was unthinkable in 1956 became policy in 1959. With no appreciable warning, and catching everyone flatfooted, Belgium announced its intention to grant independence to its colony, the Belgian Congo, but without putting any timescale on it, nor putting in place a proper transition programme. And since the Belgian Congo was demonstrably *not* a former British colony, SIS was free to set up a station there without the requirement for internal subterfuge. Bruce Lockhart approached Park and offered her the position as the first SIS head of station in Léopoldville. She would also be responsible for Brazzaville in the French Congo, located immediately across the Congo River from Léopoldville. This was a major change of direction for her. SovBloc was very much the beating heart of SIS, Africa was 'over there', very many miles distant. But Africa was where she was conceived, where she had spent the first years of her life. So she took the job. The woman whose formative years had been spent running barefoot with her African friends in Tanganyika would once more return to the continent of her childhood. But this time the games she would play would be *operational games* in a chaotic, unpredictable and extremely dangerous situation. For Park it would be the most hazardous time and coming through it unscathed would take a bucketful of courage, an ocean of *sangfroid* and more than her fair share of luck.

15

Congo 1 – Into the cauldron, 1959

When, in January 1959, Baudouin, King of the Belgians, announced Belgium's intention 'without undesirable procrastination but also without undue haste to lead the Congolese population forward towards independence in prosperity and peace', he unwittingly fired the starting gun for sub-Saharan Africa's first major face-off between the Soviet Union and the NATO allies represented by Belgium, America and Britain, in that order of influence and intensity. In so doing he continued the ignoble tradition of the Belgian monarchy of never doing well by the Congo if an alternative offered. Not that independence, as such, was a bad idea. It wasn't, but the shambolic, deceitful and venal way in which it was managed was a major contributor to the resultant chaos which over the following half-century would devastate the country and cost countless millions of Congolese lives, bringing enduring shame on Belgium. It would also ask some very pertinent questions of the intelligence services of both Britain and the United States and follow those services' two main actors in the drama, Lawrence Devlin[i] and Daphne Park, to their graves and beyond. But that was yet to come. As far as today was concerned the Belgian Congo was joining an increasing list of countries which were about to gain their independence, and the world had no reason to suppose that the Congo would fare any worse than any of the other emerging states.

As the Congo was still a Belgian colony, the British embassy in Brussels was the lead diplomatic presence, Léopoldville boasting a mere consulate-general. So it was to Brussels that Park went first in order to receive her personal briefing from the embassy SIS station which maintained good relations with the Belgian intelligence services. She is unlikely to have gained much from that meeting other than to reinforce the view that Belgium appeared determined to wash its hands of responsibility for the Congo as soon as practicable, though at the same time it was determined to retain its commercial interests in the profitable mining operations in the Congo province of Katanga, home to the world's largest copper deposits.

CIA officer Lawrence Devlin had been based in Brussels since 1957. Devlin would follow Park into Léopoldville as chief of station within days of the country's independence. The two probably met in Brussels, because by then Devlin

---

i DEVLIN, Lawrence R. ('Larry'); US Army, CIA, later to serve as station chief in Vientiane and as CIA Bureau Chief for Africa (1922-2008).

knew he was Congo bound,[1] but we do not know for certain if they did actually encounter each other at that point. By Devlin's own account he did meet a number of future Congolese political figures while attached to the CIA station in Brussels, sent to the city by the Belgian authorities in a form of pre-independence crash course in 'country administration'.

Once her Brussels business was done, Park took the train to the port of Antwerp, there to board the steamer to her destination, Matadi, sixty miles upriver from the coast on the Congo River. The sea journey took about a fortnight and made one stop en route, calling in Lobito in Angola. The voyage gave her the opportunity to study her briefing papers in some detail, augmented no doubt by extensive chats with the worried Belgian *fonctionnaires* returning from home leave with their families. It was time she would have put to good use.

In any intelligence briefing the first question posed is often 'why', as in *Why does the Congo matter?*

Park learned that the Congo mattered first because of its size: it was huge, almost the size of India. It mattered, too, because of its location. It bordered on nine other countries, many critical to Britain's interests on the continent. Whoever controlled the Congo could potentially dominate much of sub-Saharan Africa. It mattered as well because of its mineral deposits. Apart from hosting the world's largest copper mine, the Congo was rich in gold and diamonds and strategic minerals such as cobalt, coltan, tin and tungsten (the atomic bombs dropped on Hiroshima and Nagasaki had used uranium from the Congo).

Then came the 'what' question, as in *What's happening now that makes it of interest?* The modern Congo could be said to have commenced life about seventy-five years previously when Belgium's King Leopold II (Queen Victoria's uncle), secured international recognition for the 'Congo Free State'. The territory had been put together mainly through the mercenary efforts of the explorer Henry Stanley. He conducted a series of negotiations with tribal chiefs who were persuaded to exchange their presents and futures for little more than trinkets. The Belgian state did not express any great interest in its king's adventure, fearing it would be a drain on resources, so Leopold was left to run it as a private fiefdom. Not having the wherewithal to do so himself he entered into fifty-fifty collaborations with private concessionaires. These were a ruthless lot, behaving in a way that would have defied description had they not been described in some detail by Roger Casement,[i] the British consul (and Irish patriot) in the then capital of Boma.

By 1908 Leopold's time was up; that year the Congo Free State became the Belgian Congo, a direct colony ruled over by a local governor-general appointed

i CASEMENT, Sir Roger, CMG; diplomat (1864-1916).

by Brussels. The king received fifty million francs in compensation. That's how things remained until the independence announcement in January 1959. The announcement made a number of countries – including Britain – sit up and take notice; a Congo ruled by sleepy Belgium was one thing, an independent Congo, slap bang in the middle of Britain's vital African interests, was another altogether.

When Baudouin made his announcement the Belgian government had not in fact decided on the exact date of independence. Its thinking was that a staged process lasting about three years would work best, but so deep was the pent up resentment among the indigenous population that Park was told to expect full independence within months of her arrival. Even before she set foot on the ground in Léopoldville, Park realised that Belgium's attitude to its sole colony (though it also had responsibility for the trusteeship of Ruanda-Urundi, today the independent states of Ruanda and Burundi) was as different from Britain's attitude to its colonies as chalk was from cheese.

Britain had an Empire of which it was extremely (some might say inordinately) proud and which it was relinquishing with some reluctance. It had, over many years, established the structures of Empire, including a colonial civil service which it believed administered its colonies in an efficient, appropriate and equitable manner. And while many might argue the point, most Britons (at the time certainly) believed that its colonial rule was essentially benign. As Park's colleague and friend, Sir Gerald Warner, put it in his memorial address for her in Somerville College, Oxford, Park was a child of that Empire with commensurate attitudes and beliefs. So she would not have had an immediate problem with the concept of Belgium ruling over a country many thousands of miles away in another continent. How it went about that rule, though, was a different matter.

Belgium wasn't an empire and had no pretence of being one. The Belgian Congo was more a responsibility acquired from a monarch who had proved incapable of administering it, rather than resulting as a consequence of conquest or annexation. Insofar as Belgium had a colonial philosophy, it could be summed up as one of letting the Belgian settlers get on with ruling the country in what was assumed would be a decent sort of manner. And as long as the native population appeared to go along with this and were suitably quiescent *and* the revenues from the mines kept flowing, then all would be well. The settlers on the other hand, as the day-to-day rulers over the Belgian Congo, had developed a more thought-through philosophy. In their minds Brussels did not comprehend the situation on the ground at all, it was only they, the 'Belgian-Congolese', who understood the blacks.[2] For them the ideal would be akin to a father and son relationship with the Belgians playing the role of the fathers and the Africans, the sons. This is sometimes called the 'Prospero Complex'.[3]

This state of affairs was to be perpetual, for it was not intended to be a maturing relationship with the sons growing into adulthood and assuming responsibility for what was, after all, their own country. Even mentioning the *possibility* of independence was frowned upon. In 1956 Professor A.A.J. van Bilsen, an eminent sociologist and Congo expert, floated the possibility of a planned progression to independence over a thirty- year period. As a consequence he was severely reprimanded and nearly lost his government job of training civil servants for future deployment to the colony.[4] The CIA man Devlin had raised the issue himself while in Brussels:

> ... the Belgians were convinced that they were loved. I was in Brussels for three and a half years and certainly their idea was that the Congo was not ready for independence, perhaps in a hundred years. I remember pointing out what was happening in the rest of Africa, 'you don't have a hundred years,' and they assured me they did.[5]

No, independence was not part of the plan at all. And so the logic went that if it was not the intention to permit the 'sons' to grow into 'adulthood' then there was no great point in educating them beyond 'adolescence'. Thus there was no requirement for an educated professional class of Congolese teachers, doctors, engineers and lawyers (God forbid lawyers), the argument went, if those roles were and would continue to be filled 100% by the white settlers, augmented as necessary by fresh blood from home. At the date of independence there was only a handful of university graduates of Congolese origin in the Congo in a population of thirteen million (other than Congolese trained for the priesthood). There was one African doctor but not even a single engineer in a country whose principal industry was mining.

The farthest a Congolese 'son' could expect to go was to become one of the évolués. These were Africans who, in Belgian eyes, had *evolved* from having an essentially tribal orientation to forming the beginning of a semi-unified Congolese middle class. They had limited education, spoke passable French and had renounced polygamy. They were employed as tradesmen, technicians, foremen, drivers and mine workers, and in other similar occupations. In fact their technical education, up to technician level, was of a very high standard, required because of the complexity of the ore extraction and smelting machinery then in use. The role of matriarch was played by Mother Church (Roman Catholic) which had assumed semi-institutional status, its four thousand missionaries being paid by the Belgian state to provide a basic education for the évolué class. The 'European' schools admitted no more than a dozen or so African pupils, all of whom had to pass an intrusive and demeaning 'suitability test'. Nor were Africans permitted to go abroad to be educated, other than to Belgium to study for the priesthood. Many young Congolese realised that the seminary offered a chance for a better education which they took but then left as young adults, saying they had since discovered they had no vocation.[6]

And as far as the 'daughters' were concerned the Belgian view, shared by many African men, was that education was wasted on females. Such provision as there was, was patchy. A university had been established in Léopoldville in the mid 1950s to offer degree courses to both African and European students. African males, there being no female undergraduates at the time of independence, were restricted to the Arts. So far so colonial, and while the Belgian Congo did not practise apartheid with the same rigour as South Africa and indeed did not pretend to espouse it, to all intents and purposes it might as well have. Settlers, universally referred to as Europeans by the Congolese, lived separate lives in their entirety. No European would queue for service behind an African, nor have their children educated in the same school, sit in the same row on a bus or train, eat in the same restaurant or even purchase their meat from the same butcher. Europeans were paid three or four times the rate for doing the same job as an évolué. Discrimination was not just deep rooted in relation to wages, it ran right through the entire administration. For example there were eight grades in the local civil service, the top four (about ten thousand) were occupied *solely* by Belgians, the bottom four (about another ten thousand) *solely* by Congolese. Entry to the top four grades required an educational qualification not open to Africans to obtain.

For the sake of balance it should be pointed out that the Congo of 1959 was far removed from King Leopold's regime of slavery and brutality. In fact the standard of living of most Congolese was superior to that of their fellows in neighbouring states. Social security was more advanced, health services better; something that was commented on frequently by their overseers. But that wasn't enough. The évolués, weary of this paternalistic, artificially imposed limit on their lives, were now articulating demands for immediate independence. And they would get their way. The January rioting which had seen shops pillaged, women raped and Europeans in general attacked, had seen to that. Unlike Britain, Belgium did not have the stomach to counter a long drawn out Mau Mau style rebellion. Unlike Britain, it would not put up with the international odium and obloquy generated by its robust defence of Empire. Unlike Britain, at the first sign of trouble, it caved in. There was more for Park to absorb, mainly concerning the 'who' and the 'how' – *who* were the key personalities and *how* the country was run – but that could wait. She had arrived at her destination, the new consul, first secretary and head of station, and was ready to commence duty.

Arriving back in Africa a full quarter of a century since she had last set foot in it must have been an extraordinary experience for Park. The sights and sounds and smells, the hustle and bustle reawakened overpowering memories of her childhood. It would have taken quite a while to become acclimatised. All accounts of Park's career lay considerable stress on the 'African years' which in theory ran from 1959, when she was first posted to the Africa desk in Broadway, to 1968 when her focus switched to South-East Asia ahead of her posting to Hanoi. In fact, as we shall see in a later chapter, she had a continuing involvement in African affairs up to the very end of her career in SIS, even when her official responsibilities suggested otherwise.

The first eleven years of her life spent on the continent were pivotal to this. For a start they toughened her up. Eleven years spent without electric light, running water or proper sanitation is a hardening experience and even when she got to London her upbringing was still tough; there was no spare cash in that household. But those first formative years (and they are not called formative for nothing) must have given her a sense of great comfort in her new surroundings. Sights and sounds that would have been totally alien to most Europeans were bitter-sweet memories to her, reminiscent of hardship, certainly, but also reminders of childhood, of games of hide and seek in the bush, of tracking animal spoor, cooking and eating in the outdoors, reading and learning and generally just being. When allied to her naturally gregarious nature, this provided her with an ease in communicating and led to her having an instinctive understanding of how best to build relationships in that environment. This is not something that would have been taught to her in a formal sense, or even consciously observed. It must have been absorbed and lain there dormant, ready to be deployed when the moment arrived.

Africans place huge importance on personal relationships and on trust developed over time. Park was to put mutual trust rather than manipulation to good use throughout her career. Of course she had a purpose, an agenda, but so did the people with whom she would relate and do business. Espionage is an agenda-driven activity, as is diplomacy, and in Africa she was very much a spy *and* a diplomat. But it was this mutual trust that provided the essential lubrication to keep the wheels in motion. Park had the physical toughness to be able to hack it in Léopoldville. But she would need more than toughness; she would need an abundance of physical courage. Once independence came, overnight almost, the Congo descended into darkness and become a dangerous and frightening place. There was no law, no order and very little mercy. In this Congo someone from the wrong tribe found in the wrong place might be pursued and hacked to death in front of horrified passers-by. Someone with the wrong colour skin might be brutalised, raped if they were female or shot out of hand if they were a man. Park would face situations where she would be beaten and abused and where her life would hang by a thread. But she had a job to do, an important one; Broadway for once had chosen its emissary well. Park had the right make-up; her outwardly gregarious nature cloaking an ice-cold, steely resolve, an absolute determination to succeed in any task undertaken, and more than anything else a blessed certainty that her course was the right one and that the cause was just.

16

Congo 2 – On the eve of destruction, 1959-60

Léopoldville, or Léo as it was universally called, was a planned city with wide double-sided boulevards and imposing buildings rising to seven, eight and occasionally ten storeys. It was far more sophisticated, European and advanced than the capitals of most African countries at the time. It was assumed that Park would live in the European zone, where the governor-general and the twenty thousand or so Europeans, Belgians mainly, who had made Léo their home resided. But Park was more interested in establishing sources among the disenfranchised, specifically the évolués. It was from their ranks that the country's new rulers would be drawn, all of whom would be black. She knew that building rapport among the African community was going to be time-consuming and would not be helped by the regulations imposed following the 1959 outbreak of violence, which included a ban on meetings of more than three Africans. A curfew was also in place which stipulated that all African-Congolese had to exit the European residential area by nightfall. The regulation extended even to domestic servants because Belgian employers did not traditionally provide accommodation in their homes for their servants, unlike the practice in British colonies. As nightfall approached the African staff departed, leaving their employers to bolt and bar their houses, make sure their pistols and hand grenades were to hand and their Dobermans free to roam their floodlit gardens.

Instinctively Park knew that politics, at least the sort she was interested in, was likely to be an after-hours business. She envisioned informal *tête-à-têtes* over bottles of whisky and home-cooked African suppers. She saw herself hunkering down with the potential rulers and power-brokers, all of whom would by definition be black, not sitting in isolation, sipping pink gins with fellow diplomats and making idle conversation. So she plumped for a house close to the Cité Africaine where the curfew would not apply. She would live cheek by jowl with the other 380,000 inhabitants of the city who lived in circumstances that varied from the acceptable with running water, electricity and sewerage to the most basic with little or no municipal services.

The house she picked was on the road to the airport, and given that air transport was the most frequent means of countrywide travel in the Congo her home turned into a popular watering hole for various power-brokers *en route* to and from their trips. Park spoke Swahili and Lingua,[1] the main language of the

144

Congo and the one used by the military. That gave her a useful common ground, particularly with those whose French was not strong.

She didn't bother with a watchdog, nor did she arm herself. This made her domestic situation somewhat risky and she did later admit to the occasional fright when she returned home at night to her empty house. Stephen Lockhart,[i] the outgoing consul-general, and the authorities advised strongly against her decision. To the hidebound Belgians the idea of a white woman living on her own in a house in the tropics seriously infringed the rules of propriety. In fact this 'problem' was quoted by the then consul-general in Léopoldville, Harold Swan, in his submission to the ill-fated Schuster Committee in 1934 as yet another reason why women could not be admitted into the Foreign Service.[2] But Park was adamant. One result of her decision was that she was removed from the invitation list for official functions, an exclusion that didn't bother her in the slightest; she'd happily leave that to her boss when he arrived.

The house was uncomfortably hot; being at sea level it did not benefit from the gentle breeze which cooled the houses in the slightly (but crucially) elevated European quarter. But issues such as her personal comfort were of no great consequence.[3] As far as Park was concerned this was water off a duck's back as she got down to concluding some housekeeping tasks, including supervising the installation of the station infrastructure. The chancery was located in an office block on Avenue Beernaert in downtown Léo. It occupied three floors, from the fourth up. The SIS station with its ultra-secure registry and cipher-room was located on the sixth. The embassy of Liberia happened to occupy two of the lower floors. One unfortunate consequence was that it was their windows that were broken, not those of the British, when the building was attacked by mobs protesting (most often wrongly) at British 'collusion' with Katanga.[4]

As Park well knew by this time, any intelligence officer undertaking a new assignment as a station head needs to understand first and foremost just what is expected of them. How will their tenure be judged? Or, to use modern parlance, 'what will good look like?' The Congo did not offer any direct military threat to Britain. But it did, or at least might, represent a very real threat to Britain's strategic (for strategic read *significant commercial*) interests in that part of Africa. Many of those interests were concentrated in the countries immediately adjacent or in fairly close proximity to the Congo. To the east were the colonies of Tanganyika, Uganda and Kenya. Directly to the south were Nyasaland (now Malawi) – where Park's uncle, Estcourt Cresswell-George, had taken up tobacco farming – Northern and Southern Rhodesia (Zambia and Zimbabwe). Further

i LOCKHART, Stephen Alexander, CMG, OBE; diplomat, later ambassador to the Dominican Republic (1905-1989).

145

south was the protectorate of Bechuanaland (Botswana) and beyond that, independent South Africa, which at that time included Namibia.

Park would have been well aware that change was in the air. The Gold Coast (Ghana) had been granted independence in 1957. And just as the granting of Indian independence in 1947 signalled the beginning of the end for the British Empire as a whole, so Ghanaian independence sounded its more immediate death knell in Africa. Where Ghana went the rest of (black) Africa would tend to follow. The famous speech by Prime Minister Harold Macmillan to the South African Parliament in 1960, when he spoke of a 'wind of change', was only recognising a reality already well under way.[5] Not that everyone saw it like that – the history of the world is littered with people 'with eyes that do not see', and none were more unseeing than those of the White African.

When Park arrived in Léopoldville, Southern and Northern Rhodesia and Nyasaland (where her uncle Estcourt had unsuccessfully contested what was effectively a 'whites only' election in 1953) already formed the white-ruled Central African Federation (CAF). The main political thrust, in fact the *raison d'être* for the CAF, was the extension of white-only rule from Southern Rhodesia to Northern Rhodesia and Nyasaland. Estcourt Cresswell-George's party (the Confederate Party) had campaigned for an apartheid-style administration in the CAF on the South African model. The CAF was very much in cahoots with the white settlers in Katanga who were even more vociferous in their opposition to the impending independence of the Congo than were the rest of the white population. The CAF Prime Minister, Roy Welensky, had had secret discussions with representatives of 'white' Katanga about the possibility of incorporating Katanga into the CAF in the event of Congolese independence.[6] Others in the CAF spoke of linking up with Portuguese Angola and even South Africa, acting as a *cordon sanitaire* between the white-ruled and the African-ruled parts of the continent.[7] This was pure fantasy, but just because it was fantasy did not mean that serious attempts would not be made to turn some of it into a reality. Complicating matters was the fact that Britain's economic interests in the Congo, specifically in the copper-rich province of Katanga, were considerable and required minding.

The British Charter company, Tanganyika Concessions (Tanks), owned a large slice (up to 40% at one stage) of Union Minière du Haut Katanga, the principal mining concession-holder in Katanga. It was also closely linked to the giant Belgian conglomerate, Société Générale. Unilever, Shell and British American Tobacco (BAT) were also major investors in the province and the country generally. This was a two-way street; it was coal from the Wankie fields in British Southern Rhodesia that fed Union Minière's Katanga's furnaces, and it was the British-run Benguela railway that carried all of Katanga's mineral production through Angola. When it became obvious that uniting Katanga with the CAF was not going to be a runner, the second-best solution was mooted, that of an independent Katanga acting as an ordered buffer between the rest of the Congo and the British territories.

Those advocating such courses were not without influence in London and in the higher reaches of the Tory Party in particular. The chairman of 'Tanks' was Charles Waterhouse, a former Tory MP and among the leading lights of a Commons revolt over Suez in 1954.[8] Another supporter was John Biggs-Davidson, one-time (while in Oxford) communist and in later life an influential right-wing Tory MP. These were the sort of murky dealings so beloved by elements within the Tories; conjugal relations between money and politics with decidedly unpredictable and often unpleasant offspring.

It meant, though, that Park had to continually look over her shoulder in order to remain fully up to date on the activities of these Tories and their CAF chums, whose emissaries were likely to turn up skulduggery anywhere at any time. The CAF's chief skuldugger was Captain Basil 'Bob' de Quehen. De Quehen was head of its intelligence arm, the Federal Intelligence & Security Bureau (FISB). He was a former MI5 Regional Security Liaison Officer, based in Salisbury, Southern Rhodesia[9] (now Harare in Zimbabwe). He had served in the Intelligence Corps in the Second World War, transferring afterwards to MI5. He set-up the FISB in 1953, possibly on secondment from MI5, so he was well connected in security circles in London. De Quehen needed watching, and he was. In March 1960 he was observed in Élizabethville in pursuit of closer ties between Tshombe's secessionist administration and the CAF. The following May he was in Luanda, in Angola, attempting to forge a security linkup between Portugal's PIDE, South Africa's BOSS, Katanga's Sûreté and the FISB.[10] As it was to turn out, the post-Suez and much chastened Macmillan played things with a pretty straight bat and British policy remained in favour of the unitary Congo state, but it might not have been so.

So from Park's perspective 'doing good' meant protecting Britain's reputation among the African populations and administrations in sub-Saharan Africa, who were paying great attention to developments in the Congo. At the same time it meant looking after, as far as she could, her country's business interests in Katanga. All the while she had to advance Britain's main political priority. This would have been defined as something like 'maintaining a united Congo after the Belgians pull out while ensuring that the incoming Congolese administration has a make-up that is well-disposed towards Britain and its interests'. That translated as getting close to and staying close to the key political and military figures in the emerging state; keeping a close eye on the Soviets, who were not then represented diplomatically, and their Czech 'running-dogs' who were. She needed to keep a similarly close eye on the activities of the Rhodesians/CAF and of course on the Belgians, who while they might be a NATO ally, seemed to have given up the ghost and so could not to be trusted to do the right thing.

In all of this she would need to establish a positive working relationship with the still yet-to-arrive CIA station head, Larry Devlin. This may not have been as simple as it sounded. According to a report on his December 1959 African visit by her Director, John Bruce Lockhart:

> I was most struck by the strong anti-American talk I heard in East and Central Africa. This is partly due to the fact that there are a number of private American agencies operating in Black Africa, backed by a great deal of money often provided by traditionally anti-Colonial Middle Western American groups. Their activities must indeed be infuriating to the British authorities and it must be very difficult for everyone who has British interests at heart to make a distinction between the policies of the United States Government and the activities of the variously motivated private agencies.[11]

It is probably a fair assumption that the 'strong anti-American talk' referred to by Lockhart emanated from British officials in Africa in the main and probably also some of their French and Belgian counterparts who would have had a fairly jaundiced view of US policy towards the remaining colonial administrations in Africa. Lockhart also referred to the 'local suspicion of CIA agents'. Park was beginning to realise that there were many, many different interests with fingers in her particular pie.

Her first operational priority was to establish her network of agents, collaborators, informal sources and Unofficial Assistants (UAs), the term SIS used to describe those British expats who might be prepared to provide unofficial assistance to the Service in its work in overseas countries. According to Ian Scott, writing in *Tumbled House: The Congo at Independence*, there were about two hundred and fifty or so British expatriates living in Léopoldville at that time, a big enough pool to provide a few willing helpers. Park knew that time wasn't on her side. As a rule of thumb it takes a newly set-up station twelve months or so to build a network of agents from scratch. Park knew she hadn't got twelve months. So she got down to it. Her first target was the political elite; she had to figure out who were the main players that she'd need to connect with. Fairly soon she put together her leading personality reports (LPRs). Her first attempt would have been pretty rough and ready, and the personality summaries would go through much iteration during her time. Making accurate judgements about people there was difficult since there was no track record of achievement on which to base them. Accuracy was further bedevilled by the évolués' lack of education and polish.

Belgians joked that the évolués all wore reading glasses to make them appear educated and distinguished. Such cynicism reflected more on the Belgians than on the Africans. Park was well aware that the évolués were prohibited by race from advancement and so individual intellects and abilities were often concealed under their somewhat unvarnished exteriors. She had to learn – and it took some learning – that a rough-hewn army sergeant might well have the capability to lead a battalion or even an army and might be doing just that when independence arrived and he was no longer held back. Park knew she had to see behind the veneer and the way to do that was to engage in continuing discussion and debate, to draw people out, to ascertain their true views, get a handle on their abilities and on probable courses of action.

So she never missed any opportunity to meet people and make connections. One of her duties was to handle the diplomatic bag communications. Generally this was done through the high commission in Accra, though routine messages between Léopoldville and London were sent and received by enciphered telegraph. The 2,000 mile (3,500 km) trip to Accra via Brazzaville, Douala, Gabon and Lagos took about three days. She travelled by air but the delays were such that she had many enforced stops along the way. She also travelled to the other capitals of the neighbouring states for meetings with her opposite numbers in the nearby African capitals, people like Hugo Herbert-Jones[i] (Nairobi), Theodore 'Bunny' Pantcheff[ii] (Lagos), Neil Ritchie[iii] (Salisbury) and Michael Oatley[iv] (Kampala), in order to compare notes, swap intelligence, coordinate operations and, where needed, to provide operational support. Most of SIS's overseas stations were tiny – one, perhaps two officers, mostly sharing a secretary – so officers working in the same geographical area helped each other out where they could and where their assistance would be appreciated.

Whether Park met her uncle Estcourt Cresswell-George during her travels is not recorded. She may well have. He was family for a start, the only family – her mother apart – that she now had, and family mattered to Park. She would maintain contact with her African relatives up to the time of her death. He would also have provided her with an authentic White African perspective, which would have been useful if not particularly helpful. For Park the discomfort involved in these trips was an irrelevancy when balanced against the opportunities to meet people and hear what they had to stay. And so she travelled back and forth, talking and listening, forming opinions, evaluating likely scenarios, taking it all in. And all the time giving the impression she was anything but a spy:

i HERBERT-JONES, Hugo, CMG, OBE; SIS, HAMBURG, BERLIN, HONG KONG, PHNOM PENH, H/SAIGON, H/NAIROBI, H/PRETORIA, H/PARIS, C/AFRICA, D/P (Production) (1922-2014).

ii PANTCHEFF, Theodore ('Bunny') Xenophon, CMG; MI9, SIS, MUNICH, H/LAGOS, H/KINSHASA (Léopoldville), C/AFRICA (1920-1989).

iii RITCHIE, Frederick Neil; Intelligence Corps, SIS, SOFIA, AMMAN, H/DJAKARTA, H/SALISBURY, H/GENEVA (1918-d.).

iv OATLEY, Michael Charles, CMG, OBE; SIS, NAIROBI, H/KAMPALA, H/LOME, H/ACCRA, seconded to Northern Ireland Office, A/H HONG KONG, H/HARARE, C/MIDDLE EAST-C/COUNTER TERRORISM conjointly C/EUROPE (1935-).

[The car] was excellent cover, nobody ever takes 2CVs seriously. But that's not why I had it – if they'd let me loose in anything bigger I'd have been lethal. My director [John Bruce Lockhart] once told me the bravest thing he'd ever done in his life was to be driven round by me.[12]

Brave Lockhart was, for at the time she arrived in the Congo Park had yet to learn to drive, but as she said in her Royal Society of Literature lecture, 'the Congo did not have a driving test so that didn't matter'.[13] Park just got her car and commenced driving. However, there was far more than the risk of an accident or discomfort involved in her posting. By this author's count Park encountered real physical danger five times during her time in Léo. On one occasion she was driving along when she suddenly came across a machete-wielding mob. She had no room or time to turn around so she jumped out of her car and lifted the bonnet, telling her potential attackers: 'Thank goodness you've come along – I think I have a problem with my carburettor.' The men, she said, then lowered their weapons, stared uselessly at the engine until with a satisfied 'Ah-ha!' she slammed the bonnet shut, got back into her car and drove away; amusing in retrospect perhaps, but not much fun at the time.[14] On a second occasion her famous car was surrounded by a mob who attempted to drag her out through the 2CV's rollback roof. Park managed to jam herself in the opening and to the mob's amazement started to giggle. Soon they joined in and then tiring of the 'fun' moved away. To 'giggle' in such a circumstance took a degree of *sangfroid* that went way beyond the ordinary.[15]

Probably the most dangerous was the time when she was beaten by a group of soldiers and thrown into a pit. The process of execution in situations such as the Congo at that time often involved several distinct steps as the selected victim was readied for execution. It was part softening-up process, part dehumanising. Often too the executioners engaged in a process of mutual egging on as they steeled themselves for the kill. Beating the potential victim until they fell to the ground was often part of this. Throwing them into a pit or hole in the ground would achieve the same purpose. It is unlikely Park ever came closer to death than she did that day. She was exceedingly fortunate to 'talk her executioners' out of their planned course and to escape with her life.[16] The fourth (recorded) episode was when she was on her way to Stanleyville around the time of the breakout from captivity of the Congolese leader, Patrice Lumumba (see Chapter 17). Trouble started for Park when she arrived at N'djili Airport, which served the capital. Her handbag was searched and soldiers discovered a recording she had of a speech given at the official embassy party held a few days earlier to mark Nigeria's independence. The soldiers concluded it must be a speech by Lumumba and that she was a *Flamand* (Flemish Belgian) supporter of his. They decided to execute her on the spot. After lengthy negotiations Park said, 'Why don't you let me go to Stanleyville and when I come back you can shoot me?'

The soldiers thought about this. 'When are you coming back?' 'I shall be back on Thursday.' 'All right, you can go now but when you come back you will be shot.'[17] When she did arrive back in Léo a different group of soldiers was on duty so she sped away. Hard not to imagine that her heart must have been beating just a bit faster when she stepped off the plane in Léopoldville. While the story may not have lost anything in the telling it is still impossible not to be struck by the extraordinary coolness under fire that she displayed. And when she did get to Stanleyville she found herself once more in danger, as we shall see.

These encounters invariably involved mainly young, poorly disciplined troops, often under the influence of drink or drugs, fired up by a general hatred of 'Europeans' and prepared to kill. To manage to engage with them as she did took some nerve. But she always tried to play it down. As she once said:

> I must have been arrested and condemned to be shot several times. It was a hazard that I got used to.[18]

She once told her friend Jean Sackur, 'I have nothing but contempt for men who lack courage' – not something Park could be accused of.[19] The Office eventually decreed that the station commander should be issued with a pistol, mainly for protection at night when she was at home, but Park declined, lodging the pistol in the station safe, where it remained.[20]

In September 1960 Park was provided with a second officer in the person of John de St Jorre,[i] a twenty-four-year-old recently minted graduate from SIS's intelligence training course. He was to receive his own initiation into the reality of life in Léo station. Neighbouring Angola was still under Portuguese rule and at that time did not boast an SIS station. Like most African colonies it was beginning to show signs of unrest, and Park (presumably on receipt of instructions from Broadway) sent her new deputy there to report on developments.

> I went on a road trip to Angola, just before the rebellion started there and I wrote a report about the political situation. The thing I remember best from the journey is that I was arrested by drunken and drugged mutinous Congolese soldiers in the lower Congo and thought my time was up. Eventually, I managed to persuade them that I was a diplomat and they let me go. I fled towards the Angolan border as fast as I could and spent the night with Catholic missionaries before crossing. Fortunately, they had plenty of wine and cigars on hand, unlike their dreary Protestant counterparts, who were non-smoking teetotallers, and I recovered from my ordeal. I eventually reached Luanda and returned via a boat trip to Cabinda, a Portuguese coastal enclave. From there I drove to Brazzaville and took the ferry over to Léo.[21]

i De St JORRE, John; SIS, author, journalist, LEOPOLDVILLE, NAIROBI, H/USUMBU-RA, MECAS, resigned 1964 (1936-).

His welcome from Park on arrival to take up his duties may not have been as effusive as he expected:

> Daphne was a one-person band who really didn't need another officer with her, just support staff. She already had a secretary and a young male clerk who did the ciphers and other odd jobs. My French was not good while Daphne was fluent. I was assigned to run a couple of established agents who spoke English, and 'cultivate' (a favourite word) foreign businessman. I was also told to mingle with the young Congolese students at the university. However, the campus was soon shut down, so that particular field of cultivation was laid waste almost before I had started to plough it. I was also encouraged by Daphne to establish my cover and do a lot of things in the embassy that our Foreign Office colleagues did, such as general reporting and even drafting dispatches for the Head of Chancery. All in all, it was not the best way to start an SIS career although being in the Congo at that time was exciting.[22]

De St Jorre also said that he and Park were not particularly close 'either personally or professionally'. This aspect of her personality has been alluded to by others. It seems that some, at least, of her famous charisma was only there to be deployed as required, perhaps for professional or career purposes. However, while she was far from close to all who worked with her, the overwhelming impression gained was of considerable warmth and great charm.

One of the activities that caught Park's early attention was the Congolese Boy Scout movement. In that extraordinary way she had, she was quick to see and then seize the opportunity represented by it. The original Scout movement had been established in Britain in 1908 with the publication of *Scouting for Boys* by Robert Baden-Powell, a British Army general. It took off with almost 'Facebook' velocity. By 1922 there were over a million scouts in twenty-two countries. Belgium was not immune, and in fact two scouting organisations were established in the country, one Catholic and one 'neutral' or non-denominational. In 1924 the Belgians introduced scouting to the Belgian Congo. Initially it was directed at the indigenous population, the supposedly African origins of Baden-Powell's philosophy commending itself to the settlers who felt that would make it more acceptable for use in the colony. However, separate white-only scout troops were established in Léopoldville and Élizabethville.[23]

The decision was taken that only 'detribalised' Congolese would be admitted to the scout movement, évolués in other words, though the use of that word was banned in favour of 'elite'. Discipline was strict with suspension or expulsion being the norm for either 'concubinage' or 'public drunkenness'.[24] In any event there were costs associated with being a Scout that, while relatively modest, were well beyond the means of the 'non-évolué' population who, comparatively speaking, would have been living on the clippings of tin. The hope appeared

1. Daphne Park pictured shortly after she arrived in Britain in 1932. 'She wore a white lacy knitted dress, very elaborate, with a scalloped hem and petticoats beneath, white knee high socks, elaborately patterned, and white leather shoes. We were allowed to wear our hair short or in plaits. Hers was long and loose. Probably this was what girls wore in the colonies but we were astonished, for we had only seen such an outfit in a story book.' (Peggy Jeffries, Daphne Park Memorial Tributes, Somerville College 2010)

2. Daphne Park around the time she graduated from Somerville College in 1943. (Courtesy of Somerville College ©)

3. Daphne Park in FANY *c.* 1943. (Courtesy of Somerville College ©)

4. Sir Stewart Menzies, Chief of SIS 1939-52 and the canniest of 'Whitehall warriors'. (© National Portrait Gallery, London)

5. Commander Kenneth Cohen. As Chief Controller/Europe he was Park's first real boss and hugely influential on her career in SIS. 'I had the privilege of working for a very, very, great man.' (Courtesy of the Cohen Estate ©)

6. Dame Professor Lisa Hall of Cambridge University, first head of the Joint Services School for Linguistics (JSSL) where Park and other SIS SovBloc personnel (among others) learnt their Russian. (Courtesy of Jean Stafford Smith ©)

7. Sir William Goodenough Hayter, ambassador to Moscow 1953-57 and Park's 'first ambassador'. Hayter and she became close, possibly because they shared an impoverished background. (© National Portrait Gallery, London)

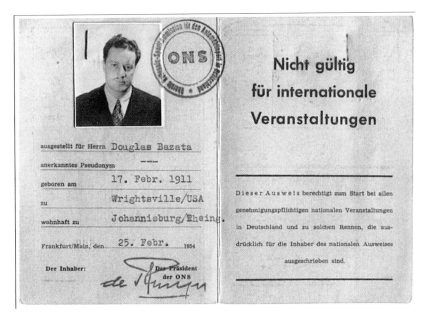

8. Driving licence used by Park's first lover, former Marine Captain Douglas DeWitt Bazata. Bazata claimed the licence was used as part of his CIA cover at the time. The address on the licence – Johannisburg – was the location of the schloss (castle) home to Baron and Baroness Mumm, where Bazata was allegedly living in a *ménage à trois*. (© Estate of Douglas DeWitt Bazata)

9. In later life Bazata was a successful artist, his admirers including Princess Grace (Kelly) of Monaco, pictured here with him. (© Estate of Douglas DeWitt Bazata)

10. Patrice Lumumba, first Prime Minister of the independent Congo, pictured as a prisoner of the army commander, General Mobutu, in 1961. Within days he would be dead.

11. British ambassador to the Congo, Ian Scott, pictured with General Mobutu, then in the process of establishing himself as the effective ruler of the Congo, c. 1961.

12. Daphne Park with SIS colleague Hugo Herbert-Jones, Head of Nairobi station, c. 1960. Park and Herbert-Jones were on an 'expedition' involving upwards of five SIS officers, who travelled from Nairobi to Usumbura, and on to Stanleyville. The nature of the operation is unknown. (Courtesy of Sarah Herbert-Jones ©)

13. Another photograph of Park on the same trip, which also included John Bruce Lockhart, John Taylor and Neil Ritchie. (Courtesy of Sarah Herbert-Jones ©)

14. Park pictured later, rather more 'glammed-up'. (Courtesy of Sarah Herbert-Jones ©)

15. John Bruce Lockhart, Director/ Middle East & Africa (Park's then director) shown on the same trip. (Courtesy of Sarah Herbert-Jones ©)

16. Daphne Park in Lusaka, a rare picture of the spy in action with customary drink in hand.

17. The Grand Kremlin Palace from the roof of the (then) British Embassy, a wonderful vantage point and an even better listening post. (Crown Copyright)

18. Broadway Buildings (pictured today) was home to SIS from the mid-1920s until the 1960s. Inside was a rabbit warren of poorly lit, cramped offices, served by a lift that stopped only on the ground, fourth and seventh floors. (Paddy Hayes)

19. Century House, referred to as 'Gloom Hall' by its occupants, was SIS's headquarters from 1964 to 1994 when it moved to its current location on the banks of the Thames at Vauxhall Cross. (Courtesy Nigel West ©)

20. The joint SIS/CIA team responsible for handling Oleg Penkovsky, possibly the single most important Western source of the Cold War; *left to right*: Michael Stokes and Harold 'Harry' Shergold of SIS and Joe Bulik and Walter Kiesvalter of the CIA. (Photo CIA Archives)

21. GRU Colonel Oleg Vladimirovich Penkovsky, agent HERO, pictured with the CIA's Joe Bulik. Later Bulik was highly critical of the arrangements put in place in Moscow by SIS to handle this prized source, leading to a radical overhaul of agent handling procedures by SIS under Shergold's direction. (Photo CIA Archives)

22. Typical Hanoi street scene, taken *c.* 1980 but remarkably similar to what it was like during Park's period in post in the city. (© Sir John Ramsden)

23. Spy station Ulaanbaatar; the British Embassy in Ulaanbaatar was referred to in SIS as 'our embassy' due to its special status whereby many of the holders of the post of ambassador were serving SIS officers. (Crown Copyright)

24. Baroness Daphne Margaret Sybil Desirée Park, CMG, OBE.

to be that scouting would help in the creation of what would be a subservient 'native elite'. Business interests were, as one might expect, naturally supportive. In 1960 Union Minière contributed 350,000 Congo francs (about $70,000) to the Catholic scouts in Élizabethville and 50,000 francs ($1,000) to the non-denominational scouts.[25]

By the time Park arrived in the Congo the movement was well established and had attracted many of the politically ambitious évolués, this despite the fact that the senior positions were open only to whites. In fairness some efforts were made to encourage contacts between whites and blacks, and by the standards that applied generally in the Belgian Congo the scouting movement was quite radical in some of its attitudes. This was grist to Park's mill and she encouraged her local scout troop to drill in the grounds of the ambassador's residence, which were extensive. That is how she made her first acquaintance with the two men who were to play a hugely influential role in the emerging country, future President Joseph Kasavubu[i] and future Prime Minister Patrice Lumumba,[ii] both of whom were active in the Boy Scouts up to independence.

As was the practice at the time, both men had scouting nicknames. Kasavubu's was Tigre Puissant (Fierce Tiger) while Lumumba's was Gazelle Russe (Russian Antelope). It would appear that even at that early stage Lumumba's sympathies were coming to the surface. Both were enthusiastic scouts but used to argue a lot, leading Park to scold them as she reminded them of the principles of the movement's founder, Baden-Powell. Once independence took place many of the scouts graduated into the youth militias and became potent and violent political forces, Lumumba's main counter to the power of the army as it came increasingly under Joseph Mobutu's[iii] control. Park was rather pleased with how her early investment of time in the two men was to turn out later to be to her advantage, and she used to cite it regularly as an example of how best to go about the spy business of cultivating future prospects.[26]

Meeting Lumumba was to lead to one of Park's more unusual experiences. This involved a journey to Stanleyville, about eight hundred miles from Léop-oldville by air. Park was, in her own words 'filling in time before independence'. She wanted to learn more about Lumumba's Mouvement National Congolais (MNC). While it is unlikely that political opinion polling, on a countrywide basis at least, was in operation at that time, people were beginning to get some sense of who was likely to feature in the final shake-out and Lumumba was definitely one of them. She took the opportunity one day to ask him if he could arrange for her to meet some of his Stanleyville-based colleagues in the movement.

i KASAVUBU, Joseph; politician, first President of an independent Congo (1910-1969).

ii LUMUMBA, Patrice Émery; politician, first Prime Minister of an independent Congo (1925-1961).

iii MOBUTU, Joseph (*aka* Mobutu Sese Seko), President of the Congo 1965-97 (1930-1997).

Lumumba agreed and suggested she contact a Monsieur Barlovatz[i] when she got to Stanleyville who would see to it. She took her flight to Stanleyville, the epicentre of the Mouvement, and duly connected with Barlovatz. She told him what she wanted and he replied that he would be happy to arrange for her to meet some of the committee members. To pass the time until the meeting he suggested that first they go on a little fishing trip. Park was game. It then turned out that the fishing was better at night so they waited until darkness fell and then went off in a small canoe. They fished, shot the rapids in the dark and fished some more. They pulled over to where some other fishermen had built a fire and were cooking some of their night's catch. These others invited Park and Barlovatz to join them. Fortunately Park had brought along a bottle of whiskey which they all shared as they chatted into the night. As dawn was beginning to break they said their goodbyes and headed back to Stanleyville in their canoe. Park thanked Barlovatz for the evening and reminded him of his promise to arrange for her to meet the MNC committee members.

'Madame, you just have,' he replied.[27]

Barlovatz, who arrived in the Congo in the 1920s from his native Yugoslavia, ran a medical clinic in Stanleyville. He explained that the committee members were under surveillance by the Belgian colonial authorities but that the surveillance did not continue after nightfall – that particular committee wasn't the first nor would it be the last to take advantage of that type of bureaucratic bungle. The story tells so much about Park, the inquiring mind, being prepared to go off into the night with Barlovatz with no security, no back-up, armed only with a bottle of whiskey 'just in case'.

Around that time she had what was to prove one of her most important long-term recruitments in March when Damien Kandolo, Lumumba's aide-de-camp, fell out of favour with his boss. Fearing that his life was in danger he put in a late night telephone call to her from a mission hospital where he was being treated for a severe beating. Park was never one to pass up an opportunity to create an obligation. She drove straight to the hospital, which was little more than a few huts. It was dark when she arrived at the hut where he was hiding and, fearing he was about to be murdered, the fugitive attacked her. When she told him who she was he calmed down. She drove him to the port in the back of her car, hidden under the jumble of clothes and blankets she habitually carried. They took the ferry to Brazzaville where he would remain until he deemed it safe to return. The favour she did him, at considerable risk, was to stand her in great stead for years to come.[28]

Someone who did not fall for her charm was the influential Andrée Blouin,[ii] later to be Lumumba's Chief of Protocol (whose every move was relayed to Park

i BARLOVATZ, Dr Alexandre, medical doctor (1896-d.).
ii BLOUIN, Andrée, the 'Black Pasionaria'; campaigner for female emancipation, nationalism and socialism in Africa (1921-1986).

by Kandolo). Blouin was *métisse* (of mixed race), something that only added to the complication of living in 'White Man's Africa'. There were approximately twelve thousand men and women of mixed parentage living in Léopoldville at the time of independence.[29] Born in what is now the Central African Republic, Blouin was separated from her African mother at the age of three and brought up in a particularly harsh orphanage in Brazzaville, one of many established by French and Belgian settlers in Brazzaville and Léopoldville to conceal the results of their libertine behaviour (often the exercise of *droit de seigneur*). Her upbringing toughened her up considerably. No fan of Blouin, Park described her as 'a very powerful and rather wicked Guinean who was right in the pocket of the Russians'.[30] This comment was made by Park to Gordon Corera fifty years after the events described; it is noteworthy for its utter lack of any softening in attitude. When Mobutu later overthrew Lumumba's government he expelled Blouin from the Congo, probably at Park/Devlin's request/suggestion. Blouin took refuge in Switzerland where she survived two assassination attempts. Her companion in exile, Dr Félix Moumié[i] – campaigner for an independent French Cameroon and referred to by name in Bruce Lockhart's report on Africa to Prime Minister Macmillan – was not so lucky. He was assassinated while in Geneva, apparently on the orders of the French government. According to Park, Blouin had earlier been 'neutralised' by the CIA,[31] the word not otherwise explained; perhaps the assassination attempts were all that was required. Anyway, unlike others so 'neutralised', Blouin reached retirement age, eventually ending up living in Paris where she died in anonymity in 1986.[32] She was once described by UN Head Dag Hammarskjold as the 'Madame du Barry' (the King of France's chief mistress) of the Congo.

One of the hazards of being female in her profession was that on occasion Park's sources thought they could take advantage and make amorous advances. One of her sources, a more informal one rather than a registered agent as such, rather fancied her and used to attempt to take things further.[33] He was quickly christened 'Lover Boy' by her station colleagues, much to her amusement. Park's solution was to insist to him that they held all their meetings in her car (a tiny and much battered Citroen 2CV). Given her reasonably ample size, the cramped conditions did not permit any hanky-panky to occur and she certainly never did anything to encourage it. On one occasion he went too far, she made her feelings known to Lumumba, and that ended it.[34]

She was a dedicated, workaholic, intelligence officer who never showed any signs of being interested in any kind of romantic activity.[35]

i MOUMIÉ, Félix-Roland; politician; his death is put down to the French secret service (SDECE) which allegedly poisoned him with thallium (1926-1960).

'Lover Boy' was an official rather than a political figure, a chief of protocol in the parliament or similar. The fact of him being a 'contact' rather than an 'agent' was part and parcel of the sometimes haphazard way that things were run.

'Intelligence' was a word with many meanings in the Congo at that time. Information acquired which was considered 'new' would be classed as 'intelligence' and sent off to Broadway as CX material. If it was considered old hat, for example confirmation of some existing information, it was simply dispatched to the Foreign Office in London via the chancery as a routine dispatch.[36] Intentions intelligence was particularly difficult to verify (as it often can be); often the initiators of particular actions did not decide themselves until the last minute, or even more often simply acted on impulse. And the country was awash with rumours. As John de St Jorre says:

> I typically would hear the rumours and then, later, have them denied or corroborated, rather like everyone else there. The only difference was that people like Daphne and Larry Devlin would hear them earlier than most people, and have more effective ways of checking them.[37]

To tap into the rumour mill Park and Devlin both entertained endlessly. Small informal suppers were her forte, or meetings in the bar of the Memling Hotel, then practically Léopoldville's only hotel and one where the worlds of the media, diplomacy and espionage intermingled. Devlin favoured more elaborate 'diplomatic' dinners, co-hosted with his French-born wife. As the situation developed did some of these dinners or suppers go from being social affairs to gatherings of fellow conspirators? They quite probably did.

As the year came to its close Park's boss, John Bruce Lockhart, arrived on his personal fact-finding mission. Harold Macmillan was scheduled to make a major visit to Southern Africa the following February and Bruce Lockhart's visit was in part preparation for that. Park was fortunate in having Bruce Lockhart as her Director. His rather schoolmasterish air disguised a keen brain and an essential decency. There was widespread sympathy for him when he was eased out in the mid-1960s. One colleague of Park's described Bruce Lockhart's management style thus:

> The man for whom I was being sent to work in London had a bad reputation with staff and JBL said to me, 'So-and-so is bright and able but sometimes very difficult. If you find you can't get on with him and it all becomes too much let me know and we will move you to something else.'[38]

As it happened that wasn't necessary:

However after a while I discovered that so-and-so's bad moods had been a result of sadness and frustration in a deeply unhappy marriage. Around the time I came to work for him he embarked on an affair with a very sexy young secretary, the sun shone, so-and-so and I got on like a house on fire, and his excellent qualities as an intelligence manager came to the fore.[39]

Park and Bruce Lockhart met a wide range of political, security and business leaders. Bruce Lockhart's discussions with officials from the Belgian Sûreté convinced him of the 'apparent abdication of the will to govern by the Belgian authorities'.[40] This confirmed what Park learned earlier on her visit to Brussels. Bruce Lockhart also encountered the mutual suspicion that was to bedevil inter-governmental relations:

> [The Director-General of Security in the Congo] pointed out that there was one important factor he wished to bring to my attention. I should know that the majority of senior officials in the Belgian Congo believed that the British Government had a long term Machiavellian plan for West Africa. They believed that the British Government were using N'Krumah [Ghana] as their 'front man'. They believed that, when the dust from the present nationalist troubles in Africa had settled, the world would find that the French and Belgian Empires had disappeared, and the British still in position, having taken over all the valuable trade concessions.[41]

When Bruce Lockhart 'contested' that view the official 'smiled wanly' and remarked:

> While he himself did not think the British capable of such machinations, his colleagues in the Congo had not had as much experience in the world as he had.[42]

That probably summed up the situation very well. The Belgians didn't trust the Africans and the Africans certainly didn't trust the Belgians; the British didn't trust the Belgians to 'do the right thing', while the Belgians were convinced that the British were working to a secret master-plan to take over all of Belgium's valuable mineral concessions. And of course no one either liked very much or trusted (at all) the Americans.

Independence was coming and with it a new ambassador-designate, Ian Scott.[i] The first Park knew about that was when she received a telegram from the Office inquiring about whether she had any particular preference for her next posting. When she replied that she was perfectly happy where she was, thanks, she was told that Scott would prefer not to have an SIS presence in his embassy, fearing that such a presence would only make his task more difficult than it already was. This attitude towards having an SIS station in embassies

---

i SCOTT, Sir Ian Dixon, KCMG, KCVO, CIE; diplomat (1909-2002).

– while changing – was still far from uncommon. Park, her once fiery temper now tempered by experience, decided to wait until he arrived before responding. That was a wise decision. Scott, despite being a little conservative, was a decent sort and when they met he agreed to leave things as they were for a time and see how things developed. Park, who already had some track record in winning over ambassadors to the cause, began to work her charm on him. One day he called her into his office and told her he was content to leave her in place (head of chancery/head of station) but first he would like a list of her agents/sources. Park realised that this was going to be the acid test of their relationship. SIS *never* reveals details of its sources to those outside the Service (and only strictly on a need-to-know basis within) other than in the gravest situations when the Prime Minister, for example, might be briefed personally by the Chief. She said as much to Scott and told him that if he could not accept that she would have no choice but to leave Léopoldville. To his credit he did accept it, and from then on the two got on exceptionally well.[43] With her ambassador now onside, and her other ducks in a row, Park was now as ready as she could be for the events that were about to unfold.

17

Congo 3 – Seven months to murder, 1960-61

About a dozen political parties contested the Belgian Congo's first general election. Voting took place over three weeks commencing in mid-May 1960. How genuinely free and fair the elections were is a matter of debate. The US certainly had attempted to influence the outcome, the State Department later admitting that:

> Even before Congolese independence the US government attempted to ensure election of a pro-Western government by identifying and supporting individual pro-US leaders.[1]

For his part Lumumba was aided by frenetic propaganda broadcasts in Kiswahili from Cairo Radio. Nasser, the Egyptian leader, was still popular in this part of Africa and he threw his full weight behind the nationalist leader. Lumumba received covert financial aid 'from Nkrumah, from Czechoslovakia, from Russia, from Yugoslavia (possibly through Dr Barlovatz)'[2] emerging as the only pan-Congolese candidate of stature. Uniquely his campaigning cut across tribal lines; his brightly painted campaign-vans, loudspeakers belting out a mixture of demagoguery, music and drumbeats, could be seen and heard throughout the Congo while those of his rivals stuck to their individual tribal areas. When the votes were counted it was seen that only Lumumba's MNC and the PNP had taken seats outside their own tribal areas. Lumumba's party won seats in five of the six provinces, the only party to achieve this level of cross-tribal representation. But while the MNC grouping was the largest, it was well short of commanding a majority, with just forty-nine seats out of the one hundred and thirty-nine seats in the Lower House. A coalition of sorts was formed between the MNC and his rival, Kasavubu's ABAKO group. The two former Boy Scouts would lead the country; Lumumba (Gazelle Russe) would be Prime Minister while Kasavubu (Tigre Puissant) would hold the largely nominal post of President. The combined groups would have a majority of six. Their scouting nicknames turned out to be on the ball.

The Independence Day ceremony took place as scheduled on 30 June 1960. The first speech, by Baudouin (King of the Belgians), was reported to have been both patronising and inappropriate – the monarch was either carelessly advised or careless with his words. Either way, he clearly aroused the ire of the assembled Africans, which was hardly the intent. By way of contrast President Kasavubu was conciliatory and self-effacing. Lumumba was not scheduled to speak, but when apprised of the contents of the monarch's address, he insisted unwisely, if unsurprisingly, on being heard. Lumumba's words were 'hard, bitter, accusatory and xenophobic', according to the report by Ian Scott, now elevated to ambassador to reflect the fact of the Congo being an independent state:[3]

> 'We have known the contempt, the insults, the blows which we have had to suffer morning, noon and night because we were niggers. Who can forget that "*tu*" was used to a black man and "*vous*" reserved for the whites? We have seen that there was one law for the whites and another for the blacks.'[4]

The Belgian contingent threatened to walk out. Lunch was delayed for two hours while they considered what to do, eventually allowing themselves to be mollified. But any chance of a post-election reconciliation between Lumumba and his former colonial masters was doomed. Lumumba had confirmed the worst suspicions the Belgians had about him. Notwithstanding the slight glitch, four days of exuberant independence celebrations followed which were surprisingly peaceful and trouble-free. They would be the last such days for many months; this Prime Minister would enjoy no hundred-day honeymoon. In fact he would be in office for just seventy-one days. For the following seventy-nine he would be in a form of limbo before entering the hell that would be the final forty days of his life. This three-act tragedy took just seven months to play out, with Park at the front and centre throughout.

Author's Note: what follows is not a comprehensive account of the cataclysmic events which followed the declaration of independence of the former Belgian Congo. This has been well documented elsewhere. The author's intention is to give the reader a feel for the chaos and confusion – some orchestrated, some not – which erupted, and the role of the CIA and SIS in particular in the events that led up to Patrice Lumumba's downfall and murder.

The first act, 1 July to 14 September 1960; seventy-six days

Independence commenced with Prime Minister Lumumba boiling with rage. What prompted this rage was his discovery that all of the key levers of power – the intelligence service (Sûreté Nationale), the police, magistrature and army – remained in European hands. For that matter neither was the Force Publique, now renamed the Armée Nationale Congolaise (ANC), too happy with European control remaining in place. On 5 July, the day after the independence celebrations ended, rumours swept the capital of trouble in the ANC. Lumumba and General Émile Janssens (the Belgian commander of the ANC) were reported to have had a bitter row over the ANC's future role, Janssens saying, in effect, 'independence changes nothing', Lumumba saying 'it changes everything'.[5] The next day, the Léopoldville-based units of the ANC rebelled against their white officers. Janssens resigned because he was refused permission to use the Belgian troops that he also had under his command to put down the mutiny.[6]

Lumumba, ever the populist, announced an increase in wages of 30% for all government employees except soldiers, who instead were promoted by one rank. He ignored the fact that the state coffers could afford neither gesture. He then announced that all officer posts were to be Africanised without further notice. The former army warrant officer turned journalist, Joseph Mobutu, who had been appointed as minister for defence, was made chief of staff with the rank of colonel. Seven hundred and fifty Belgian officers were dismissed with a small cadre being retained as advisors. Mobutu was given responsibility for appointing new officers, though some were to be elected in 'soviets'.

But the reforms did not quell the unrest. On 8 July there were reports of full-blown mutiny among the soldiery. The trouble commenced in Camp Hardy, one of two army bases in Thysville, ninety miles downriver from Léopoldville. A number of wives of Belgian officers were raped, causing the remaining Belgians to flee at once to Léopoldville by whatever means open to them. The panic extended to the capital as news spread like wildfire, confirming the former colonialists' worst nightmares. River steamers that were normally used for ferrying goods and passengers on the thousand-mile up-river journey to Stanleyville were pressed into service to take fleeing refugees across the river to Brazzaville. Ambassador Scott's residence was besieged by British and Commonwealth subjects fearful for their lives. Most, according to Scott, stayed on, but many of the men sent their wives and children to safety.

Within two days the army mutiny had spread throughout the country. Stanleyville was particularly badly affected. According to a telegram to the Foreign Office in London from Ambassador Scott, the jobs of the ten thousand or so direct and indirect employees of British American Tobacco (BAT) were being threatened as the company considered ceasing tobacco production and repatriating its key (European) staff.[7] In fact the rumours of rape and pillage were more widespread than their actual incidence. According to Park, relatively few Europeans in Léopoldville were seriously harmed.[8] However, whether through rumour or otherwise, the result was an exodus of Europeans. Twenty thousand had left by this stage, with a consequent impact on the country's infrastructure and its state-owned transport company OTRACO in particular. And not just infrastructure, government departments too were stripped of their experienced officials, all of whom were white. Paralysis descended.

It was at this point that Larry Devlin, the brash, tough as teak, new CIA head of station, arrived on the scene. The US consulate had been re-opened in 1958, the US having had an on-off diplomatic presence since the mid-1920s.

There were substantial numbers of Protestant American missionaries based in the Congo, and of course its enormous mineral wealth made it 'of interest'. Devlin commenced his CIA career working under non official cover (NOC), the term used to describe a CIA officer working outside the umbrella of a diplomatic mission. Devlin's cover was as a roaming European editor for Fodor,[9] the well-established publishers of travel guides and sometime provider of operational cover for CIA officers.[10] Prior to his arrival Devlin was briefed about Lumumba's 'commie' tendencies and was already looking at him with a pretty jaundiced eye. Devlin's briefing also included a warning by one previous incumbent to be sure to bring a dinner jacket for the socialising and to expect to be on the golf course every day by two in the afternoon. That illusion quickly vanished as he found himself one of the very few heading *for* Léo from Brazzaville, rather than the other direction. And when he stepped off the ferry he could understand why, experiencing a pretty rough welcome from mutinous Congolese soldiers before he made it to the relative – and that's all it was – safety of the US embassy.[11]

Once there he dumped his kit and set about figuring out what he needed to be doing. His CIA complement was tiny, probably just himself and a secretary and a communications specialist plus one NOC officer, Howard Imbrey,[i] who had arrived just ahead of him. Imbrey's cover was as a public relations consultant specialising in government affairs. NOCs are useful because they are not readily identified as acting on behalf of the US. Given what Devlin had in mind, he needed such people. One of the first people he met, outside his own country's officials, was Park, so that he could be brought up to date with the political situation from the British perspective at least. One of their most difficult tasks, they quickly realised, would be separating truth from rumour. In the febrile atmosphere of the city there were rumours about everything and anything; tracking down the truth was going to be extraordinarily difficult. Quite early on they picked up reports from Mobutu that the 'running dogs' in the Czechoslovak consulate were orchestrating the army mutiny. They were not able to prove it. Another concerned a Polish vessel that was supposedly due in the port of Matadi with a cargo of weapons for the ANC. There appeared to be no truth in that but Park and he would have had to check it out all the same.[12]

By this stage several hundred Russian troops and specialists had arrived through N'djili Airport, so upping the tension. Devlin was so concerned that he had installed an agent in the airport to monitor their arrival and count the numbers: 'any European getting off a Russian plane is a Russian'. Soviet aircraft had also landed in Stanleyville, Lumumba's home base, giving even further cause for alarm. Devlin and Park, and the authorities generally, were afraid that the aircraft might be used to transport troops loyal to Lumumba to Léopoldville

i IMBREY, Howard; CIA (1921-2001).

in the event of a military standoff, thus altering the balance of forces in the Prime Minister's favour. This finally decided Devlin that the interests of the United States did not include having Lumumba stay on as Prime Minister. On 18 August he sent a cable to CIA headquarters summarising his view of the situation, raising the spectre of the Congo 'becoming another Cuba'. The cable was top secret but its contents were revealed in the Church Committee Senate Hearings in 1975. Those hearings threw some rare and welcome light into the shadows, illustrating some aspects of what the CIA (and by extension SIS) was up to at the time.

EMBASSY AND STATION BELIEVE CONGO EXPERIENCING CLASSIC COMMUNIST EFFORT TAKEOVER GOVERNMENT. MANY FORCES AT WORK HERE: SOVIETS * * * COMMUNIST PARTY, ETC. ALTHOUGH DIFFICULT DETERMINE MAJOR INFLUENCING FACTORS TO PREDICT OUTCOME STRUGGLE FOR POWER, DECISIVE PERIOD NOT FAR OFF. WHETHER OR NOT LUMUMBA ACTUALLY COMMIE OR JUST PLAYING COMMIE GAME TO ASSIST HIS SOLIDIFYING POWER, ANTI-WEST FORCES RAPIDLY INCREASING POWER CONGO AND THERE MAY BE LITTLE TIME LEFT IN WHICH TAKE ACTION TO AVOID ANOTHER CUBA. (CIA cable: Station Officer, Léopoldville to Director, 18/8/60)[13]

Devlin knew how not to mince his words and must have been gratified by the response:

IN HIGH QUARTERS HERE IT IS THE CLEAR-CUT CONCLUSION THAT IF LUMUMBA CONTINUES TO HOLD HIGH OFFICE THE INEVITABLE RESULT WILL AT BEST BE CHAOS AND AT WORST PAVE THE WAY TO COMMUNIST TAKEOVER OF THE CONGO WITH DISASTROUS CONSEQUENCES FOR THE PRESTIGE OF THE UN AND FOR THE INTERESTS OF THE FREE WORLD GENERALLY, CONSEQUENTLY WE CONCLUDE THAT HIS REMOVAL MUST BE AN URGENT AND PRIME OBJECTIVE AND THAT UNDER EXISTING CONDITIONS THIS SHOULD BE A HIGH PRIORITY OF OUR COVERT ACTION. (CIA cable: Dulles to Station Officer, Léopoldville, 26/8/60)[14]

Unusually for the time the cable was signed personally by CIA Director, Allen Dulles. Devlin responded with enthusiasm and ramped up the station's anti-Lumumba activities to the point where nothing less than the full destabilisation of his regime became the aim. The CIA complement was increased by one embassy-based officer, Bill Jeffers, who was rostered as Devlin's second-in-command, and a few NOCs of suitably poor provenance. Devlin wanted no-conscience, no-nonsense political fire-setters for his Operation WIZARD, the CIA's plan to destabilise fatally the administration of Patrice Lumumba.

Devlin and Park could access the full complement of 'party tricks' that both SIS and the CIA had available to accomplish this. They ranged from simple bribery, to inserting forged letters in newspapers alleging various kinds of malpractice, to spreading rumours about corruption and even allegations of witchcraft, to organising work stoppages and 'spontaneous' demonstrations against the administration, and on occasion to blowing up bridges and other key pieces of infrastructure.[15] In her address to the Royal Society of Literature, Park speaks of testing stink bombs sent to her for use in the Congo (they were designed to disperse crowds) with a colleague named only as 'Hugo' (it was probably Hugo Herbert-Jones). The aim generally of campaigns of this sort was to create a climate of fear and uncertainty, to portray an administration not in control of its own country. For example, when Lumumba hosted a meeting of foreign ministers of independent African states it was disrupted by serious rioting orchestrated by Imbrey and other NOC officers, so destroying Lumumba's plan to use the occasion to enhance his standing among the local population and fellow African leaders.[16]

At the end of August Park received a telegram from Dick White in London confirming that Macmillan had instructed her station to cooperate with the US in Project WIZARD.[17] White may not have been particularly enthusiastic but it is unlikely that his reluctance was shared in any sense by Park or by Bruce Lockhart, the archetypal robber-baron and Park's direct boss. Bruce Lockhart was pretty gung-ho. He told her that the SIS station was being augmented and to expect the arrival of another officer (John de St Jorre).

In September, with Lumumba now in office for some sixty days, President Kasavubu announced on radio that he had dismissed his Prime Minister and asked the more moderate Joseph Ileo to form a new government. Lumumba retaliated by announcing he had dismissed Kasavubu. Technically under the constitution Kasavubu had the authority to dismiss Lumumba, while Lumumba did not have the power to dismiss Kasavubu. To overcome this Lumumba appealed to parliament where he was supported by a vote in both houses, the legal status of that vote being uncertain. Park and Devlin could not have cared less about its legality or otherwise; the two concentrated on steadily increasing the pressure. They knew the key to controlling the state was the army. The ANC was a bit of a raggle-taggle force but, much like the one-eyed man in the land of the blind, it was the only one available and whoever 'owned' it owned the country. Britain was asked for money but there is no record of it offering any; however Devlin arranged for the US to provide $1,000,000 to pay soldiers' wages, to be handed over through the UN.[18] Belgium provided another $400,000 for the same purpose. Mobutu was now in control and no doubt he knew to whom he should be grateful.[19]

But even more robust actions were also under consideration. An agent codenamed WI/ROGUE was dispatched to Léopoldville under non official cover. A CIA cable stated:

* * * HEADQUARTERS [HAD]* * * INTENT TO USE HIM AS UTILITY AGENT IN ORDER TO (A) ORGANIZE AND CONDUCT A SURVEILLANCE TEAM; (B) INTERCEPT PACKAGES; (C) BLOW UP BRIDGES; AND (D) EXECUTE OTHER ASSIGNMENTS REQUIRING POSITIVE ACTION. HIS UTILIZATION IS NOT TO BE RESTRICTED TO LEOPOLDVILLE. (CIA cable: Headquarters to Station Officer, Léopoldville, October 1960)[20]

A week later, with the active encouragement of both Park and Devlin, who were beginning to despair of him, Mobutu seized power for the first time. He immediately suspended all governmental institutions but retained Kasavubu as titular head of state. Lumumba's residence was encircled by two rings of troops. The inner, UN (Ghanaian), to protect him from attack; the outer, ANC, to ensure he stayed where he was. His seventy-six days as Prime Minister were over.

The second act, 15 September to 2 December 1960; seventy-nine days

The SIS station was reinforced, as promised, by the arrival of John de St Jorre from London by way of Paris and Brazzaville, N'djili Airport being closed. It was de St Jorre's first overseas assignment for SIS. He would need to be a fast learner. Mobutu had (nominally) transferred governmental power to a College of Commissars, quickly renamed College of Commissioners on Devlin's advice, fearful of the reaction of the US Congress to the word 'commissar'. It had six members: Damien Kandolo, Lumumba's former chief of cabinet, now effectively minister for the interior, Cyrile Adoula, Justin Bomboko, Victor Nendaka, Mobutu and Albert Ndele. Most were also linked through having been educated by the Belgian White Fathers. It is worth noting that while Kandolo[i] and Nendaka[ii] were extremely close to Park[21] and Devlin[22] respectively (and received substantial amounts of money from them), that did not imply they were agents in the sense that they could be given orders that they would follow. Mobutu likewise would have had a similar relationship (though more bountiful) with the US.[23]

It wasn't totally one-way traffic, however. In retaliation for his effective incarceration Lumumba supporters and allies were making for Stanleyville by all means available in order to regroup. Antoine Gizenga, Lumumba's former

---

i KANDOLO, Damien Lopepe; Commissioner for Internal Security following the overthrow of Lumumba (1927-1978).

ii NENDAKA BIKA, Victor; Director Sûreté Nationale du Congo (Congo's Security Service) 1960-65 (1923-2002).

deputy, announced his intention to reconstitute a central government containing a number of former ministers. What the West most feared appeared to be happening, the fragmentation of the Congo. Orientale Province was now under the control of Gizenga, Katanga was under Tshombe (as a Belgian surrogate) and diamond-rich South Kasai was threatening to break away as well. That result would have been catastrophic for the remaining rump centred on Léopoldville, leaving it without any proper tax base and financially unviable.

The Soviets upped the ante by announcing that it was their intention to recognise the Stanleyville-based (Orientale) administration as the 'legitimate' government of Congo. The United Nations (UN), caught between a rock and a hard place, did not recognise Mobutu's regime *de jure* but they dealt with it on a *de facto* basis. To the extent that the UN had any sort of coherent policy it was to crush Tshombe, crush Gizenga, dissuade South Kasai from going it alone, and restore the Congo to central rule as a unitary state. Park's instructions from London were to support this. In July the minister of state, John Profumo (who would later feature in the notorious 'Profumo Affair') made it abundantly clear that Britain was opposed to secession, saying, 'a state truncated of its richest province would become just the sort of African slum in which communism would be most likely to take root'.[24] The Commissars – now officially called Commissioners – had by then taken up their positions so a cabinet of sorts existed. All were in the pay of the CIA, though according to Imbrey the sums weren't huge.[25]

But even a locked-up, marijuana-puffing Lumumba still represented a potent threat, and the day after Mobutu's coup Devlin sent a cable to Washington reporting that he was serving as an advisor to a Congolese effort to 'eliminate' Lumumba owing to his 'fear' that Lumumba might have in fact been strengthened by placing himself in UN 'custody'. Devlin concluded:

ONLY SOLUTION IS REMOVE HIM FROM SCENE SOONEST. (CIA cable: Station Officer, Léopoldville to Director, 15/08/1960)[26]

Headquarters, Langley, responded five weeks later:

WE WISH GIVE EVERY POSSIBLE SUPPORT IN ELIMINATING LUMUMBA FROM ANY POSSIBILITY OF RESUMING GOVERNMENTAL POSITION. (CIA cable: Dulles to Station Officer, Léopoldville, 21/09/1960)[27]

As each political group attempted to consolidate its position there followed several attempts on Mobutu's life, apparently orchestrated by allies of Antoine Gizenga, now holed up in Stanleyville. Park's boss, Ambassador Scott, cabled London with a suggestion that Lumumba be prosecuted for complicity in this attempted 'murder/treason'. Scott also claimed Mobuto was being irresolute in prosecuting his coup. He suggested that Lumumba be either jailed or made ambassador to Moscow, anything to get him out of the country.[28] Perhaps Mobutu was being irresolute, but he was beginning to show his steel. One of his first acts was to close the Soviet embassy. According to a KGB report cited in the Mitrokhin Archive, when the Soviets were being expelled Mobutu amused himself by putting the KGB resident, Boris Sergeyevich Voronin, up against a wall and personally conducting a mock execution.[29] This rather contradicts Scott's account, where he says the departure of the Russians took place 'without ... the slightest personal inconvenience or molestation'.[30] God bless his naivety.

At the end of the month the situation in the Congo was discussed at a meeting in the Foreign Office in London. There was little support among those present for Scott's suggested remedy. He was considered to be a generally decent sort but probably not best suited for the sort of rough-house the Congo had become.[31] Notwithstanding this, he and Park got on very well together and in later life would be firm friends.[32] The assistant head of the Africa Department, Howard Smith – a toughie if ever there was one – prepared a minute of the discussions. In the minute he referred to the difficulty caused by Lumumba's continuing presence on the scene:

> I see only two possible solutions to the problem. The first is the simple one of ensuring Lumumba's removal from the scene by killing him. This should in fact solve the problem since, as far as we can tell, Lumumba is not a leader of a movement within which there are potential successors of his quality and influence. His supporters are much less dangerous material ... My preference (though it might be expressed as a wish rather than a proposal) would be for Lumumba to be removed from the scene altogether because I fear that as long as he is about his power to do damage will only be slightly modified. (Howard Smith,[i] 28 September 1960)[33]

This was the infamous 'death' minute. A.D.M. Ross, an assistant under-secretary in the Foreign Office, appeared to agree with its broad thrust, saying:

> There is much to be said for eliminating Lumumba, but unless Mobutu can get him arrested and executed promptly, he is likely to survive and continue to plague us all. (A.D.M. Ross, 28 September 1960)[34]

Ross did go on to say that he did *not* think it wise to authorise Ambassador Scott to put pressure on Kasavubu or Mobutu to take strong-arm action against Lumumba or to ask any of Scott's colleagues to do so. The word 'colleagues' was almost certainly a coded reference to Park as the senior SIS representative. The

---

i SMITH, Sir Howard Frank Trayton, KCMG; diplomat, later Director General of MI5 1979-81 (1919-1996).

future Prime Minister, Edward Heath MP, was Lord Privy Seal (effectively a minister of state in the Foreign Office) at the time. He too was circulated with Smith's 'death' minute. He thought that Scott 'and his colleagues' should be encouraged to contact Kasavubu and Mobuto 'discreetly' in order to ascertain the lie of the land regarding the Lumumba problem.

The timing of the Foreign Office 'death' discussions is interesting because earlier in the month Dr Sydney Gottlieb, a CIA scientist, arrived in Léo armed with a lethal poison concealed in toothpaste, which Devlin was supposed to find a means of having administered to Lumumba. Gottlieb, who travelled under a pseudonym and introduced himself as 'Joe from Paris', was at the time head of the Agency's wonderfully named 'Health Alteration Committee' – it was certainly that.[35] The delivery of the poison and its intended use were confirmed in evidence given to the Church Committee.[36] What was *not* given in evidence to the committee, nor referred to by Devlin in his book, was Devlin's response. According to CIA officer, Howard Imbrey, Devlin sent the poison back with an angry note saying:

> Don't you know the Belgians are going to kill him [Lumumba], what do you want us to do? [37]

To date this is the nearest material yet unearthed of a smoking gun linking the CIA with Belgium's decision to have Lumumba murdered. It must have been among the more significant pieces of evidence *not* revealed at the Church hearings. It would be interesting to know why Imbrey wasn't called; his testimony could have been used to challenge Devlin's.

In early October the political machinations orchestrated by Park paid another dividend when twenty-five Senators and MPs from Lumumba's MNC issued a statement saying they no longer supported their leader, whom they described as 'Khrushchev's No. 1 Apostle' and 'friend of Ghanaian and Guinean leaders Nkrumah and Sekou Toure'.[38] This was a good example of Park's approach, expressed a little indiscreetly perhaps in a television interview some years later.

> Once you get really good intelligence about any group you are able to learn where the levers of power are and what one man fears of another ... you set people discreetly against one another. They destroy each other, we don't destroy them.[39]

The Belgians too were becoming increasingly active. According to Imbrey (contradicted by Devlin[40]) they were in close contact with the CIA 'though our programs were different'.[41] But perhaps not so very different; the next day the Belgian Minster for African Affairs, Count D'Aspremont Lynden, sent a telegram to the Katanga administration. He wrote that the principal objective of Belgian/Katangan policy from then on was to be the 'élimination définitive' of Patrice Lumumba 'for the sake of Katanga, Congo and Belgium'.[42]

Responding to the continuing pressure from Park (on London's instructions), Mobutu attempted to arrest Lumumba. There were reports of the UN troops guarding the deposed premier 'resisting' and talk of a 'pitched battle' followed by a stand-off between the UN and the Congolese. So for the moment at least, Lumumba was safer behind his double *cordon sanitaire*.

Safer but not necessarily safe, with all three governments tossing around the words 'eliminate' and 'remove' like snuff at an Irish wake. In fact Lumumba knew he would only be really safe if he could get to Stanleyville where his loyal deputy, Gizenga, was now in control. Gizenga had been arrested in Léo by Mobutu but his release was demanded by UN who safeguarded him until he was able to arrange his departure to Stanleyville.[43] The UN, probably not wanting a total break with Mobutu, refused to do the same for Lumumba but neither would it hand him over, so he remained stuck there. However, someone in his inner circle revealed his thinking to either Park or Devlin because on 14 November Devlin reported to CIA headquarters that he had information that Lumumba was planning to break out from his confinement:

POLITICAL FOLLOWERS IN STANLEYVILLE DESIRE THAT HE BREAKOUT OF HIS CONFINEMENT AND PROCEED TO THAT CITY BY CAR TO ENGAGE IN POLITICAL ACTIVITY***DECISION ON BREAKOUT WILL PROBABLY BE MADE SHORTLY. STATION EXPECTED TO BE ADVISED BY ———— OF [*sic*] DECISION WAS MADE***STATION HAS SEVERAL POSSIBLE ASSETS TO USE IN EVENT OF BREAKOUT. AM STUDYING SEVERAL PLANS OF ACTION. (CIA cable: Station Officer, Léopoldville to Director, 14/11/1960)[44]

On 24 November a combination of threats, bribery and bullying by Britain and the United States resulted in the United Nations General Assembly voting by fifty-three votes to twenty-four to recognise the regime of Kasavubu as the lawful government of the Congo. Three days later Kasavubu arrived back in Léopoldville in triumph wearing the gleaming white uniform of a lieutenant general to formally assume power as the official nominee of the UN. Lumumba must have known he had no time to waste. Later the same day, at around 8 p.m., he escaped from the residence during a massive thunderstorm. His destination was Stanleyville. As soon as the rumours spread about his possible escape Ambassador Scott took up the diplomatic cudgels on Park's behalf. Park (and Devlin) needed to know that their quarry was on the loose and thus within their grasp:

I telephoned the UN Headquarters and said that this was not an acceptable situation: either the UN must officially and at once declare that Lumumba was still in the official Prime Minister's residence, guarded by their troops, or else they must admit that he had escaped (with or without the connivance of his UN guards) ...

within the hour the UN troops had gone, the Congolese had searched the house and found that indeed Lumumba was not there.[45]

The operation cooked up by Park and Devlin swung into action at once. Devlin headed straight for Mobutu's headquarters to be on hand to monitor the hunt for the fugitive. Park had the much more dangerous job of travelling to the rebel stronghold of Stanleyville. In *Tumbled House*, Scott refers to 'a woman member of my staff who *happened* [author's italics] to arrive in the airport that morning' (Scott provides the date, 27 November).[46] The 'woman member' referred to was undoubtedly Park. In her own account of the incident as related to Caroline Alexander (and others), Park herself simply refers to her being on a 'fairly routine' visit to Stanleyville. She does not, for obvious reasons, link her reason for being there to Lumumba's escape.

Trouble started for Park when she arrived at the airport. As stated in the previous chapter, her handbag was searched and in it was a tape recording of a speech given in the embassy to mark Nigeria's Independence Day celebrations. The soldiers mistakenly thought it was Lumumba giving the speech and so assumed that Park was one of his supporters, reason enough to execute her. Unbelievably she managed to talk her way out of the situation and was allowed to board her flight to Stanleyville. When she arrived in the city she found a chaotic situation; foreigners were being rounded up on various pretexts, some being dragged from their beds in their nightclothes, brutalised and held in appalling conditions without water or sustenance. Park was roughed up and held in the blazing sun before being rescued by the French vice-consul. Eventually she found herself in front of a senior official whom she knew from her *tête-à-têtes* and she was able to negotiate her own release and secure some betterment in the conditions of the prisoners generally. It was a dangerous, unpleasant and risky experience and, as it turned out, it was not necessary because Lumumba never made it to the city.

This was a bitter irony, because despite the forces ranged against him Lumumba could still have made sanctuary. He had a head start and the Congo was a vast and difficult country to search. However, his pursuers knew his ultimate destination and that he would have to cross the river to make it home. So they watched the river-crossings he was most likely to use. He still could have made it, though, had the demagogue resisted the temptation of speechifying at every opportunity. But he could not: nature will out, so the fugitive halted a number of times to give passionate speeches to his supporters, some running into hours. He was to pay with his life. On the evening of 2 December Lumumba's convoy arrived at the Sankuru River, a tributary of the Congo. The ferry was moored on the far bank. A party which included Lumumba was dispatched in a rowing boat to secure the services of the ferryman to bring the rest of the party across. Lumumba returned with the ferryman to collect his wife and child when Mobutu's forces appeared from the darkness accompanied by a detachment of UN troops.

Lumumba appealed to the UN to take him into protective custody. The UN troop commander consulted with UN military command in Léopoldville by radio. Léopoldville consulted with New York. The decision was taken that since Lumumba 'had voluntarily absented himself from UN protection' he was no longer the UN's concern. Had, as a Mafioso might have put it, 'the UN been got to'? We cannot be certain; what we do know is that having voluntarily absented himself from its protection the Prime Minister would not be allowed to 'un-absent' himself. The UN detachment commander at the river bank signalled to Mobutu's men that they were free to go with their prisoner. Lumumba was now in the custody of his enemies. The second act was over.

The third act, 3 December 1960 to 17 January 1961; forty-six days

Now a prisoner, Lumumba was returned to Léopoldville by air. He appeared to have been severely beaten. Eyewitnesses (including then SIS officer John de St Jorre) spoke of him being chained in a truck while being displayed to journalists and photographers, all the time being kicked and struck with rifle butts. UN observers did not intervene. Gizenga, unable to help directly, concentrated on consolidating his control of Stanleyville and Orientale Province. Tshombe did likewise in Katanga. Mobutu decided that it would be safer to move Lumumba to the military prison in Thysville, which was considered secure. Lumumba's supporters increased the pressure to have him released, at one stage threatening to 'behead' all Europeans in Stanleyville unless Lumumba was freed within 'eighteen hours'. Mobutu refused to budge.

In January Mobutu appeared to have decided to resolve the situation. The Belgian government had promised to equip one airborne battalion and supply 120 million Belgian francs ($2.4 million) a month to him in 'aid', but only if the situation with Lumumba was resolved. The urgency for that was reinforced when word was received in Léopoldville of a mutiny in Camp Hardy in Thysville. The soldiers were demanding increased wages. To reinforce the threat they began raping the wives of their African officers. It appeared that Lumumba had been released from custody but was still in the base. Europeans in Léopoldville panicked, with many attempting to escape across the river to Brazzaville, their standard response. Mobutu, Nendaka, Bomboko and Kasavubu met the threat head-on. The four leaders went to Thysville and confronted the mutineers face to face. They persuaded them to return to barracks and to place Lumumba back behind bars.

The Belgians decided that there was no further time to waste: Lumumba must be executed. Mobutu was unwilling, for political reasons, to order the execution directly, so the Belgians exerted considerable pressure on their Katangese surrogate, Moïse Tshombe. Tshombe was not concerned about murdering Lumumba, whom he hated, but did not want to be seen to be cooperating openly with Léopoldville. Belgian African Affairs Minister, Count D'Aspremont Lynden, broke the impasse when he sent a handwritten message to Colonel Vandewalle, the former head of the Colonial secret service and now the 'secret' head of the Gendarmerie in Élizabethville (Katanga), instructing him to tell Tshombe that 'he personally insists that Lumumba be transferred to Katanga without delay'.

On 16 January sources close to Mobutu indicated that the decision had been taken to resolve the issue regarding Lumumba finally. His destination would be Élizabethville and not Bakwanga, as originally mooted. His fate would likely have been the same in either case. The next day, 17 January, Patrice Lumumba was flown to Élizabethville where he was murdered. It was the day before John F. Kennedy was inaugurated as President of the USA. Within days if not hours Devlin received a report via the CIA office in the city confirming that Patrice Lumumba was dead, executed in the presence of Katangan premier, Moïse Tshombe. Later Victor Nendaka would provide details of Lumumba's final hours, confirming that the former Prime Minister had indeed gone to his grave.[47]

Author's note: What most people consider to be the most accurate and comprehensive account of the events immediately prior to Patrice Lumumba's death is contained in Ludo De Witte's book, The Assassination of Lumumba, *on which the following is based.[48] Where other sources are used they are specifically cited.*

Damien Kandolo (Park's agent/contact) and Victor Nendaka (Devlin's agent/contact) were the two men who set in train the events leading directly to Lumumba's murder.

> It was Damien Kandolo and André Lahaye [Belgian advisor to Victor Nendaka, Chief of Security for Mobutu] who presided at the meeting, Nendaka who was in his office in Léopoldville when Kandolo came in with a note showing him the flight plan. André Lahaye came a couple of minutes later. So we found out that it was Lahaye who presided at the meeting. Kasavubu signed a letter asking Nendaka to go bring Lumumba from Thysville.[49]

Nendaka had, some months earlier, taken advantage of a power vacuum and appointed himself head of the Sûreté Nationale. The Belgians arranged for Kandolo's and Nendaka's children to be flown to Brussels, something that 'would encourage them to carry on' according to the accompanying signal.[50] It was agreed that Nendaka would be the one to go to Thysville where Lumumba was back behind bars. Lumumba trusted Nendaka, who had been his personal secretary.

When Nendaka arrived he told Lumumba that Mobutu had been deposed in a coup and that he (Nendaka) was there to escort the Prime Minister back to Léopoldville in triumph. Lumumba, while suspicious, agreed to leave the army base. Accompanied by two of his closest supporters, Maurice Mpolo and Joseph Okito, they drove to a nearby airfield; during the drive Nendaka's escort attacked Lumumba, beating him severely. They boarded an aircraft. By then Lumumba realised what lay in store. Once the aircraft took off the guards began to beat him and the others again. They were so violent that the pilot was forced to leave his cabin and warn them that they were endangering the flight. On arrival in Moanda he was transferred to the custody of Baluba guards where they boarded another aircraft for the flight to Élizabethville. During the flight he was beaten to the extent that his hair was pulled out in tufts and he was forced to swallow it.

When the plane landed in Élizabethville he was 'kicked down the steps of the aircraft'. Swedish UN troops at the airport were kept away though that would not have taken much. Everything was now happening under the supervision of Belgian officials who brought the three prisoners to a private residence, the Villa Brouwe, owned by a wealthy Belgian. The Belgians set up a security cordon, fearful of attempts to free Lumumba if the word leaked out where he was being held. Here the beatings and the torture continued for several hours. Lumumba was then visited by Tshombe and a number of his cabinet colleagues who also participated in the beatings (Tshombe's suit was described later as being 'covered in blood'). At ten o'clock that night Lumumba, Mpolo and Okito were taken from the villa and driven at high speed deep into the bush. The convoy drew up before a large tree where three separate firing squads were waiting. The police commissioner, Verschurre, a Belgian, now took charge. At his command Lumumba and the two others were shot, each by a different squad. The executions were witnessed personally by Tshombe. Lumumba apparently maintained his dignity throughout. They were buried in shallow graves but the next morning Godfried Munongo, the Katanga interior minister, ordered that the bodies be destroyed. They were exhumed by another Belgian police officer, Gerard Soete, who dismembered them, then submerged the remains in acid before finally burning them in a large pot. The whole business took two days, conducted in a drunken haze.

Patrice Lumumba was dead. He was thirty-five years old. Act three was over.

A week later, on 25 January, Park and Scott left the Congo for Washington for a round table conference with Ambassador Timberlake and Devlin and their higher-ups. The focus of the meeting was the situation in the Congo now that the 'Lumumba business' had been resolved.[51] The death of Patrice Lumumba was officially announced on 13 February 1961. Mobutu returned power to Kasavubu, who in turn appointed Mobutu commander of the army.

18

Congo 4 – Who killed Cock Robin?
Not I, said the spy, 1961

To understand the place of Daphne Park in the events surrounding the death of Patrice Lumumba, the roles of the principal players need to be established. In essence it was a quadripartite affair. The Congolese nationalist politicians in Léopoldville and Élizabethville were first in line; it was they who (figuratively and literally) pulled the trigger on the deposed Prime Minister. The government of Belgium gave the command which instigated the process. The government of the US provided the encouragement, not to say the backbone for the Belgians to act, while Britain acted as America's loyal, if junior, partner. It is important as well to understand that the situation on the ground in the Congo at the time was chaotic and inherently unpredictable. While Lumumba's reign – such as it was – might be characterised as a play in three acts as set out in the previous chapter, it was a play without central direction. It was more like a series of scenes, each acted out without much reference to what had gone before or any certainty of what was to follow, until time ran out and it eventually reached its bloody climax. Lumumba exerted an almost unholy hold on people, even on his enemies, who seemed to feel that only a stake through his heart at midnight would be sufficient to end his extraordinary influence. And finally, while Mobutu, Kandolo and Nendaka were in receipt of money from the CIA and SIS (and the French and the Belgians and God only knows who else) they were far from being pliant lapdogs ready to do their masters' bidding. These were tough, hard men, loyal only to each other if even that.

The evidence shows that physical act of killing and the gross brutality preceding it took place on the direct orders of the Katanga administration with the active participation of the province's Prime Minister, Moïse Tshombe. This happened after the captive Prime Minister had been handed over to the Katangan authorities on the orders of Joseph Mobutu, the *de facto* leader of the Congo. Belgium was the governing power right up to the day before independence and still retained significant political power and influence. Among the external governments it was best placed to determine the fate of the Prime Minister. It had the power to call off the dogs; it chose instead to unleash them. Its actions throughout were directed by its African Affairs Minister, Count D'Aspremont Lynden.

André Lahaye[i] (Léopoldville) and Lieutenant Colonel Frédéric Vanderwalle[ii] (Élizabethville) were the Count's lead executive agents on the ground. The third party in the mix, the US government, was 'once removed' (though barely) in that its actions were designed to undermine the Lumumba administration and make the country ungovernable while reserving the 'right' to take unilateral action to end Lumumba's life if the Belgians were too tardy. The US campaign was prosecuted through acts of sabotage, bribery, conspiracy and cajolement. The lead executive agent in the Congo for the US was Lawrence R. Devlin, COS/LEOPOLDVILLE. The fourth and final element, 'twice removed' so to speak, because its direct role was mainly to support the CIA's undermining campaign of sabotage, bribery, conspiracy and cajolement, was Britain and its lead executive agent on the ground, Daphne M.D. Park, H/LEOPOLDVILLE.

The Belgian government has accepted responsibility for its role, the United States partly, others noticeably less so and in varying degree.

> Some members of the government, and some Belgian actors at the time, bear an irrefutable part of the responsibility for the events that led to Patrice Lumumba's death. (Belgian Foreign Minister Louis Michel, 6 February 2002)[1]

While the Belgians, the Americans and the British were the prime external forces in the affair, they were not the only ones. The Soviet Union was active in the Congo, seeing it as a prize of great value. So were the French, their interest piqued by problems of their own in their West African colonies, one of which bordered on the Congo. The Israeli government had a bit of skin in the game too; it was keen to ensure supplies of uranium for its new nuclear bomb programme and had an active Mossad station based in its embassy which maintained close contact with Devlin and Park.[2] The Chinese, operating under the cover of the National China News Agency (NCNA), were attempting to woo the African nationalists away from their dependence on Moscow, with some success.[3] And finally there were the governments and colonial administrations of the various other countries, such as the Central African Federation (CAF), which bordered on the Congo. The number of different players, all with their own agendas, made making sense of things difficult. As John de St Jorre told this author:

> The UN, or bits of it, had their own agendas, which complicated things even further. Rajeshwar Dayal was doing one thing, the Ghanaians and Guineans something else, and the Nigerians, Malays, and a few others in the Western camp doing yet something different.[4]

---

i LAHAYE, André; agent 070a of the Sûreté de l'État (Belgian Security and Intelligence Service).

ii VANDERWALLE, Lieutenant Colonel Frédéric J.L.A.; Reserve Colonel in the Force Publique, appointed effective head of the Gendarmerie in Katanga Province in 1960 (1912-1994).

Lumumba was considered generally to be a dangerous individual by the three governments best placed to do something about him. The issue then became which of the three would take the initiative and do the needful. As mentioned above, the obvious candidate for the job was the Belgian Sûreté. The Americans were next in line; they certainly had the 'moral purpose' to initiate an assassination plot. The British were a fairly long way back. It is not at all certain that Whitehall would have felt Britain's national interests were so imperilled that instructing SIS to assassinate a foreign leader would be justified, nor indeed that the Service under White would have followed such a directive. However progress was slow and it appears that by the autumn of 1960 the Americans had lost faith in the Belgians and decided they were not to be relied upon to bite this particular bullet. The US began actively planning Lumumba's death.

One of the first things the US did was to ensure that Britain was onside with whatever it was it planned. It didn't need physical assistance from Britain; it was more that Britain, then as now, was useful in providing political cover, to make whatever it was they were planning look less like American imperialism and more like the concerted actions of a group of 'responsible countries' (*pace* Iraq and Afghanistan 2003 perhaps). In August 1960 Harold Macmillan wrote to Dick White instructing him to support the CIA efforts to destabilise the Lumumba regime.[5] A reluctant White duly passed on the instruction to Park. At around the same time (autumn) the CIA's main protagonist in this affair, Richard Bissell,[i] visited White in London. It would be reasonable to assume that the fate of Lumumba was discussed and perhaps that certain understandings were reached.[6] White would have been prepared, having been apprised of the likely Soviet threat by Bruce Lockhart as early as the previous December:

> The Soviet Bloc will want to establish a base nearer Central and Southern Africa and it is a reasonable bet that they will make a big effort on 1960 to exploit the rapidly deteriorating situation in the Congo.[7]

Park confirmed as much in her pre-independence dispatches in June 1960 when she reported that Lumumba and his deputy, Antoine Gizenga, would align the newly-independent country with Moscow.[8] Bissell's visit was an important part of the sequence of events. Bissell was the principal architect and driver of the CIA's assassination policy. As Deputy Director/Plans (head of operations) it was he who drew up the target lists and managed the political approval process, even at one stage 'loaning' his personal assistant Justin O'Donnell to see the Lumumba project through to completion. In later life after he left the Agency, Bissell bemoaned the shoddy professionalism of the CIA and even expressed

---

i BISSELL, Richard Mervin; CIA, Deputy Director/Plans (effectively director of operations) 1958-62 (1909-1994).

doubts about the wisdom and/or the necessity of the assassination policy, but he never appeared to harbour any moral qualms.

With the CIA satisfied that it had Britain on board, the hard planning commenced. The Agency was satisfied it had the US President's explicit authorisation for its actions, certainly up to the point of actually pulling the trigger. The secure and highly sensitive communications between Washington and Léopoldville, which were in furtherance of that objective, have been made available. These were given the codename PROP. PROP cables were restricted to four named senior officers in CIA headquarters and were directed solely to the station officer (Larry Devlin) in the Congo. As part of PROP the Agency dispatched Dr Sydney Gottlieb[i] to Léopoldville where he passed over to Devlin CIA-manufactured toxins to be administered to Lumumba. Devlin, according to his own account, did not want to be so directly involved in the assassination and so disposed of them. A specialist contract agent, codenamed QJ/WIN,[ii] operating under non official cover, was dispatched to the Congo to be on hand to assist in any eventual assassination. The cable informing the station of QJ/WIN's arrival was deemed by Washington to be too sensitive to be retained in the station and carried the instruction 'this dispatch should be reduced to cryptic necessary notes and destroyed after first reading'.[9] With Devlin still showing little enthusiasm for the PROP project, a decision was taken to send another CIA officer, Justin O'Donnell, to Léopoldville to progress it. O'Donnell refused, on legal and conscience grounds, to plan the assassination of the Congolese Prime Minister, causing something of a stalemate. 'Murder corrupts,' O'Donnell said.[10]

At around this time, however, there seems to have been a sea change in the CIA's position, for despite not being willing to participate in an assassination plot, O'Donnell was still posted to Léo. The most obvious conclusion is that the Belgians made it known to the Agency that it was after all prepared to do the needful and get rid of Lumumba itself, and the Agency figured that having O'Donnell on hand might facilitate that.[11] The evidence we have of Belgium's new attitude comes from the mouth of CIA officer Howard Imbrey. Imbrey was an experienced, long-established CIA officer who had been sent to Léopoldville under non-official cover. It was he who said, decades later when asked about Gottlieb's visit:

> Devlin sent the poison back with an angry note saying, '*Don't you know the Belgians are going to kill him* [Lumumba], *what do you want us to do?*' [Author's emphasis].[12]

We do know from the evidence to the Church Committee that sometime around the time of the visit planning appears to have shifted from direct 'assassination

---

i GOTTLIEB, Dr Sydney; head of the CIA's 'Health Alteration Committee' (1918-1999).
ii MANKE, Jose Marie Andre; CIA contract agent.

mode' to what might be termed 'facilitating-the-assassination-of' mode. O'Donnell was senior in rank to Devlin, but he agreed to report to his station chief (Devlin) in everything but the PROP operation. Somewhat Jesuitical in his thinking, O'Donnell had indicated that while he was not prepared to have Lumumba assassinated he was prepared to facilitate Lumumba being taken from the protection of the United Nations and into the custody of the Congolese, which amounted to more or less the same thing.[13] That then became the new Plan A, though the assassination option remained on the table and available. In effect this meant persuading Lumumba to abandon the protection offered by the UN's protective security cordon or otherwise facilitating his removal. The agent QJ/WIN spoke of the need to 'pierce Congolese and UN guards' and to enter Lumumba's residence and 'provide escort out of residence'.[14]

Britain, it seems, was quite comfortable with this as long as its hands were not actually dirtied. For a start it thought it was probably the best solution, all told. Even more importantly it was only four years after the disastrous breakdown in Anglo-US relations caused by Suez. So it quite suited Macmillan to cosy up to Washington and play the role of loyal ally. And while White was not an enthusiast for this type of action he wasn't the only person in the picture. John Bruce Lockhart was Park's Director and he took considerable interest, visiting her twice during her time in Léo. As her Director he would have had significant influence over her actions, and he was very much in the 'affirmative action' school of intelligence. On 14 November Devlin sent a cable to the CIA in Washington (reproduced in the previous chapter) informing headquarters that Lumumba was expecting to break out from UN protective custody 'shortly' and that the station expected to be informed of the exact date. On 27 November Lumumba broke out. The next day Devlin sent a cable to Washington stating:

[STATION] WORKING WITH CONGOLESE GOVERNMENT TO GET ROADS BLOCKED AND TROOPS ALERTED [BLOCK] POSSIBLE ESCAPE ROUTE.[15] (CIA cable: Station Officer, Léopoldville to Director, 28/11/1960)

This would appear to confirm that Devlin was actively involved with the Congolese in coordinating the hunt for Lumumba. It is interesting though that in his direct evidence to the Church Committee hearings he played down his role in the hunt. In his book, *Chief of Station, Congo*, he speaks of being ordered to leave the Congo in the middle of the hunt in order to brief his CIA superiors attending a CIA meeting on African affairs in Rome.[16] Park, on the other hand, 'found' herself en route to Stanleyville on the morning of Lumumba's planned escape and before he had made his breakout. This is explicitly confirmed in Scott's book, *Tumbled House*, where he gives the date she arrived in Stanleyville as 27 November.[17] Scott also recounts how, once rumours commenced that Lumumba had flown the coop, he put strong pressure on the UN locally in Léo to confirm that Lumumba had in fact escaped. It is reasonable to infer that he was doing so at Park's (and indirectly at Devlin's) request. They needed to know it was time to let loose the hunting dogs.[18]

The theory that best fits with the established facts is the both Devlin and Park had advance knowledge of Lumumba's planned escape. Devlin, who was building a close personal relationship with Mobutu, remained on hand to assist the hunt while Park headed to Stanleyville in a pincer movement, to be available should he escape the dragnet and pitch up there. The agent QJ/WIN, an enthusiast obviously, offered to proceed to Stanleyville in order to be on hand in that eventuality and to carry out his original assassination assignment.[19] Given Park's and Devlin's detailed knowledge of the scene, given their closeness to Mobutu's interior minister Damien Kandolo and his head of intelligence Victor Nendaka,[20] it seems they could not have been other than aware of the probable outcome, i.e. Lumumba's death. And that in fact this was the outcome they desired. Devlin came close to admitting that when he told the Oral History Conference:

> I saw it very likely that it would result in Lumumba's death. I never talked to the Binza group about what they were going to do, because that was their business and I was not there to decide anything. I knew what US policy was and I knew that I was not going to implement it, but I would not have tried to block it. (Larry Devlin, speaking in 2004)[21]

In his book Devlin describes Park in glowing terms as 'one of the best intelligence officers I have ever encountered'. He then goes on to follow the CIA convention of not linking any foreign intelligence service with any specific CIA activity when he says 'Daphne and I worked separately and did not have any joint operations' before concluding that the two had come 'to similar conclusions about ... Lumumba'.[22] While very gentlemanly of Devlin, this does not accord with the facts. Park was rather more direct: when asked (in 1989) by Caroline Alexander, 'Who killed Lumumba?', she answered, 'The CIA of course' (see below).

Operationally, Devlin and Park shared pretty much everything while they were in Léopoldville, meeting almost daily to swap notes.[23] They had a job to do, and doing it together made far more sense than going their separate ways. The Congo was the beginning of an intertwining professional and personal relationship spanning almost five decades. This is not necessarily an indication that they agreed on everything but suggestive certainly that they never disagreed on what really mattered, which was thwarting the Soviets. According to a former SIS officer who knew Park well, she was resolutely anti-Soviet in her attitudes, a complete Cold War warrior, and remained so throughout her career.[24]

Separately there is also the reported conversation between Daphne Park and Lord Lea which, according to a letter Lea sent to the *London Review of Books*, took place shortly before her death. Lord Lea states that Park admitted to him that she arranged Patrice Lumumba's killing in 1961 because of fears that he would ally the newly democratic country with the Soviet Union. Lea wrote: 'I mentioned the uproar surrounding Lumumba's abduction and murder, and recalled the theory that MI6 might have had something to do with it, "We did," she replied, "I organised it."'[25] There is no other evidence to support that admission. Jean Sackur, a lifelong friend of Park, says that at that time Park was on heavy medication for her cancer and that she had behaved 'strangely' in a number of ways.[26] Lord Lea's letter prompted Caroline Alexander, whose long and intimate interview with Park is the most accurate summary of her non-SIS life, to write to the magazine. In her note Alexander says that she too asked the same question of Park. The reply was, 'The CIA, of course.' Alexander finished her note by saying that 'Daphne Park, a master of inscrutability, may have said one thing to one person, and another thing to someone else. But if she were dissembling in our interview, she was indeed a brilliant actor.'[27]

In July 1961, following intense negotiations, the British ambassador, Ian Scott, the US ambassador, Claire Timberlake, and the UN representative to the Congo, Rajeshwar Dayal, were withdrawn and replaced by politically more acceptable appointees. While it was denied at the time that this was an agreed 'plan' (and Scott later denied it in his Congo memoir) it was obvious to all that it was the price for a fresh start on the ground.[28] In August a new government was formed with Kasavubu remaining as President and with Cyrille Adoula as Prime Minister, both men on the CIA's payroll. Antoine Gizenga agreed to surrender power in Stanleyville and serve as deputy Prime Minister of the central government. His fellow Lumumbist, Gbenye, would serve as minister of the interior. The Soviet Union admitted it had lost the play and recognised the new administration in a letter from Khrushchev on 31 August.

In October Park returned to London, with the award of the standard SIS gong, an OBE 'for her role in protecting UK citizens'. In reality it was recognition for courage under fire and for a job well done. A month later de St Jorre also left Léopoldville for Nairobi. Devlin stayed on until May 1963.

And that is how it turned out. The consequences for the Congo have been appalling. What by rights should be one of the world's most prosperous countries is in fact one of its poorest. It has been riven by corruption, kleptomania and more recently by a civil war of unimaginable brutality. Six million people have died to date with hundreds of thousands subjected to forcible amputation or rape, both in widespread use as weapons of war.

What Park finally thought of her work in assisting Mobutu's rise to power we do not know. She was very critical of the Belgians in private but she never publicly criticised Mobutu or his regime or expressed regret for her part. When asked by this author about Lumumba she replied that 'he was an able and dangerous man'. Devlin too was unrepentant to the end, seeing the excesses of the Mobutu regime as a price worth paying for seeing off the Soviets. He remained personally close to Mobutu until the dictator's death in 1997. He did not enjoy being tainted with the reputation of being a political assassin (nor did Park) and in 2007, a year before his death, he published his account of his time as CIA station chief in the Congo. Devlin denies being an agent in Lumumba's death, but in that he is only technically correct. Neither Park nor Devlin pulled the trigger or gave the order to the firing squad, but they conspired to bring about a situation where the most logical, indeed the only possible outcome would be the death of Patrice Lumumba.

In a somewhat ironic footnote to history, the former SIS officer John de St Jorre, Park's number two in Léopoldville, was hired as ghost writer for Devlin's Congo memoir. De St Jorre describes Devlin as being 'anxious' to complete the work, to get his side of the story on the record. His emphysema was well advanced by the stage and he was connected to a portable breathing apparatus twenty-four hours a day, but that did not stop him enjoying a cocktail or two to help with the reminiscences. Interestingly, when de St Jorre challenged Devlin's recollections of some events he found the former CIA man reluctant to change anything, in part because he had cleared the contents with the CIA (something he did not acknowledge in his text) and in part because he had decided that this was how he wanted it told. 'That is not how I recall it,' he would say when challenged.[29]

Finally, some comments about Park and her period in the Congo. One comes from a close friend and former academic colleague, Barbara Harvey, of Somerville College:

> In answer to a question from me, Daphne claimed she never did anything of which she was ashamed. But I thought that she would have been capable of *anything* if duty demanded.[30]

And from lifelong friend Jean Sackur:

> At the end of the day Daphne was a soldier, if she was ordered to do something, she would have done it.[31]

And from Park herself:

> Yes, I have been involved in death, but I cannot speak about that.[32]

19

Bewitched, bothered, bewildered ... and betrayed, 1962-64

Members of a nation's Intelligence Service (its spies), of whatever persuasion, typically share a number of character traits. Perhaps the most common is that they are invariably imbued with a love of their country coupled with an instinct for public service and a desire to influence, even if in a limited way, their country's decisions and policies. Evidence of the presence of those attributes would have been sought as part of their recruitment process. Spies play a key part in their country's defences, reaching far beyond its borders to detect and deflect hostile actions. For this reason entry to almost every nation's foreign espionage service is open only to those who are its citizens from birth. The Soviet Union's KGB emblem of 'the sword and shield' captures this aspect well; the shield to defend (in the KGB's case the Party) and the sword to smite down its enemies. It follows therefore that the most heinous crime a member of an intelligence service can be suspected of, is that he or she has gone from being a keeper of their service's secrets to being a betrayer of them. No other crime even comes close, and the punishment reflects that. For the KGB invariably it was death; for the CIA it was life imprisonment without the possibility of parole; for SIS it was the longest prison term ever imposed in Britain for any crime.

In 1964 an SIS counterintelligence officer, detailed to investigate the loyalty of his colleagues as part of the most in-depth search for a traitor ever conducted by Britain's security services, determined that Daphne Park was a Soviet agent, a betrayer. Unbeknownst to her, Park now faced the greatest threat to everything she held dear. If the suspicion were elevated to the status of a formal Security Service investigation then even if no proof of guilt was discovered (and it could not be discovered because she was not a traitor), her career, her reputation, her friendships would be at risk as never before.

To understand how this situation came about we must first go back to the 1960s, to the decade of rock 'n roll, of revolution and of betrayal. For the people of Britain the previous decade, the 1950s, could be characterised as a perplexing time. They were perplexed by how slow and painful was the recovery from the war, with food rationing continuing for almost ten years after its end, which 'we had *bloody* won, thank you'. Perplexed by how their Empire, that great bulwark in their lives, seemed to be disappearing under the very waves over which Britannia was supposed to rule forever; perplexed because they didn't really believe Harold Macmillan when he told them that 'they'd never had it so good'.

Then the 'swinging sixties' came. Being British was suddenly hip, as the country basked in a global pop-driven cultural renaissance. The Beatles, The Stones, Carnaby Street, Cilla, The Kinks, 'You'll Never Walk Alone' – on it went and on. Sixties Britain saw the term 'the permissive society' thrillingly enter conversations as sex went from being the unmentionable 'below the waist' to being the subject of seemingly endless, ever-more frank, television and radio discussions, newspaper and magazine articles. Sixties Britain was the era of the *Lady Chatterley's Lover* obscenity trial which enthralled the chattering classes with its end-of-epoch-defining remark to a bemused jury: 'is it a book that you would even wish your wife or your servants to read?'[1] This was when Sean Connery lit up our cinema screens as James Bond in *Dr No*, a candidate for the first ever global cross-media cultural phenomenon and certainly the first to feature such an overt mix of sex, sadism and snobbery. But it wasn't just talk; because the icing on the cake was the Pill. Soon everyone was *doing it* as sexual intercourse went from being the preserve of the marriage-bed to the rear seat of the Mini. Yet the sixties was also a time of conformity and uniformity, when the forces of conservatism, rallied by the revanchist opinion formers of the *Mail*, *Express* and *Times* made their stand before retiring bloodied and bowed, to fight another day perhaps but not without taking some notable scalps along the way.

For the Service this was a lesson in not believing your own PR, for enamoured as the world may have been with Bond and the idea of an omnipotent British secret service, the reality was chillingly different. Within SIS the 1960s will never be described as the Service's finest hour. For behind Broadway's opaque facade was a whiff of treachery and decay, and much, much more than a whiff of suspicion.

All that lay ahead. It was now January 1962 and Park was back in London, back from the Congo. She had settled into her new flat in 15A Wimpole Street in Marylebone, a better part of town than Epsom and much closer to Broadway. Life was good. She knew she had done well and had her OBE to show for it, an honour not handed out like sweets at a children's party, and particularly not to one of the tiny number of women members of the Intelligence Branch.[2] Park was a Production Officer (P Officer), which involved handling the flow of traffic between Head Office sections and her stations and representing each to the other, obtaining resources, writing briefs and submissions or forwarding the latter from the stations, all under the supervision of her Director, Godfrey 'Paul' Paulson.[i]

i PAULSON, Godfrey Martin Ellis; HM Forces, SIS, VENICE, SINGAPORE, H/BEIRUT, H/ROME, C/NORTHERN AREA, D/MIDDLE EAST & AFRICA, later consul-general in Nice (1908-1990).

Park was still in D/P2 (Directorate of Production/Africa), which had since come under the direction of the well established robber-baron Paulson, known to be another staunch defender of Philby. Paulson had recently returned from the job of H/BEIRUT, where Philby, who had not yet bolted, was regarded by Paulson 'as being a useful asset'.[3]

Park's domain was the West and Central African stations. West Africa included Ghana, Nigeria, the Gambia, Sierra Leone and another dozen or so smaller nations, where few if any would have boasted SIS stations. Central Africa included the Congo and its neighbours in the soon-to-be-abolished Central African Federation (the two Rhodesias and Nyasaland), Angola, Cameroon and half a dozen other smaller entities, again few would have had any permanent SIS presence. But between the two there were enough big beasts to matter. Since her clutch of stations included Léopoldville she took a particular interest in how her replacement, Bunny Pantcheff, was getting along and whether his second-in-command, John Sackur,[i] was coming up to scratch. Park knew Sackur from West Berlin and she had scant regard for him. Later, after his divorce, she used say to his wife Jean:

The best thing the Service got from hiring John was having you for his wife.[4]

The P Officer's job was to back up her or his stations in Head Office. They had no controlling function, so were more staff than line, the heads of station being directly responsible to their Directors. But of course they could sometimes guide or influence their heads of station or tip them off if something they were doing was proving unpopular back at the ranch. She was not their senior, certainly not their superior, the whole idea was that the heads of station 'did their own thing' subject only to the dictates of their Director/Controller, which the cannier learned, with practice, how to circumvent. That said, it would be a foolish head of station who disregarded what his/her P Officer had to say, though the bolder among them might then set about refuting or disregarding it.[5]

Africa was now a major preoccupation for SIS. There is some dispute about whether this enthusiasm was shared by Dick White. Tom Bower suggests it was not,[6] but sources spoken to by this author do not agree with that assessment and claim that White was in fact quite consumed by events on the continent.[7] The former colonies were now independent states, or in the process of becoming so, and enjoyed flexing their foreign policy muscles. Some, like Ghana, had moved out of the British orbit and aligned themselves with Moscow. Others, like Kenya and Nigeria, remained loyal. But all had to be minded, to a greater or lesser extent. And this had to be done in the teeth of continuing interference from the Commonwealth Relations Office (CRO).

---

i SACKUR, Christopher John; SIS, BERLIN, LEOPOLDVILLE, SALISBURY (1933-1986).

For Park this reached its nadir in pre-UDI Rhodesia when the CRO permitted the establishment of an SIS station in Salisbury but demanded, and got, a veto over its targeting. It was thus able to prevent the penetration of the Rhodesian National Front by the local station. This meant that Broadway (and so White-hall) was ignorant about the advanced planning for the Unilateral Declaration of Independence and were caught by surprise when it took place three years later.[8]

Yet even as Park got stuck in to her new responsibilities she could not help but realise that something was seriously amiss. She had been in Léopoldville when news of George Blake's arrest broke and was deeply affected by it. She knew him well and her identity as an intelligence officer was certainly compromised, but she had by this stage established herself in D/P2 so her career prospects remained undimmed. But the scale of Blake's betrayal had left her shaken. Now she would be forced to confront the cancer that had been eating away at SIS's core. It is still difficult to sequence the series of events that so shook SIS and the rest of the intelligence establishment in the first half of that decade because many had quite a long tail, but the Blake episode, though not the first in time, was arguably that with the most savage impact.

Everyone who was in SIS at the time remembers when they first heard about George Blake's betrayal, the Monday morning in April 1961 when two 'deci-pher-yourself' telegrams arrived from Broadway carrying the stark words:

[Telegram 1] THE NAME IN THE FOLLOWING TELEGRAM IS A TRAITOR
[Telegram 2] GEORGE BLAKE

For those who were not in the Service it is difficult to imagine the destructive impact of that message. Blake wasn't as senior nor as 'establishment' as Philby, he was never slated to become Chief, but internally and certainly to mid-ranking staff, his defection was the more shocking. Confirmation of Philby's betrayal had seeped into SIS's bloodstream like a slow poison. By the time he was officially revealed for what he was, he was twelve years out of the Service. To many he was history. But Blake was current, Blake was a thunderbolt. One day he was the well-liked, well-regarded, tall, urbane, professional officer 'who'd done bloody well in North Korea in those dreadful camps'; the next the detestable one-of-our-own who had gone over to the enemy. The damage to SIS operations was grave, for those more directly involved it was traumatic.

According to Blake's own account, he betrayed the identities of hundreds of agents inside East Germany, wiping out SIS's complete war intentions intelli-gence net. The Berlin Tunnel, probably SIS's finest technical achievement to that point, was betrayed even before it became operational. And the Service's entire order-of-battle, its sources, methods and priorities were presented to the Soviets on a plate.[9] For years afterwards officers withdrawing files from the registry would see their covers stamped with the legend 'COMPROMISED BY BLAKE' (or Philby).[10]

John Quine, one of Blake's interrogators, was given the unenviable job of rating each member of the Intelligence Branch as either compromised, 'CRUET RED', or uncompromised, 'CRUET GREEN'. As a reward for completing this task Quine earned the internal sobriquet 'Quine the Swine'.[11] Some of those graded 'Red' by Quine decided to leave at once, while others, such as John Sackur, hung on for a while before finally throwing in the towel. Sackur had been scheduled to go to the Middle East on anti-Soviet operations, and had completed a course in Arabic in Durham University in preparation. Quine's 'Red' rating of him ended that plan and the disgruntled officer was instead sent to Africa.[12] This was a peculiar decision given that most IB officers tended to be known or at least suspected by the KGB after a few years service and it did not seem to affect their careers.[13]

Even today, fifty years on, the sense of betrayal among those then present is palpable. For White, the new broom, the man sent into clean up SIS, it was a particularly bad day in the office. One of the factors upsetting him was that a regulation existed in SIS at the time which stipulated that an officer freed from a period in enemy captivity should not be allowed to return into a sensitive post, at least not until after a lengthy period of quarantine. White had to carry the can for that omission. If that was all it was, then that is all it would have been, but there was more bad news to come.

The arrest of Blake was followed by the arrest the following year of John Vassall,[i] a clerk in the Admiralty. In 1954, the same year as Park, Vassall had been assigned to Moscow as an assistant to the naval attaché. His sexual orientation was not of course officially known, nor could it have been, homosexual acts being a criminal offence in the UK at that time. Sigmund Mikhailsky was a locally employed embassy interpreter and unofficially a provider of sexual services (to both genders), black-marketeer and general fixer. He had been inserted in to the embassy by the KGB. Mikhailsky befriended Vassall and quickly established his sexual orientation. Next he commenced a homosexual affair with the clerk. With everything now in place, General Oleg M. Gribanov,[ii] head of the KGB 2nd Chief Directorate and a skilled practitioner in sexual blackmail, decided to bait his honey-trap.

Mikhailsky introduced Vassall to some new 'friends' who invited him to join them for dinner in a restaurant near the Bolshoi. Mikhailsky made his excuses

---

i VASSALL, William John Christopher; British Admiralty (KGB) (1924-1996).
ii GRIBANOV, General Oleg Mikhailovich; KGB (1915-1992).

and did not join them. On arrival in the restaurant Vassall was escorted into a private dining room. He was, according to his confession, plied with 'strong brandy' and soon the dinner turned into a drink-fuelled homosexual orgy. A few days later Vassall was invited to the flat of a Russian officer, again introduced to him by Mikhailsky; the officer excused himself and two men entered the room. The attaché was first of all threatened with jail in Moscow, then with having the photographs sent to his mother, and finally to his employers and the police. Rumours suggest that the person Vassall least wished to know of his condition was the ambassador's wife, of whom he was something of a favourite (in his own eyes). He caved in without too much argument, it seems, agreeing to spy for the KGB. He commenced at once, passing over whatever secret material he could lay his hands on in the embassy. When he returned to Britain in July 1956 he continued on for a total of seven years passing over a wide array of classified material, mostly related to naval weapons development.

However in 1962 the seemingly inevitable occurred and he was betrayed by a fellow betrayer, a CIA agent in the KGB. Vassall was arrested, charged, convicted and sentenced to eighteen years' imprisonment. What made his arrest so fascinating, apart from the espionage angle, was his homosexuality and his connections, which were fairly tangential, to some of the upper echelons in British society, to 'toffs' in other words. This enabled the press to speak of honey-traps in plush Moscow restaurants, of homosexual orgies in Mayfair flats and squalid debauchery in luxurious Tuscany villas. Countless column inches were devoted to the idea of this 'ring of queers' penetrating the upper reaches of society with God only knew what consequences for public morals.

Within the Service the betrayal by Vassall, while regrettable, was not seen as particularly catastrophic, more as the price one paid for being in the game. For a start Vassall wasn't SIS, but more importantly, as Nicholas Elliott put it to John Le Carré:

Ah well *Vassall* – well he wasn't top league was he?[14]

Then, in January 1963, as if scripted, someone who was most definitely 'top league' was revealed to have been a betrayer. Kim Philby bolted. The bolter had been living in Beirut working for the *Observer* newspaper whose editor David Astor was a long-term SIS collaborator. All the while Philby was on a retainer from SIS which 'saw him as a useful asset'.[15] The immediate cause of his decision to flee was a visit to the city by Elliott, one of his closest friends and – up to then – supporters. Elliott left Philby in no doubt but that the game was up and that Philby was staring at a deeply unpleasant future. Elliott offered him immunity from prosecution but only on condition that Philby cooperated fully with his interrogators and spilt the beans totally, giving up everything he knew about

Soviet intelligence. If at any point SIS decided that he was withholding it would be free to institute criminal proceedings, in which case he could expect the same sort of 'lock him up and throw away the key' sentence as had been visited on George Blake.

There has been some speculation that White, who had not favoured charging Blake in the first instance, and certainly did not want a repeat performance in the Old Bailey, engineered matters so that Philby felt he had no choice but to bolt. SIS sources spoken to by this author discount that and claim it was a case of 'cock-up rather than conspiracy'. But in any event, pushed or not, bolt the bolter did. A few days after he confessed his betrayal to Elliott, he disappeared from Beirut on board the Soviet freighter, the *Dolmatova*. On 1 July the Soviet authorities issued a statement announcing his arrival. A month later they announced he was receiving 'political asylum' and being granted Soviet citizenship.

What made the Philby business so much worse was that the Service was discovered to have been lying about him. Attempting to cover up mistakes and misdeeds is an institutional norm and SIS was no different in that regard. But the fact of it being an organisation that operated in secret arguably placed upon it a greater obligation to own up to any mistakes it made. In recognition of this SIS had always made great play of its honesty, claiming that its straight dealing was the crux of its relationship with Whitehall.[16] This was patently untrue: 'old' SIS would deny that the sun rose in the east if it thought it could get away with it. So, true to form, it hadn't owned up over Philby. It played down his importance on one hand, denying that he was one of those who might ultimately have been in the frame for the job of Chief, while mounting a sustained, and for a period a successful, defence of his reputation on the other. Even when it finally knew beyond doubt of his betrayal it didn't come clean. It concealed the fact that Menzies (about to retire) and Sinclair (about to succeed him) had agreed that Philby be appointed as number three in the Service with a view to succeeding to the Chief's slot eventually. The move was prevented (peculiarly on grounds of intuition) by Patrick Reilly,[i] the noted diplomat who had extensive connections with British Intelligence and was highly regarded within the Foreign Office. Reilly recommended that Dick White, then Deputy Director-General of MI5, be appointed in Philby's place. That was blocked by Menzies and Sinclair who managed to install Easton as number three with rights of succession.[17] But, as has been shown previously, that piece of succession planning came unstuck after the Suez affair.

i REILLY, Sir Patrick D'Arcy, GCMG; diplomat (1909-1999). Reilly was the (effective) Foreign Office representative to SIS at a critical period during the Second World War. He also served as chairman of the Joint Intelligence Council before becoming ambassador to Moscow in 1957 and Paris in 1965.

As bad again was Elliott telling Philby he need only confess to his misdeeds 'up to 1949', thus excluding those committed on US soil and avoiding the possibility of him being extradited to face trial in the US with attendant odium. White (C) then wrote to the FBI's Hoover, claiming that Philby had ceased spying for the Russians in 1946, and persuaded the head of MI5, Sir Roger Hollis, to co-sign the letter.

> In our judgement [Philby's] statement of the association with the RIS [Russian Intelligence Service] is substantially true. It accords with all the available evidence in our possession and we have no evidence pointing to a continuation of his activities on behalf of the RIS after 1946, save in the isolated incidence of Maclean. If this is so it will follow that damage to the United States' interests will have been confined to the period of the Second World War.[18]

The truth was that the six-year period from 1945 to 1951 was when Philby did by far the greatest damage. The White/Hollis letter was patently a falsehood. Coming clean to the Americans about the true extent of Philby's betrayals would have enabled the CIA to identify and review the operations compromised by the betrayer (twenty-five major operations at least, according to one CIA officer quoted in Ben Macintyre's book, *A Spy Among Friends*) and allowed the Agency to take whatever steps might be open to it to ameliorate any damage. Not doing so had the reverse effect. But that was not the SIS priority; all that mattered was to cover up its mistakes. For a Service that habitually lied to its own government, lying to the US was hardly going to cause it sleepless nights. For the Americans, though, it was the final straw. SIS's supporters in the CIA, rapidly diminishing in numbers anyway, were mortified, exposed as naive Anglophiles, placing their trust in an ally who was simply not to be believed. While the increasing number of Anglophobes, including Hoover, who was never a particular friend to Britain anyway (the dislike was mutual),[19] were confirmed in their prejudices. For White it was one more mountain to climb. Trips across the Atlantic to explain to an increasingly sceptical CIA about the latest British traitor were becoming almost routine.

And there matters might have mouldered away but for the arrival on the scene of Michael Goleniewski[i] and Anatoli Golitsyn,[ii] for the traffic in betrayals is rarely in one direction. Goleniewski (UB/Polish Intelligence) betrayed Blake. He also betrayed a clerk who worked in the Underwater Weapons Establishment in Portland, called Harry Haughton, and his girlfriend/co-conspirator, Ethel 'Bunty' Gee. Golitsyn (a KGB officer) was Vassall's betrayer and provided enough information to confirm Philby's treachery ('There is a ring of five spies recruited

i GOLENIEWSKI, Michael, codenamed 'SNIPER' and 'LAVINIA'; UB (SIS) (1922-1993).
ii GOLITSYN, Anatoli Mikhailovich, KGB (CIA) (1926-).

in Cambridge before the war'). The actual catalyst for Philby's uncovering was a report to MI5 from an old, but now 'reformed', Marxist friend called Flora Solomon. She was outraged by the spy's treatment of his wife Aileen, whom she had introduced to Philby, and so told MI5 about his attempt to recruit her all those years ago. Philby wasn't the first, nor the last, spy to be undone by being unable to keep his flies buttoned.

But Golitsyn went further. Prior to his defection he had spent sixteen years in the KGB's strategic planning department which had given him a detailed overview of the organisation's global strategy. There was something akin to panic in KGB ranks when he defected. Fifty-four KGB residencies were ordered to report to Moscow on the implications for their local operations. On arrival in the US, Golitsyn was interviewed by James Jesus Angleton,[i] the omnipotent head of CIA counterintelligence. In confirming the existence of the five spies (the Cambridge Ring) he lit the blue touch-paper on the great KGB 'strategic deception' conspiracy. Angleton knew Philby from the Second World War, from the time when he had served in London with the OSS. He had been among those most seduced by Philby's charm (though he later denied it) and who felt personally the most let down, scalded in fact. When Golitsyn went on to tell Angleton of this 'strategic deception' initiative, of which Philby was but one small part, Angleton seized upon it. Something seemed to fuse inside him as he listened to Golitsyn outline how the KGB had recruited key intellectuals, not just in Cambridge, but in the top universities in Britain and the US in the 1930s and how those 'super-sleepers' were now holding key positions in Western intelligence services and government administrations. 'The CIA,' Golitsyn declared dramatically, 'has been penetrated and its most significant operations are being controlled from Moscow.' No defectors, unless personally approved by him, were to be trusted; all should be considered 'plants'. As cottage industries go, Golitsyn's 'strategic deception' play was up there with the best of them.

Was this the Holy Grail that Angleton had been searching for all his life? Quite probably, for in retrospect it seems he had discovered an epic cause to which he could devote himself body and soul. If someone as clever as *he* was could be fooled, he reasoned, then it was axiomatic that *everyone* was fooled. Angleton was quite extraordinarily clever, but like more than a few such he had precious little nous when it came to day-to-day reality. He launched into a decade and a half long mole hunt codenamed HONETOL, a near-acronym of *Ho*over and A*natoli* Golitsyn.[20] In so doing Angleton almost wrecked the institution he was sworn to protect, caused the premature ending of the careers of hundreds of perfectly innocent CIA officers, did enormous damage to the Agency's operational capability, and stopped only when he was summarily dismissed.

i ANGLETON, James Jesus; OSS, CIA (1917-1987).

Given that it had all started with Blake and Philby, the Golitsyn/Angleton disease soon spread across the ocean. Almost overnight the prevailing attitude in London went from one of 'denying everything' to one of 'denouncing everyone'; the 'traitors whoever they may be shall be rooted out'.[21] Keen to internationalise his cottage industry, Golitsyn came to London in 1962 and after pressure from Angleton was given access to a number of MI5 files. He quickly drew up a list of 'suspects', mainly MI5 but SIS did not escape unscathed. Naturally most suspects were juicily senior; senior as in Harold Wilson, the Labour Party leader and future Prime Minister, senior as in Roger Hollis, head of MI5 and Graham Mitchell, his deputy. Michael Hanley, another future head of MI5, was also to come under suspicion as did many more, about forty all told.[22]

The problem was that Golitsyn's accusations were, in a practical sense, almost impossible to *disprove*. The slightest inconsistency in an officer's career could be seized on as 'proof' of their infidelity. Officers in both the UK and US who dismissed the theory as 'unproven fantasy' could very quickly find their own loyalty questioned. For example, his accusers declared that Hollis had spent the early part of his career in China, where he had been 'got to'. The KGB 'had assassinated Labour Party leader Hugh Gaitskell'[i] in order to pave the way for their 'stooge Wilson', they declared. They went further, claiming that Gaitskell too had been a traitor (why then the KGB thought it necessary to murder one traitor, Gaitskell, to make way for another, Wilson, was not explained).

In Mitchell's case so certain (wrongly) were his accusers of his guilt that they arranged a 'barium meal'. This is an established counterespionage technique whereby material is shown to a suspect in the hope it will cause them to hotfoot it to their handler where they can be caught in the act. Hollis passed on a piece of 'hot' intelligence to Mitchell, such that he and the investigators were certain that Mitchell would hotfoot it to his 'KGB controller'.[23] Fearful that its own watchers would be known to Mitchell, MI5 asked SIS for assistance in springing the trap. The following account is provided by one of the former SIS officers involved:

> We were asked to establish a surveillance team which watched Mitchell on his way home from the office, reporting having been arranged for him to see which the [MI5] team were confident would make him call for a contact with his [KGB] case officer. Of course he knew the MI5 watchers so we were called in to assist.[24]

The trap was never sprung. Mitchell did not hotfoot it to anywhere, and was eventually cleared. For while Golitsyn accused, he did not, apart from the initial

---

i GAITSKELL, Hugh Todd Naylor, CBE, PC; politician (1906-1963). Gaitskell died from lupus; those with a penchant for conspiracy claimed his condition was a result of deliberate infection by the Soviets.

revelations in his 'intelligence dowry', provide proof. As one MI5 interrogator noted, 'his knowledge ranges over a wide field but nowhere has it any great depth'.[25] Even Peter Wright, who rivalled Angleton in the intensity of his belief in the mole theory, admitted that 'the vast majority of Golitsyn's material was tantalisingly imprecise, it often appeared true as far as it went, then faded into ambiguity ....'[26]

In 1964 White established a dedicated Directorate of Counterintelligence & Security (D/CIS) in SIS under Maurice Oldfield.[i] He also agreed to the creation of a joint MI5/SIS working group called FLUENCY to investigate the Golitsyn/ Angleton accusations. The group had five members drawn from MI5 and two initially from SIS, others would join later.[27] Arthur Martin of MI5 was its operational boss. This was when Park entered the picture. One of the SIS officers attached to the FLUENCY investigation was Bunny Pantcheff, her replacement in Léopoldville. Another was John Sackur, who had been Pantcheff's number two in the Léo station. Pantcheff had returned to London from Léo and had been drawn into the orbit of the mole hunt. He was assigned to work with Peter Wright[ii] of MI5. Wright was arguably MI5's most ardent believer in the Golitsyn/Angleton theory. According to the author Nigel West, Wright and Pantcheff started with the file of Walter Krivitsky, a pre-war Soviet defector.[28] Krivitsky had tantalisingly identified the *fact* of Maclean's and Philby's betrayal but not in enough detail for either betrayer to be identified. This was despite Krivitsky travelling to Britain from America in 1940 where he was questioned in detail by MI5's Jane Archer.[29]

Park was only sixteen when Krivitsky defected in 1937[30] and therefore she could not have featured in his testimony. Next they turned to the case of a retired SIS officer, Dick Ellis. Ellis was interrogated by Wright and Pantcheff and report-edly admitted to passing information to the German *Abwehr* while he was posted to Paris before the Second World War. He did this for money, he claimed, and he wouldn't have been the first pre-war SIS officer to have augmented his meagre living by unapproved means. Ellis refused absolutely to concede that after the war he had spied for the Russians, though Wright and Pantcheff reported that that was their conclusion and wrote it up as such.[31]

It appears that sometime after that Pantcheff identified something about Park that made him suspicious, something that convinced him that she had been turned and was a Soviet agent. What the basis for that belief was is not known and Wright's book (*Spycatcher*) does not contain anything that

---

i OLDFIELD, Sir Maurice, GCMG, CBE; Intelligence Corps, SIS, SINGAPORE, C/FAR EAST, H/WASHINGTON, D/CIS (Counterintelligence and Security), VCSS, Chief 1973-78, later Security Coordinator Northern Ireland (1915-1981).

ii WRIGHT, Peter Maurice; MI5, Assistant Director, author of *Spycatcher* (1916-1995) .

might help other than Park's attendance at the Joint Services School for Linguistics (JSSL) at Cambridge. She had been posted there in 1951 to be taught Russian in advance of her Moscow posting. According to Wright, MI5 viewed the School as a KGB recruiting ground. In his book he claims that this was confirmed by Golitsyn who studied the files of those who had attended in an effort to pick out any possible KGB agents, so perhaps it was he who first pointed the finger.[32] Certainly the KGB would have been aware of the JSSL and its purpose from George Blake, who attended, and it would be natural to assume that it was on its target list. Attendance at the school was hardly a cause for suspicion of itself though, given that five thousand *kursanty* (language cadets) had passed through its doors.[33] However, if suspicion was subsequently aroused then such were the times that the simple fact of a person's attendance might well have served as a form of corroborating 'evidence'. On the other hand Christopher Andrew's official history of MI5 (*Defence of the Realm*) does not contain any references to MI5 suspicions about the JSSL being penetrated by the KGB.

Another pointer, in Park's case, could have been Philby's bolt from Beirut. When MI5 learned that he had escaped from the city it became convinced that he had been tipped off by yet another mole in SIS, starting a hunt that was to last for a further two decades.[34] Nicholas Elliott was the initial suspect and he was interviewed at length by MI5's Arthur Martin before being cleared, 'just about'.[35] Elliott was now Park's superior, having been appointed Deputy-Director Middle East and Africa. Elliott could never be described as closemouthed. Did he perhaps blab to Park about the real reason for his trip to Beirut, or did Pantcheff just think that he might have? Elliott certainly blabbed it to the Colchesters, Halsey[i] (H/ATHENS) and his wife Roxanne, when he broke his journey to Beirut in Athens.[36] Did Pantcheff surmise that Park too knew the real purpose of Elliott's visit to the city and so 'alerted' her 'KGB handler' in the same way MI5 had hoped Mitchell would after being fed his 'barium meal'?

Or it is possible that Golitsyn had heard some rumour about a KGB recruitment of a British source around the time Park was stationed in Moscow? The KGB had made one successful recruitment certainly, that of John Vassall, but Park's unusual behaviour (referred to earlier in the chapters on Moscow) might well have been enough, when recalled later, to have raised doubts about her loyalty.[37] Whatever the reason, Pantcheff was suspicious, as the following account – provided by an SIS officer who served contemporaneously with Pantcheff – illustrates:

---

i COLCHESTER, Halsey, CMG, OBE; SIS, H/ZURICH, H/ATHENS, H/PARIS (1918-1995). Following retirement from SIS in 1972 he was ordained into the priesthood, becoming vicar of Great and Little Tew in Oxfordshire.

Daphne herself fell under serious suspicion. I recall, when stationed in ——, being taken aside on a lonely road in —— by a visiting member of the 'Golitsyn cabal' to be warned that she was almost certainly a KGB agent and that he firmly believed that she was.[38]

The visiting member dropping this bombshell turned out to be none other than Theodore 'Bunny' Pantcheff.

Theodore Xenophon Pantcheff aka 'Bunny' was much liked by those who worked under him, a warm and loveable person except for those, like me, who distrusted his 'born again' zealot commitment to the anti-com struggle and distrusted his judgement. He was altogether too keen on spying for my taste. It was Bunny who stopped me on that lonely road in —— to tell me that Daphne was almost certainly a KGB agent. I doubt whether she knew of these suspicions at the time and think it most unlikely that she was confronted with them. The dangerous circumstance in all these cases, whether Wilson, Hollis, Mitchell, Daphne, was that those who harboured those suspicions were convinced of the Golitsyn/Angleton message. Thus they knew, for a certainty, that there must be spies at all levels occupied by those who were old enough to have been 'thirties recruits. Given that starting base they had no need of evidence to identify a suspect, it was more a question of who was *not* a spy and that anyone who came within certain parameters and could not convincingly be eliminated must be brought into consideration. Then they dug for material to fill out the case. Something totally innocent in Daphne's history, as in Hollis's or Wilson's or Gaitskell's, provided them with tenuous pieces of straw to which they clung. It was a wild time![39]

Pantcheff, while making it clear his belief that Park had been turned, did not, however, reveal the source of the information that led to that conclusion nor did he indicate with whom else he shared his suspicions. Jean Sackur, whose husband, John, worked under Pantcheff in Léo, and who knew Pantcheff well, says that never, either by word or deed, did he as much as hint to her that he had any suspicions about Park. That suggests that the suspicion arose after Pantcheff returned to London in 1963 and joined the FLUENCY team.

A former SIS counterintelligence officer from that period told this author that Pantcheff and Co thought that the Russians 'were ten feet tall' and were total espionage aces. Nothing would do for them but a full 'clean out of the traitors'.[40] Another told of encountering 'grizzled old officers coming in and out of the lifts in Head Office, none of whom would ever hint at what they were doing'.[41] In 1969 Pantcheff was officially 'seconded' to the Ministry of Defence.[42] This was probably to continue his work on FLUENCY. Christopher Phillpotts had succeeded Maurice Oldfield as head of Counterintelligence & Security (CIS). Phillpotts was a convinced molehunter and another Angleton disciple. As head of CIS Phillpotts was responsible for a number of SIS officers, including Andrew King, having their employment terminated on grounds of 'suspicion'. Later Pantcheff worked with MI5 assisting that organisation to develop its counter-IRA capability as the troubles broke out in Northern Ireland.[43] In 1977 Pantcheff was made CMG and appointed Controller/Africa. He retired the same year as Park, in 1979. Whether he still held the same views about her is not known.

What is perhaps the most poignant aspect of the affair is that these suspicions were held by a man whom Park held in such high regard. Julian 'Jules' Harston[i] was a former SIS officer who succeeded Park in Hanoi (1973):

> Daphne was very kind to me and gave me a lot of help when I was preparing to go to Hanoi in 1973. She helped not just because of my posting but because I was a protégé of Bunny Pantcheff, *whom she adored and trusted* [author's emphasis].[44]

In conversation with this author Daphne Park was vehement in her rejection of what she occasionally referred to as the 'John Le Carré' view of SIS, as a place of 'intrigue, betrayal and double-dealing'. Park's SIS was a place of loyalty; loyalty to one's colleagues, to one's agents in the field and above all to one's country. Had she been confronted with Pantcheff's suspicions she would of course have defended herself vigorously, but she would also have been deeply hurt that one she held in such high esteem could think so lowly of her.

Those were indeed extraordinary times. Within SIS and MI5 suspicion was rampant; the proven treachery of Blake and Philby, the revelations about Anthony Blunt and John Cairncross had rocked confidence, shoulders were no longer for clapping but for looking over, the Golitsyn/Angleton imbroglio only added to the paranoia. Former SIS officers spoken to by this author tended in the main to be reasonably blasé about the affair and affected to be not terribly shocked; and indeed most were not affected directly by it at all. Perhaps this nonchalance was due the passage of time, because the overall attitude seemed to be 'these things happen'. One reason perhaps is that proof of guilt in espionage cases is so terribly difficult to find. A former head of security in SIS put it like this:

> All you can do is to study the file, then conduct the interrogation. When the interrogation is concluded you must ask yourself in which direction your mind has been moved, towards guilt or innocence? You cannot really expect anything more, this is not Perry Mason.[45]

Whether Park was ever confronted with these accusations we do not yet know. Probably not, but if she was been she remained silent about the confrontation to the grave.

And sanity did return.

i HARSTON, Julian ('Jules'); SIS, H/HANOI, H/BLANTYRE, H/LISBON, H/HARARE, H/GENEVA, H/BELGRADE, later Assistant Secretary-General of the United Nations (1942-).

20

Back in the field, 1964-67

Despite the interest and scope of her role as a P Officer, Park longed to be back in the field. So she must have been delighted when news of her posting to Lusaka came through. In general the Personnel Dept in Petty France (near Westminster) was reputed to work in mysterious ways, its appointments rationale often quite difficult to fathom, as Jean Sackur put it:

> It was said that they [personnel] spent their time on two projects, moving people around till they could: a) fill the Embassy in Beirut with people with bird names – Sparrow, Robin etc., and b) fill the Embassy in Ouagadougou [Burkina Faso] with people who spoke Japanese.[1]

However, in this instance sending Park back to Africa made good sense. She knew the ground. Zambia (formerly Northern Rhodesia) was a good posting for her too. The country was readying itself for independence; it would be the ninth African state to be granted self-determination by Britain. The Belgian experience in the Congo had served as an added encouragement for the Colonial Secretary at the time, Iain Macleod, to initiate the process of freeing Britain's colonies sooner rather than later.[2] However matters in its southern neighbour were far from settled and were a cause of increasing disquiet in London. For this reason, at White's insistence, SIS was permitted to bypass the Attlee Doctrine and establish a station in Lusaka. Even so the CRO successfully battled to ensure that the SIS station in Salisbury, capital of Southern (soon to be just plain) Rhodesia, remained subject to its stifling writ.

John Sackur, who had been the station number two in Léopoldville, had been posted to Salisbury the previous year in an attempt to beef things up a bit. Unfortunately he had been over-enthusiastic and had been arrested leaving the home of the nationalist leader, Joshua Nkomo, in Bulawayo. The Rhodesians accused Sackur of a 'provocative act' and expelled him as a *persona non grata* (PNG), diplomat-speak for a spy. What his wife Jean, who was eight months pregnant at the time and was already the mother of two children, thought of his expulsion is not recorded. The welcome he received from Park on his return home can hardly have been the warmest either though the fact that there was no publicity surrounding the incident probably helped a little. Sackur left the Service a few years later, disillusioned with the life of a spy.[3]

Park's station was one of three focused on the deteriorating political situation.

Pretoria was the lead station in Southern Africa; it would cover the relations between Salisbury, the capital of Rhodesia, and the South African government. Issues such as war aid, munitions support, sanctions busting and the developing political situation would come under its bailiwick. The Governor's office in Salisbury was the location of the second station, the British government maintaining representation in Salisbury for a number of years until UDI was declared. The third, Park's station in Lusaka, was the main listening post for nationalist Black Africa and the emerging guerrilla groups which would wage war against the illegal regime after UDI.

Park's appointment as H/LUSAKA was not universally welcomed. When she went across to the CRO to be briefed she was greeted by Costley-White with the words 'Have you jailed any more British businessmen this week, Daphne?' The reference was to Greville Wynne, the British businessman (and unofficial assistant for SIS) who had just been jailed by the Russians over the Penkovsky[i] affair.[4] It was quite an extraordinary statement, indicative of the state of relations between the CRO and SIS. The Penkovsky affair was still pretty raw in SIS and, as a relatively recent Moscow hand herself, Park was in no mood for jokes about the subject. She replied with something unprintable and stormed out. Back in Broadway she went up to see the Chief, White. She told him of her encounter. White to her amazement suggested she might apologise to Costley-White for losing her temper. Park refused absolutely to apologise and eventually received a grudging one from the CRO man. She did not forget what she later described as 'White's cowardice' over the affair.[5]

The British High Commissioner in Lusaka, Sir W.B. Leslie-Monson,[ii] a CRO appointee of course, was another disapproving voice. He informed her on her arrival *en poste* that she had no business being there:

> On arrival in 1964 she was told by the High Commissioner she might as well go home for there was no job for her, and anyway Africa was no place for a woman. (Sir Gerald Warner)[6]

But Park seemed to have a special way with ambassadors, and much as she had turned an ambassadorial sceptic into a friend in Moscow in 1954 and in Léopoldville in 1960, she worked her charm on Monson and turned him into a strong supporter. Cultivating ambassadors was something that some station commanders did and others didn't bother with. Park did bother. In fairness,

---

i PENKOVSKY, Oleg Vladimirovich, GRU (SIS/CIA) (1919-1963). Penkovsky was a senior officer in Soviet military intelligence when he began spying for SIS and the CIA. In his two-year career as a spy he handed over thousands of pages of top secret papers, mainly to do with Soviet rocket development.

ii LESLIE-MONSON, Sir William Bonnar, KCMG, CB; diplomat (1912-1993).

Monson was quite knowledgeable about the situation in the country, having been head of the Foreign Office's East African desk for a number of years prior to his appointment as High Commissioner.

As usual Park's first task was to get the station set up and organised and to figure out how she should go about achieving her task. She had done exceptionally well in both Moscow and Léo so the bar was set high if she was going to improve on either. Léopoldville had been a political-action led post and such intelligence as was collected was done principally to support the political aim of destabilising the Lumumba administration and replacing it with one more friendly to Western interests. Her first task in Lusaka was also one of political action: it was to assist the election campaign of Kenneth Kaunda who was adjudged the least undesirable of the candidates for President.[7] Channelling money to election candidates is grade school stuff for an intelligence service and Kaunda was duly returned as the independent state's first elected President.

Park then set about getting close to him. Kaunda was a deeply religious family man, not a *bon vivant*, not particularly sociable, and he lived a protected existence in the well-guarded presidential compound in Lusaka. The city itself was as different from Léo as one could imagine. There were few buildings over three or four storeys and the paved roads quickly gave way to rougher surfaces on the city's outskirts, lined by sellers of roasted groundnuts. At first sight the President and Park had little in common and little occasion to meet other than at official functions. Whether Kaunda was fully aware of her role in Lumumba's disposal we cannot say, but he knew Lumumba and admired him and that alone would not have brought him closer to her. Kaunda and Lumumba had met in Tanzania in 1958 at the All Africa Peoples' Conference, the forerunner to the Pan-African Freedom Movement for East & Central Africa (PAFMECA), and probably subsequently.

And Park did not have the field to herself. The Security Service was not letting go of its Commonwealth links lightly, and dispatched its Deputy Director-General, Sir Martin Furnival Jones,[i] to Lusaka a few months ahead of Park's arrival to negotiate the establishment of a security liaison office in the capital. The security liaison officer (SLO), Eric Leighton, was now on the ground. He was an experienced officer who had previously been SLO in Kuala Lumpur.[8] Park knew that Leighton would be a serious rival for Kaunda's 'affections'. Leighton had served in Malaya alongside Maurice Oldfield,[9] with whom Park was very friendly, so she'd have got the low down on her rival from him. Relations between SIS officers and SLOs could be fraught. One of Leighton's successors in Kuala Lumpur had demanded that the local SIS station commander hand over a list of all his sources in the country. When the officer refused the SLO secured the

---

i FURNIVAL JONES, Sir Martin, KCB; Director General of the Security Service (MI5) 1965-72 (1912-1997).

backing of the High Commissioner (Viscount Head) for the demand. The SIS officer had to threaten to close down his operations if they persisted, and the request was reluctantly withdrawn.[10]

Then along came a stroke of good fortune. Park picked up intelligence that suggested that a *coup d'état* was in the making with a view towards toppling Kaunda. She had a problem, however. It arose from the fact that the plotters were probably better disposed towards Western interests than was Kaunda. But some instinct told her that Britain's long-term interests would be better served by sticking with Kaunda rather than risk being seen to be plotting to dispose of another elected government. This is how Sir Gerald Warner described it:

> She discovered a plot close to the president of which she might have taken short-term advantage. Instead she took the longer view and the more straightforward course and told him of it, thereby demonstrating that, against expectations, she could be trusted to act honourably even when it was not in the UK's short-term interests. It was a crucial example that the British could be trusted. Word got about, not only in Zambia, and the ability of our Service to influence events was accordingly much enhanced.[11]

Probably influencing her decision was a series of army revolts in the newly independent states of Kenya, Uganda and Tanzania (the East African Revolts). All took place without even the faintest rumour of trouble reaching the ears of MI5's SLOs and had the potential to 'Balkanise' that region of Africa. All required the support of the British Army if they were to be suppressed. White laid the reason for the failure of intelligence as being the Attlee Doctrine, which required that intelligence in these countries remained the responsibility of MI5's SLOs and not of the local SIS station.[12] The SLOs perceived their role more as advisors to the indigenous law enforcement agencies rather than being in the SIS business of intelligence acquisition, running agents and so on. In this they were encouraged by the various high commissioners, all CRO appointees.

Park's decision to side with Kaunda had significant consequences. Kaunda decided that Zambia needed a fully professional intelligence service and asked her if she could help to put one in place. For any intelligence service being asked by a host government to assist in the establishment of said country's new intelligence service represents the pinnacle of achievement. And Park knew just the chap to undertake the task. She turned to Denis Grennan, founder of the Ariel Foundation. Ariel was one of those organisations which operate in that half-world between fully independent non-governmental organisations (NGOs) and what are often little more than fronts for intelligence agencies (usually referred to as a 'proprietary'). The Ariels of this world function in part as cut-outs, enabling the agencies to funnel money to people and causes without being identified as the source.

Grennan wasn't known to possess any particular expertise in establishing an intelligence[13] service (a rare enough skill anyway) but that didn't hinder the man who was also reported to be a 'personal friend' of Kaunda. He took up the post as special advisor to Kenneth Kaunda with the task of getting the Zambian intelligence service off the ground.[14] A decade later Grennan's and Park's paths would once more cross when Grennan was special advisor to James Callaghan, the then Foreign Secretary, and Park was Controller/Western Hemisphere, and they had a communist revolution in Portugal to sort out.

Meanwhile, a thousand miles to the north-west in the steamy jungles of the Congo, Park's former comrade-in-arms, Larry Devlin, was hard at work. He returned to the Congo for a second stint in the middle of 1965. Shortly after he arrived *en poste* Devlin learned that the Cuban revolutionary, Che Guevara, and a small band of followers had infiltrated the Congo and intended to contact the Simba tribesmen whose violent rebellion Devlin had been instrumental in putting down the year previously. For Devlin, one Simba rebellion was enough and anyway the CIA had plans for the Congo which did not include its fracturing into a number of pieces. Devlin made it his business to ensure that Guevara's latest adventure did not take hold. The National Security Agency (NSA) positioned a ship fitted out with sophisticated listening gear in the Indian Ocean off the coast at Dar-es-Salaam. It was able to pick up Guevara's inbound and outbound communications. Between that and other more direct actions Devlin killed off Guevara's African adventure, which appeared to be ill-thought out from the start. It lasted only for about six months.

Devlin also gave the lie to Kent's[i] famous First Law of Intelligence, '*that any coup about which you have heard in advance never takes place*'. For it strains belief to think that Mobutu's seizure of power five months after his good friend, Larry Devlin, returned to the Congo was undertaken without at least a nod of approval from the direction of the US embassy. The Park and Devlin show was up and running again – a coup aborted in Lusaka, a coup enabled in Kinshasa. Mobutu and Kaunda were both very different men with radically different political ideologies, but both, supported by their British and American patrons, would hold power until the 1990s. Park also kept up her contacts with the local CIA personnel. According to Prof. Eunan O'Halpin (TCD), she and the Lusaka station chief, the legendary Angus Thuermer,[ii] took advantage of a shared passion for horse-riding to meet while both were out for their Sunday morning canters.

i KENT, Sherman; CIA (1903-1986). Kent was a legendary CIA intelligence analyst and head of the CIA's Office of National (Intelligence) Estimates (ONE) for fifteen years. He framed a number of intelligence 'laws' of which the first (quoted above) is the best remembered.
ii THUERMER, Angus McLean; US Navy, CIA (1917-2010).

That same year saw a long threatened event finally come to pass as (Southern) Rhodesia made its Unilateral Declaration of Independence (UDI). Tanzania's President Nyerere immediately blamed Britain and broke off diplomatic relations with London. Harold Wilson responded, in part, by attempting to put together an ill-fated Commonwealth mission to act as peace-brokers in the Vietnam War. This was Wilson at his worst. The Americans weren't the least bit interested, US President Johnson remarking bitterly in a late night telephone call to Wilson, 'If you want to help us in Vietnam send us some men ...'.[15] The Commonwealth heads of state saw it as a ploy to distract them from the Rhodesian crisis, while the North Vietnamese settled for extracting as much propaganda value from it as possible but without ever attempting to engage seriously with it. Perhaps it was this that sparked Park's interest in Vietnam, to be given expression a few years later when she was posted there.

The Rhodesian declaration certainly had the effect of elevating Park's relationship with Kaunda to a strategic level. Kaunda was personally hugely influential; he was also closest to Nyerere among the key African leaders of the so-called frontline states. This meant that some form of conduit could be maintained whereby London was privy to Nyerere's thinking. This was critical because Tanzania, despite not bordering on Rhodesia, soon became the political focus of resistance to UDI and home to a proliferation of resistance groups. In some respects Tanzania was, at that time, a bit like an African Cuba. It was through its territory that Che Guevara had infiltrated his band into the Congo. Tanzania's closeness to the Chinese communist government was also a cause for major concern. In February 1965 Kaunda had sent a representative to Downing Street to warn Number 10 of the likely consequences for Nyerere of his anti-American and anti-West German rhetoric.

This was an environment for Park at her best, an intelligence officer consumed with building the relationships that could really assist her country's foreign policy objectives, not stealing secret blueprints from ministers' safes. As Warner put it:

> For she well understood that in Africa influence was more important than intelligence, and that our service had special opportunities to exercise it.[16]

Park was by now exceptionally close to Kaunda, so much so that the relationship gave rise to (completely unfounded) Foreign Office gossip that she and Kaunda were lovers.[17] This was the risk that single women, and not just those in the SIS, ran: any perceived closeness to a male was considered grounds for tittle-tattle and speculation. Park did not let the gossipers hinder her work and she continued her schmoozing. She even gained her High Commissioner's permission to spend an afternoon picnicking in the company of the Soviet ambassador to Zambia where the two alternately drank whisky and vodka.

> The most important thing I learned that afternoon was that relations between staff on the Soviet *Kolony* were even more dysfunctional than in the High Commission.[18]

Park also remained close to events in the Congo, by her own account visiting the country while she was based in Lusaka, mainly to provide much needed operational and moral support to her successor.

> Later on when I was in Zambia I used go up to the Congo from time to time to see our Consul-General [SIS station head] who was very beleaguered. One day I got there, having had a slightly lively time getting there, because there had been bandits on the road and they had built a great big barrier that they were hiding behind. So I got out, looked around and said, 'Oh, it must be a document check,' in a loud voice. So they came out and so I took the papers from my handbag – it was always full of them – and gave them each one. And they were a bit bewildered but they looked at them and by the time they were through they had really lost the will to live. So I gave them a beer and drove two of them – maybe unwisely – near to where I was going. And when I got there, the Consul-General, who was a wonderful man, was very agitated because he had a British subject who was a black Rhodesian who had been arrested by the Congolese for something and the Congolese were going to hang him the next day and he'd been allowed out the night before into the hands of the consul. So we decided we obviously couldn't let him be hanged. So we decided to remove him instead and I knew all of the border guards very well, I used give them nice things to eat and drink and tell them about their families and so forth. So we set off in convoy with Bill in front in his large handsome consular car with nothing in it but Bill. And me in my little *Deux Chevaux* with a man on the back seat or rather under the back seat. And we arrived at the border and of course all the men at the border took great pleasure in taking Bill's car to bits and looking for all sorts of interesting things there. They didn't take any notice of me because I was their chum and they said 'how are you?' and we drove through and we got to the other side and we finally got to Northern Rhodesia [Zambia] where we parted company with my guest and said to him 'now you can look after yourself'. Now the sad thing is that twenty years later I read a book about African leaders and one of them was a ZANU/PF man who said that at one stage of his life he had been about to be killed by the Congolese and he had been rescued by a rather strange diplomat called Delphine [*sic*] Park and unfortunately I've lost the book so I've no proof of this but I thought you'd like to know that when I drove I drove to some purpose.[19]

It is a bit more Buchan than Bond, sounding like a 'spiffing jape', getting one over on 'these blighters' who are all set to hang 'one of Her Majesty's subjects'. The reality was probably a bit more complicated and not nearly as much fun as Park makes out.

Over the next two years the Rhodesian situation continued to deteriorate and dominate everything. In 1966 the Rhodesian Bush War commenced. Since Zambia was the only nationalist state with a common border with Rhodesia it soon became home to fighters and political representatives from the nationalist organisations ZANLA/ZANU and ZPRA/ZAPU.[20] Establishing and maintaining connections with both those organisations consumed more and more Park's time and energy. She received a backhanded compliment for her work when she was attacked several times on Rhodesian Radio as 'a friend of terrorists'. It was while she was in Lusaka that the importance of Africa within SIS was finally recognised and it was made a Directorate in its own right under the first Controller/Africa, John Taylor (see Chapter 19).

One of Park's visitors was Oliver Wright, with whom she had had that conversation about their respective career trajectories late one night (over a bottle of whisky one suspects) in West Berlin, Park picked up where they had left off ten years previously:

> I was in Lusaka busily organising things when [Harold] Wilson [PM] was shuttling back and forth to Salisbury trying to persuade Ian Smith and there was Oliver as his chief-of-staff – the Jonathan Powell job – which was a minister's job. He came to see me and said, 'Here we are again,' and I said, 'well I don't know how you are doing but I am having a wonderful time,' and I said, 'by the way you can be useful,' 'useful,' he said, 'yes, I've been talking to the High Commissioner about you, we have got a submission on the table in London, something we want to do and they've been very troublesome about it, you can make sure that the Prime Minister signs it off.' So he said, 'okay,' and he did so we got our operation. It was one of the more satisfying moments of my life.[21]

Nine times out of ten Daphne 'got her operation', it seems. The Foreign Office gossips would have been amazed to learn that Park had in fact fallen in love while she was in Lusaka, but not with Kenneth Kaunda. Park had fallen for a British military officer working alongside her in the city. Her second great love affair had begun.

As 1967 came to its end she knew she had some serious thinking to do about her future. But for now her tour was over and time to return to London, to a Service that was barely recognisable as the one she had left behind just three years earlier. Dick White, aware that his time was running out, had moved firmly and decisively at last.

21

Reform at last, 1967-69

On returning from Lusaka in 1967 Park first had to familiarise herself with the new Head Office set-up. In her absence SIS had left Broadway, its home since 1924, and been moved (it was most certainly not its choice) to the twenty-storey speculatively-built office block called Century House, located on Westminster Bridge Road in unfashionable Lambeth. White did, however, manage to maintain the Chief's rather plush residence in Queen Anne's Gate adjoining the former Broadway Head Office. The choice of Century House, immediately christened 'Gloom Hall' by its occupants, was a pointed statement from Whitehall about where SIS stood on its totem pole of estimation. On the 'wrong' side of the Thames, far from the clubs of Pall Mall and St James's, it was, in the words of one stalwart, 'in a part of London a gentleman would rarely have occasion to be'. SIS had truly been cast into the outer darkness.

Like it or not, Park had no choice but to settle in as her next overseas posting wasn't due for a couple of years; it would be to Hanoi in North Vietnam, about as far removed from the socialisation of Lusaka as it was possible to get. We don't know exactly when Park was offered the Hanoi post, or why particularly – quite possibly out of desperation, the Hanoi post being very difficult to fill. Her knowledge of French and Russian would have been seen as an asset, but probably her greatest advantage was that she was willing to take it. It was a change from Africa but personnel policy was (and remains) to expose SIS officers to a range of geographical and operational challenges over the course of their careers. And while it was not unknown for an officer to be, for example, a SovBloc specialist for virtually their entire time in the Service, it was not the preferred option. So Hanoi it would be.

The scandals that had buffeted SIS and British intelligence generally continued. The most lurid was probably the 'Profumo Affair' in which the priapic minister of state in the War Office entered into a brief dalliance with a 'party girl' called Christine Keeler. Keeler was also occasionally sharing the bed of a hard-drinking, womanising Soviet military attaché called Yevgeni Ivanov.[i] For a combination of reasons the linked affairs eventually reached the ears of the press. To the owners of the *Mail*, the *Mirror* and the *Express* newspapers in particular it was a gift from the Gods.

---

i IVANOV, Captain Yevgeni; GRU (1926-1994).

Motivated in part by a witches' brew of malevolent vindictiveness, obsessive hatred and hypocrisy, and desperate to reverse the declining newspaper sales brought about by the launch of the commercial television channel, ITV, the press barons seized upon this empty vessel with the joy of the shipwrecked seeing rescue on the horizon. This was the type of sex scandal that *proved* just how *right* they had been to lament the decline in moral standards of post-imperial Britain. That said, given the preoccupations of their readers, it was understandable that they might take advantage. The Profumo affair featured lurid country house sexual orgies with beautiful young women cavorting naked in swimming pools. This was the 'highest in the land' behaving like the lowest, consorting with 'pimps, procurers and prostitutes' (none of which any of them were) and simultaneously sharing their favours with 'Russian spies'. If they had made the whole thing up it couldn't have been any better.

Britain may have been fascinated by the Profumo Affair, but the puritanical Americans were anything but – this was proof, if proof was needed, of the rotten state of post-Empire Britain. In the words of the American statesman Dean Acheson, 'Britain has lost an Empire but has yet to find a role.' The Americans could understand sex and they could understand spies; what they found hard to grasp was Britain's insistence on linking the two activities together.[1] But they were determined to find out. The State Department decided to conduct some espionage on its own account. It asked the US ambassador to London, David Bruce, to set up an Irish-American playboy, Tom Corbally, in a Mayfair flat, with a chauffeur-driven limousine, lavish expenses and whatever else was required to play the role of a big-spending dissolute man about town. With film-star looks and appetites to match Corbally was well up for the task, which was to penetrate the louche end of London High Society and report back to Ambassador Bruce on the sexual shenanigans of ministers and their assorted friends and companions.[2] The CIA may have turned down the assignment, possibly on the grounds that it involved spying *against* Britain as opposed to simply running operations on British soil, though it wasn't usually so finicky. Perhaps it wasn't asked, because it was certainly interested and its London chief at the time, Archie Roosevelt,[i] was told to make sure that Langley was kept fully briefed, even sending daily cables at one point. The reason for the intense Washington interest (apart from being keen to see how it impacted on domestic British politics) was a rumour (that's all it was) that the then President John F. Kennedy may have enjoyed a brief fling with Christine Keeler during a short visit she made to New York in 1962.[3]

Corbally, whose grandfather was an Irish New York policeman who made millions in retirement from hiring out armed strike-breakers during the Great

i ROOSEVELT, Archibald Bulloch, Jr.; CIA, COS/ISTANBUL, COS/MADRID, COS/LONDON (1918-1990).

Depression, had the necessary connections for the assignment, into which he reportedly threw himself into wholeheartedly. He soon made contact with Stephen Ward, who confessed the entire Profumo-Keeler affair to him. Corbally reported his findings to the ambassador,[4] who arranged for them to be passed on to Prime Minister Harold Macmillan and of course to the State Department.[5] For the Americans this was the final straw. Spurred on by James Angleton, the new US President, Lyndon Johnson, demanded action. He got it in the form of a top secret US investigation into the effectiveness of Britain's intelligence agencies and their combined abilities to counteract the Soviets.

Two men were appointed to carry out this investigation, Gordon Gray and J. Patrick Coyne. Both were members of the US President's Foreign Intelligence Advisory Board (PFIAB). Both knew their stuff. Gray had served on the Psychological Strategies Board, the State Department body that authorised covert operations. He had been Secretary to the Army and later Assistant Secretary for Defence under President Truman. President Eisenhower appointed him as his National Security Advisor from 1958 to 1961. In that role he had been a member of the Special Group (of four) in the National Security Council (NSC), responsible, *inter alia,* for US policy on the Congo. He was thus intimately involved in the decision to eliminate Patrice Lumumba from the scene. Gray wasn't known to have shied away from taking tough decisions, then or later. Coyne was a former Assistant Director of the FBI specialising in intelligence and internal security who transferred to NSC in 1948. Over the next sixteen years he served 'in various intelligence capacities' in the Truman, Eisenhower, Kennedy and Johnson administrations. The two would be assisted by the CIA's Cleveland Cram, his colleague Archie Roosevelt and various other US worthies. This was to be a cold-eyed study, devoid of all sentiment. They would send their assessment directly to the President. None of the British services under review were to be advised about the investigation in advance.

The two men went about their mission with a will. They lunched and chatted and dined and chatted and met and just chatted with a wide range of MI5 and SIS officers and their Whitehall 'customers', without of course revealing the nature and purpose of their enquiries. As very well-connected Americans with impeccable credentials and letters of introduction signed by the US President, every door was opened to them, every question responded to. When their findings were complete they reported them to Johnson, and their report was scathing. It found that in neither their recruitment policies, nor their training programmes, nor their application of resources and core competencies, were MI5 and SIS capable of doing the job that was required of them. They reserved particular criticism for Roger Hollis of MI5, whose resignation they demanded.

Of course the contents of the report had to leak. Angleton showed it to

Christopher Phillpotts,[i] then H/WASHINGTON. Phillpotts briefed White. After some hesitation Johnson passed the report to the Prime Minister, now Harold Wilson, thus confirming Wilson's worst concerns about the efficacy of his intelligence agencies. In fact Angleton's main purpose behind Gray-Coyne was to enable the CIA to secure a form of *de jure* control over the operations of SIS and MI5, rather than the *de facto* one that US power and money semi-facilitated anyway.

The initial British reaction was one of anger, outrage and humiliation. For months MI5's Hollis refused to talk to the Americans. SIS remained in contact, but Angleton's star had now lost its lustre. However, the more farseeing within the two British agencies and the majority of those outside – that is, those exclusive few who were in a position to know – saw that fundamental change was indeed needed, and if not now then when? Already the Soviets regarded Britain with contempt as 'broken-backed'. As Peter Wright put it, 'as a general rule the Russians respect only iron fists, ideally theirs'.[6] And Britain's intelligence fist was far from being iron.

White, aware that his time was coming to an end, lobbied hard for the changes he had wanted almost from the beginning of his tenure but had not had the clout to insist on when he had the balls to act, nor later the balls to act when he had the clout. Now possessed of both, he summoned his hatchet-man John Briance back to his side and over Christmas and the New Year of 1965/66 the two drew up a list of those who needed to be weeded out. Among the many offered golden handshakes were Paul Paulson and John Collins. James Fulton was sidelined; John Bruce Lockhart had already been retired, Young had long gone.[7] White also reorganised the various Controllerates into the form they would retain until the end of the Cold War.[8]

Controller Europe (C/EUR)
Controller Soviet Bloc (C/SOV)
Controller Western Hemisphere (C/WH)
Controller Far East (C/FE)
Controller Middle East (C/ME)
Controller Africa (C/AF)
Controller UK (C/UK)

Nicholas Elliott was spared in the cleanout, possibly because of White's misgivings about his own role in unearthing Philby. Elliott was given Europe but soon after

i PHILLPOTTS, Christopher Louis George, CMG, OBE; HM Forces, SIS, MALMO, COPENHAGEN, H/ATHENS, H/PARIS, H/WASHINGTON, D/CIS (Counterintelligence & Security) (1915-1985).

kicked upstairs to D/Requirements, an administrative job he hated. He decided it was time to 'hand in his musket'. Within three years of the cleanout he too was gone, to a job in the City at the age of fifty-three. Harold Shergold was given SovBloc while John Taylor was made the first Controller for Africa (C/AF). Even more significantly, at Harry Shergold's suggestion a joint MI5/SIS section was set up to target Soviet operations in the UK. Shergold reasoned that this way would avoid jurisdictional issues and share both expertise and resources. The section would report jointly to SIS's C/UK and to MI5's KY Branch. Tony Brooks of SIS was made its first head,[9] securing the defection of Oleg Lyalin in 1971 but later allowing his obsessive suspicions about Harold Wilson's loyalty to divert his energies and to a degree sully his reputation, though he and Park remained close all their lives.

As noted earlier, a Foreign Office under-secretary had been brought in to take over the Service's administration and finances and a Foreign Office officer of counsellor rank installed in Head Office as Foreign Office Adviser to C. But the White-inspired reorganisation did not stop there. Over the next couple of years the changes continued, marking it the most significant reorganisation of Britain's overseas intelligence structures since the end of the Second World War. The Joint Intelligence Committee (JIC) which in 1957 had moved from the control of the Chiefs of the General Staff to that of the Foreign Office, would hereafter come under the remit of the Cabinet Office, coming in effect within Number 10's orbit where it has remained. However the chairmanship would continue to be provided by the Foreign Office (later the FCO). The pivotal position of Secretary – though how and in what way, depended on the office holder – was taken from the FCO and given to Brian Stewart,[i] an experienced SIS officer (and one-time contender for the position of Chief). Stewart occupied the role from 1969 to 1972. He was succeeded in turn by representatives from GCHQ, MI5, etc.

The Cabinet Office's dominance in intelligence affairs was further cemented with the establishment inside the Cabinet Office of the Intelligence & Security Secretariat (ISS). The secretariat was to be headed up by a new position of Intelligence & Security Co-ordinator to the Cabinet Office and would have adequately resourced Assessments Staffs to service the JIC. White would be the first holder of the post. The CIA (along with representatives from the Australian, Canadian and New Zealand services) was to have the right to attend the weekly meeting of the JIC. The Agency had been excluded in the run-up to Suez. The visitors would attend for the first part of the meeting, then withdraw as 'purely British matters' were discussed. The CIA was granted the right to participate

---

i STEWART, Brian Thomas Webster, CMG; SIS, RANGOON, H/BEIJING, H/SHANG-HAI, H/MANILA, H/KUALA LUMPUR, H/HANOI, H/HONG KONG, D/ST (Science & Technology) (1922-).

in the drawing up of the JIC's annual National Intelligence Requirements Paper (NIRP). This paper fed directly into the SIS Red Book, its targeting and intelligence priorities schedule. The relevant portion of the Red Book was sent to each overseas station. The CIA was given *carte blanche* to open stations in any African country without reference to MI5, ending the situation where they did not have stations in commonwealth countries. SIS too was given the freedom to open stations in Britain's former colonies at will.

Recruitment of new intelligence officers in SIS was to be conducted on a strictly professional basis rather than on an informal 'recommendation' basis. Here is how one former SIS officer described the old system:

> Around that time my tutor in Oxbridge, the SIS talent-spotter, sent three of my most brilliant but wildly unsuitable friends to be interviewed [for SIS] and neglected to send me who, with hindsight, proved eminently suitable for the contemporary requirement. (Luckily for me my friends, although still quite unclear about what they had encountered, told me enough about it for me to express interest a year or so later.) When some years afterwards I met the tutor I asked him why he had made these choices and he told me that he had been in military intelligence during the war and had met former SIS officers who were 'more like them than like you'.[10]

Enhanced positive vetting (as opposed to the 'nothing known' passive/negative vetting) was to become the norm for new recruits, repeated on five-yearly cycles for the holders of some senior posts. Positive vetting was also introduced for new recruits into MI5. SIS's registry, it was agreed, needed reorganising; when the FLUENCY investigation commenced the registry was discovered to have been a bit of a shambles with no central cross-indexing. Arthur Martin of MI5 was transferred to SIS in 1967 and given the task of creating a fully modern filing and retrieval system.

Angleton did get one part of his dream. A formal counterintelligence-sharing arrangement covering Canada, Australia, New Zealand, Britain and America (CAZAB) was put in place, being formally commissioned in November 1967. Its successor organisation remains in operation, though today referred to as 'Five-Eyes'. However, rejected were polygraphs (lie-detector tests) and a proposal that the CIA's London station would be increased substantially with the bulk of the increase posted as resident 'liaison officers' inside SIS Head Office. A similar arrangement was proposed for MI5 with the FBI providing the additional manpower, 'the better to assist'. That last was seen as a bridge too far, it would have placed Britain's intelligence services on the same footing as that which the East European satellites enjoyed with the KGB.

The reforms also went to the very heart of the way SIS ran its networks of agents. Shergold in his role as C/SOV set about reorganising how SIS approached that task. Shergold had been responsible for the British end of the Penkovsky operation and he felt that lessons needed to be learned from it, the US view and one shared by many of the British was that poor tradecraft by SIS was the immediate cause of Penkovsky's downfall. And not just Penkovsky, the failure of the SIS's Egyptian networks at the time of Suez was hugely damaging and was due in part to how SIS ran its agent networks and in part to the unthinking arrogance of the SIS officers in Cairo station.

Shergold decided on a total overhaul of the agent-handling system. What became known as 'Moscow rules' were introduced for the handling of agents in hard target areas. Shergold also decided that agent networks would be a thing of the past.[11] Traditionally agents were organised in 'rings' or 'circuits'. Each ring would be made up of a head agent and sub-agents. The sub-agents in the ring might include support agents who would be limited to actions such as posting letters or delivering messages. There would be a dedicated communications agent whose sole responsibility would be communicating between the ring and SIS, usually by clandestine radio.

For Shergold this system had serious drawbacks. For a start, assuming long-term false identities wasn't practical in many post-war environments and relying on the concept of a head agent located in the operational territory offered very poor security. For example if the head agent was identified he could be placed under observation and over time lead his watchers to his complete circuit, or he could be picked up and forced to reveal the names under interrogation. That was what happened in Egypt where virtually the entire SIS agent network was rolled-up after a number of head agents were arrested and tortured. It also happened in East Germany where, aided by information from George Blake, the Stasi were rounding up agent after agent (four hundred in all, according to Blake, but he may have been exaggerating for effect). SIS did not know or even suspect the cause at the time, but it did see the result.

So Shergold introduced the practice, which exists to this day, of each agent being handled on an individual basis by a designated case-officer. Communications between the agent and SIS were on a one-to-one basis and virtually never through an intermediary. The case-officer might be based in the operational country (typically under diplomatic cover, like Park) or travel to it to meet the agent clandestinely, posing as a tourist or businessman (visiting case officer/VCO). If the agent had the freedom to travel he would arrange to meet the case-officer in a third country. Otherwise the agent would receive his coded instructions by radio from the numbers station such as the Lancashire Poacher, referred to earlier. This was called a One-Way-Voice-Link; the agent would purchase a specified model of an 'ordinary' domestic radio, one capable of receiving short-wave signals, and listen in at prearranged times. Stolen documents would be passed from the agent to SIS by dead drops and the like. Each agent's identity remained a closely guarded secret, known to as few as possible and never disclosed to other agents.

For SIS the change was revolutionary, altering decades of established trade-craft. It took the CIA some time before they too followed suit; the KGB had already introduced it, ahead of both services. The pre-war Cambridge spy ring model, where agents knew one another, and knew one another to be spies, had been abandoned in favour of the one-on-one approach. For example, neither Blake nor Philby were aware of each other's existence as Soviet agents until it was revealed in the press.

So, twenty years after Park had entered Broadway for the first time, the SIS was reaching the point where it was truly 'fit for purpose'. The dead wood had been largely cleaned out, its structures reorganised, its operations streamlined. Never again would the Service be penetrated before the end of the Cold War. In some respects SIS had the KGB to thank for its reorganisation. The Russian intelligence service was the most implacable foe ever faced by the Service; it was also its first global threat. SIS knew it had to codify its systems, streamline its organisation, and tighten up its operational security; an enemy of the calibre of the KGB demanded nothing less. As one SovBloc officer put it, 'where the KGB was we were and where it was not we needed a bloody good reason to be'.[12]

Park also had to think about the implications of her love affair. Achieving a transfer from the General Service into the Intelligence Branch had not been without its complications, one being that should she marry she would not be permitted to stay on in SIS (or the Foreign Office for that matter). When the Gowers Committee met in 1945 to determine the condition under which women would be permitted entry to the Foreign Service it was seen as axiomatic that married women could not be sent overseas and would be required to offer their resignation on marriage. If Park was to insist on her lover divorcing his wife, assuming he was prepared to and the two of them then married, it would mean her resigning the Service.[13] There was another complication. He was a family man with children, Park did not want to be the marriage-wrecker, the 'other woman' responsible for the break-up of another woman's family. So she decided. She and he would remain lovers, theirs would be a full and loving relationship, but it would not end in divorce and re-marriage. Daphne Park would remain single.[14]

She also decided she would keep the existence of the relationship secret from the Office, a decision that was a serious security breach, the rule in SIS (and the Foreign Office) being that significant relationships with the opposite sex had to be declared. It was a rule more honoured in the breach than the observance, with relatively few officers in either service choosing to declare their illicit love affairs. Her decision was understandable. At the time, despite attitudes changing, there would have been little tolerance within SIS for a flagrant love affair with a married man. And of course as a serving officer his position would have been untenable. But Park had the skills for deceit, telling only a few close friends from outside the Service (until after his death, when she became a tiny bit more open). So successful was she that one former colleague, who would have considered himself a friend, told this author that she (Daphne) had never had any affairs. In that he was quite wrong. While eventually, in around 1980, secretaries and junior staff generally were allowed marry and keep their jobs, Intelligence Branch female staff could not do so until after the end of the Cold War.[15]

This was the price people like Daphne Park and Hilary La Fontaine and others chose to pay. It might well be their decision not to marry was a lifestyle choice that had nothing to do with their SIS careers. It is equally true that career-oriented women like Daphne Park could not have had the SIS careers they did had they married. Park made very few public references to her unmarried state. One she did make may give a clue to her state of mind at the time. In a 1983 interview with the Diplomatic Service Wives Association magazine she said, 'A woman has to make a choice. I made a choice in the other direction.'[16] She once said to fellow peer Lord Glentoran,[i] 'I was a spinster, Robin, so I was always free to go to to wherever they wished to send me.'[17]

The name of Daphne Park's lover is not revealed in this book. Her friends, to whom this author spoke about the affair, were adamant that revealing his name would cause only hurt to his family and not achieve any significant purpose. He was not a public figure in any sense, simply a mid-ranking officer in the service of his country's armed forces.

This, then, was the Service that Park would represent as the next H/HANOI. She would have prepared for her posting with some trepidation but much excitement; preparations would have included spending time with her predecessors including John Colvin,[ii] Gordon Philo[iii] and Brian Stewart, learning the lie of the land, ensuring that when she arrived she too would be 'fit for purpose'.

---

i DIXON, Major Thomas (Robin) Valerian Dixon, 3rd Baron Glentoran, 5th Baron Bally-menock, CBE; Grenadier Guards, politician (1935-).

ii COLVIN, John Horace Ragnar, CMG; Royal Navy, SIS, NORWAY, VIENNA, KUALA LUMPUR, H/HANOI, H/ULAANBAATAR, H/WASHINGTON (1922-2003).

iii PHILO, Gordon Charles George, CMG, MC; HM Forces, SIS, ISTANBUL, H/KUALA LUMPUR, H/HANOI (1920-2009).

22

Hanoi 1 – Spy station Hanoi, 1969-70

The British consulate-general in Hanoi was no ordinary diplomatic outpost. Though described as a consulate-general, it was in fact an SIS spy station. Described even more accurately, it was an intelligence outpost concealed inside a barely functioning *faux*-diplomatic mission in the capital city of a country at war.

Consulates were to some extent a hangover from a previous era when many countries had two quite separate forms of diplomatic representation. The senior branch were the embassies and legations which were the preserve of the moneyed class; traditionally wealthy well-connected aristocrats. The embassies were almost exclusively concerned with diplomatic representation with no wish to soil their hands by involving themselves in the *business* of consulates. For their part the consulates tended to be located in ports and trading centres and were much closer to the (often insalubrious) hustle and bustle of daily life. Their primary purpose was not diplomacy but to foster trade. Consulates issued visas, renewed passports, were sources of information about tariffs and import levies, and tried, to the extent that they could, to look after the interests of a country's citizens abroad. And traditionally British consulates, much like passport control offices, also provided cover for SIS officers who would have been regarded by the diplomats as being very definitely 'trade'. The Consular Service was absorbed by its senior partner – the Diplomatic Service – in 1943, but the distinction remained, consulates being located in lots of strange places for many and varied reasons.[1]

The particular situation in Hanoi arose out of the 1954 Geneva Conference which was established to resolve a number of international conflicts, including, quite late in the day, the future of French Indochina. After fractious negotiations bedevilled by Cold War hostility, the Geneva Accord (of sorts) was reached. The accord stipulated that France would withdraw from the region leading to the creation of three separate states, Laos, Cambodia (both formally independent since 1953), and Vietnam. As colonial legacies went, it was up there with the worst. Vietnam would not even commence its independent existence as a single entity; it would be divided temporarily into two, North and South. Elections would be held by 1956 to determine the future government of a unitary state. However, and not for the first time, what was decreed to take place at some future date never came to pass. No elections took place; in fact neither South

213

Vietnam nor its principal international backer, the United States, signed the Accord which really agreed on little more than the ceasefire – and that wasn't to last too long either.

The leader of the South, Ngo Dinh Diêm, argued that free elections could not possibly take place in a communist state, which the North was. Accordingly he declared a republic, the Republic of South Vietnam (RSV). In retaliation the Viet Minh in the North also refused to hold elections, becoming instead the Democratic Republic of Vietnam (DRVN) under the leadership of Ho Chi Minh.[2] The populations in both halves were given a period to choose which regime they preferred to live under. Some one million (mainly Catholics) moved to the South from the North, many courtesy of transport provided by the US and French navies, while ten thousand or so made the journey in the other direction. The CIA-orchestrated operation was called Operation Passage to Freedom, one of its slogans being 'The Virgin Mary is moving South'. South Vietnam was formally recognised by most Western powers including the US and Britain, whose Foreign Secretary, Anthony Eden, had co-chaired the conference. Both Britain and the US refused to recognise the communist regime in the North, though the Soviet Union, China and most other Eastern Bloc powers did.

When the dust settled in 1955, to the extent that it did, Britain still had its consulate-general in Hanoi, now the capital city of the DRVN. Originally a plain 'consulate', it had been upgraded to a consulate-general during the Geneva talks as a gesture to the North and in recognition of Eden's role. The Americans also maintained a consulate in Hanoi but soon closed it. This was in retaliation for a decision by the North Vietnamese authorities to ban the consulate from using its radio to transmit outbound messages and simultaneously declaring its outbound telegrams to be 'undeliverable'. Having no communication facilities made nonsense of the mission and so the US consul, Thomas J. Corcoran,[i] was instructed to shut up shop and leave Hanoi.[3] The Foreign Office in London was minded to do likewise. While the mission was still viable, not suffering the indignity of having its communications cut off, from the Foreign Office perspective maintaining any form of representation in a state one did not recognise was illogical and an ineffective use of scarce resources. This was particularly so given that the consul-general's perceived role as Anthony Eden's (co-chairman of the Geneva talks) personal representative had come to an end.[4]

Hanoi is a carbuncle on the hide of our diplomatic representation, declared the Foreign Office (though probably more diplomatically), and will have to go. SIS, in the person of Sir Stewart Menzies, disagreed heartily. The Service had a fondness for operating in out of the way places. For instance it established a station in the Iraqi port of Basra in 1951 which more than paid its way in

---

i CORCORAN, Thomas James; diplomat (1920-1994).

intelligence terms, being closed down only in 2013 – a decision doubtless objected to by SIS. Hanoi had been opened in 1946, shortly after the Second World War[5] when it became obvious to SIS that the region would be in turmoil as it entered the post-colonial era. Nothing SIS had seen since indicated that the turmoil was likely to ease anytime soon.

As intelligencers the Service saw great value in having trained eyes and ears in sensitive parts of the world, even if running agents from them might be difficult or impossible, and whether or not others saw the logic. So a compromise was reached; Hanoi would remain open but be paid for in part from the SIS budget rather than from that of the Diplomatic Service.[6] Fine, said Menzies, our budget, our man (or words to that effect), and so it was agreed that as paymasters SIS would have the right to nominate one of the two personnel who would make up the mission.[7] But maintaining a consulate did not mean that Britain would recognise the DRVN, on that the Foreign Office remained adamant. So the consulate-general would be a non-diplomatic diplomatic mission and the consul-general would be a non-diplomatic diplomat who would be accepted by the host government as being one though not recognised as such. In fact the North Vietnamese regarded the British consul-general from the beginning not as a diplomat but as a 'private unofficial foreign resident'.[8]

Perhaps because of the US pull-out, the North Vietnamese decided to allow the British mission to remain, figuring perhaps that one 'imperialist lackey' outpost in their city could do little harm and might actually convey some benefit. For its part the North Vietnamese regime also benefited. It could maintain its consulate in London, which was useful for propaganda and intelligence purposes, and also keep open its four-man office in Hong Kong, then under British administration, which was a useful facility for the DRVN as well. Intelligence reports suggested that it was, *inter alia*, the main base for securing supplies of foreign currency to support the guerrilla war in the South.[9] However the North made clear its strong preference for recognition and the establishment of formal diplomatic relations between the two countries, without which the British representatives could expect few if any *tête-à-têtes* on the consular verandas. And few indeed there were.

The wisdom of SIS's decision soon became apparent. The North Vietnamese were distinctly unhappy with the outcome of the Accord. From their perspective they had not engaged in the 'French War' only to see their country partitioned. So they commenced a campaign to systemically undermine the South, which by general agreement (though never publicly admitted) was ruled over by a corrupt and unrepresentative regime. By the early 1960s the situation had deteriorated to the point where a communist-led takeover of the South appeared inevitable. The new US President, John F. Kennedy, decided to intervene by providing aid to South Vietnam in the form of military hardware and military 'advisors', who eventually numbered about sixteen thousand. In 1963, when it was obvious that the aid wasn't doing the job, Kennedy decided to permit/facilitate a coup to oust Diêm and replace him with a leader that the Americans (wrongly) hoped would be more effective. Kennedy was assassinated before he could follow through on his policy but his successor, Lyndon Johnson, did. Furthermore Johnson ordered that ground troops be sent to Vietnam. The Vietnam War began in earnest.

After six years of bloody fighting, Johnson's successor as President, Richard Nixon, seeing that ground troops accompanied by large-scale aerial bombing campaigns weren't the answer either, decided to reduce the ante, announcing a reduction of thirty-five thousand in US troop numbers and a cut in the draft (conscription). The process would accelerate in the coming years as the US concentrated its efforts on disengaging from the war, a process known as 'Vietnamisation'. So, by September 1969, when Park was due to take up her duties, the outcome of the 'American War', as it is referred to in Vietnam, was pretty much determined. America would lose and North Vietnam would win. All that remained to be decided was how to end the fighting and permit the combatants to disengage. The North, however, refused (at least from the US perspective) to play ball and negotiate a settlement that would allow the US forces to depart with their dignity intact. So US strategy was directed at forcing that process along, summed up in the phrase, 'bombing them back to the negotiating table'.[10] That process would take a further five years, almost doubling the period of formal combat.

Fortunately for Park, there was a pause in the bombing of the city at the time she arrived. Even so, Hanoi was going to be a tough station in every sense. Because Britain did not recognise the DRVN, the North Vietnamese government refused to issue a certificate of *exequatur* which is the normal legal basis for a diplomat's presence, guaranteeing diplomatic immunity and the associated rights and privileges that go with it. Since one of the rights was the right to import pretty much anything for their personal use, conventional diplomats were able to overcome most of the shortages of Western consumer goods which were simply not available in the North other than to a select group of highly privileged Communist Party officials.

The British consul-general did not enjoy that as of right, so Park was advised to draw up a list of the items she would be permitted to import on arrival. She was advised that during her tenure the North Vietnamese authorities would formally permit only one importation of personal effects for the duration of a posting, though in practice that varied depending on the political climate at any given time. Other than that she would live the life of the local population, relieved only by an ice-box or two brought back from the monthly consulate trips to Saigon with the diplomatic bag. Her list should be heavily biased in the direction of hygiene, she was advised, and a visit to the dentist prior to departure was an absolute must. She was told to expect power cuts, poor to non-existent medical treatment and constant surveillance.

The journey to Hanoi commenced with the long haul flight to Bangkok to be briefed by the British ambassador to Thailand and the local SIS station commander. Thailand was the core US ally in the region and critical to sustaining the US war effort in Vietnam. Most land-based bombers and fighter bombers engaged in Vietnam took off from USAF airbases in Thailand and it was the centre for the CIA's massive paramilitary operations in the region. From Thailand it was a relatively short flight to Saigon, capital of the South. Park's flight arrived in Than Son Nhut Airport, a huge military/civilian complex which had been expanded tenfold to handle the massive military traffic generated by the war. The airport was subject to regular attacks by Viet Cong guerrillas and the surrounding land, levelled to provide clear fields of fire, was pockmarked with shell and bomb craters from previous engagements.[11]

Park would have found the heat and humidity almost overpowering, as was the stench of aircraft fuel from the countless helicopters, fighters and troop transports that were landing and taking off in a never-ending brain-deafening roar. And everywhere there were columns of helmeted troops, arriving, departing, guarding or simply waiting. In the not far distance could be heard the steady drumbeat of war, the crump, crump of air-delivered bombs exploding in quick succession mixed in with the bang-boom of artillery rounds and the occasional crack-crack of small-arms fire carried on the wind. Was Park reminded of the old adage, *if you can hear the sounds of war you're probably too close?* She probably was. She was met at the airport by a representative of the Saigon SIS station who brought her to the ambassador's residence where she would stay for the duration of her brief stopover.

When Park had got her bearings the first thing she would have noticed was how Saigon had yet to recover from the assault on the city in what was known as the 1968 Tet offensive.[12] The damage was widespread and it was clear that nervousness remained, with heavily armed foot patrols of soldiers of the Army of the Republic of South Vietnam (ARVN) troops visible on every thoroughfare. The city itself was an extraordinary mix of the traditional and the modern with the most garish advertising hoardings sitting side by side with Buddhist shrines and Catholic churches amid the endless honking of car horns and the phut-phut of a million 50cc motorcycle engines. The streets teemed with life but stank of corruption – prostitutes on every corner, drug-pushers in mirrored sunglasses on every other, hawkers, bars, brothels and bazaars; everything and everyone was for sale.

The streets were of course thronged with GIs, the REMFs (Rear Echelon Mother-F******), sleek, well fed, dressed in crisp fatigues, arrogantly eyeing up the merchandise of whatever kind. The frontline troops, there on errands or to snatch some R&R, were a breed apart: skinny to be point of being almost feral, gaunt-faced, sometimes unshaven, often drunk or stoned, blacks with blacks, whites with whites. And there were Australian and New Zealand forces milling about as well, though not in the same numbers as the Americans. The bar girls touting for business liked to taunt the Aussie soldiers about how mean they were compared to the high-spending Yanks. The sight of an Australian was enough to bring out the chant:

> Uc-dai-loi [Australian] cheap Charlie
> He no buy me Saigon tea
> Saigon tea cost many, many P [piastre]
> Uc-dai-loi cheap Charlie.

Over the next couple of days Park would receive her briefings. By convention the first would be from the ambassador, John Moreton.[i] Moreton was an experienced hand, having spent a good few years in various African posts, and the two got on famously.

Park was then briefed by 'Tinker' Bell[ii] (H/SAIGON) and by his second-in-command Andrew Fulton.[iii] She learnt from them how US Army discipline was disintegrating. Drug-taking was rife, as was the practice of 'fragging' senior NCOs or officers (originally, rolling a fragmentation grenade under their bunks, usually with fatal results) who were seen as being too gung-ho or who were otherwise on their case. Racial tensions were another issue, often breaking out into semi-open conflict, and there was talk of weapons being fired at fellow soldiers. All in all, the picture they painted was not likely to have been either positive or pleasant.

US Military HQ (Military Assistance Command Vietnam/MACV) would have been different, naturally. Everyone in MACV appeared to want to tell everyone else what they wanted to hear. And what the military wanted to hear was that the war was being won. Anyone on the American side, soldier, civilian, reporter, who offered a contrary view was quickly advised how unwelcome that was. They even had an expression to cover it: *If you're not part of the solution, you're part of the problem.* The military, as are armies generally, was in favour of more: more troops, more weaponry, more aggression. *You can't win a war with one hand tied behind your back,* summed up the attitude. *The way to finish the war was to bomb the Red River dikes, every paddy field in the North would be flooded, every village made uninhabitable, every road impassable, kaput.*[13]

i MORETON, Sir John Oscar, KCMG, KCVO, MC; diplomat (1917-2012).
ii BELL, Alfred Edwin ('Tinker'); SIS, RANGOON, TOKYO, BENGHAZI, H/SAIGON (1923-1987).
iii FULTON, Robert Andrew; SIS, SAIGON, ROME, H/EAST BERLIN, H/OSLO, H/NEW YORK, C/EASTERN EUROPE, H/WASHINGTON (1944-).

The CIA's station head, Ted Shackley,[i] *aka* 'the blonde ghost', might have painted a more subtle picture, though from her chat with Bell and Fulton, Park would have learned that the CIA was being sidelined as far as Vietnam policy went. The key decisions in the war were being taken by a triumvirate of interests representing the White House, the State Department and the Pentagon, the Agency being relegated to the role of local spy-runners and counterinsurgency operations, tasks it was not carrying out particularly well. It had no human sources of significance in the North Vietnamese intelligence or military administration and was reliant for the bulk of its human-sourced intelligence on the interrogation/torture of captured, relatively low-level North Vietnamese Army (NVA) regulars and Viet Cong (VC) guerrillas. It also had a number of associated activities, such as 'Phoenix Program' which aimed at executing suspected Viet Cong supporters/members among the civilian population.

Once her business in Saigon was done, it was time for Park to make the next and final leg of her journey, to Hanoi. The only way to get to Hanoi was by a special flight operated by the International Control Commission (ICC), a legacy of the Geneva Accord. The flight went first to Vientiane, then to Phnom Penh, and on to Hanoi. The Americans, who were still bombing the North on a daily basis, though not above the 20th parallel, interrupted their bombing runs once a week for just long enough for the aircraft to navigate the approach to Hanoi in safety. Vietnam was divided in two at the 17th parallel; the 20th was therefore well inside its borders but some miles distant from the capital Hanoi. The Pathet Lao guerrillas likewise halted their anti-aircraft missiles. Or so the theory went. Park made it in one piece on board a propeller-driven Stratocruiser – an aircraft originally intended to be the gold standard for trans-Atlantic crossings but now well past its best and held together by prayers and its French crew of pilots/mechanics.[14] As a previous holder of the post put it, 'All one could do was concentrate on one's reading and hope for the best.'

One of the first people Park would have called on during her stopover in Vientiane was Larry Devlin, now CIA station chief in Laos. Devlin was heavily involved in supporting the Hmong hill tribes in their war with the North Vietnamese Army (NVA) and their allies, the Pathet Lao guerrillas in Laos. The war was centred in the north of the country, the region bordering on North Vietnam, and was a dogged slugfest with up to sixty thousand NVA regulars involved at its peak. This was the largest paramilitary operation in the CIA's history, and it ran for thirteen years in all. No US ground troops were involved but the USAF flew thousands of sorties against the communist forces aided by Air America transports and by substantial numbers of volunteer Thai forces paid

i SHACKLEY. Theodore G. ('Ted'), Jr.; CIA (1927-2002).

for from CIA budgets. It was in many respects a mini-Vietnam, with broadly the same aim: to prevent (in this case) Laos falling into communist hands. From the NVA's perspective the main aim was to protect their supply lines inside Vietnam. They figured, correctly, that once they were victorious in Vietnam, Laos would fall into their hands.[15]

As station chief Devlin was the link between the main CIA paramilitary command post in Udorn in Thailand and the US ambassador to Laos, William Sullivan. Sullivan was responsible to the White House for the prosecution of the war in Laos, to the point where it was referred to as 'Sullivan's War' in Washington.[16] Devlin held the station job for four years, from 1968 to 1971. A tough no-holds-barred posting for a tough no-holds-barred man. Park would have had her cards well marked by Devlin by the time she left Vientiane for Phnom Penh and then on to Hanoi (this would be their third collaboration). Park's flight arrived in darkness and was escorted, passengers were told, by MiGs of the North Vietnamese Air Force. Ten minutes before the landing the aircraft started its spiralling combat descent into Gia Lam Airport, Hanoi.

For the uninitiated, entering any totalitarian state is something between intimidating and interesting; entering one in the middle of an all-out war will definitely incline the visitor towards the former. Prior to commencing her journey, Park had to complete an extraordinary array of documents. Scowling immigration officials now inspected these with exaggerated care and had her complete a further long green-coloured landing card. It was clear they considered her to be from an enemy state and not from the fraternal socialist fellowship. Eventually she was passed through and exited into the tall columned hall to where her number two, Warren Townend,[i] the vice-consul, and her outgoing predecessor, Gordon Philo, waited. Philo would depart later on the aircraft on which Park had arrived. He must have looked mightily pleased – almost as if he feared she might have funked the flight at the last minute and left him in post for a few months more. They shook hands, then bade each other farewell.

Despite his wartime Military Cross, there was a fairly widespread view within SIS that Philo wasn't really cut out for the work of SIS, as the following might indicate. Personnel Department always found filling the Hanoi post difficult. It was a tough station in every respect. Spartan accommodation, bad food, socially appalling (and usually unaccompanied) and during bombing raids quite dangerous. Desperate to find someone to take the post, Personnel asked an incumbent to approach Philo and sell him the idea of taking Hanoi. The incumbent agreed to approach Philo next time he was back in London. The day arrived. It was miserable, cold and grey, and the incumbent began to sing the praises of Hanoi to Philo – endless sunshine ... free and easy ... your

i TOWNEND, Warren Denis; diplomat (1945-).

own boss – and even showed him photographs of that year's Queen's Birthday Party with everyone seemingly in the highest of spirits. Philo fell for it and applied for the post. For as long as he remained in the Service Philo never again addressed the officer who had suckered him.[17]

Park and Townend left the airport in the mission's sole car, a Ford Escort which had just enough petrol left in its tank to make the return journey to the residence. Their journey was interrupted by another major inspection of documents at a checkpoint on the oft-bombed Paul Doumer Bridge. The bridge spanned the Red River and was the gateway into Hanoi proper. A blackout was in place so Park would have seen little of her surroundings. Thirty minutes later they pulled up outside the official residence. The consul-general had arrived. The residence, faintly pagoda-like in design, was located in a quiet tree-lined road near the centre of 'downtown' Hanoi. The locally employed staff (provided by the Department for Servicing Diplomats) included a driver called Tien, who according to John Colvin[18] was a hypochondriac and *fainéant* (lazy) with it. Colvin said Tien could usually be found seated in the stationary consulate car, a blazing metal box, enjoying temperatures of up to 120°F/48°C. There was a major-domo/general factotum called Monsieur Dong (referred to by Park in the passage that follows), a blind gardener, a not terribly good cook, and a first class secretary/translator called Monsieur Xuan who had been working for the consulate for at least seventeen years. All had to be considered to be spies for the regime; each quite vociferously accused the others of so being and in any event would have had little choice in the matter. Such was life in any outpost in a communist state. This is how Park described the residence:

> The Residence was formerly a house of ill fame. Handkerchiefs are boiled in the saucepans, other dirty clothes in the dustbin. When the household cat disappeared, opinion was divided whether she had been eaten by the neighbours or the rats. When even more water than usual flooded the bathroom floor, and even less (though more noisome) water came from the tap, and the plumbers eventually came, they withdrew for three days to attend cadre meetings before removing the dead rats they found in the pipes. No rodent extermination service exists because, officially, rats have been eliminated. Unfortunately the rats do not know this. When Ambassadors come to dinner and it rains, the drawing room floor is covered with buckets and saucepans to catch the water from the ceiling. The major-domo at the Residence has been at some earlier time an inmate of a mental institution; the misfortune is that he was ever released.[19]

Surprisingly the Hanoi post was not, apparently, considered a 'hardship' post by the Foreign Office up to the time Park went there. A hardship post attracted a fairly modest additional stipend and some other benefits. Park set about to securing that, as much for her successors, one imagines, as for her own benefit. In her opening salvo she used the same phrase as in her valedictory dispatch (quoted above), but with the addition of an extra one, as recounted to this author by former SIS officer Hugo Herbert-Jones:

> Daphne set out to convince the Foreign Office that Hanoi should be treated as a 'hardship post' qualifying for modest extra pay. Her chosen method was to start her initial Despatch with the words 'My Residence was once a house of ill-fame, and has a bidet in every bedroom'. It became a celebrated text, and she got her extra allowance.[20]

A short distance away was the office of the consulate-general, in Ly Thuong Kiet. It was a neat two-storey building, not unattractive, with a canopied entrance, blue shutters, and a small balcony on the first floor. There was an office for Park, one for her vice-consul, a strong-room and a secure cipher/radio room, plus some general facilities for the locally employed staff. The vice-consul lived in a separate apartment nearby. The contrast with Saigon was total. If Saigon was crowded streets, teeming traffic, endlessly honking horns, packed bars, teenage prostitutes and drunken off-duty American servicemen, then Hanoi was a city of low rise unpainted buildings, uniformly constructed from yellow sandstone, pockmarked from bomb shrapnel, and instead of cars and motorbikes the streets teemed with cyclists wearing pith helmets. There were some motorbikes but practically no civilian cars at all. What the American bombs had not already laid waste appeared to her eyes to have been destroyed by years of neglect. Perhaps a deliberate act of rejection of their French legacy by the administration, though despite everything some signs still remained of Hanoi's original grace.

To Western eyes the people appeared undernourished, poor and shabbily dressed, whole families sleeping in doorways and shelters – anything, apparently, to get away from the stifling heat which even at night barely diminishes.

> ... we are nearer to them, for we walk far more, and especially at night when the children who in daylight pursue us shrieking Lien Xo (Russian), and leave us black and blue with inquisitive pinches, are gathered round the family brazier on the pavement, eating their rice, or are already asleep. Young and old, like battered bundles, sleep in the hottest months on the steps of the Ministry of Foreign Trade, on the pavement, in doorways, anywhere out of the stifling courtyards and the houses where they live, a family to each room. The rats run over them as they sleep, fight over scraps of garbage, and sometimes drown in the water which gathers in the open concrete shelter-holes; and at flood time when the drains overflow and the streets for a while are two or three feet deep in rushing water, they swim along in the brown muddy flood with the leaves, twigs and rubbish. There are rats even in the cinema.[21]

Daphne Park was no longer in any doubt, if she ever had been, that this posting would stretch even her legendary *sangfroid* to its limits and beyond.

23

Hanoi 2 – 'Though never quite enough to ask for another year', 1969-70

The consulate-general's in-between status manifested itself almost immediately in how Park was officially received. Rather than present her credentials to the Foreign Minister, as would befit a consul-general, she would instead present them to the External Affairs Bureau of the Administrative Committee of the Hanoi Municipality, which was rather like being greeted in London by a functionary of the (then) Greater London Council. The mayor of the city, a relatively important personage, would not deign to meet during her stay.

In fact, as was made clear to Park, she would not be granted meetings with North Vietnam's leadership other than of the most fleeting kind at state or diplomatic receptions. The DRVN leaders trusted no one outside their own intimate circle and they most certainly did not intend taking Park into their confidence. Such conversations as she had with any were of the briefest duration and restricted to social pleasantries. Members of the Politburo (senior North Vietnamese government ministers) and Foreign Ministry officials would have no absolutely truck with Park or the other holders of the British post and made it clear they saw no value in using the consul-general as some sort of informal back-channel to the Americans. They viewed Britain as 'imperialist lackeys'. In an interview in 1965 with the journalist James Cameron, the North Vietnamese Premier Pham Van Dong stated, 'The British government's attitude is now so clearly a permanent reflection of Washington's that it can have no standing as a mediator whatever'.[1] Nothing that happened since seems to have altered that viewpoint. As the final snub she was told she would not be permitted to access a range of facilities reserved for overseas diplomats and the Communist Party elite. These included the Tong Dan special store, the ICC Club, swimming pool, use of a small retreat outside Hanoi, free importation of goods for personal use, etc.

Park had also to accommodate herself to her movements being controlled through the simple expedient of denying her any means of transport other than 'shanks's pony'. The only vehicle transport was the consulate car which was provided only with petrol for the monthly journey to and from the airport for the diplomatic bag and little else, other than by special arrangement. Bicycles, the mode of transport for the majority, were not permitted for consulate staff 'on safety grounds' though bicycle permits were applied for annually as a matter of

223

course. Once during her tenure the authorities relented when Park suggested that she be allowed a trishaw on which a representative of the DRVN security bureau could also travel, thus ensuring no improper advantage was secured by virtue of her being semi-mobile. This went swimmingly until one afternoon Park arrived at an official reception on her 'chauffeur-driven' trishaw with a Union Jack flag affixed to the handlebars, thus signifying her 'official' status. The privilege was at once withdrawn.[2]

She was allowed to walk about, but told she must restrict her walking to a two-square-kilometre block in the city centre, though the centre was not precisely defined. She was also to avoid areas forbidden to foreigners which, likewise, were neither marked on maps nor identified by signage. That said, practically every street had its own appointed lookout that would be quick enough to wave away any foreigner if they were trespassing on forbidden territory. One of her successors as H/HANOI, Julian Harston, described that aspect thus:

> The *de visu* reporting that could be done in Hanoi itself and on rare visits out was all fresh for our US cousins, and despite being limited to two square kilometres there were key places that could be visited on afternoon walks (I had five separate routes). Passing the rubbish bins outside the military hospital could give a good estimate of the number of soldiers being recruited just by counting the used syringes used for inoculations.[3]

One SIS holder of the post who stepped out of the permitted zone in order (he claimed) to visit one of the four Christian churches that were supposedly open was arrested. He was questioned and eventually released at four in the morning when he explained that visiting a church on Christmas Eve (which it was) was something Christians do.[4]

Photographs were permitted, but not of any sensitive installation nor of any particularly poor or deprived area. Photographs were to be in black and white only, to be developed locally and be available for inspection if required.[5] Of course every effort was made to circumvent those restrictions. Another of Park's successors, vice-consul Alan Prosser, was upbraided by the head of the Security Police in person for 'inadvertently' including in an 'innocent photograph of a lake' some of the people made homeless by US bombing and forced to live in air raid shelters.[6] According to Harston, Prosser was:

> ... an ex-SAS trooper who was an unusual SIS officer, whose love of Welsh rugby had kept him going in difficult times. On [our] arrival in Hanoi my wife and I quickly realised that he [Prosser] had spent his entire year in a sleeping bag on the living room floor ... Welsh chapel or SAS had taught him that comfort was sinful.[7]

Contact with Vietnamese at official level was tightly controlled, while at the level of the ordinary citizen it was non-existent. For a start no ordinary citizen would dream of calling on the consulate; to have done so would have invited detailed questioning from the Security Police and possibly a spell in jail. And even though there was not a policeman posted at the entrance to the consulate (because it was not an official diplomatic mission), it was monitored by the policeman who stood guard outside the nearby Algerian mission. Any formal meeting with an official, for example to request a particular facility or to iron out some issue or other, would be in the presence of a witness and conducted in Vietnamese in that person's hearing. There were no exceptions, for example on one occasion a medical consultation involving the wife of one diplomat and a local doctor had to be conducted in badly interpreted English to Vietnamese in the presence of the ubiquitous witness despite both the diplomat's wife and the doctor being fluent in French. To have attempted otherwise would have seen the consultation terminated at once. Park also had to come to terms with the slew of petty restrictions coupled with the sheer difficulty of navigating and negotiating life in the city. In her valedictory dispatch Park describes – with obvious feeling – this aspect of her situation on Hanoi:

> Nearly every necessity of life must be imported, though only upon receipt, after some months, of import permits listing each jar of herbs, each bundle of toothpicks. The Director of Customs has sometimes refused a permit, or proposed to allow in only part of the order, on the ground that H.M. representative 'has had enough this year' and does not need it. The presents most prized by local staff, when they dare to accept them, are razorblades, bicycle repair outfits, bottles (empty), and Aspro.[8]

Learning to deal with this bureaucracy was part and parcel of the life in Hanoi, as Park put it in one of her regular dispatches to London:

> In my dealings with the External Affairs Bureau, the Customs, the Police and so on I have always maintained ... a bland and amiable optimism and an apparent belief in the relatively good intentions and good sense of the Vietnamese officials. If things go wrong I assume that their only wish in life is going to be to help me solve the problem; looking somewhat surprised, they occasionally do, even according a certain amused respect to my tactics ... But although it is not part of their policy to squeeze us out they will make no major concessions and will continue to use a variety of tactics to secure [diplomatic] recognition ... *I have found a certain satisfaction in not noticing harassment when it happens* [author's emphasis] and I hope my successors will feel the same way.[9]

Sometimes the dealings had an almost 'Alice in Wonderland' aspect to them. On one occasion two fridges, imported in order to be able better to cater for the Queen's Birthday Party, were seized by customs. Due to a clerical error the fridges had been missed off the incoming aircraft's cargo manifest. The External Affairs Bureau official accused the consulate of involving them in 'condoning a felony' while the customs refused a suggestion that the fridges be exported and then re-imported on the grounds that the fridges were no longer consulate property but 'forfeit to the state'. A face-saving solution was eventually found and the drinks at the birthday party were suitably cold.[10]

Another 'Alice occasion' required desperate measures to get messages to the right people. Colvin was directed by London to hand a particularly important message directly to the Foreign Ministry. Unfortunately the DRVN Foreign Ministry refused all contact with the consulate. Colvin's solution was to approach the rear of the ministry building which boasted a fine garden tended by a gardener. Colvin attracted the man's attention, then stuck his arm through the barred gate and handed the startled gardener the missive from London, scarpering before the amazed man could do anything about it. Another holder was given a personal message from the then Foreign Secretary, Michael Stewart, to the DRVN leadership, with the usual instruction 'see that this gets to the right person, etc.'. He arranged to meet his usual contact in the Municipal Affairs office. When the meeting was over he stood up to leave the room, and as he said his farewells he thrust the letter, addressed to the Foreign Ministry, into the hands of the startled official, then scarpered – Colvin-like. He thought it probably got to the right person, but one could never be certain.[11]

Consular communications were closely scrutinised. The consulate was permitted to receive enciphered telegrams via the central Telegraph Office but not to dispatch anything other than *en clair* (plain text), presumably on the basis that to receive confidential instructions was permissible but to transmit outbound secret intelligence was not; and who was to say that was unreasonable?[12] The ban on outbound ciphers had been introduced after John Colvin made a fundamental error. He submitted a report in code to London on the aftermath of a particularly severe bombing raid by the USAF. In a follow-up report which he sent *en clair* he referred to the contents of the previous coded message in such a way that it was clear he had been secretly reporting on the effect of the US bombing. The DRVN authorities reacted predictably by banning all future outbound coded messages.[13] It was a bad mistake by Colvin and the result was a serious drawback; secure coded two-way communications are the lifeblood of any intelligence outpost, and diplomatic ones for that matter. Park's immediate predecessor, Gordon Philo, had once attempted to test the water by including a couple of enciphered sentences in an outbound telegram but had been refused.[14] The same rule applied to radio transmissions: the consulate was permitted to import and operate a radio *receiver* but not a *transmitter*.[15]

Even though it was not a recognised diplomatic outpost, the consulate had official use of a diplomatic bag on a monthly basis. However, this was not considered frequent enough for adequate reporting so undeclared use was made of a special weekly Canadian diplomatic 'red' bag which went out via Vientiane to Saigon and was always accompanied by a courier. This was used, not just for SIS messages, but to forward copies of the North Vietnamese newspapers to the Joint United States Public Affairs Office (JUSPAO) in Saigon[16] where they were eagerly scanned for even the slightest hints of changes in North Vietnamese attitudes and thinking. The authorities appeared to be aware of this unofficial practice. John Liudzius,[i] Park's immediate successor, once remarked 'on the additional interest displayed by the Security guards both near us and outside the Canadian office in our visits to the office on bag day'.[17] However interest was all it was; neither he nor Park (nor their vice-consuls) were interfered with in any way.

The monthly bag trips to Saigon had another advantage; they meant that Park and her vice-consul, Warren Townend (replaced by scientific officer Alan Smith when Townend's tour came to its end) could get some relief from Hanoi (and each other) by alternating who escorted the bag on each trip. They could replenish their personal effects and enjoy a couple of days of hot baths and a change of scenery. The journey went by way of Vientiane, giving Park the chance to catch up with Devlin during the stopovers when it was her turn. One person who looked forward to her visits to Saigon was Ambassador John Moreton. After Park died he wrote:

> Daphne's visits were like a breath of fresh air. She made light of all her difficulties, radiating optimism and always full of intellectual curiosity. It was a particular pleasure to learn of her plans to hold a Queen's Birthday Party in war-torn Hanoi, and to be shown the hat and dress bought specially for the occasion. British birds adorned both hat and dress. What a privilege, to have known her.[18]

Park had her Queen's Birthday Party (UK diplomatic equivalent to most countries' 'National Day') and it was attended by the Soviet ambassador, Ilya Shcherbakov,[ii] with whom, according to Gerry Warner, 'Daphne ... got on famously'.[19] As the Dean of the Diplomatic Corps, Shcherbakov's presence provided a form of 'diplomatic blessing' that helped ease her relations with other missions and open the door to conversations from which scraps of information might be gleaned. According to John Liudzius, Shcherbakov was 'not known for underestimating his own importance'. That said, he was an influential figure, thought to have the ear of Brezhnev. He was later ambassador to the People's Republic of China (PRC) at a particularly sensitive period in Sino-Soviet relations. The other missions were potentially fruitful sources of sometimes well-informed gossip, sometimes not, but all had to be mined. As Julian Harston commented:

---

i LIUDZIUS, 'Big' John Michael, OBE; Intelligence Corps, SIS, HELSINKI, SEOUL, RANGOON, H/HANOI (1916-1999).

ii SHCHERBAKOV, Ilya S.; Soviet ambassador to Hanoi 1964-74.

I always ended at the Thon Nghat hotel. Ghastly rat infested dump, where all visitors to Hanoi, and some embassies were ... Access to a bored and incestuous diplomatic community two or three days a week enabled the collection of personality and political assessments of a large number of dips, SovBloc and others.[20]

Shcherbakov and Park also met from time to time to exchange views, their conversations aided of course by her obligatory bottle of whiskey and her ability to converse in both French and Russian. Shcherbakov returned the favour and invited Park to a number of Soviet embassy receptions from which her predecessors had been excluded, giving her the opportunity to chat, if only at a surface level, with some senior DRVN ministers. But such receptions came with their own price, described by Park:

Very few weeks pass in Hanoi without a national day, an Army day, or a day to commemorate some socialist event. On those days, at seven p.m. precisely, the long line of official cars disgorges diplomats and cadres at the International Club. Between March and October, when the temperature in the shade may stand at 110 degrees, and the humidity at an unvarying 98%, shirtsleeves are worn, and like unhappy overheated penguins a long way from water, the socialist Ambassadors line up at the top table on the right of the host and the Dean, flapping their paper fans: on the left stand the Vietnamese. The arc lights burn, the mosquitoes whine, as the speeches are made – in Vietnamese with no translation, in Bulgarian, or Polish, or Russian, with Vietnamese translation only – and the diplomats cautiously clap with one eye on the Dean. Toasts are offered and a curious Nuts in May ceremony is observed; first the diplomats file past the Vietnamese, clinking glasses, then the Vietnamese return the compliment. After that both parties eat, wise diplomats confining themselves to the soup and the bread, the rest laying up worms and worse; the tables groan with dishes full of what may at best be sliced dog, of pork rolls, and mudfish from the paddies, and bright yellow ice cream. These rituals last two or three hours. Throughout, the Vietnamese stay on the left, the diplomats on the right of the hall; and crossing over is not encouraged. These occasions represent, in microcosm, the co-existence without contact which is diplomatic life in Hanoi.[21]

But it wasn't just receptions; Park's extraordinarily gregarious nature manifested itself in so many ways. Here is Harston again:

... Another example was the relationship she had with the younger members of the Soviet Embassy, whom she met at their regular film evenings. She spoke Russian as taught by White Russian émigrés in Paris, which for the young Soviets was fascinating. A voice from history was how one young second secretary described it.[22]

Here is this 'diplomat' known by the Soviets to be a British spy, yet welcomed into their regular film evenings to chat in old-fashioned Russian to the young diplomats. It was almost like a rehearsal for the chats she would later have with fascinated undergraduates in Somerville when she became Principal, though the Soviet embassy in Hanoi was no Oxford college.

As America's eyes and ears in Hanoi, Park was in a unique position to provide the US with practically its only human sourced intelligence from the heart of the enemy's capital. For their part the North Vietnamese authorities were aware of her role and were determined to prevent her from reporting anything that could damage their war effort. There was an element of cat and mouse about it, as Park once remarked: 'I went for a walk every day, and in the middle of the war, there's a lot you can see.'[23]

But Park had to tread warily. To have done otherwise would have been as unwise as it would have been difficult. She was a known member of SIS since her time in Moscow. In fact the true occupations of most of the SIS officers posted to Hanoi would have been known to the Soviets, betrayed by Blake or Philby or established through observation while on other foreign postings. It was a given that the Russians would, in the spirit of socialist fraternity, have passed that information to the North Vietnamese. For the SIS nominee to have been caught while engaged on overt espionage activity would, in all likelihood, have resulted in the closure of the consulate. In a worst case it could have led to the imprisonment of the consul-general since the holder of that position did not enjoy diplomatic immunity. One of Park's predecessors, Myles Ponsonby,[i] once came across a useful map containing some information about defence installations, which was duly passed on the Americans. The map whetted their appetite for more of the same, a request that drew a fairly curt response from the Foreign Office in London:

> Any task of this kind, particularly if it involved Ponsonby in a perceptible departure from his daily routine ... *could be dangerous to him personally* [author's emphasis] and could jeopardize the value for other purposes of keeping him in Hanoi.[24]

Despite the restrictions and the danger, a couple of sentences in a letter to the embassy in Saigon sent by Liudzius (like Park a well established SIS officer) hint at the possibility that there may have been some spy business contemplated if not actually undertaken.

> They [DRVN] probably assume that the post is used for extra-diplomatic purposes in UK, and probably in US interests, but calculate that no great damage can be done to them by this. There has certainly been no evidence of inordinate surveillance beyond the measures applied to most other missions ... *I have come*

i PONSONBY, Myles Walter, CBE; SIS, CAIRO, NICOSIA, BEIRUT, DJAKARTA, NAIROBI, H/HANOI, H/ROME, H/ULAANBAATAR (1924-1999).

across no indications of surveillance directed specifically against any of us [author's emphasis] except in the context of the weekly [diplomatic] bag dealings with the Canadians.[25]

The man who was to follow Liudzius into Hanoi, Joe Booth Wright, put the issue even more directly (Wright was not a member of SIS. During his tenure as consul-general the SIS job of H/HANOI was held by the vice-consul):

We *have no impression of an increase in surveillance, nor indeed of any deliberate attempt to dog our footsteps, or check on our comings and goings* [author's emphasis]. The guard opposite the residence generally sees us leave but has no means of knowing where we are going.[26]

An SIS officer with experience of Hanoi remarked that Wright's note to London betrayed the naivety of the diplomat. All that the DRVN authorities would have needed to do was install a bell push in the sentry hut for the soldier on duty to press anytime he spotted the consul leaving the building, so alerting the surveillance team on stand-by.

On the other hand, is it too fanciful to imagine that these innocent-appearing words contained a hidden meaning? These were official communications from the capital of an adversary, if not quite a declared enemy. The contents were considered and thought through and circulated at a very senior level in London. Copies and/or summaries were made available to the Americans and were eagerly awaited. It is possible that SIS (or the CIA) had recruited a North Vietnamese diplomat or official while he, or less likely she, was posted to an overseas country. The main targets (wish-lists more like) would have been any member of the Central Committee of the ruling Lao Dong Party (the Politburo), or officials in its secretariat. Next would have been the Central Office for South Viet Nam which coordinated political activity directed towards the South. Finally there was the DRVN's principal intelligence agency, the Central Research Agency (CRA).

To have successfully penetrated any of those organisations, and there is no evidence to say that either the CIA or SIS succeeded in that, would have to have been by means of an overseas recruitment. The intense scrutiny surrounding all interactions between Park and North Vietnamese officials made the possibility of a recruitment pitch, to or from either side during an official encounter, a practical impossibility. The same would have applied to senior people such as members of the Politburo or the apparatchiks. Three sentences were about as much as she might expect to have with a senior minister if he even deigned to acknowledge her presence during an official reception. Accessing really senior people overseas wasn't any easier. Their career path rarely included any substantial time spent abroad (other than as members of well guarded delegations, etc.). In all communist countries time spent overseas was politically disadvantageous and career limiting due to the perceived risk of 'contamination' from prolonged exposure to Western 'values'.

Recruitment was therefore invariably from the ranks of diplomats, intelligence officials and a tiny handful of specialists of one kind or another who were permitted to travel overseas. In all probability any approach would have been initiated by the betrayer (most are anyway) and probably in one of the neutral countries where North Vietnam was represented, such as Sweden or India, and where SIS and more probably the CIA would have had the required operational freedom to carry off the recruitment, London and Hong Kong being two other possibilities. Such a person could have filled a dead letter box (DLB) with secret material for later retrieval by the person handling them, whoever it might be. A dead letter box/DLB (dead drop in CIA parlance) would have been essential – they are used to pass information between an agent and the intelligence service on whose behalf she/he is spying. Its use obviates the necessity for face-to-face transfers, which are inherently dangerous.

Typically in Hanoi there was up to twelve hours of darkness daily, in theory cover enough for her to have serviced the drop and left instructions and special requests. It would have been extraordinarily risky, politically so too, but that was, after all, the business SIS was in. The only direct reference we have to agent running from Park is contained in an interview she gave in 2008, two years before her death. Accompanied by another former SIS officer, Baroness Meta Ramsay, Park was interviewed for the *Daily Telegraph* by journalists Rachel Sylvester and Alice Thomson. Sylvester and Thomson's report includes this sentence:

> As one of the Secret Intelligence Service's most senior controllers for more than 30 years, Lady Park, 88, *ran agents in Hanoi during the Vietnam War* [author's emphasis], smuggled defectors out of the Congo in the boot of her Citroen 2CV and was posted to Moscow when the KGB was at the height of its powers.[27]

The reference to running agents was made by Park during the interview.[28]

Running an agent in that environment would have taken extraordinary guts and courage. Park was a Westerner and a woman, whose considerable presence on any street would have been cause for immediate notice and comment even when engaged on the most innocent of activities. As stated earlier, every Hanoi street had its official lookout whose task it was to report the presence of foreigners or other unusual happenings; Daphne Park strolling down some alley definitely met that criterion. It would have taken every ounce of tradecraft she possessed, knowing that if she made the slightest error and was discovered it would have meant certain death for her source and quite possibly for his entire family and the loss of a possibly vital source of intelligence from inside the North's regime. Julian Harston doubts that Park was running agents in Hanoi.

I would be astonished if she ran agents in Hanoi, unless she was allowed to run agents in the diplomatic community (who had already been recruited elsewhere), but I doubt even that. The lack of any kind of opportunity to be in control of the environment meant that any kind of truly clandestine activity was out of the question ... Add to this that white people were very, very unusual and easily spotted whatever they were doing. No diplomats drove their own vehicles, not even the Soviets.[29]

However, Harston then goes on to mention a specific request from the Americans to service a dead letter box in Hanoi, a request he turned down.

On a de-briefing visit to Saigon I was asked by the Americans if I would consider emptying a DLB (dead letter box) in Hanoi. My reply was a gentle enquiry about their sanity ...[30]

In some regards this is contradictory information, but at the very least it provides an indication that the Americans may have had an agent in place in Hanoi at that time. Theodore Shackley, who was the CIA's station chief in Saigon during Park's time in Hanoi, spoke of how useful having a foreign diplomat in 'Hanoi or Beijing' on its books was to the CIA.[31] Might Park have responded differently than Harston says he did to such a request, particularly if it came from her old mate Larry Devlin or her wartime buddy, Luc Conein? She might indeed. Either way, SIS has never commented on the existence of any such agents among North Vietnamese officialdom, but then it hardly would.

The Americans were of course the ultimate (and probably principal) customers for any intelligence she could glean. One aspect of significant interest to the US was intelligence relating to the whereabouts and treatment of the US prisoners of war held close to Hanoi, mainly downed airmen. The prisoner issue was a topic of major domestic political concern in the US with rumours of torture and neglect rife, rumours that later turned out to be true.

The main POW holding centre was Hoa Lo prison, *aka* the Hanoi Hilton. The prison was a short stroll from the consulate. Hoa Lo was home to several hundred US POWs held in appalling conditions. The US had contingency plans for urgent intervention in the event that the POWs lives were physically threatened at any stage. Separately it was also planning at least one specific prisoner rescue attempt at the time Park was in Hanoi and would have asked her to get as much intelligence as she could about that site. The target for that attempt was Son Tây prison, about twenty miles from the centre of Hanoi. That was presumably considered to be a more feasible target than a large, well guarded prison in the middle of the city. The raid on Son Tây took place on 17 November 1970, a few weeks after Park returned home. It was successful up to a point. Successful in that the site was seized and brought under control of the US rescue force, but unfortunately the sixty-five US prisoners held there had been moved out of the camp a week or so before the rescue attempt due to flood damage. So the raid was in vain. The rescue force withdrew, suffering no fatalities.

But there would still have been focus on the main prison. While the US had high quality aerial surveillance photographs of Hoa Lo, 'walk-by' observations with details of guard posts, how many sentries, their alert state, weaponry, availability of motor transport for pursuit or escape and so on would have been useful. According to Julian Harston, the street was blocked off to pedestrian traffic, but that may have occurred after the raid on Son Tây. An SIS officer who served in the region at the time was pretty certain that Park provided useful intelligence to the Americans regarding Hoa Lo.

When she was in Saigon on one of her regular visits to the city, Park, in common with other holders of the post, spent a lot of time in the company of CIA officers, being debriefed and trying as best she could to answer their questions. The British consul-general was one of their very few pairs of live 'eyes' on the ground in the enemy capital. Park, personally, was also very much a known and admired quantity to the Americans, not simply 'another Brit intelligence officer'. She was the woman to whom Lucien Conein had turned when he wanted his Jed teams in Algiers to be readied for their mission. He had joined the CIA after the war and was heavily involved in the Agency's work in Vietnam. He had resigned by the time she arrived but was still based in Saigon, and Park spoke of meeting him there.[32] And another former Jed trainee, future CIA head Bill Colby, was also around, leading the Phoenix assassination program, aided and assisted by none other than Douglas Bazata, a man who knew something about killing. And there was Devlin in Vientiane. So Park was 'plugged into' the Americans in Saigon in a way many SIS colleagues might not have been. They used her to their utmost and she used them in return, telling Martyn Cox that she had no problem dropping Bill Colby's name (particularly after he was appointed Director of the Agency) if she needed a favour done from some CIA officer.

It wasn't all work and Saigon was a chance to relax. Because of the security situation a curfew was in place from 10 p.m. to 6 a.m. Partygoers had to ensure they were back in their living quarters by curfew time; if not they were stuck in the party until dawn (there were worse fates). Some of the more youthful, such as Andrew Fulton, the SIS station's number two, would head straight from the party to the golf course and get a round in before the heat became unbearable. A scratch golfer, the twenty-six-year-old used to enjoy 'taking some money off the American officers'.[33] Fulton probably built up some useful connections while he was at it, useful then and later on for his two stints in the US.

Park attended quite a few of the parties, but she was not a huge fan and rarely let her hair down fully. On occasion the parties turned into very heated debates. More than once Park and reporter Clare Hollingsworth[i] (the first war correspondent to report the outbreak of the Second World War) exchanged heated words. Hollingsworth was not a great admirer of US involvement in the Vietnam War, so the two 'alpha females' used spark off one another. On another occasion one of those attending a party – a girlfriend of Andrew Fulton who had been on home leave from her job as a nurse to US forces in Saigon – brought back with her the just-released Beatles LP, *Abbey Road*. That was one of the nights when the curfew was missed and the assembly passed the time playing and replaying the LP, probably at maximum volume. Park (then almost fifty and well past her pop music days) said nothing, but on her next visit to Saigon she had a present for Fulton. She had been attending an SIS meeting in Singapore (SIS regional headquarters) and used the opportunity to buy an LP of a Mozart string quartet. This she gave to Fulton, a subtle reminder to the young SIS officer that there was more to music than the Beatles. He later appreciated the way she gave him the message, no dressing down, no complaint to his boss, just a point made.[34] Park had some justification for her chiding. The parties, usually held in either the louche Caravelle Hotel or its slightly more straight-laced neighbour, The Continental, were attended by 'interesting' people, a mixture of journalists, diplomats and stray military types and spies, all mingling, swapping gossip and drinking too much. Polish diplomats attached to the International Control Commission (ICC) might venture out to them occasionally. Many of the partygoers, and certainly the Poles, were of significant intelligence interest to the local SIS station, so its members would have been expected to have been alert to the possibilities the parties presented and not simply be there bopping the night away to overloud pop music (that being Park's view anyway).

One of the factors impacting negatively on the ability to gather 'casual' intelligence (as opposed to the highly dangerous business of agent-running) was the perennial lack of Vietnamese speakers in the consulate. Park referred to this in one of her dispatches, suggesting that FCO appointments to Hanoi be made earlier thus enabling vice-consuls in particular to be taught the rudiments of the language. That way they might be able to read building names and *notices* [Park's emphasis].[35] Her point was well made, for the communist administration made widespread use of street posters and notice boards to exhort, advise and inform the populace of matters of significance to the leadership. Being able to comprehend the content of such notices would have been an obvious advantage, as would have been the ability to read local newspapers. Park applied to the authorities for permission to hire a language tutor to learn Vietnamese while she was there but was refused. It didn't stop her from attending whatever publicly accessible fairs, museums and exhibitions were open to her, carrying on the tradition established by her and her colleagues in Moscow to such good effect.

By definition anything written about specific espionage activities, as opposed to general observations, diplomatic reporting etc., that might have been undertaken by Park, is in the realm of speculation. That said, Park was a spy and 'a spy is, what a spy does'. There would have been little point in sending a trained spy to Hanoi if all she was expected to do was act like a conventional diplomat. Unlike a duck, a spy operating under diplomatic cover might well talk like a diplomat and walk like a diplomat but he or she is most definitely *not* a diplomat (most prefer the term 'intelligence officer' to describe what they do, but they are really spies). The pressure on intelligence officers (some self-generated) to secure secret intelligence is considerable; they do not want to spend their time *en poste* 'telling their beads'.

Park was sent to Moscow to spy and we know that she did spy. Her actions in Léopoldville were those of a spy and quite separate in purpose and effect from those of her diplomatic colleagues. It can be assumed, or at least presumed, that she was sent to Hanoi to spy as well and that she did. What she actually got up to, in detail, is locked in the vaults of SIS. So we cannot say for sure if she was able to get to close Hao Lo prison and secure some useful intelligence. But might she have tried? Might she have serviced a dead letter drop if asked to by Larry Devlin or Bill Colby? You can bet your bottom dollar she would.

We do know that she never gave up in her attempts to forge some form of connection with the leadership of the DRVN and in that she was eventually rewarded by being granted very occasional but invaluable access.[36] She gave a description of one such meeting to the MP Chris Mullin:[i]

> [Park] described how one morning a senior member of the politburo turned up unannounced at her house, and spent six hours chatting on her veranda. 'We have agents in every ministry and every village in the south,' he boasted. 'In that case,' inquired Park, 'why do you find it necessary to hang village headmen?' 'Because we are Leninists and Lenin believed in revolutionary terror,' was the chilling reply.[37]

Park's report of that meeting would make interesting reading. It is, however, not contained in the Foreign Office files for Hanoi for that period in the National Archives, either because it was withheld or because Park had a direct communication line to SIS in Century House for ultra-secret material and so it never got to the Archive in the first place.

The thirteen months passed and in October 1970 her posting came to its scheduled end. For Park it was a career-defining posting, if not a life-defining

i MULLIN, Christopher John; politician (1947-).

experience. She had arrived weeks after the death of Ho Chi Minh and at a pivotal time in the Vietnam War. Isolated in Hanoi, she was cut off from the saturated Western news media's coverage of the war and was forced to rely on diplomatic pouch bulletins, long-wave radio broadcasts and sterile North Vietnamese propaganda for her information. But as she observed, the mere fact of being there was illumination in itself. It is interesting that years later she concluded that the US decision to pull out, while understandable in context, was the wrong one:

> The writing might have been on the walls in the South, but it was on the North Vietnamese walls too. If the Americans hadn't succumbed to the tremendous pressure at home, history might have been different.[38]

Park was fortunate in that her tour took place during an interregnum in the US bombing of the city. In fact the evacuated schoolchildren were returning to their parents in Hanoi as she arrived, though within two years they would be evacuated again. It must have struck her as ironic given that she too had been evacuated, in her case during the Blitz when Rosa Bassett School was moved to the English countryside. Joe Wright, whose tour followed on that of her immediate successor, John Liudzius, mentioned reading official DRVN circulars to the effect that diplomats killed in US bombing raids might have to be buried in their embassy grounds. So she was spared that possibility at least.[39]

For Park, almost fifty years old by then, it was more the steady wearing away that took its toll. The difficult day-to-day life, the effort it took to secure the simplest thing from the North Vietnamese bureaucracy, the stress of rarely knowing for certain whether the action or inaction was politically motivated or just the result of plain inertia. Some idea of the stress associated with the job was how the hair of one of her successors (Hilary La Fontaine) turned white over the course of her posting. As one (unnamed) holder of the post remarked, perhaps a little bit contradictorily:

> '... it [the Hanoi post] was known in the office as the worst post in the world at least 10 years before I got there (that is, in terms of acute discomfort, health risks, limitations, isolation and general beastliness)' ... However, this is not to say that Hanoi was not sought after by FCO personnel, for 'it was also a fascinating post politically, an immense challenge, and deeply interesting'.[40]

A former SIS officer who worked closely with Park during her time in Hanoi told this author that he formed the impression that she had not enjoyed her time in Hanoi very much if at all, and who could blame her? However, even if true, it was not something that Park would have wished to admit. She spoke of an experience that she would not have missed, as she put it in her valedictory dispatch:

Like me, most of them have wanted to come here and left with some regret – though never quite enough to ask for another year.[41]

And as so often with her, her timing was impeccable. Her tour in Moscow coincided with Budapest and Suez; Léopoldville for the first major face-off between East and West in post-colonial Africa; Lusaka in time for Rhodesian UDI; and Hanoi at the most critical turning point in the war. As she said:

When I arrived here thirteen months ago buffaloes grazed on the grass in front of the Consulate General, the factory defence militia practised unarmed combat and grenade throwing there, an occasional battered *cyclo-pousse* creaked past carrying a family and its chattels, and at night the bats swooped and the cicadas were noisy. None of this has changed. But the sentry outside the Algerian Embassy has planted a garden round his sentry box, Hanoi is full of new lorries, the shape of Ho Chi Minh's mausoleum is under debate, and the State Plan for 1970 has allowed the Residence roof to be mended; my successor will not need to catch the drops in the drawing room. A new kitten appeared at the Residence this month, and may one day kill rats if it survives. We have moved a few steps out of Limbo for we have been allowed to travel, and perhaps even Hell is a little less hot than before. The children are back from the country and Hanoi is a year further from the war. I do not yet know, and neither do the Vietnamese, whether that means they are a year nearer to peace.[42]

Commenting on this, Saigon-embassy based Donald McD. Gordon observed with some prescience:

The South Vietnamese cordially dislike Northerners ... whom they resent as being forceful, arrogant, insensitive and efficient. The Southerners combine a streak of indolence (and often corruption) with a sense of humour and a sense of local (Cochin-Chinese) national identity. They have no desire to take over the North. Unfortunately the traditional North Vietnamese *Drang nach Süden* (Urge for the South) seems to remain as strong as ever. In the longer if not the shorter term, it is going to take a lot of stopping.[43]

And it wasn't stopped. On 30 April 1975, four and a half years after Gordon's memo, North Vietnamese Army units took final control of Saigon. The last word goes to the Deputy Under-Secretary, Sir Frank Tomlinson,[i] who observed, on being circulated with Park's valedictory dispatch:

An illuminating dispatch which enhances my admiration for Miss Park's fortitude (and her prose style!).[44]

We do not know if Park ever encountered Douglas Bazata during any of her visits to Saigon. If she did it certainly did not lead to any rapprochement. Park

i TOMLINSON, Sir Stanley Frank, KCMG; diplomat (1912-1994).

returned to London in November 1970 to be awarded the CMG for her work in Hanoi, to add to her OBE. That level of award certainly signified *something*. CMGs are awarded for meritorious overseas service and usually to those of a higher rank than Daphne Park had attained at that time. Park was the first ever woman officer in the Service to be so honoured.

24

What Daphne did next, 1970-74

The bones of what Park did in the four years between leaving Hanoi and being appointed as Controller/Western Hemisphere (C/WH) in 1975 are known, but as bones go they are pretty bare.

The standard curriculum vitae used by the FCO and others to chart this period of Park's career states that in 1971 she took a sabbatical year from the FCO during which time she was an Honorary Research Fellow in Kent University in England. In the spring of the following year (1972) she then went to Ulaanbaatar, capital city of Mongolia, as *chargé d'affaires* for barely three months. When she returned to London she did what Gerry Warner said[1] were a couple of 'operational jobs', before her appointment as Controller (C/WH). That's true, as far as it goes, but it leaves a bit to the imagination.

One explanation offered for her stint in Kent University was she was there to write an account of her time in Hanoi (an explanation offered in passing to her friend Jean Sackur, and a facility granted from time to time by the Service), and perhaps to use the time to recover from the ordeal of Hanoi which obviously had taken its toll. When interviewed by Caroline Alexander for *The New Yorker*, Park mentioned this, saying she had completed the first six chapters when asked to drop everything (which she did with some relief) and go to Ulaanbaatar. An alternative suggestion is that she was in Kent in order to learn Mongolian as preparation for replacing the incumbent John Colvin as ambassador in the spring of 1972. However Kent University did not offer Mongolian as a subject at that time (the University either can't or won't say how it was she spent her time there). In her interview with Caroline Alexander Park maintains she 'never expected to be called' to the Ulaanbaatar post. Nor does this take account of the fact that John Colvin had only taken up his appointment in Ulaanbaatar in 1971 so for him to leave in 1972 would have been ahead of the normal three-year stint. If Park was a temporary replacement for Colvin, that too was unusual: it was not normal Foreign Office practice to send a replacement head of mission to a post to cover for the incumbent's annual leave which in any event would not normally amount to three months. It may be that Colvin was on extended home leave for compassionate reasons or because he was in need of medical treatment. However he makes no mention of either in his book, *Twice Around the World*, where he describes his time in Mongolia in some detail.

Perhaps there is a less innocent explanation. While Park was in Ulaanbaatar she made a trip to Beijing, staying as a guest of the British ambassador at the time, John Addis.[i] The ambassador relates an amusing anecdote about Park wishing to purchase some small gifts to give to the locally employed staff of the ambassador's residence.[2] Addis gives as the reason for Park being in Beijing that she was 'on leave from her lonely posting in Mongolia'. Perhaps she was, but her 'lonely posting' lasted about three months (Park's first dispatch to the FCO in London was dated 29 March and her last is towards the end of May), so she wasn't really there long enough for the loneliness to become unbearable. Ulaanbaatar was not Hanoi. One explanation could be that Park was in Beijing for operational reasons, meeting with SIS colleague Gordon Barrass[ii] perhaps who was stationed there at the time, and that that was the reason why she was sent to Ulaanbaatar as Colvin's temporary replacement in the first place, to run an operation, perhaps one that required Russian which Colvin was not known to speak. All we can be certain of is that by 27 June Colvin was back in Ulaanbaatar 'from leave in London'[3] and Park had returned home to Britain. Colvin stayed until 1974 when he was replaced by Myles Ponsonby, also of SIS and, like both Colvin and Park, a veteran of the Hanoi post.

Mongolia, brief as the posting was, was going to be an interesting appointment, not least because it was another one of those 'unusual' quasi-diplomatic, quasi-espionage outposts. The Foreign Office viewed the country as a Soviet colony and so not worthy of separate representation. SIS didn't agree. Stuck between China and the Soviet Union, it was precisely the sort of place where it wanted to be. Matters came to a head in an unusual way. In 1962 an SIS officer en route back to London from his posting in Beijing decided to travel overland to Moscow via Ulaanbaatar (in so doing he was breaking about a dozen rules, travelling through the Soviet Union unaccompanied being the least of them). He had no particular reason, other than that at the time the tensions between China and the Soviet Union were rising and that made Ulaanbaatar 'interesting'. Some of the tension was ideologically driven; some was a remnant of ill-feeling over border settlements between the two states which the Chinese felt were unfair. The combination of the two was enough to stir his curiosity (good spies are incessantly curious) and he was an adventurous sort. When he arrived in Ulaanbaatar he presented himself to the authorities, this despite having no official status whatever, there being no diplomatic relations between the two countries. The Politburo made him royally welcome; he sat in an honoured position at the National Day parade and had some interesting discussions. After ten days of this he went on his way. When he arrived back in London he submitted a report recommending that consideration be given to opening an embassy in the country.

i ADDIS, Sir John Mansfield, KCMG; diplomat (1914-1983).

ii BARRASS, Gordon Stephen, CMG; SIS, HONG KONG, BEIJING, BERNE, C/SOV-BLOC (1940-).

Perhaps the matter was under consideration in any event, but the report seems to have stirred things up and negotiations commenced in Beijing between the Mongolian and British authorities. In fact Mongolia had been effectively (if not technically) subsumed into the Soviet Union as far back as 1924, so the FCO's point that it was not a separate political entity had some merit. But an embassy offered a number of things, all valuable in their own right. First of all flashpoints are inherently interesting to SIS and a flashpoint between Russia and China was way up the totem pole in terms of interest. It could also serve as a listening post to be staffed by GCHQ technicians that would enable Britain to eavesdrop on sensitive Chinese and Soviet military communications, and that was potentially extremely useful. It could also provide a door on which any KGB officer thinking about defecting could knock. That last was critical to SIS, because it had come to realise that in most if not all cases of defection, the running was more than likely to be made by the defecting party. Pitching for defectors was proving to be a bit of a mug's game, but having a ready door on which anyone considering defection could knock had some prospect of success and had become SIS's default strategy.

The Foreign Office still wasn't convinced, but SIS pressed. Well, you can pay for it then, said the Foreign Office, probably quite sniffily, and so in 1963 the Service gained what it liked to refer to as 'its' embassy.[4] Granted, it was the smallest one in the stable though it did contain a well staffed listening post (confirmed by Park[5]). Not all heads of mission were SIS officers but a number were, including Colvin, Ponsonby and Roland Carter, who had served with Park in Moscow. The cost was split between SIS and the FCO.

For Park, arriving in Ulaanbaatar would have been like going back, if not a century, then maybe two. There were no organised farms, no effective postal service, no telephone or telegraph system, no national transport infrastructure. And this was a big country, six hundred thousand square miles. Ulaanbaatar itself, with a population of less than a million, was not huge but it was well spread out. There was very little traffic and what there was, was mostly official or military. After leaving the airport, she would have passed beneath a giant oriental arch to reach the outskirts of the city that went on for miles and consisted of rows and rows of gers, the traditional tent-like Mongol dwellings. The city itself had smokestack factories billowing black smoke and blocks of shoddy high-rise apartment blocks, similar to what she would have seen in Moscow. In the background were towering mountain ranges whose peaks were snow-covered throughout the year.

The chancery was a surprisingly elegant building on Peace Street, the main thoroughfare. It had been the home of the Cuban embassy, but they had been slung out by the Mongolian authorities for not paying their rent and the building had become vacant. For once the FCO had moved with some alacrity and secured it for HMG's use, thus freeing the embassy from the 'awful' Hotel Ulaanbaatar, its previous home and the then current home of the French mission.

Ruled over by the despotic Yumjaagiin Tsedenbal since 1952, Mongolia was a police state in the best traditions of such institutions, with the (not so) hidden hand of the Department of State Security (DSS) everywhere. Contact with foreigners was banned except as part of a person's official duties. Travel was highly restricted. Native Mongolians were permitted one visit to the countryside a year to see relatives; other than that they were confined to the city (and this in a nomadic society!). Park would have more freedom of travel than the inhabitants; she was permitted to go up to forty kilometres from Ulaanbaatar without special permission. Travel to the rest of the country was allowed, other than to the border zone. The Russians, who permeated official life, lived in their own zone located behind the British embassy, consisting of block after block of uniformly grey high-rises, shoddy and in poor repair. They had their own shops to which entry was prohibited to non-Russians, their own entertainment, hospitals, and so on. Conceptually it was similar to the US practice of creating 'little Americas' in their overseas posts, but about fifty years behind in terms of amenities. There were no bars in Ulaanbaatar and few cafés, but there was one thing that was plentiful – mutton. All holders of the post remarked that the Mongolians had found uses for every conceivable part of the twenty million sheep that grazed there. The only meat served was mutton, the only fabric was wool, the only lamp oil was tallow from mutton. By the time you returned from your Mongolian posting everything you had smelled of sheep.

At the time of Park's assignment East-West relations were icy. The Vietnam War was still raging with the North Vietnamese receiving substantial amounts of aid from both Russia and China. The bombing of Hanoi, suspended during Park's time in the city, had been resumed in earnest. The Sino-Soviet split and how it was being played out were the dominant features of the embassy's reporting. US President Nixon visited Beijing in March and Moscow in May, so Park was well placed to report on reactions from both countries' ambassadors to Ulaanbaatar. A number of Park's dispatches are available in the UK National Archives. Interestingly none contain the sort of musings about life that so dominated her dispatches from Hanoi. However in her interview with Caroline Alexander for the *New Yorker* she provides some insight:

The beauty of the situation in Mongolia was that although the regime was Communist, it was a country with twenty million animals and one million people. If you have got only one million people and you want to spread them over industry and agriculture and education and you want to send them abroad to conferences, there aren't many left over that you can put in jail or a camp. You have to be very selective. Therefore, up to a point the Mongols – I wouldn't say they got away with murder, but they could drag their feet quite spectacularly. I remember talking to an unfortunate technical adviser from Hungary, or Rumania, or somewhere, who got rather drunk and told me that he had been there about fifteen years, and had originally been sent in to help the Mongols set up a factory – representatives from the bloc countries were frequently sent in to set up shoe factories or carpet factories, or some such thing. The theory was that they would be there for six months to teach the Mongols how to do the work, and then they would leave, and the Mongols would supply the Eastern-bloc countries with boots, or carpets.

But the Mongols didn't see it that way, because in the summer all sensible Mongols spent their time on the steppe riding and making children and drinking koumiss. That's what you did. It was a very short summer, and you didn't waste it on anything but that. The winter was very long and rather cold and uncomfortable, and so you hibernated as much as possible. You stayed at home and kept warm, and probably drank quite a lot, because the food wasn't very remarkable in its variety – mutton, mutton, and mutton. As a result, there were never enough Mongols to run the factories. They couldn't be forced to go there, and if they did they fell asleep in the corners. So, years later, all these unfortunate Hungarians were still running the factories.[6]

Later, in a dispatch to the Foreign Office, she does though recount a film evening held in the Soviet embassy, probably as a part of the celebrations marking the end of the Second World War. Her style is unusually acerbic:

Not for the first time I was obliged on May 6th, to sit through a Soviet so-called documentary film, made in 1970, which perpetuates the lie that – *Kak Vsem Izvestno* – the Soviet Union won World War II entirely on its own ... I had at first the doubtful pleasure of Colonel Larionov[i] as a neighbour. Crushing me sideways, he blew unwanted explanations in my ear through the usual Russian miasma of stale cabbage, garlic, vodka and the current version of the disagreeable Soviet aftershave which used to be known (to us) as Stalin's Breath. However, when he told me as an Englishwoman I could have no idea of what the war had meant since the Germans had left us alone and thrown their whole weight against the Russian people, I remarked tartly that on the contrary the bombed cities of England, from London to Coventry, had some very direct experience of war. But at that time, when we were fighting the war alone, the Soviet Union was still of course enjoying a very rewarding alliance with the Nazis; it must have been a nasty shock to be attacked by their ally in 1941. Colonel Larionov left me rather abruptly after that so I was not able to continue his education ...[7]

A few days later Park attended the wreath-laying ceremony. This time what caught her eagle eye was Mrs Tsedenbal, the wife of the Mongolian leader:

I had not met before the wife of Tsedenbal. Wearing one of those fearsome Russian hats for the well-dressed woman conceived of a union between a hairy sombrero and a shovel, she looked and behaved like a matron in a Soviet sanatorium, and her notion of an archly smiling but reproving look seemed to shrivel all but the blandly cheerful leather faced Mongols.[8]

i LARIONOV, Valentin V. (later General Major); Red Army.

Park's final dispatch from Ulaanbaatar is dated 27 May. It is a routine report of a conversation she had with the Chinese ambassador to Mongolia who had called on her on the previous day. There is no reference to her leaving her post soon, no hail and farewell, though perhaps the reason why the ambassador was calling on her was to do with the fact that she was leaving.

By the end of June 1972 Park appears to have been back in London because Colvin had resumed his dispatches. Her next post was as H/UKC. UKC was the Africa 'natural cover' station which ran UK-based third country operations directed at African targets. This section, known colloquially within SIS as 'Africa Attack', operated separately from the Africa country stations.[9]

The SIS term 'natural cover' approximates to the CIA's 'non-official cover' and is used to describe officers and operations which are not embassy based but operate under the cover of business executives, journalists, aid workers and so on. Because of past colonial links there was a substantial presence in the UK of African 'persons-of-interest' to SIS. These would have included people active in African politics, some perhaps fomenting opposition to the increasing number of despotic regimes on the continent, others keeping an eye out for the regime's interests, and various journalists, reporters, lobbyists, diplomats and other key influencers. This responsibility was shared with the Security Service with whom Park's section cooperated on a day-to-day basis. UKC also trawled through the student lists at UK universities seeking potential recruits from among the future African elite. Most of the major intelligence services favour this method of recruitment.[10] Candidates for possible recruitment can be assessed at leisure for their current or more often their future potential while the recruitment process itself is relatively risk-free and operationally straightforward. Park had one other operational job during this period, possibly as head of all UK stations. She was now living, if not quite above the shop, then at least very close to it, in a small flat in Vauxhall Bridge Road, across the street from the SIS London station and quite near the SIS head office building, Century House, at 100 Westminster Bridge Road.

Her secret love affair continued, in secret as always, now into its second decade. It had perforce to remain secret. For while in February 1973 the FCO formally rescinded Diplomatic Service Regulation No. 5 on marriage and so ended the marriage bar, it was, quite extraordinarily, still retained by SIS and would not be abolished there until after the end of the Cold War.[11] Whether by this time Park and her partner would have chosen to marry we do not know, but in the event that option wasn't open to her if she wished to see out her service in SIS. So a secret lover she remained in the secret service of her country.

25

C/WH 1 – Spymaster, 1975-77

In 1975 Daphne Park, now living in Ashley Gardens near Victoria, was appointed to what was to be her final post in SIS, as Controller Western Hemisphere (C/WH). It was a signal honour, an assurance, if such was needed, that the Service had no doubts about her fealty. She was also the first woman officer to reach that rank, an extraordinary achievement. SIS Controllers were and probably still are the top dogs, the equivalent of the CIA's Divisional Directors. Controllers were SIS's most senior line managers, the spymasters of lore, responsible for the successful prosecution of the Service's intelligence agenda in their area. Here is how one officer described it:

> At that time the regional bosses were Directors. Later re-organisation under the influence of the FCO turned those jobs into Controllers and inserted functional rather than area directors above them, *viz* Support Services (science and tech.), Counter-Intelligence and Security, Personnel and Administration, Requirements and Production.
> However the Controllers continued to be responsible directly to the Chief, rather than to the Director of Production who mainly shadowed the Chief in relations with the FCO. Controllers negotiated and were responsible for their own budgets and staffing and continued effectively to run the Service as an operational entity, leaving its administration to the Directors. It was a quite marvellous job; we were the princes – or in Daphne's case the princesses – what we wanted we got – at once![1]

Maurice Oldfield held Park in high regard and as Chief would have been instrumental in her getting a Controller's position – the appointment would certainly have required his approval. As Vice-Chief to John Rennie,[i] he had also been instrumental in her getting the equally interesting but rather more arduous Hanoi position. Perhaps Oldfield recognised a kindred spirit or simply enjoyed the prospect of working with her; he would be her effective boss for most of her time as Controller, only being replaced as Chief by Dickie Franks[ii] in 1978.

It was not a particularly good time to be taking up the appointment. Although the Service had emerged from the torpor and trauma of the 1960s, it was subject to a series of continuing budget cuts by successive governments determined to

i RENNIE, Sir John Ogilvy, KCMG; diplomat, Chief of SIS 1968-73 (1914-1981).
ii FRANKS, Sir Arthur Temple ('Dickie') Franks, KCMG; HM Forces, SOE, SIS, CYPRUS, TEHRAN, BONN, Chief 1978-82 (1920-2008).

contain public spending, as Professor Philip Davies puts it in his account of the organisation of SIS:

> ... [providing] virtually definitive evidence that the UK intelligence community, and the SIS in particular, had been run down to such a level that they could no longer defend the Realm from Third World dictatorships, let alone the USSR and its satellites ... the western hemisphere [controllerate] had suffered more heavily from the operational cuts ...[2]

In some respects it was a contradictory situation. While the Service was definitely better organised to carry out its work, its ability to do so was materially affected by its continuing lack of financial resources. This was a malaise that affected far more British institutions than just the SIS, but since it operated out of public sight it was an easier target. This was a tough time for the economy; a threatened run on the British pound was only halted by swingeing public expenditure cuts and a $3.9 billion IMF loan, then the largest ever applied for, though because of increasing North Sea oil revenues the full amount was never drawn down.

It wasn't all bad, though. The decade had commenced with the defection of KGB officer Oleg Lyalin and the subsequent expulsion by the Heath government of a hundred and five KGB/GRU officers from London. The two London intelligence residencies had collectively formed the Russian intelligence services' largest overseas intelligence collection operation and were a principal centre for the Soviet's successful technological and scientific intelligence acquisition programme. The expulsions dealt a hammer blow to the Soviets' intelligence ops because henceforth the intelligence services would have to compete for the available diplomatic slots with the other government departments. The expulsions and a more aggressive pursuit of the policy of refusing diplomatic accreditations to known Soviet intelligence officers (thus reducing the pool of experienced KGB/GRU officers available for posting to the UK) sent a strong signal that MI5 and its government masters still had some teeth and were not totally 'broken-backed'.

Three years later and just before Park took up her post as C/WH, the Service's 'open door' policy paid off when it welcomed its first senior defector-in-place in the KGB, Oleg Gordievsky.[i] The recruitment was not before its time. According to Hugh Bicheno:

> In 1963 after Blake and Philby the top brass in SIS decided that the only way of ensuring SIS was not penetrated was to penetrate the RIS. Dearlove and Scarlett played key roles in that.[3]

i GORDVIESKY, Oleg Antonovich, CMG; KGB (SIS) (1938-).

Former Chief Richard Dearlove[i] and John Scarlett[ii] have come in for some, probably justified, criticism for their participation in Tony Blair's 'sofa' government and their apparent acquiescence in the infamous '45 minutes' Iraq invasion dossier. But in recruiting Gordievsky they went straight to the top of the class.

Like the well-regarded Oldfield, they knew that 'spies betray spies'. Blake had been betrayed by a Polish intelligence officer, Goleniewski. Philby knew he could be betrayed at any time; in fact it was a minor miracle they he hadn't been by Krivitsky or Orlov[iii] or Volkov[iv] (any one of whom could have blown the whistle on him). The stress induced by this fear of disclosure undoubtedly contributed signally to Philby's prodigious drinking. In the end his fate was sealed by another defector, Golitsyn. Dearlove and Scarlett figured that if they got their own spy inside the KGB then he could betray any spy the KGB had in SIS, as long of course as he got in before the other fellow.

Thus the Gordievsky recruitment was critical, not just because of the intelligence it produced, some of the most important of the Cold War, but because in recruiting, running and protecting Gordievsky for eleven years, SIS could be certain it was no longer penetrated by the Russian intelligence service. He was SIS's 'ring of confidence' (to borrow a phrase) to the extent that when the hunt to identify the MI5 betrayer Michael Bettaney[v] commenced in 1983 the Security Service team decided, against their DG's specific instructions, to ask Gordievsky's handlers in SIS to assist in the hunt, secure in the knowledge that they were proven to be 'sound'. This was the time when Gordievsky was posted to the KGB's UK residency, bringing its usefulness as an intelligence collection station to an end. As a Controller, Park would have been briefed on Gordievsky and she would need to have been, for as the Service's chief interlocutor with the CIA[4] (i.e. responsible for inter-service liaison between SIS and the CIA) it would have been her job to put in place the arrangements for sharing his 'product' with the Agency.

---

i DEARLOVE, Sir Richard Billing, KCMG, OBE; SIS, NAIROBI, PRAGUE, PARIS, H/GENEVA, H/WASHINGTON, D/OP (Operations), ACSS, Chief 1999-2004 (1945-). While posted to Prague 1973-76 Dearlove, despite being subjected to extraordinarily close surveillance, managed to recruit a senior source within the Czech security services.

ii SCARLETT, Sir John McLeod, KCMG, OBE; SIS, MOSCOW, NAIROBI, H/PARIS, H/MOSCOW, Chief 2004-09 (1948-). Prior to being appointed Chief of SIS, Scarlett chaired the Joint Intelligence Committee.

iii ORLOV, General Aleksandr Mikhailovich, the most senior KGB official ever to defect, fled to the US in 1938 (1895-1973).

iv VOLKOV, Konstantin Dmitrievich, in 1945 the KGB officer based in Istanbul, planned to defect to the West and in so doing identify Kim Philby. Philby was made aware of Volkov's plan and alerted his KGB handlers. Volkov was returned to Russia where he and his entire family were liquidated.

v BETTANEY, Michael John; MI5 (KGB) (1950-).

Queen of Spies

Park would have had a hand in the decision not to disclose Gordievsky's identity to the Americans, though the *fact* of his recruitment quickly became known. Her judgement was sound. Eventually the CIA was able to figure out the spy's name from an analysis of the intelligence passed on to the Agency by SIS. Fortunately it took until 1985 for this to happen, but when it did Gordievsky too was betrayed by one of the greatest betrayers of all, the CIA's Aldrich Ames.[i]

Park's Western Hemisphere Controllerate was directly responsible for the US/ Canada (P7), Latin America (P8) and the Caribbean (P10). But what made the Controllerate so important was not the intelligence product *per se*, which was actually fairly modest, but rather its closeness to the CIA. While the day-to-day liaison between the Agency and SIS was the job of the Washington-based 'schmoozer' of the day (H/WASHINGTON), to Park would fall the higher-level responsibility as the chief interlocutor between SIS and the Agency. But in choosing her, Oldfield had chosen well. The Agency knew Park and rated her highly; in fact Bill Colby, her wartime Jed trainee, was now the CIA Director (retiring in 1976) and her old buddy, Devlin, had only retired the previous year.

By agreement the US was not an SIS intelligence target, nor was Canada. SIS was not permitted to run operations in either country without the permission and cooperation of their hosts. This was something that J. Edgar Hoover of the FBI was never likely to grant, though the Canadians were more relaxed on the issue. Both Washington and Ottawa were (and remain) Area Coordination Offices for SIS operations.

When Park took up her post Guy Bratt was H/WASHINGTON.[ii] Bratt was followed in 1977 by schmoozer-in-chief, John Colvin. Colvin was a *bon vivant* with a particular affection for decent hock and the finer things in life and, some claimed, no great affection for the 'down and dirty' side of SIS life. Park knew him well, both being veterans of Hanoi and Mongolia. Amusingly, much to the reported chagrin of the then British ambassador to Washington, the Americans used to address Colvin as 'Ambassador Colvin' in accord with the American protocol by which former office-holders continue to be addressed by their past titles.[5]

Park had stations in Havana, Buenos Aires (Hugh Bicheno[iii]) Santiago (David Spedding, the future Chief, had just departed), Rio de Janeiro, Georgetown in

i AMES, Aldrich Hazen; CIA (KGB) (1942-). Ames is serving life imprisonment without the possibility of parole.

ii BRATT, Guy Maurice, CMG, MBE (Mil); SIS, BERLIN, BRUSSELS, H/VIENNA, H/ GENEVA, H/WASHINGTON (1920-2006).

iii BICHENO, Hugh; SIS, BUENOS AIRES, resigned 1978 (1948-).

248

the former colony of Guyana (Oz Robinson[i]) and Guatemala. That was pretty much the extent of her empire. Most of her stations would have had two officers; one declared and one covert, and a secretary or two. An exception was a one-and-one station in Guatemala, established because of Guatemala's claim to sovereignty over British Honduras (now Belize).[6] SIS had effectively withdrawn from the Caribbean in Dick White's time. White had accepted the Americans' offer to let the CIA provide SIS with whatever intelligence it required from the region, sub-contracting if you will.[7] The Joint Intelligence Committee (JIC) remained similarly relaxed about South America and about the intentions of Argentina in particular, a misconception that was to lose the FCO its powerful chairmanship of the JIC in 1983 after the Falklands War (and after Park's time). Nor was South America perceived to be the global provider of illicit drugs it was to become. Other countries in South and Central America were looked after on an ad hoc basis.

Given the unpredictable security situation, station security was tight. In every station the secret of secrets was the 'copper room'. This was the communications centre, which was exclusively for the use of SIS. It was built so that it was isolated from its surroundings, sitting on a cushion of air. All computer terminals were 'Tempest' protected by copper shrouds (hence the name) to avoid electronic emissions being detected by 'hostiles'. Entry to the room was through four sets of combination-locked doors. The first led into the chancery, the second from there to the registry (where the files were kept), the third to the SIS registry (where the SIS files were kept), and the fourth finally to the copper room. In a number of missions SAS troopers were on hand to provide armed security and on occasion to act as bodyguards. Hugh Bicheno recalls a trooper telling him one day, 'You are the pistol, I am the bullet.'[8]

Cuba was officially the number one SIS priority in the region, and as a reflection of that the country had its own dedicated 'attack section', Cuba Targeting and Counterintelligence (TCI/Cuba). It was one of only four such attack sections in the entire Service, the other three being TCI/SovBloc, TCI/Eastern Europe and TCI/China.[9] The rationale for TCI/Cuba was not that Cuba was seen as a key British intelligence target; on that basis alone Cuba might not even have warranted a station. TCI/Cuba was initiated at the request of the Americans. The UK budgetary constraints meant that SIS's dependence on intelligence handouts from the US had reached critical levels, so the 'request' was acceded to. As Hugh Bicheno said:

i ROBINSON, Oswald ('Oz') James Horsley, CMG, OBE; Royal Engineers, SIS, RANGOON (Highlands), MEXICO CITY, QUITO, BOGOTA, H/GEORGETOWN, H/BANGKOK (1926-2009).

The only reason we did Cuban ops was to have something to give the Americans in part exchange for the enormous amount of Intel they gave us.[10]

TCI/Cuba could be seen as a makeweight, offering some compensation for the vast intelligence trove provided to the UK by the Americans. There was also the issue of Cuban adventuring in Africa, which mattered to Britain, and in Asia, which mattered less. However, as Bicheno said, sucking up to the Americans was the key. As a consequence TCI/Cuba was considered a bit of a joke within SIS.[11]

For its part the US hadn't altered its attitude to Cuba much, if at all. It was still seen as a potential base 'for a Soviet attack on the US'. The missionary zeal with which Castro prosecuted his self-appointed mission to spread the Marxist message in South and Central America, America's back garden, was a cause for great concern in 'domino theory' Washington. Britain had maintained diplomatic relations with Cuba after the Castro rebellion and had opened an SIS station there when diplomatic relations between the US and Cuba were severed by President Eisenhower in 1961. Park's role was to know what it was the Americans wanted, brief her station chief accordingly, and monitor progress. The Agency needed British assistance; according to Bicheno, the DGI (Cuban intelligence service) had totally penetrated all CIA operations on the island and was effectively running them under Castro's personal direction.[12] This assertion is at least partially confirmed by Ted Shackley, former CIA Associate Deputy Director for Operations, the Agency's third most senior post. Shackley writes that in 1979 a US senator, Richard B. Stone of Florida, revealed the presence of a Soviet combat brigade on the island and asked what was known about its presence and purpose. According to Shackley, the Agency 'had no agents in place on the Island to task to provide the answers'.[13] Presumably it asked Park if SIS could assist.

Attempting to help the Americans monitor the activities of the DGI both domestically within Cuba and internationally was seen as a critical but difficult task, given the scale of DGI activity. The DGI operated stations in New York, Ottawa, Montreal, Toronto, Mexico, Peru, Venezuela, Guyana, Panama, Ecuador, Jamaica, Britain, France, West Germany, Italy, Portugal, Spain and thirteen African countries (unnamed in the source document).[14] That said, TCI/Cuba managed to organise the monitoring, for a period at least, of all arrivals and departures through Havana's José Martí airport. The details were passed on to the CIA in Langley.

Most of the DGI illegals deployed in Latin America left Cuba first for Czechoslovakia, which served as a staging post, where they could assume their false identities before going operational. To give an example, over one four-year period a total of six hundred and fifty Cuban illegals passed through Czechoslovakia from Cuba en route back to Latin America to take up operational assignments. Most carried Venezuelan, Dominican, Argentinean or Columbian passports which were genuine issue apart from the substitution of false names.[15] Probably the most effective Cuban-directed intelligence gathering operation was a sophisticated signals intercept facility located within the embassy confines and operated by GCHQ technicians. (In the early 1990s the intercept station was responsible for the Columbian authorities' arrest of a Provisional IRA explosives training team en route to a meeting with FARC terrorists and travelling under the guise of 'birdwatchers'.)[16]

The DGI was also of interest to Park because the KGB often sub-contracted out its intelligence operations to the Cuban agency. After the mass expulsion of a hundred and five KGB/GRU intelligence officers from London in 1971, the DGI took on responsibility for running a number of KGB operations in Britain.[17] The KGB maintained 'operational contact' with the DGI in six foreign capitals and cooperated with it in targeting potential leads on the US mainland.[18] The head of the DGI at the time, Méndes Cominches, was a regular attendee at Soviet Bloc intelligence meetings.[19] But the Cuban leader Fidel Castro was nothing if not ambitious and he had plans to expand Cuba's influence beyond Latin American into Asia. He had offered to send combat troops to North Vietnam to join the war against the Americans. The offer had been turned down by the DRVN, afraid that the presence of Cuban 'mercenaries' would dilute the appeal of their struggle.[20] During Castro's visit to Hanoi in 1973 the then H/HANOI, Julian Harston, had to listen to a three-hour speech from the Cuban leader, delivered in Spanish (which Harston did not speak) and translated into Vietnamese (which he didn't speak either).[21]

Brazil was naturally seen as important and SIS maintained a station in Brasilia, probably one of the least sought-after posts in the entire Service. At weekends everyone who had the means abandoned the city for the pleasures of Rio, leaving only the (relatively) poor and destitute, and that included most overseas diplomats. The country was still ruled over by a right-wing military dictatorship which was taking a fairly muscular attitude to any potential rivals, real or imagined, past or present. In Park's second year as C/WH the junta was suspected (never confirmed) of ordering the murder of two former civilian Presidents, Juscelino Kubitschek and Joáo 'Jango' Goulart. In 1978 a shifting of chairs within the junta saw Joáo Figueiredo take over the reins. As a former National Director of Intelligence (SNI), he had been cultivated by successive station heads and one in particular. That cultivation was to prove its worth when the Falkland crisis broke out in 1982: not to the extent of persuading Brazil to support the British action, for it was firmly on the side of Argentina, but in other ways. In a military dictatorship having a friend running the presidential palace is rarely to one's disadvantage.[22]

The first signs of the Falklands crisis came in 1977 when fifty-five Argentine 'scientists' landed and set up camp on the island of South Thule. An analysis of the action and of the accompanying rhetoric suggested that this could be a precursor to an attempt by the Argentine junta to seize the Falkland Islands themselves, though as stated above, the FCO remained resolute in its view that the Falklands was safe from invasion. In London the Labour government of James Callaghan considered the situation and decided to dispatch a small naval force to the region under the codename Operation JOURNEYMAN. The mini-taskforce consisted of a couple of frigates, two support vessels and, most critically, H.M.S. *Dreadnought*, a nuclear-powered submarine, not that anyone was contemplating launching nuclear tipped missiles at anybody.

Callaghan later claimed that JOURNEYMAN's purpose was *not* a display of force *per se*, as in gunboat diplomacy. Rather he intended that this would be a clandestine deployment, but the decision to deploy and the force's rules of engagement would be leaked to the Argentines as a means of discouragement, allowing them to disengage from the islands without any public loss of face. In 1982, when the invasion that led to the actual Falklands War took place, the issue surfaced amidst much debate as to whether the deployment was, as Callaghan claimed, a clever move to discourage the planned invasion or some sort of bluff, an insurance policy to be relied upon should preparations for an invasion be ramped up to the point of action. For it to function as a deterrent would require that the Argentine government be made aware of its presence, officially or otherwise. If it was to be an insurance policy then it could be deployed in a clandestine manner to be used or not as events unfolded.

In his testimony to the Falkland Islands Review of 1983, also known as the Franks Report, the now former Prime Minister Callaghan claimed that he had briefed Maurice Oldfield in 1977 on the deployment and asked him to find a means of making the Argentines aware *of its deployment and its orders for engagement* so that they might pull back from the brink.[23] He later claimed that this tactic was the main reason why the earlier threatened invasion was called off. His son-in-law, Peter Jay,[i] supports this account, though he does not quote any independent evidence to support it.[24]

David Owen, the Foreign Secretary at the time, disputes Callaghan's memory of events, saying that 'no evidence was ever found that Oldfield had either been instructed by the Prime Minister or acted on such an instruction'.[25] Owen maintained to this author that his relations with Oldfield were such that he could not believe that the head of SIS would not have told him of such an instruction from Callaghan. Owen and Oldfield used to meet on a regular basis, as was becoming

i JAY, Peter; broadcaster, journalist and diplomat (UK ambassador to Washington 1977-79) (1937-).

the norm for the Chief and his Foreign Secretary. Hugh Bicheno, stationed in Buenos Aires during the supposed incident, goes further and insists that Callaghan 'lied' when he made the claim.[26] He also states that Park told him that 'nobody at head office did [told the Argentines] either'.[27] Another former officer, one with direct experience of Latin America at that time, concurs with this view.[28]

However, a former senior SIS officer, one known to be close to Oldfield, asserted to this author unequivocally that Oldfield told him that Callaghan *did issue such an instruction and that it was acted upon.*[29] On balance it appears that Callaghan did remember correctly and that the deployment of the ships was, not as David Owen said, 'an insurance policy that did not of itself deter',[30] but a successful strategy, orchestrated by the then Prime Minister and executed in total secrecy by the then Chief of the Service, Maurice Oldfield. It appears that Oldfield bypassed the Western Hemisphere Controllerate and used some other means to deliver what was a top secret message that was in effect threatening war. The Argentines heeded the warning.

One consequence of the affair was an insistence by Park that the SIS in Latin America be provided with emergency radio communications to London in the event that the SIS radio net physically located inside the embassies became unavailable. SIS always maintained its own independent radio net for communications from stations to London and never relied on the FCO embassy net.

> She insisted on providing emergency communications in South America, which proved their worth during the Falklands War.[31]

Park obviously thought that the junta might have another go and it was better to be prepared. Alternative communications were installed in the house of the SIS head of station in Brasilia.[32]

Park also spent much of her time getting close to the Argentines in London. She used to entertain them regularly on the rooftop of her flat in Ashley Gardens in Victoria and in the Naval & Military Club in St James's, better known as the 'In & Out' because of its entrance gates. During her time, while women were permitted at the club, they were not allowed use the main entrance. Park deputed one of her staff to greet her guests at the main door while she had to scuttle round to the side.[33] We don't know what she thought of this procedure, not a lot one would imagine, but her attitude of 'if that's what it takes then I'll do it' was one she maintained throughout her career. And that particular affront to her gender would have been the least of them.

And always the charm, that irresistible and irrepressible Daphne Park charm. This is an account (given to the author by one of her former subordinates) of one classic Park episode that occurred during her time as C/WH:

We had this operation for which approval was required. Her P officer had put together a paper and was running it by Daphne before going over to the FCO to see the relevant under-secretary for final go-ahead. We really wanted to do this op but it was potentially tricky. Daphne suddenly stood up and said,

'I will come along with you if you don't mind.'

'Not at all,' the P officer said and waited while Daphne went over to this tiny mirror she had in her office. She dabbed on some lipstick, brushed at her hair, pulled on this ratty cardigan with a hole in it and finally plonked a hat down on her head. Off to King Charles Street the two of them went to meet the under sec. When they had completed their pitch Daphne looked across the table at him and cocking her head to one side gave this irresistible come-hither smile and said,

'Fine then, have we the go ahead?'

The under secretary looked at her then shook his head as if in bewilderment and gave the okay. The op went ahead and it worked. She was so irresistible, this plump, untidy, middle-aged vamp![34]

Another spoke of the great care she took in composing telegrams to be sent to officers in the field. Park understood the loneliness of the life, how vulnerable officers could be and the damage to their morale that a carelessly worded telegram from head office might cause. She insisted on seeing many of the telegrams at the drafting stage and never hesitated to suggest they be altered. In that regard she wasn't particularly good at delegating, but then most managers in SIS weren't, the nature of the organisation didn't lend itself to it. Eventually the issue had to be addressed by training.[35]

Ireland did not come under Western Hemisphere, and of course America's influence over events in Ulster was enormous. Forty million Americans claimed Irish ancestry, so Ireland mattered in domestic political terms, not with the same degree of intensity as Israel did (for which most Irish diplomats were profoundly grateful), but it mattered. When Park took over in 1975 the conflict in Northern Ireland was at its most violent with the cumulative death toll reaching a thousand during the year and a particularly vicious sectarian murder onslaught in full swing. There was a ten-month ceasefire brokered by SIS in 1975 before the province once more descended into violence, leading to the 'no wash/no slop-out' protests which in turn led to the hunger strikes of 1980 and 1981.

The diplomatic arena was the responsibility of the Washington embassy, and Callaghan would later install his son-in-law, Peter Jay, as ambassador to the US in 1977 to oversee it. Much of the attention was directed towards keeping onside the 'Four Horsemen' – Hugh Carey (former Governor of New York), Senator Daniel Patrick Moynihan of New York, Speaker of the House Tip O'Neill and Senator Edward Kennedy, both from Massachusetts. These were leaders of moderate Irish-American opinion and wielded considerable influence over the Democrats and the incumbent President, Jimmy Carter (from 1977). They were also a strong political counterweight to the principal Republican fundraising (in the widest sense) arm NORAID (Northern Ireland Aid).

The other side of the coin was arms shipments. America was not the main provider of arms for the Provisional IRA. That dubious honour belonged to the Gadaffi regime in Libya, but America was a consistent source of high grade weapons, including the infamous Armalite rifle, machine guns, pistols, ammunition and explosives and of course cash, without which terrorist campaigns cannot be sustained. One route for shipments of US origin was via passenger or cargo ships from eastern seaboard ports to Liverpool or Southampton, then onwards to either Northern Ireland or the Irish Republic. Sympathetic Irish-American longshoremen could be relied upon to turn a blind eye to bundles of arms and ammunition concealed in stripped-down pieces of furniture or other bulky household items. Countering that activity was mainly the job of domestic law enforcement with the FBI in the lead role. MI5, which also had a significant presence in the Washington embassy, had the primary responsibility for managing relations with the Bureau.

But SIS was interested and so was Park, whose father had been a Belfast Protestant. Even more importantly, so was the Secretary of State for Northern Ireland (SOSNI), Roy Mason.[i] Mason was probably the most consistently hard-line SOSNI ever to occupy that post and the one who came closest to defeating the Provisionals militarily. He was not a great advocate of a political solution to the Ulster problem, nor did he go out of his way to pursue one. His attitude is best summed up by the following remark, which has been attributed to him: 'We are squeezing the terrorists like rolling up a toothpaste tube. We are squeezing them away from their safe havens. We are squeezing them away from their supplies of many explosives.'[36]

Mason was not joking; christened 'stone-mason' by the Provisionals, he authorised the maximum possible use of legitimate force against the PIRA. Perforce, this meant ramping up the intelligence war. Much of the available intelligence on arms and explosives shipments and clues to the identity of the main perpetrators came from agents on the ground in Ulster. A little of this was secured by SIS while it was operational during the 1970s and most by agent-running military intelligence groups such as the highly-effective Force Research Unit (FRU) and MI5. Agent-supplied intelligence was augmented by communications intercepts, both telephone and postal between America and Northern Ireland, and probably between the US and the Irish Republic, and certainly between the UK and the Republic.

Encouraged (directly or otherwise) by the Secretary of State, there would have

---

i MASON, Roy, Baron Mason of Barnsley, PC; politician, Secretary of State for Northern Ireland 1976-79 (1924-2015).

been a strong temptation to use this intelligence to infiltrate Irish-American groups and if needs be to run sting operations. But Park knew she had to tread carefully. Hoover was a fearsome enemy and if any such operations came to light he would have made his displeasure not only known but felt. Passing the leads on to the FBI was the safer route and the one usually followed. However SIS did run a number of illegal intelligence operations in the US during Park's tenure as C/WH, under what might be termed the 'spies will be spies' dispensation.[37] The CIA did likewise on occasion in the UK when it felt that circumstances either justified or necessitated it.[38] Neither country was running operations directed *against* the other, simply availing itself of the other's soil. Another former SIS officer described the SIS actions in the US as 'easing the machinery'[39] (of US law enforcement), nudging it along in other words.

Overseas was more straightforward. That was the CIA's responsibility. The Agency was far more Wasp (White Anglo-Saxon Protestant) than the Bureau and was naturally more sympathetic to Britain's interests. Park would have encountered few roadblocks in seeking Agency assistance to identify anything that might inhibit the flow of arms and explosives to the Republican terrorists. This meant monitoring international arms dealers, many of whom were unscrupulous about whom they would supply and who were well capable of forging the necessary 'end user certificates' without which arms shipments cannot be legitimately shipped. Libya's Gaddafi was a separate problem. The authorities knew that despite the extensive seizures of arms, ammunition and explosives from the PIRA, the organisation's ability to mount operations had been scarcely dented. Intelligence told them that the Provisionals had been successful in landing industrial quantities of arms and explosives from Libya which had then been dispersed in secret dumps throughout the island. SIS had good sources which it used to intercept the Libyan-originated shipment on the M.V. *Claudia* in 1973, but would have welcomed any CIA assistance. Groups such as the Palestinian Liberation Organisation (PLO) were also naturally sympathetic to the IRA and they too needed to be watched.

The relationship with the CIA was SIS's single most important connection, and for the four years she was in the post it was Park's responsibility. In some respects it was a case of the CIA's priorities becoming those of SIS, and her job was to be aware of them and support (or at least not hinder) the CIA as far as was appropriate and feasible. The CIA's global list of tasks and priorities was summarised in what the Agency termed key intelligence questions (KIQs).[40] When Park took up her post there were sixty-nine KIQs in all, of which about a third were concerned with the Soviet Union.[41] Park also had the equal and opposite task of seeking to take advantage of the Agency's vast intelligence gathering capability in Britain's own interest. The role placed her in a unique position to influence SIS relations with its American 'cousins'. As the main high-level link she could influence the messages going *to* the Agency from SIS and interpret, to a degree at least, messages *from* the Agency to SIS ('I think what they mean is this ...'). And, as one former colleague put it, 'as an activist she could be expected to put her slant on things'.[42]

The left-wing revolution in Portugal was one of the more important of these 'things'. A non-C/WH issue, but one where both the CIA and SIS had some skin in the game and where Park needed to ensure that CIA actions were aligned with those of the UK and its socialist European allies, to the extent that the irascible US Secretary of State, Henry Kissinger, would permit. The 'Carnation' Revolution of 1974 had overthrown the Estado Novo (New State) dictatorship in Portugal and handed power to a cadre of left-wing army officers, the Armed Forces Movement (MFA) *aka* the Junta of National Salvation (JNS). Within days of the revolution Portugal's leading left-wing politicians, Álvaro Cunhal and Mario Soáres, returned from abroad to be greeted by rapturous crowds of supporters. But while both were left-wing, each had a different definition of what that meant. Cunhal, who had been imprisoned for thirteen years by the Salazar regime, was a hard-line Soviet loyalist. He had been one of the first Western communist leaders to come out in favour of the Soviet-led invasion of Czechoslovakia in the 1968 crushing of the Prague Spring.[43] Despite their differences, however, Cunhal and Soáres agreed to participate in a series of 'provisional' coalition governments, with Soares assuming responsibility for negotiating the independence of Portugal's overseas colonies.

One of the immediate actions of the first provisional government was to establish diplomatic relations with the Soviet Union. Ambassadors were exchanged and soon there was a KGB residency up and running in the Soviets' new Lisbon embassy. Within days Cunhal was meeting clandestinely with the brand new KGB resident, Svyatoslav Fyodorovich Kuznetsov, and passing him thousands of pages of sensitive intelligence documents, including those relating to NATO and links with Western intelligence services. At their first meeting, held in a safe house belonging to the Portuguese Communist Party (PCP), so fearful were the two of being bugged by British or American agents that the entire meeting was conducted in silence, handwritten notes being used to communicate.[44]

They were right to be concerned. The CIA had an active mid-sized station in Lisbon with about sixteen officers under John Stinard Morgan.[45] SIS had a more modest set-up, probably the standard two plus two with Stanley Galsworthy[i] as H/LISBON. The two station heads would have had a pretty good idea between them of what was going on, and that would have included keeping an eye on both Cunhal and Kuznetsov. Whatever the two were up to, neither Morgan nor

i Pseudonym.

Galsworthy liked it much. Nor did the American ambassador, Frank Carlucci,[i] and he made it his business to support the two stations in their counter-coup activities. Park and he knew each other, as he had served in the Congo during her time there.

Overhanging everything was a shared concern about Spain and the 'domino theory'. General Franco, the Spanish dictator, was known to be in poor health and not expected to live much longer. When he died Spain would be considered vulnerable to a communist takeover. That country already had a sizable left-wing element in its population and bitterness over the civil war still ran deep. It was assumed that any communist-leaning regime in Portugal would support the establishment of a similarly oriented administration in post-Franco Spain, and quite possibly work towards it. Henry Kissinger shared this concern. He continually chided Western European leaders about the need for action in order to secure 'pluralistic democracy' in Portugal.

The situation worsened considerably after the elections of April 1975, in which the communists under Cunhal received only 12.5% of the vote. Cunhal shrugged off the vote, confident, he said, that real power would remain with the MFA. He went so far as to tell one interviewer, 'I promise you there will be no parliament in Portugal.'[46] The Labour government of Harold Wilson joined with other Social Democratic leaders in Europe and in August 1975, as matters were coming to a head in Portugal, they met in Stockholm and formed the succinctly-named Committee for Friendship and Solidarity with Democracy and Socialism in Portugal. Chaos continued, with six provisional governments formed between April 1974 and July 1976. The socialists consistently achieved up to 35% of the votes in the parliamentary elections, by far the largest single block, the communists never achieving more than 12-14%. Throughout this period the CIA, SIS and West Germany's BND (Bundesnachrichtendienst) were on the ground, reflecting the increasingly influential role of Kissinger, Jim Callaghan and Willi Brandt, who though he had resigned shortly before as Chancellor of West Germany (due to a spying scandal) was still a hugely influential figure. Large sums of money were pouring into the socialists' coffers, including donations from Britain, according to former FCO mandarin, Stephen Wall:[ii]

> I do know that Callaghan as Foreign Secretary arranged for money to be taken to Mario Soáres, who was the main person who stood for genuine democracy in the face of a very real threat of a Communist take-over.[47]

i CARLUCCI, Frank; State Department, CIA, White House (1930-).

ii WALL, Sir Stephen, GCMG, LVO; diplomat, principal private secretary to the Foreign Secretary and private secretary to the Prime Minister, ambassador to Portugal and permanent representative to the EU (1947-).

Wall did not profess any knowledge of a further intervention by Callaghan, in particular the intervention described to this author by the former Foreign Secretary in person (see below).[48] In November 1975 General Franco died, thus bringing Spain potentially into play. Within days there was a second attempted military coup in Portugal, organised by elements supporting the Communist Party. This was put down by a counter coup led by moderates with the support of the three Western intelligence services. The cooperating CIA, BND and SIS Lisbon stations played a big part in organising forces to suppress the attempted communist coup. Park would have been at the heart of the London end. In any event Britain, the US and West Germany decided that they needed to act. According to Callaghan's account, after speaking to Brandt and Kissinger he had arranged for the Russians to be told that unless they backed off in Portugal the British and their allies would support armed intervention in the country and would halt at once any further cooperation in establishing the Organisation for Security Cooperation in Europe (OSCE) a key Soviet political objective.

Callaghan did not say how the threat was passed on or precisely how it was couched. In any event it is likely that SIS, and quite possibly Park, would have been involved in its delivery. A communication threatening military action would, in circumstances such as these, be delivered outside conventional diplomatic channels. Callaghan did say what form the intervention would take: he told this author that the RAF would drop weapons from the NATO GLADIO stockpile (in RAF Chicksands) to members of the armed forces loyal to the West. Brezhnev got the message and responded appropriately. Whether due to Callaghan's intervention or not, free and fair parliamentary elections were held, and in July 1976 the first post-coup constitutional government headed by Mario Soáres took power. Spain too made the successful transition to democracy under a constitutional monarchy. The Iberian Peninsula was saved.

There is no independent verification of Callaghan's story. A number of (British) Cabinet papers from the Prime Minister's office dealing with relations between Britain and Portugal at the time are still withheld from public release, and another, possibly one of the more interesting, a letter from Henry Kissinger to Number 10, is 'missing'.[49]

Might Callaghan have 'disremembered', as was (wrongly) suggested over the Oldfield flotilla warning to Argentina? That is certainly one possibility. Or was he embroidering for reasons best known to himself? That too is possible. On the surface, however, there seems little reason for either. This was less than ten years after the event so his memory was still fresh. The conversation took place on the margins of a conference when Callaghan was taking a leisurely tour around Dublin, killing time before he went on the podium. It was he who brought up the issue. It appears his memory was correct about the Falklands, so perhaps it was correct about Portugal too. He also said candidly one other thing:

> Do you know what Paddy? I was talking to Brandt and Kissinger last week. The three of us have decided that none of us will accept any further speaking engagements for less than £12,000, we've been selling ourselves too cheap.[50]

C/WH 2 – Finale: Rhodesia and the ending of UDI, 1978-79

There is an expression popular in Ireland, which probably has its equivalent in many cultures: *you can take the man out of the bog but you can't take the bog out of the man (or woman).* In Daphne Park's case it was reversed, in that while it seemed you could take Africa out of her, you could not take her out of Africa. And even though her responsibilities were now firmly fixed on her Western Hemisphere Controllerate (C/WH), Africa was to play a continuing and increasing role in her career right up to the point of retirement. Some of this was to do with her interlocutor's role, but it was more driven by the intimacy of her connections in sub-Saharan Africa. Her involvement in the efforts to bring about a peaceful settlement to Rhodesia's Unilateral Declaration of Independence (UDI) meant that she was effectively seconded to that effort for the final twelve months or so of her career.

> She [Daphne Park] was called in to brief the Prime Minister, Margaret Thatcher, before a crucial Commonwealth Conference in Lusaka [in August 1979]. We were told it was a difficult meeting. Daphne was told that she would have 10 minutes; in the end she had two hours. As was her wont, the PM led from the front: Lusaka was full of terrorist organizations – Freedom Fighters by another name – and therefore President Kaunda himself was a terrorist. The PM would have no truck with him. Daphne suggested that life was not quite like that, and advised a rather more diplomatic approach, with much toing and froing about the causes of colonial and postcolonial conflict. The PM was unmoved and gave no ground whatsoever. But at CHOGM [Commonwealth Heads of Government Meeting, 1979] and without any acknowledgement in any direction, the PM conducted herself very much as Daphne had advised – and indeed earned plaudits in Africa through a widely circulated photo of Kaunda and herself on the dance floor![1]

This rather understates what actually happened and downplays considerably Park's pivotal role in the UDI negotiations. But that is to be expected. SIS protocol demands that the achievements of deceased former colleagues – when referred to at all – are mentioned in only the most oblique terms.

Formerly known as Southern Rhodesia, with the status of a semi-independent British Dominion, Rhodesia had declared its full independence in 1965. This was after months of fruitless negotiations with the government of Harold Wilson aimed at securing a negotiated constitutional settlement which would have led to black majority rule. UDI was the creation of a hard-line white supremacist, former RAF pilot Ian Smith. Smith had been elected by the two hundred thousand or so white population, while the seven million plus black population were effectively disenfranchised. The move was rejected by Britain and greeted with general outrage among most African countries, with the principal exception of South Africa, which was similarly governed, and the administrations of the Portuguese colonies of Mozambique and Angola. Britain decided that force would not be used to end the illegal declaration; instead a series of increasingly tough economic sanctions would be applied, effectively cutting off Rhodesia from world trade. The sanctions regime would be mandated by the United Nations, thus giving it the force of international law.

Since Rhodesia shared a border with both South Africa and Mozambique the efficacy of the sanctions was limited, so black nationalist groups based in the neighbouring states of Zambia, Tanzania and Malawi commenced a campaign of armed resistance. Called the Rhodesian Bush War, this war of attrition was designed to make ordinary day-to-day existence impossible for the white population. There were two main externally-based nationalist/guerrilla forces, nominally united under the banner of the Patriotic Front. The larger, the party of the Shona 85% majority of the population, was led by Robert Mugabe, widely considered to be Marxist in his orientation. It was called ZANU, with a military wing, ZANLA.[i] The second group, ZAPU, was led by Joshua Nkomo, the party of the 15% Ndebele population. Its military wing was ZPRA.[ii] It was ZPRA which began the liberation war in earnest in 1972. Britain did not recognise this guerrilla war as legitimate.

The declarations of independence of both Mozambique and Angola in 1975 altered the balance of power in the region, making the continuation of the white regime in Rhodesia impossible. ZANU/ZANLA alone had eleven thousand armed guerrillas engaged on the ground in Rhodesia supported by a further fifteen thousand in Zambia and Mozambique, which had gone from being a sanctions busting ally to the base for attacks across its borders on Rhodesia.[2] The appetite among the white population for a war that was seeing more and more of their young men killed and wounded was disappearing fast. Whites were 'voting with their feet' and abandoning Rhodesia in increasing numbers, to the point where the continuing viability of both the armed forces and the civil service was in doubt.[3] Soon even Smith recognised that the campaign was becoming unsustainable and began behind the scenes negotiations to end the conflict.

i ZANU/ZANLA; Zimbabwe African National Union/ Zimbabwe African National Liberation Army.

ii ZAPU/ZPRA: Zimbabwe African Peoples Union/ Zimbabwe People's Revolutionary Army.

The first serious attempt at a negotiated solution was the Geneva Conference of 1976, held under British chairmanship. This was the first time that delegations from the Smith government and the Patriotic Front met face to face. Julian Harston (then H/BLANTYRE) describes the opening:

> Later at the Geneva talks on Rhodesia (the first time Mugabe was involved) there was an extraordinary scene at the opening in the Palais in Geneva when the art deco lobby to the conference room was full of 100 excited black faces and about six or seven white, all of them MI6 officers ...[4]

The conference fell at the first hurdle and was adjourned after a couple of weeks of wrangling, never to meet again. Park was not involved. FCO policy became to support the idea of an 'internal settlement', i.e. an agreement reached between Rhodesia-based moderate black nationalists and the regime. This plan had little appeal to the wider world which viewed it as a form of 'apartheid-light' because it excluded the groups who were prosecuting the war and who were in effect forcing Smith to the negotiating table. Predictably the settlement was condemned by the UN and by most African states. However the British foreign secretary, David Owen, working in conjunction with US secretary of state, Cyrus Vance, was hatching up a hidden plan to use the internal settlement as a lever towards a final solution. But it was not the settlement that had been cooked up by the Smith regime, something that was seen as 'flawed and dishonest'. Instead Owen and Vance wanted something which would lead to free and fair elections and international acceptance. It was thought that Mugabe would come round if the process could be got off the ground.[5] As Owen's then private secretary, Stephen Wall, said:

> [On] Rhodesia ... there was an Anglo-American plan: David Owen and Cyrus Vance travelled the world together, it was very seductive.[6]

Even so opinions were still mixed. Dr Hastings Banda, the President of Malawi, made his views clear to SIS's Harston in Malawi.

> Even Doctor Banda was telling Nkomo, Sithole, and others at that time that they had to get used to the idea of Mugabe as Prime Minister.[7]

Owen and Vance decided to press on: the Americans very definitely had a dog in this particular fight. Africa remained a Cold War battleground and the US had set its face firmly against the illegal Rhodesian regime. The US had considerable leverage over South Africa, which it regarded as a staunch ally in the fight against communism and so supported militarily and economically. According to Wall, Vance's role in the scheme was to put pressure on South Africa to reduce its support for Rhodesia to the point where Smith would be forced to sign the settlement treaty. With that in the bag the second phase could then begin.

Owen and Vance felt that the internal settlement, but only as amended, could be the basis for a long-term solution if it could be 'legitimised' by the inclusion of Joshua Nkomo, the more moderate of the two guerrilla leaders, to the initial exclusion of the Marxist Mugabe, who was by general agreement considered to be 'bad'. In Owen's words, Nkomo was the sort of African politician Britain could do business with, as Owen said:

> Bad but our sort of bad, a bit corrupt, hand out for the money, but okay to do a deal with.[8]

The two set about making this happen with the assistance of SIS. Oldfield dispatched Park to meet Owen who would brief her on what he wanted her to achieve. He did this despite her being C/WH, so by-passing Pantcheff who was Controller Africa (C/AF) at the time and the logical choice for the job. Owen told this author that he was not aware that Park was C/WH and he assumed from her detailed knowledge of the situation on the ground that she was a senior officer in the African Directorate. Presumably that was down to her ensuring that she was fully briefed on all the necessary details before going to meet her foreign secretary.

It is noteworthy that SIS did not choose to tell Owen that Park was being seconded to the effort. In fact it was routine for SIS to make use of its officers' existing connections even when they had moved on in their careers. Owen certainly feels (in retrospect) that SIS was making good use of her extensive network of high-level contacts with key African players, in particular with President Kenneth Kaunda of Zambia. Owen said that Park seemed instinctively to understand the importance of relationships among Africans: 'once trust is established,' he said, 'bonds can become very strong.'[9]

SIS refers to this form of secret negotiations as *parallel diplomacy*. It requires considerable skills and often the sort of trust that is built up over a considerable period of time. The Service considered itself quite accomplished at this and saw it as a key weapon in its armoury. As Julian Harston says:

> MI6 [SIS] was deeply and very successfully involved and was to all intents and purposes leading UK foreign policy ... I was personally in touch with all the Zimbabwean leaders, whose only point of entry to Zimbabwe was through Blantyre Chileka airport.[10]

Owen and Vance's plan called for Nkomo to be appointed *acting* PM ahead of the elections scheduled for the following March. This would give him a critical advantage and virtually guarantee his victory. Park's role was to persuade

Kenneth Kaunda to go along with the plan. Politically this was a huge risk for the Zambian leader and Park would have expended much of her political capital on it. Trust was pretty thin on the ground at the time. In fact most of the key African leaders, including Kaunda, were far from assured about Britain's *bona fides*. As Julian Harston put it:

> The UK was concentrating more than 40% of its foreign policy effort on Southern Africa. Yet world opinion was still firmly of the belief that the UK was in bed with South Africa ...[11]

But persuasion was Park's stock-in-trade and she brought Kaunda around. His participation was vital. Not only was Kaunda hugely influential, he had an especially close relationship with the guerrilla leader of which Park was aware. Of course nothing takes place in a vacuum. For his part Kaunda wanted to remain onside with Britain and the United States in particular. On the other side of his western borders in Angola a fierce civil war was raging between the Marxist MPLA and the more Western-oriented UNITA/FPLA movements. It wasn't going well for the West, as twelve thousand Cuban troops had been airlifted to Angola by the Russians who had equipped them to fight a modern war. On his eastern border another civil war was raging in Mozambique and the Western-oriented groups weren't likely to prevail there either (nor did they in either country). Kaunda was in regular contact with the US government about Rhodesia, Angola and Mozambique, he needed them as much and more than they did him.

The secret meeting between Kenneth Kaunda, Joshua Nkomo and Ian Smith, with Joe Garbo (Nigeria's foreign minister) also present, took place in Lusaka in August 1978. Julius Nyereré of Tanzania, whose left-wing orientation made him sympathetic to Mugabe, was not told of the scheme and was excluded from the meeting at Kaunda's insistence.[12] The plan was for agreement to be reached on the appointment of Nkomo as interim PM of Rhodesia-Zimbabwe. He would leave the meeting at dawn, fly to Salisbury where he would be greeted and saluted by the Rhodesian army's chief of staff, General Walls, taking over as acting PM with Smith's agreement and cooperation. The support of Cyrus Vance of the US was critical but had to be kept secret. US President Jimmy Carter did not approve of the internal settlement, but Vance assured Owen that if he pulled off the Nkomo deal he would be able to bring Carter along with what would have been a *fait accompli*.[13]

According to Owen, Nkomo messed his part up and agreement was not reached. This may have been the occasion referred to by Stephen Wall, then assistant private secretary to Owen:

I do remember a guy from Century [SIS] coming with one of them [Park's reports] to my home in the middle of the night and he and I then went off in his official car to Limehouse to report to David Owen. Quite why all this had to be done at 1 o'clock in the morning I cannot now recall but it may have been that she was seeing Kaunda again early the following morning and needed an answer.[14]

If it was, it was to no avail. Nyerere heard about the meeting. He was predictably outraged and the entire deal was scuppered. Park's role was kept secret even from fellow former SIS officers who were closely involved with the negotiations, as Julian Harston, who was one of them, says:

She [Park] did not feature at all in any of the stuff I was involved with on Rhodesia/Zimbabwe, and it is still not absolutely clear to me what role she played at that time.[15]

Harston continues:

We were in direct sometimes daily contact with 7 (at least) Heads of State and speaking on behalf of HMG.[16]

So knowledge of Park's involvement was kept within a very tight circle; perhaps even Bunny Pantcheff was excluded.

Even though the plan was not a success, Park was not finished with Rhodesia, though by the time she was involved again Jim Callaghan was no longer PM, having been replaced by Margaret Thatcher in the post-'winter of discontent' general election of 1979. In Owen's place as foreign secretary was Lord (Peter) Carrington. With the internal settlement effectively doomed to failure, attention turned to the possibility of staging the postponed (from 1978) Constitutional Conference. Carrington decided to convene it in Lancaster House in London in the autumn of 1979. Prospects for success were not considered great, but it was a better alternative than simply doing nothing and risking total anarchy.

The conference would be preceded by two meetings, thus providing the opportunity to line up a few ducks and organise some political choreography. The first meeting was the previously mentioned Commonwealth Heads of Government Meeting (CHOGM) scheduled for Lusaka in early August. Newly elected Prime Minister Margaret Thatcher was a fairly unknown quantity, but what was known was not seen as particularly encouraging. She was thought to believe that ZANU and ZAPU were 'terrorist' organisations on a par with Provisional Sinn Fein and the IRA; that Mugabe and Nkomo were 'terrorists', and that since Kaunda's government played host to both these men that made him pretty much a 'terrorist' too. As a negotiating position about a month or so before a proposed settlement conference it wasn't perhaps the best.

According to David Owen,[17] Thatcher was not at all certain that the Queen should even attend the Lusaka get-together. The guerrillas were known to possess surface-to-air missiles and would use them to shoot down two Rhodesian passenger aircraft in the coming months. The absence of proper control over these and over anti-aircraft batteries generally was a cause for serious concern, with fear that the Queen's aircraft could be mistakenly targeted by trigger-happy crews. Of course non-attendance by the monarch would have been seen as a deliberate snub and might well have scuppered the conference before it even got off the ground. When Thatcher spoke to the Queen about her concerns she was told that the Queen was attending, full-stop, and that only a formal order by the government prohibiting her attendance would prevent her.[18] A senior RAF officer was dispatched ahead of time and effective control of all anti-aircraft batteries handed over to him for the duration.

It was obvious that Thatcher needed to be 'got at' in order to ameliorate her tone. As Stephen Wall said:

I had the impression in Lusaka that Mrs Thatcher was surprised to find that Kenneth Kaunda and Nyerere were such educated and cultured men, and Daphne Park would very probably have started that process of education before CHOGM. Unlike a generation of Labour Leaders such as Jim Callaghan, who were intimates of the front line leaders, Mrs Thatcher had no experience of abroad and her views were, instinctively, pretty sympathetic to the Smith regime.[19]

Park was entrusted with that bit of 'parallel diplomacy' noted earlier in the extract from Warner's address, and she was obviously successful. A critical CHOGM objective was the agreed Lusaka Declaration on the Commonwealth on Racism and Racial Prejudice, a key part of the political choreography. The meeting finished with a party at which Margaret Thatcher took the floor and danced with President Kaunda. The symbolism of that dance should never be underestimated, according to Julian Harston:

This was a very clever piece of theatre which actually worked, and began a process which led to closer ties with Kenneth Kaunda and then with [Samora] Machel [President of Mozambique], which were to play a very important part in the eventual settlement at Lancaster House.[20]

CHOGM was considered a great success. Agreement was reached among those present supporting Britain's plan for the Lancaster House conference and for the proposed British approach to the negotiations. Given where everyone originally came from, that was no mean achievement. Park's ability to bring Thatcher through an almost 180° turn in attitude turned out to be central to this success and was testimony to her quite extraordinary powers of persuasion.

The second key meeting was a Non-Aligned Movement summit scheduled for Havana that September, immediately ahead of the Constitutional Conference. There would be ample opportunity for the relevant Commonwealth leaders to meet on the margins of the summit and it appears that Kaunda in particular was seeking some assurances about the likely British approach to the negotiations. Kaunda had been seriously embarrassed by the Smith-Nkomo debacle. London was aware of this, as a note from Carrington's private secretary, R.M.J. Lyne, to Downing Street explained; Kaunda 'burned his fingers badly in arranging the Smith-Nkomo meeting last year' and understandably wished to avoid a recurrence.[21] Once again Park was dispatched to calm the waters and execute some more parallel diplomacy. She flew to Lusaka where, in conditions of great secrecy, she met Kaunda for almost two hours (19.45 to 21.30) on the evening of 27 August. She would report directly to Thatcher in Downing Street via the Lusaka station's comms.[22]

From Britain's perspective Park's main objective was to secure backing from Kaunda for a step-by-step approach to the negotiations; first agreeing a constitution, then moving on from that to the issue of elections, and only then addressing the thorniest issues – ceasefire, separation of forces, etc. She appears to have been largely successful, with the exception of the issue regarding a commonwealth military force to guarantee free and fair elections and to secure order. She pleaded with Kaunda to accept Britain's *bona fides* in that regard.

SECRET
CONTINGENCY PLANS FOR A COMMONWEALTH FORCE?

7 THE PRESIDENT WAS CLEARLY GREATLY EXERCISED ABOUT THIS ISSUE. HE WAS PARTICULARLY CONCERNED ABOUT THE TIME IT WOULD TAKE TO ASSEMBLE A COMMONWEALTH FORCE, IF THAT WAS WHAT WAS ENVISAGED. AT THIS POINT, ENCOURAGED BY MARK CHONA, HE ASKED ME POINT-BLANK WHAT HMG'S PLANS WERE IN THIS REGARD. I SAID HMG WAS FULLY AWARE OF THE CRUCIAL IMPORTANCE OF THIS PROBLEM, WHICH HAD UNDOUBTEDLY BEEN UNDER CONSIDERATION, BUT THE FIRST REQUIREMENT WAS TO GET BOTH SIDES TO THE CONFERENCE TABLE PREPARED TO BE CONSTRUCTIVE. THE OBJECT OF MY VISIT HAD BEEN TO EXPLAIN AND SECURE HIS SUPPORT FOR THE STEP-BY-STEP APPROACH AMD THE GENERAL PRELIMINARY THINKING OF HMG. THE FACT THAT I WAS NOT ABLE TO GIVE HIM ANY CATEGORIC ASSURANCES ON HOW HMG PROPOSED TO DEAL WITH THE QUESTION OF ENFORCEMENT AND GUARANTEES DID NOT MEAN THAT SERIOUS THOUGHT WAS NOT BEING GIVEN TO THIS; BUT HMG WISHED ABOVE ALL NOT TO HAVE TO PREJUDGE SUCH ISSUES BEFORE THE CENTRAL ISSUE OF THE CONSTITUTION HAD BEEN RESOLVED BY ALL PARTIES. (CX (extract) from Daphne Park to SIS London, 27 August 1979)[23]

Kaunda, while he had reservations, seemed reasonably happy and told Park that he felt that the Havana summit would go well (thus lining up the next political duck) and that any resolutions relating to Rhodesia would be

CONDITIONAL, I.E. IF THERE ARE NO RESULTS FROM THE LONDON CONFERENCE, THEN … (CX (extract) from Daphne Park to SIS London, 27 August 1979)[24]

Park and Kaunda met again the following day, leading to Kaunda to write to 'my dancing partner' on 29 August thanking the PM 'for sending your special envoy to Lusaka, I found your message very useful'. It appears from Kaunda's note that the parallel diplomacy had worked but had reached the end of its usefulness, for the time being at least:

> It is therefore important that we return to normal diplomatic channels of communications – either through my high commissioner in London or your own in Lusaka, my change of mind on this subject is due to the obvious importance of the matter over which we are exchanging views. (Kenneth Kaunda to Margaret Thatcher, 29 August 1979)[25]

It is noteworthy that in her opening paragraph in the above telegram Park refers to Mark Chona, Kaunda's special political advisor, being present 'clearly by the wish of the president'. In the second to last paragraph (10) she states 'because of the presence of Mark Chona I laid no specific stress on his [Kaunda's] relationship with Nkomo and he, too, spoke throughout of the Patriotic Front, but it was clear that Nkomo was meant'. It would appear that the Kaunda/Nkomo relationship had contained elements that were not even for the ears of the President's special advisor. Park concluded by requesting that the PM acknowledge Kaunda's message by way of an interim reply including some sign that the meeting he requested with the PM in London, ahead of the Conference, would take place. Thatcher did not accede to the request, at least not at that time.

That last bit of parallel diplomacy appears to have concluded Park's role. The conference was a success and Rhodesia's UDI came to a peaceful end. The role of intelligence had been crucial in getting the conference off the ground and it continued to be in securing final agreement. But by then Daphne Park had resigned from the SIS, her thirty-one-year career as a secret servant to her country's cause had come to its end.

27

Return to Somerville, 1980-89

In the late 1950s SIS brought the retirement age for officers down from sixty to fifty-five. Not, as has been mooted, as a cunning plan by Dick White to weed out the robber-barons, rather an acknowledgment that the Service's age profile was a bit askew and that intelligence work was better suited to the young than the middle-aged (or even to the middle-aged rather than the old). Because Park had joined in 1948 her retirement age was unaffected and she was free to stay on until her sixtieth birthday in 1981. She chose instead to retire two years ahead of that time, in the late autumn of 1979. We are not certain why she took that decision; it was perhaps a combination of factors, as such decisions often can be. She told her friend Jean Sackur that she felt that her gender would prevent her being made Chief and that she had probably reached the pinnacle of her career. A move to a different Controllerate may have been on the cards, but a Controller's job entailed considerable travel and her mother's illness made that difficult. A Director's slot may equally have been on offer but that role is essentially an administrative one with little or no operational aspects and that might not have appealed, as administration was never her strongest suit.

Park heard about the position of Principal of Somerville, her old college, and decided to apply. She telephoned Jean Sackur (Professor Emeritus, London School of Economics) and asked her to write her a reference. Sackur did as asked, but has since had some regrets, not on her own account but due to Park's unhappiness with her time at Somerville.[1]

Park's first two years were particularly difficult due to the combination of moving house from Guildford to Oxford, trying to get on top of her new job (with its totally new way of working) and her mother's illness. Maggie Fletcher,[i] her former secretary in SIS (before Park went to the Congo) was summoned from retirement in order to provide her with some much needed administrative support; Park's filing and correspondence was mainly filed on the floor. Barbara Harvey, Vice-Principal at the time of Park's time in Somerville, sums it up thus:

> When, in 1980, Park became Principal of Somerville, she did not leave behind all the *Difficult Places* that she included in her entry in *Who's Who* as a form of recreation, but the particular ways in which Somerville was, for a time at least,

i FLETCHER, Margaret ('Maggie') Mary; SIS, MILAN, NAIROBI (1929-2014).

such a place were new to her. Her own views were carefully formed, and often proved in the event to be prophetically right for the College. It was, however, a new experience for her to find herself without a defined place in a hierarchy, but only first among equals and possessing influence but not power. And it was a cause of some amazement to her that the fellows of Somerville disliked telephone calls when teaching or researching – two exclusion zones that seemed to cover most of the day – and preferred the written note as a form of communication. Later, e-mail would solve this problem, but to the end of her life, Park never used this method of communication.[2]

There is speculation that Park felt that among academics she was not even first among equals. Her 2.1 was not a top level academic-level qualification and would not usually have qualified her for a teaching post in the university. Somehow this extraordinarily confident person, more than capable of setting her own Prime Minister on the straight and narrow when it came to how to deal with African leaders, was herself lacking in confidence when it came to her dealings with academia. She once expressed the view that she thought they saw her simply as an 'administrator', a category of person not held in high esteem among their kind.[3]

'They live in a thermos flask,' Park once said of her academics, 'they can behave just like MPs.' She then continued, 'If confronted by a piece of paper their instinct is to analyse it, to take it to bits, but not to be constructive about it. They want to look at so many sides of the question that sometimes it is difficult to get decisions. Here as head of the house you have total responsibility and absolutely no power.'[4]

She did accept that eventually she was able to lever her influence into something approaching power, but it was hard work and if she slipped up they might say, 'of course Principal, that is your diplomatic way of doing things' and it wasn't meant as a compliment.[5] Park was not the only former Foreign Office official to find the transformation from international diplomacy difficult. The current Principal of Somerville (at the time of writing), Dr Alice Prochaska, put it like this: 'academics prefer one of their own'.[6]

Park's uncertainty, if not insecurity, manifested itself in a number of ways. Barbara Harvey spoke of how Park, when meeting with the College's Governing Body or otherwise in formal session, would read from prepared notes and when this was completed would not engage in further debate or discussion.[7] For someone whose greatest skill was 'speaking and listening' and who, to use an Irishism, 'could chat the hind legs off a donkey' this was strange and confining. Her first portrait too reflected this insecurity. She insisted on being painted with an open book in her lap because she 'wanted to look academic'.[8] The general consensus is that that first painting was not a great success. The second work, completed just prior to her completing her term almost ten years later, was seen as being a much better representation. Park herself remarked to Dr Mai Yamani,[i] a doctoral student with whom she became very friendly:

I will look much better in this than in the first one despite being older.[9]

Against this were her relationships with her students. Mai Yamani was far from the only student who admired her, as Barbara Harvey said, 'Park loved her students and they loved her.' She was always available to them, offering words of cheery encouragement and advice. Yamani spoke of how Park almost 'pursued' her to complete her doctorate, so convinced was she of Yamani's intellectual gifts. And she succeeded; the young married mother returned to Oxford with her one-year-old baby girl and obtained her doctorate.[10] Rachel Sylvester, the *Times* journalist, describes Park as being one of her 'heroes'. And this sentiment is far from unusual.

The issue of Park's being an ex-spy was also a factor during her time in Somerville. When she was appointed her real role in the 'Foreign Office' was explained to a few people in Somerville, but as far as the rest were concerned she was what she appeared to be, a retired diplomat.[11] Some would have guessed. The Congo was subject to intense media interest during Lumumba's brief reign. It was among the first of the world's global trouble spots where the forces of international diplomacy media and intelligence converged and there really wasn't anywhere for someone like Park to hide. Soon the savvier among the British reporters had formed their own judgements about her true role, as did the American reporters about Devlin. Following a number of newspaper reports she was listed as a former member of SIS in the 1983 espionage exposé *British Intelligence & Covert Action*[12] and her principal career postings outlined. So from then on at least it is probable that the information slowly percolated through the Somerville community. Certainly by the end of her time as Principal her mischievous side occasionally came to the fore and she would joust occasionally with the academics about her prior history as a spy.[13]

Whether and to what extent her intelligence background influenced attitudes to her is difficult to say. Park both liked and admired Margaret Thatcher who was Prime Minister throughout her tenure as Principal. In 1983, shortly after being re-elected for her second term, Thatcher, accompanied by her daughter Carol, visited Somerville presumably at Park's invitation. To her dismay the PM was greeted by the sight of hundreds of Somervillian (and other) undergraduates vociferously protesting against her presence, in the main due to her government's economic policies. Afterwards Thatcher sent Park a her 'bread and butter' letter telling her how much she enjoyed her visit, but one suspects that was mainly for form.[14] The PM cannot have expected that what was billed as an occasion for

i YAMANI, Dr Mai, who completed both her MSt and DPhil at Somerville (1956-).

some nostalgia to turn into what was close to a mini-riot. Park would not have enjoyed it much either.

Worse was to come. In 1985 it was suggested that Margaret Thatcher be honoured with the award of an honorary degree. The suggestion caused controversy among the dons. Thatcher's overall economic policies, in particular her government's attitude towards the universities and higher education generally, aroused fierce opposition. Park, naturally, was firmly in favour of the proposed award, arguing that the achievements of the woman should be separated from purely partisan political issues. The fact of Thatcher being the first woman Prime Minister only added to that. A vote was held and the proposal turned down by a resounding 738 votes to 319. Park did not even carry her own college, Somerville. So Thatcher became the first Oxford-educated Prime Minister since the war not to receive such an honour. The result was a huge loss of face for Park, who was reportedly 'shattered' by the negative vote of her own academics in particular; for her it was 'a question of decorum and patriotism; even in extreme circumstances you do not humiliate the British Prime Minister'.[15] Coming less than a year after her mother's death, it was a bitter blow.

Another divisive issue was the question whether Somerville should retain its 'women-only' status. More and more Oxford colleges were abandoning their 'men-only' policies, in part because of the changing mores and more significantly because of the system of central grants which had the effect of penalising single-sex colleges. This meant that women who planned on attending Oxford had a far wider choice than had obtained heretofore and in some ways meant that the need for a women-only college was much reduced, if not eliminated altogether. Park's initial attitude was in favour of retaining the distinction, but when the financial and other realities were explained to her and how the college would suffer from the reduced central support, she converted and began to lobby for the change. However, when it went to a vote the College decided to retain its single-sex status. When she made the announcement of the result there was nothing in Park's demeanour to suggest that she had ever been in favour of anything else, to the extent that most thought she was actually in favour of the retention. With Daphne Park there were no *arrières pensées*.[16]

Spy or not, academic equal or not, Professor Anna Morpurgo Davies was in no doubt about the quality of Park's overall contribution to Somerville:

In 1980 Daphne inherited a demoralized institution which felt that through no fault of its own it had lost its academic status as well as its raison d'être, its fundamental role in the education of women. Admittedly Somerville had produced the first woman Prime Minister, a matter for rejoicing, but here too the college was divided in the assessment of her policies. And yet in these circumstances we soon discovered that Daphne's optimism was for real. It quickly translated into a programme for action. The financial position was bad: so money had to be found.

The college's status had declined: a new public persona was needed and the college had to be better known. The students worried about their future: they had to be given employment opportunities. Daphne had never done any fundraising but now she started in earnest ... nobody was more surprised than she was when she succeeded. By the end we managed to have a new quad and a new set of buildings largely built with the money that she raised. ... In the background there was her inexhaustible energy – she never gave up – and her irresistible cheerfulness. But the impressive thing – again with hindsight – was the way in which she used the multiple problems of Somerville. The question of finances, academic status, unemployment, were all looked at together and made to help each other. Daphne exploited her communicative skills to the maximum. Future benefactors or simply benevolent grandees were invited to dinner; fellows helped to entertain them, undergraduates and graduates were invited to meet the guests after dinner in the lodgings. Drinks were produced and, after the inevitable sticky silences, slowly this ill assorted group of industrialists or bankers, diplomats, academics, tongue-tied undergraduates, earnest graduates, began to gel. One of Daphne's stories broke the ice, the atmosphere changed (whisky helped) and when late at night the party dispersed undergraduates and grandees were friends. Daphne's warning to the industrialists that a letter would soon arrive was received with equanimity. The letter arrived and yielded fruit. There were also evenings for industry in which the great firms participated and the undergraduates turned up to meet them. In fact Daphne opened a new world where the dividing line between academic and non academic pursuits disappeared. At the same time the college received a constant stream of visitors: ambassadors and ex ambassadors from various and often colourful parts of the globe, revolutionaries of one or the other type, millionaires and refugees: the variety was striking and, though we occasionally complained, it was also exciting.[17]

Dr Yamani's account dovetails with this. She speaks of being invited by Park to attend fundraising dinners. Park, whose passion for Turkish Delight was reflected in her rather stout figure, was normally quite a sloppy dresser and completely uncaring about her appearance, but she would dress up and look the part for these occasions. And they worked. Park, Yamani said, assembled a group of about thirty rich and influential Arab business leaders who not only contributed generously but who in turn opened doors to others, including Nemir Kirdar, founder and CEO of the Bahrain-based hedge fund managers, Investcorp. Park's influence was also pivotal in securing significant support for the controversial Saïd Business School in Oxford (named after Wafic Saïd, the Saudi-Syrian billionaire who has donated up to £70 million to the school). Yamani's own influence (she is the daughter of Sheikh Yamani, the billionaire former Saudi Arabian oil minister) should not be underestimated, but she emphasised that Park never crossed the boundaries and did not use her connection to Mai to approach the Sheikh for donations, 'unlike others', she added.[18]

Soon it was time to stand aside. To say goodbye to her students and to her fellow staff who by 1989 had come round to Park practically without exception and recognised what an enormous contribution their Principal had made to their college. She left behind a new quad, many new buildings, a fully computerised college, a renewed sense of purpose and vigour and much more. By way of tribute she was offered that famous second portrait, marking not just her change in attitude to her college but its change in attitude towards her.

Before she left she had one final matter to attend to. It was to thank Mary Chambers, the daughter of the Anglican archbishop of Dar-es-Salaam and organiser of the correspondence course that had introduced the young Daphne to the world of English literature and the Classics. It was Mary Chambers who had written to Doreen Park in 1932 and suggested that the young Daphne be sent to England for some proper schooling. Later in her life Chambers had left Tanzania and settled in Britain where she had read of Park's appointment and got in touch.[19] One can only guess at the emotions present on that occasion; for Daphne Park to meet the woman who, more than any other, had helped set her course in the world, and for Mary Chambers to see at first hand, as so few of us ever do, the truly extraordinary result of her intervention all those years previously.

And then without a backward glance Daphne Park was gone. She had fresh fields to conquer.

Daphne Park: a life extraordinary

Daphne Park's active life did not end on her retirement from SIS, nor did it when she left Somerville. In fact during her time in Somerville she was appointed by the Prime Minister, Margaret Thatcher, to the Board of Governors of the BBC, a precursor perhaps to her later elevation to the House of Lords, also on Thatcher's watch. The BBC appointment came in 1982. This was relatively early in Thatcher's premiership (and in Park's principalship) and was a time of considerable strain in relations between the BBC and the Conservative government and, coincidentally, between Park and her Somerville academics.

Thatcher was determined to sort out the BBC. She knew too that the sorting would be tricky. The Corporation occupied a very special place in British life and to be seen to be interfering overtly with it could be damaging politically. But something needed to be done to tame the unruly beast. One way was to have her placemen at the BBC, to redress, as she saw it, the left-wing bias in the organisation. Park fitted the bill on a number of fronts: she was very much a known quantity, a staunch Conservative and not the slightest bit 'wet'. Her history suggested too that she was an above-the-parapet sort of person; if something needed saying you could rely on Park to say it, if it needed doing, to do it, no bystander she. So the 'former diplomat and academic' (she was actually neither) was duly appointed.

Park more than justified her choice, serving Thatcher well in her role as a Governor (board member). She was still at the height of her intellectual powers, just turned sixty, and she went about her work with a will. She confronted the then Director-General, Alasdair Milne, with unremitting vigour. It is probable that Milne knew what he was up against. Milne was a career BBC man and it seems likely that some BBC journalist would have had the connections to fathom Park's past role in the 'Foreign Office' and pass that little titbit to the DG. But if Milne knew he didn't allude to it in public. He played the establishment game, referring to her in his memoirs simply as 'a diplomat who had worked in far flung places like Hanoi and Lusaka'. A hint there perhaps, but that was all.

The two locked horns over issues like key internal BBC appointments, Park always alert to the placing of 'yet another' left-leaning programme controller in a key slot. They clashed too over programme content, Park describing one proposed programme as being in the 'Hitler loved dogs', category,[1] while Milne described her as 'almost spluttering with fury' over the issue.[2] She had a point, perhaps: the programme in question, *Real Lives*, was to feature a sympathetic interview with the then Provisional IRA leader Martin McGuinness, whose organisation had attempted to blow Thatcher and her Cabinet to smithereens a few years previously and was still engaged in all-out war with Britain. A 1984 *Panorama* special report, *Maggie's Militant Tendency*, on links between Tory MPs and extreme right-wing groups, did little to further endear the Corporation to Thatcher or indeed to Park.

Milne was to discover, as many had before, that it is rarely wise 'to take on City Hall'. Thatcher would have her way. While Park was not appointed in order to overthrow Milne in some SIS-style conspiracy, she probably played a part in the *coup* that eventually saw him off. She had the experience for it at least, and it is unthinkable, given her political proximity to the PM, that she would not have been consulted by the BBC chairman Marmaduke Hussey before he plunged in the knife. Plunge it he did, and deep. On 28 January 1987, four months after he had been appointed chairman, Hussey summoned Milne to his office and told him to pack his bags that day. 'It is time,' Hussey said, 'for your lawyers to speak with my lawyers.'[3]

Milne may not have seen it coming, but he did see beyond Park's 'Miss Marple' exterior. As he put it in his account of his stewardship in the BBC, Park's 'strong resemblance to recent characterisations of Agatha Christie's Miss Marple concealed a tough and uncompromising view of life'.[4] Milne variously referred to her as 'deeply suspicious' and 'deeply sour'.[5] Friends they were not.

Thatcher may have had other reasons for having her people on the BBC board. The intelligence services maintained much closer links to the BBC than was advertised or generally known. All permanent applicants for positions on the editorial/ programme content side were vetted by MI5. The vetting operation was run by a Home Office appointed former military intelligence officer, Brigadier Ronnie Stonham.[i] Stonham headed up a small team based in Room 105 in Broadcasting House. Applicants who failed the vetting process had their file stamped with a Christmas tree-like symbol, a sign to the initiated that the subject was not suitable for hiring.[6] In 1983 a total of 5,728 applicants for positions with the BBC were referred to MI5 for vetting at Stonham's request (*Daily Telegraph*). Michael Nelson (ex-Reuters) claimed in a letter to the *Times* in August 2014 that in a total of one hundred non-governmental organisations were subject to vetting by MI5.

MI5 also briefed the corporation on the activities of known and suspected 'subversives' in Britain. If, for example, subversives were thought to be behind a particular labour dispute, this would be made known to the DG and through him to the head of news and current affairs. A summary of current intelligence on the status and activities of organisations considered by MI5 to be subversive (or significantly penetrated by subversive elements) was delivered every quarter

---

i STONHAM, Brigadier Ronald ('Ronnie') L.; Royal Signals, BBC (MI5) (1928-2014).

to the BBC from MI5's F Branch. That way, senior BBC news editors would be made 'aware of the background issues'. Particular regard was paid to what were seen as 'politically motivated' industrial relations disputes.[7]

SIS was also involved in providing secret intelligence to the BBC. The BBC's external broadcasting headquarters, Bush House, was the recipient of daily intelligence briefings, routed through the Foreign Office. The material reportedly included 'telex traffic from British ambassadors' and analysis of secret intelligence 'collated from MI6 and GCHQ'. According to a source quoted by the *Observer*, 'you can see they have some very well placed people in foreign governments and it's obvious they're reading their letters and so on'.[8] *Plus ça change*, then. The BBC reciprocated by providing a service to SIS reminiscent of its Second World War special messages collaboration with SOE. Any SIS officer who wished to impress a potential agent or collaborator could arrange to have a special message or piece of music played at a pre-arranged time on the appropriate BBC station. It was a very effective means of demonstrating to the potential collaborator that they were indeed in contact with the 'man' (or 'woman').[9]

Three years after the Milne affair, in 1990, the year after she completed her Somerville post, Daphne Park was made a life peer by Margaret Thatcher, then in the sunset of her own career. She was the first senior officer in SIS to be so ennobled other than a former Chief. The honour was not solely because of her work in SIS, though her role in the secret UDI negotiations and her personal briefing of the PM in 1979 would not have been forgotten by Thatcher. Her role as Principal of Somerville College, her extensive record of voluntary public service, the fact of her being a woman, and of course her politics, all played into the decision. Barbara Harvey (her Vice-Principal) summed up better than most what this meant to Park:

> When, in 1990, Daphne received a life-peerage, she entered on what she once called her fourth career, and it was one of unalloyed pleasure. She loved everything about the House of Lords: the formality and courtesy of its proceedings, the occasional pageantry, the importance of its work as a revising chamber for legislation, and other things beside these. At first, she hesitated to accept the honour when it was offered and felt obliged to tell Margaret Thatcher, the Prime Minister, who had nominated her, that although she wished to take the Conservative whip, she might not always be able to support Conservative policies. Having received what she described as a 'brisk' encouragement from the Prime Minister to differ whenever she wished to, she accepted. ... She was moved to tears by the admission ceremony. At the time, I did not fully understand her emotion, though I felt moved myself by the matchless prose forming part of the ceremony. ... Daphne was moved because she felt that she was once again a public servant, able to express her love for her country, and to do so now with no need for concealment. She was in her defining role again but in the open, where she had perhaps often wished to be in the past.[10]

Had Daphne Park accepted the offer of a position in the Treasury or the Foreign Office when she was offered it during the Second World War it is likely that her natural talents would had seen her achieve senior rank and her career of 'colonial girl made good' would have been rightly lauded. But she did not. Instead she wriggled her way into the Special Operations Executive via a reluctant FANY where she trained the bravest of the brave in the use of the codes on which their lives would depend when dropped behind enemy lines.

After the war she was refused entry into SIS but she persisted, snuck around to the side door and gained entry on the second time of trying. But it was not entry to the elite Intelligence Branch but to the more humdrum General Service. So she wriggled some more, befriended her boss and soon found her way into the Intelligence elite, where she would have felt she belonged all along. But then she discovered that within that elite there was a further elite, SovBloc, so she wriggled some more until she was accepted into that and posted to Moscow. And on it went from there, positions of increasing responsibility as she rose through the SIS ranks to its highest operational position, that of Controller, the plummiest of plum jobs.

She did perhaps have a vain streak in her. Don't we all? As we have seen, she insisted for her first portrait in Somerville that she be painted with an opened book on her lap in order, she said, to appear 'more academic'.[11] While she was discreet about her exploits in SIS, she certainly seems to have enjoyed the aura that came from being known to have been a spymaster for her country's Secret Intelligence Service. She would joust mischievously with her academics in Somerville over her past and she wasn't above burnishing the legend occasionally. According to author Steven Dorril, who was a consultant to the programme, it was Park who approached SIS for permission to appear on *Panorama* in 1994, not as is often said (by her), the other way round. Her lifelong friend and former PA, Maggie Fletcher, described by Barbara Harvey 'as the most reticent person I ever met' was also, according to Harvey, 'quite disapproving of Daphne speaking to the media'.[12]

Her two great love affairs were hugely significant in her life. Her first, with Douglas DeWitt Bazata, affected her deeply. For him it appears to have been just a wartime fling. For her it was true love and the hurt stayed with her for a long time. In interviews later in her life she referred to one great affair that 'ended in death'; there is some speculation that it was the death of her love to which she was referring, not a fatality. Bazata was one of those people who start off 'crazy' and who then go slowly mad. Apart from being dashing, handsome, brave and daring he was *trouble*. A talented artist, he exhibited internationally, being collected by the Duke and Duchess of Windsor and by Princess Grace of Monaco. The latter befriended Bazata to the point of becoming (reputedly) his muse[13] and mounting a *vernissage* (showing) for him on at least one occasion.[14] Most fittingly of all, Bazata had his portrait painted by Salvador Dali in a piece called 'Homage to Bazata' in which he appeared as Don Quixote. Perhaps Dali foresaw Bazata's bizarre claim, made in 1979, that he had been hired by his boss in the OSS, the legendary 'Wild' Bill Donavan, to murder General George S. Patton. The claim is given little credence. His final job was in the Reagan administration as counter-terrorism (special assistant) to Secretary of the Navy John F. Lehman, Jr. This was a job he was 'well suited for', according to Lehman, and one he did well. 'Set a thief to catch a thief', Lehman concluded (to this author), rather enigmatically.[15] Lehman also said that he and Bazata visited the Special Forces Club in London a few times when Park was a member. He recalled Bazata introducing him to a number of women who had been involved in Special Forces during the war but could not recall whether their number included Daphne Park. After Bazata's death a semi-coherent 'diary' written by him was discovered in which he claimed to have been a sort of hitman for quasi-governmental agencies. That claim too is given little credence. He died in 1999 at the age of eighty-eight.

Park's second great love, which commenced when she was in her mid-forties, was a more enduring one. And in the best spy style she managed to keep it secret from all or practically all her colleagues. One, who would claim to have known her well, spoke to this author of 'Daphne being a virgin when she died'. He wasn't the first to see a middle-aged woman or man and not to see that under that plump exterior had once lurked a passionate individual, since in the words of Jean Sackur, Park did experience 'a full and loving relationship'. Park herself actually spoke about it to one or two outside the Service – Jean Sackur was one, Mai Yamani another – mentioning her 'secret love'. Whether marriage between them was ever discussed we do not know. He was already married with children, so a divorce would not have been without consequences for his family. That certainly weighed on her mind, according to Jean Sackur. Perhaps it was that she was too late in life to want to change (Jean Sackur certainly thinks that might have been a factor), or perhaps the secret love life fitted with her secret work life.

On every Valentine's Day up to the time he died her lover sent Park a Valentine's card. Park did not attend his funeral. She wanted to dearly but felt that her presence would have been noted and would have intruded onto his widow's grief. So she chose to grieve alone.

Park was in effect an only child (brother David dying at fourteen), as were both her parents. She appears to have had little or no contact with her relatives in Northern Ireland. No Parks are listed as having attended her memorial service. That said, she was decidedly pro-Ulster Unionist in her outlook, far more so than the average Tory peer, according to Paul Bew,[i] an academic and political observer (and fellow peer) who got to know her quite well. Unusually for Westminster she was, according to Bew, a regular attender at Northern Ireland briefings given to parliamentarians by various Secretaries of State for Northern Ireland, but neither by word or deed did she indicate to Bew (or Glentoran for that matter) that she had antecedents from Belfast.[16] During Maurice Oldfield's short-lived appointment as Security Coordinator for Northern Ireland (1979/80), Park acted as his sounding board in London but was never involved operationally in the Province. Park herself was vehemently opposed to the IRA, telling a friend of the author that she would relish the opportunity to confront the former Provisional Gerry Adams if he ever showed his face in Westminster.[17] In later life she was also active in campaigning against the practice the Provisional IRA had of 'expelling' from Northern Ireland those who acted counter to its wishes. Whether her Northern Ireland Protestant ancestry was a factor in her overall attitude we do not know.

On the African side it was different, which, given her involvement with the continent, is no surprise. Her grandmother (Anne Cresswell-George) was from a decent-sized Monmouthshire family who settled mainly in South Africa, Northern Rhodesia (now Zimbabwe) and Nyasaland (now Malawi). Park maintained contact with them throughout her life. Cousins, Wayne Parham and Pamela Millar, used call on her during their occasional visits to Britain. Park in turn visited Parham in Zimbabwe very late in her life (she was eighty-one at the time, according to Barbara Harvey), slipping across the border to meet him and at risk of being jailed if discovered. Parham was a substantial landowner in Zimbabwe but had much of his holding seized by the Mugabe administration. The African side of her family was well represented at her memorial.

Of course Daphne Park wasn't perfect; she had her moments as most people have. She could, according to some former colleagues, 'be a good hater'. She was very unforgiving of Dick White's stance over the perceived insult from Costley-White of the CRO, in retirement describing White to a former colleague as a coward.[18] She certainly detested the Russians; she made that clear to this author when they met. Another acquaintance spoke of an incident that took place in the mid 1990s at the height of the 'thaw' between Western intelligence services and their former Soviet counterparts. A conference was held in St Antony's College at which former (and current) British, American and Russian spies assembled to talk about past times and previous deeds (lots of ghosts present as you can imagine). Daphne Park was invited and duly turned up. However when one former KGB officer stood up to speak she paled and became so upset she had to leave the room. Once outside she could no longer contain her fury; 'That man tried to

i BEW, Dr Paul Anthony Elliott (Baron Bew) (1950-).

murder my friend,' she hissed through gritted teeth. It took some time for her to compose herself and return to the room.

Nor did she like the French very much:

Daphne disliked the French quite intensely but spoke the language superbly and enjoyed showing it off, for example at the annual *Maison Française d'Oxford* party. (Barbara Harvey)[19]

But she did admire the Americans:

They get things wrong from time to time but at the end of the day it is on America that we depend on for our freedom.[20]

And at her memorial in Westminster among the hymns she chose to have sung was the stirring 'Battle Hymn of the Republic', a choice she shared with Winston Churchill. Perhaps it was a nod to her old mucker, Larry Devlin, or to her old flame, Douglas DeWitt Bazata.

On the other hand she didn't have time for Stella Rimington, the former Director of MI5 who published her memoirs:

Stella Rimington is a disgrace. I disapprove of that woman so strongly. All the people who might be preparing to stick their necks out in a dangerous situation will think; I'm not going to talk to that lot because they write their memoirs. And the silly woman wrote as if there had never been a woman in MI5 before – well, there had been plenty before her. The only time I ever experienced sexism is when an African chief gave me a special gift of a hoe, instead of a spear.[21]

John Le Carré (David Cornwell) didn't tickle her fancy either:

... John le Carré I would gladly hang, draw and quarter. He dares to say that it is a world of cold betrayal. It's not. It's a world of trust. You can't run an agent without trust on both sides.[22]

Not all her colleagues sang her praises:

As for Daphne, she was charismatic and loved by the people who worked for her. I was never, myself, an admirer. I never worked for her, so my perception was from a distance, but she seemed too much a Cold [War] Warrior for me and a little rigid in her thinking ... [though] she was clearly an extraordinary person. I don't know how she came to be an intelligence branch officer. She must have had a tough fight to make her way.[23]

We weren't close, professionally or personally ... I have always thought of Daphne as a blend of Margaret Rutherford, the bosomy and motherly actress, and Rosa Klebb, the cold-eyed KGB dragon-lady with a poisoned blade in her shoe. (John de St Jorre)[24]

But most did:

> The English can recognise integrity but we find it difficult to be articulate about it. We just call it by name and esteem it. Daphne showed us that her integrity was simple: she integrated her faith and values into her personality and into her behaviour. She was what she believed: she was a living value. Her friends could not but think, 'if all this matters so much to Daphne, why doesn't it matter like that to me?' Hence her own power of leadership. (Sir Mark Allen[i])[25]

Daphne Park was quite reserved and remained something of an outsider all her life. In SIS she wasn't one of the lads (or lassies), frequenting the bar in Century House only on rare occasions. Nor was she a 'shoulder to cry on' for her male colleagues or subordinates. Hugh Bicheno speaks of her being as 'tough as nails' on him when he once stepped out of line. Jean Sackur adds that for a woman to rise as high as Park did in as male-dominated an organisation as the SIS she could not do so by being everyone's 'favourite auntie'.

In fact Park did not make friends easily, not in school (as recalled by Daphne Helsby) and not afterwards either. While hugely popular with the students in Somerville, it was the popularity afforded a 'Mr Chips' rather than the friendship of equals.

> The 'Queen' [Daphne Park] wasn't 'huggable' ... she could be very intimidating; I could imagine her slowly killing someone with her smile. (Dr Mai Yamani)[26]

> [Park] invited me to lunch and introduced me to a great many members. She was obviously well respected because everyone acknowledged her ... just before our first course I asked her 'Lady Park, how should I address you?' I was thinking that she might say 'just call me Daphne' or something similar but without a moment's hesitation she replied 'Lady Park'. I didn't think her pompous and I wasn't in the slightest offended. (Bill Duff, former RUC Detective Superintendent)[27]

And regrets? Yes.

In later life she deeply regretted the fact that she had not had a closer relationship with her mother from whom she had been parted at the age of eleven, not seeing her again until she was in her late twenties. Park speaks of writing dutifully to her mother 'until she was eighteen' but of having transferred her love and affection to her two great-aunts, something to be expected given the circumstances. It was nonetheless a cause of deep hurt to her mother when she came to Britain and discovered it (and from what one can gather the home environment in Cedar Road in Sutton had its moments, if being asked to parade around Croydon dressed in a Pierrot costume 'in order to eliminate her self-consciousness' is any guide).

i ALLEN, Sir Mark John Spurgeon, CMG; SIS, MECAS, ABU DHABI, CAIRO, H/BELGRADE, C/ME (1950-).

Park told Caroline Alexander that she had a sort of romantic view of her father, the man 'who had trekked across Africa'. On the other hand she had 'resented her mother', describing the absence of a full relationship with her 'as the black spot' in her life. She had not realised until almost too late that it was her mother, through her enormous drive and determination and the sacrifices she had made, who had set her on the road to the career that she enjoyed. However, it was a career that took Park away from her mother for extended periods on foreign postings for ten of the first twenty years that the nearly blind Doreen Park lived in Britain. Perhaps part of Park wanted to escape because she only called a halt to the travel in 1972, when her mother was seventy-three and in extremely poor health. And while her mother was proud of her daughter's achievements, Park's career orientation was mystifying to her. She wanted her daughter to be 'gay and flirtatious' and marry and have someone look after her, not pursue a Whitehall career.[28] Park's close friend, Jean Sackur, described this aspect of Park as:

> Not maternal, not maternal at all, but then you'd hardly expect her to have been, having effectively lost her mother when she was eleven.[29]

While Park did not fear death, she did not welcome it either, saying wistfully:

> And yet there are all sorts of things I would like to do. One never stops learning. If there is nothing to learn, nothing stimulating, one begins to die a small death. I would like to go to Burma – it is my Kathmandu, my Timbuktu, a place that simply attracts me. This is a marvellous world. I wish I could go on and on.[30]

It is difficult to sum up that combination of personality, values, strengths, weaknesses and priorities that governs someone's behaviour over the long term. Perhaps the extract below from her 1983 interview with the Diplomatic Service Wives Association (DWSA) magazine comes closest to defining Daphne Park. When asked what qualities she would wish for her students in Somerville, she answered:

> The qualities I would wish them (which I am not sure I can give) are courage, stamina, intellectual curiosity, the desire for excellence, an adventurous spirit and above all an abiding belief in the decency of human beings.

That could probably serve as her epitaph.

Daphne Park's achievements should never be underestimated. From the moment the eleven-year-old girl set foot on British soil in 1932 she never once faltered. The Service she joined in 1948 was a chauvinistic, militaristic mens' club. In fact all of the men who mattered were members of clubs which did not admit women as policy. The one club that did grant her admittance still insisted she enter the building by the side door. As someone who'd had to do that all her life she obviously didn't let it bother her. Because whether by the front door, side door, or back door she persisted until she got what she considered to be her due.

For this author finding those doors has been a task. Park was a spy and spies are careful. There are very few photographs of Park from the thirty-one years she was in SIS. 'She preferred not to appear in photographs,' said her friend Jean Sackur. Nor are there many personal letters from her overseas postings. 'She didn't write,' said Jean, 'just telephoned when she had arrived back in London.'[31] These were the discretions drummed into her by years of secret work: 'leave nothing more than a footprint in the sand' might have been her motto. In tracing her life I have had to seek out those footprints, many already almost completely washed away, others fast fading from sight. But enough have been left, I hope, for some idea of the extraordinary person who was Daphne Park to emerge.

Daphne Park passed away on 24 March 2010. For some time she had been suffering from arthritis, confining her to a wheelchair. She then was struck down by cancer. A former SIS officer who knew her well said of the last couple of years:

> Sometime before Daphne's death an angel appeared who ministered to Daphne for the last years of her life. If the angel turned out to benefit in some way from the ministering, then perhaps that was the price that needed to be paid.

As the Ides of March 2010 passed, realising the end was near, Park told her doctors it was time to 'let her go'. One of the last to visit her was Sir Gerald Warner, a former colleague, a warm and close friend, and himself a renowned SIS personality.

> 'Goodbye dear Gerry,' she said and then as if to reassure him, 'It's all right you know.'[32]

Acknowledgements

Biographies of the deceased usually depend on what biographers describe as 'the trove', a cache of documents that can be mined for those nuggets that will bring to life the author's description of the subject. Diaries are an ideal component, as are volumes of personal correspondence, official documentation of any kind, letters, reports, journals, inquiries, expenses claims, if it comes to that.

It can be assumed that during the thirty-one years of Daphne Park's service in SIS she generated her due share of such documents, just as it can be assumed that 95% of them remains safely under lock and key in the vaults of the organisation she served so well.

So, like the poor of old, this biographer was forced to rely on the generosity of friends (Daphne's, not his own) for the source material in *Queen of Spies*. Leading the donors were Jean Sackur (*née* La Fontaine, a lifelong friend of Daphne's), and John de St Jorre (her former SIS station colleague in Léopoldville). Without Jean's and John's extraordinary insights, generously given, the book would have been very much the poorer, if it could have been written at all.

A significant number of Daphne's former SIS colleagues gave of their time and their memories; a few, like (the late) Hugo Herbert-Jones, Julian 'Jules' Harston and Hugh Bicheno, can be named; the rest prefer to remain anonymous: to you all go my thanks. The same gratitude is expressed to the other unnamed contributors to this book and of course to all who assisted the author in his quest for information. The UK National Archive in Kew and its wonderful staff deserve a special mention.

Somerville College, its Principal, Dr Alice Prochaska, and Vice-Principal Emeritus, Barbara Harvey, were pivotal. As was Martyn Cox, the independent television producer and renowned expert on SOE and the French *résistants* who gets a special word of thanks for his extraordinary generosity. Not to forget Steven Kippax, the doyen of the Yahoo 'Special Operations Executive' group whose members provided much needed detail on that period of Daphne's service to her country.

Daphne Park was interviewed by Caroline Alexander for *The New Yorker* (30 January 1989). Of all the interviews Park provided, Alexander's was the most revelatory, offering a rare glimpse of the inner person behind the public facade of diplomat, spy and college principal. The author acknowledges the contribution made by this interview.

Britain is well served by its cadre of intelligence authors and I acknowledge the assistance from superb works by Christopher Andrew, Nigel West (Rupert Allason) and Stephen Dorril in particular among the many. Nigel and Stephen were also personally very helpful. Tom Bower's magisterial biography of Dick White, *The Perfect English Spy,* proved an invaluable reference.

My agent Andrew Lownie is *the business.* Andrew possesses endless energy, radiates optimism, is extraordinarily well-connected and really knows his literary onions. How fortunate I am to be a part of his stable. My publishers, Duckworth Overlook, are superb to work with. Their team, including the book's two editors, Andrew Lockett and Deborah Blake, brought their unique expertise to bear in excising the superfluous, the grammatically incorrect and the tautological from the text; those blemishes that remain are my responsibility and mine alone. The same applies to any errors of fact that have slipped into these pages; given the subject matter much of the material can be difficult to verify. Grateful note will be taken of any errors brought to my attention to be corrected in future editions.

To my friends in the Longtable writing group who helped so much over the years and to its founder John Kelly go my gratitude and affection. To my daughters Rachel and Aoife and my wife Helen (Keogh) goes my undying love. Without Helen this book could not have been written, without her it would not have been worth writing.

Paddy Hayes

Appendix

Timeline of Daphne Park's life

1921 Born 1 September, Kingston, Kent; parents: John Alexander Park and Doreen Gwyneth Park (*née* Cresswell-George)

1922 Returned to Africa with her parents, first to Nyasaland and then to Tanganyika where the family settled

1932 Left Tanganyika to live with great-aunts in London

1933-39 Rosa Bassett School, Streatham, London

1939-43 Somerville College, Oxford (Modern Languages, 2.1)

1943-46 Special Operations Executive (SOE), on secondment from First Aid Nursing Yeomanry (FANY)

1943 RF section SOE

1944 (January) Jedburghs, Milton Hall, head of coding instruction

1944 (April) RF section, coding instructor

1944 (August) Jedburghs, Massingham, briefing officer

1945 Special Allied Airborne Reconnaissance Force (SAARF), Virginia Water, Surrey, head of coding

1946 FANY

1947 Field Intelligence Agency Technical – British Intelligence Objectives Subcommittee (FIAT-BIOS) on continuing secondment from FANY

1948-79 Secret Intelligence Service (SIS)

1948-49 General Service in administrative role

1949-50 Staff officer to Kenneth Cohen, Chief Controller/Europe

1950 Stay behind officer, Germany, Austria, Switzerland

1951 Transferred to intelligence branch (IB) on Operation GLADIO in France

1951-52 Joint Services School of Linguistics/Newnham College, Cambridge, Certificate in Russian

1952 Immersive Russian language tuition, Paris

1952-54 Press attaché to head of UKDEL NATO, Fontainebleau

1954 General Tradecraft course, London and Hampshire

1954-56 2nd secretary, head of station and deep cover officer, Moscow (H/MOSCOW)

1957-58 Production officer (P Officer), West Germany stations

1959 Sub-Saharan Africa desk, London

1959-61 1st secretary and consul, Léopoldville (H/LÉOPOLDVILLE)

1961 Appointed OBE

1961-64 Production officer (P Officer), Central and West Africa stations

1964-67 Consul and head of station, Lusaka (H/LUSAKA)

1967-69 Far East Controllerate

1969-70 Consul-general and head of station Hanoi (H/HANOI)

1971 Appointed CMG

1971 Sabbatical as Honorary Research Fellow at the University of Kent

1972 (March/April/May) *chargé d'affaires ad interim* Ulaanbaatar, Mongolia, (H/ULAANBAATAR)

1972-75 Head of UK Africa stations, London (H/UKC)

1975 Controller/Western Hemisphere (C/WH)

1979 Retired from SIS

1980-89 Principal of Somerville College, Oxford

1982-87 Governor of the British Broadcasting Corporation (BBC)

1983-89 Member, British Library Board

1984-90 Chairman, Lord Chancellor's Advisory Committee on Legal Aid

1985-89 Pro-Vice Chancellor, University of Oxford

1989-90 Director, Zoo Development Trust

1989-94 Chairman, Royal Commission on the Historical Monuments of England

1990-2010 Baroness Park of Monmouth, of Broadway in the County of Hereford and Worcester

1991-92 Trustee, Royal Armouries Development Trust

1994-96 Member, Forum UK

1994-2010 President, Society for the Promotion of the Training of Women

2003 Patron, Action Congo

2010 Died 24 March, Radcliffe Hospital, Oxford.

Member, Royal Asiatic Society

Member, Special Forces Club

Member, Margaret Thatcher Foundation

Governor, Ditchley Foundation

Trustee/Patron, Great Britain-Sasakawa Foundation

Trustee, Jardine Educational Trust

Trustee, Lucy Faithfull Travel Scholarship Fund

Fellow, Royal Society of the Arts (FRSA)

Fellow, Chatham House (RIIA)

Founder, Military Commentator's Circle

Notes on Sources

Introduction

1. '*C*': *A Biography of Maurice Oldfield* by Richard Deacon was first published in 1985. Tom Bower's biography of Dick White (*The Perfect English Spy*) was published in 1995, but White was not a career officer in SIS, never having served in the organisation prior to his appointment as its Chief.

Chapter 1

1. Outbound UK Passenger Lists (UK National Archives).
2. Lawrence E.Y. Mbogoni, *Aspects of Colonial Tanzania History* (Mkuki na Nyota Publishers Ltd, 2013), p. 38.
3. Ibid., ch. 2.
4. Author interview with Jean Sackur (*née* La Fontaine).
5. David Clive Nettelbeck, *A History of Arusha School Tanzania* (Department of Education, University of Adelaide, 1974).
6. Author interview with Jean Sackur.
7. The birth of Estcourt Cresswell-George's son (and Park's cousin) Michael was the beginning of that arm of Park's family to which she remained close all her life. In turn that family was to include the Parham brothers (Wayne and Gary) and their sister Pamela.
8. UK Incoming Passenger Lists do not record Daphne Park arriving onboard any vessel from Africa between 1930 and 1935. Records were not kept for passengers arriving from Mediterranean countries. Park may have sailed to Suez and onwards by a different vessel, or, may have made her landfall in a port such as Marseille. In either case no immigration record would have been completed (source: National Archives). A popular alternative means of travelling from the colonies home to Britain was to make the European landfall in France, often in the port of Marseille. That way avoided the Bay of Biscay where rough waters made the passage uncomfortable. That was in the days before passenger vessels were fitted with stabilisers.

Chapter 2

1. Daphne Park's grandfather William Herbert Cresswell George had three sisters: Mary Elizabeth Jane, Mary Anne Josephine and Emily Clara Josephine (George). Two of the sisters married, but the youngest, Emily Clara (whose engagement was broken), remained single all her life. It is not possible to state definitively which of the two sisters looked after Daphne, but records suggest it was Mary Elizabeth (married to John George Trembeth) and Emily Clara, the single sister (in the role of paid companion).
2. Daphne Helsby, *née* Whittle, Daphne Park Memorial Tributes (Somerville College, 2010), p. 17.
3. Memorial Address (29 May 2010) by Sir Gerald Warner, Daphne Park Memorial Tributes, p. 22.
4. Daphne Helsby, Daphne Park Memorial Tributes, p. 16.
5. Caroline Alexander, 'A Profile of Daphne Park', *The New Yorker*, 30 January 1989, p. 59.
6. Caroline Alexander, p. 60.
7. Funeral Address (29 May 2010) by Barbara Harvey, Daphne Park Memorial Tributes, p. 5.

8. Pauline Adams, *Somerville For Women* (OUP, 1996, p. 243), quoted in the Daphne Park Memorial Tributes, p. 18.

9. Daphne Park interviewed by Martyn Cox for *Our Secret War*, filmed Oral History Project.

10. Ibid.

11. While the sign outside read Women's War Work Enquiries, it was officially The Ministry of Labour and National Service Registration and Employment Office for Women. The Office assigned women positions in one of the armed services' women's branches (WRNS, ATS or WAAF) or into war factories, hospitals or farming. As it happened the Office also kept a quiet look out for suitable candidates for FANY.

12. Park interview with Martyn Cox.

13. Ibid.

14. When the Second World War ended the two Gamwell sisters went back to their farm in Northern Rhodesia (Zambia). In 1964, after Zambia had gained its independence, the two decided that life there 'was not to their liking' and returned to the UK, living out their final years in Jersey.

15. Park interview with Martyn Cox.

Chapter 3

1. Park interview with Martyn Cox.

2. Leo Marks, *Between Silk and Cyanide* (Harper Collins, 1999), p. 332.

3. Hazel Yeadon, 'I was selected to train as a coder!' (from the BBC's *WW2 People's War* website (http://www.bbc.co.uk/history/ww2peopleswar/), contributed by Hazel Yeadon, 23 January 2006.

4. Park interview with Martyn Cox.

5. Marks, *Between Silk and Cyanide*, p. 475.

6. Park interview with Martyn Cox.

7. Ibid.

8. Laurent Joffrin, *All that I Have* (Arrow Books, 2005), p. 25.

9. Ibid., pp. 24-5.

10. Anne Keenlyside blog, *Memoirs of MUMMAWUN* (29 October 2007).

11. Stories about the infamous Beaulieu seductresses were legion. There was at least one other, a woman called Marie Chilver, improbably codenamed Agent FiFi, whose file was opened (with redactions) by the UK National Archives in September 2014. Rumour (or wishful thinking perhaps) had it that the seductresses were prepared to 'go all the way', in an effort to get trainee agents to break their cover stories, the punishment for which was usually expulsion. When France was liberated and Beaulieu closed, SOE sent Wicken to India to join its operations there. After the war she was reported to have emigrated to South Africa rather than returning to her pre-war role as a secretary with coal brokers, John Hudson & Company.

12. Maj. Elliot J. Rosner, *The Jedburghs: Combat Operations Conducted in the Finistere Region of Brittany, France from July-September 1944* (United States Military Academy, 1976), p. 26.

13. William Colby, *Honourable Men: My Life in the CIA* (Hutchinson, 1978), p. 37.

14. Park interview with Martyn Cox

15. BCRA – Intelligence and Operations Central Bureau, forerunner to the SDECE, the post-war French equivalent of the CIA.

16. Park interview with Martyn Cox.

17. Gen. Paul Aussaresses in a letter to Lt.-Col. Will Irwin quoted in Lt.-Col. Will Irwin, *The Jedburghs* (Public Affairs, 2005), p. 62.

18. Capt. Stanley Cannicott, *Journey of a Jed* (Special Forces Club/Imperial War Museum, undated).

19. The story was submitted to the BBC's *WW2 People's War* website by Jane Pearson, a volunteer from Age Concern, Dorchester on behalf of John Cook Montague (deceased), and has been added to the site with the permission of his daughter, Cilla Claire Maine.

20. Park interview with Martyn Cox.

21. The BIGOT list originated in a wartime flight to the island of Gibraltar, the passengers all being privy to the date of the D-Day landings. For security reasons the passenger list name was changed from TO GIB to BIGOT. It stuck and became used for all people who were subsequently indoctrinated into the D-Day secret. In later years it became used to describe any list of people who were cleared to know about any particular operation or code name.

22. Park interview with Martyn Cox.

23. Ibid.

Chapter 4

1. Ibid.

2. Ibid.

3. Ibid.

4 Aaron Bank, *From OSS to Green Berets: The Birth of Special Forces* (Presidio Press, 1986), p. 14.

5. Cannicott, *Journey of a Jed.*

6. Marks, *Between Silk and Cyanide*, p. 418.

7. Description of Spooner attributed to Colonel Buckmaster by Leo Marks in *Between Silk and Cyanide*, p. 308.

8. Noor Khan was sent in to France in June 1943 and was captured the following October. After interrogation by the Gestapo she was sent to Dachau Concentration Camp where she was later executed. It was ironic, but Spooner's reservations about her turned out to be correct. In strict contravention of every SOE rule in the book she retained copies of all her sent messages which fell into the hands of the Germans on her capture, doing irreparable damage. That is not to take away from her bravery.

9. Spooner would have preferred it if women were not sent into battle, especially behind the lines. However, if it had to be done then such women should possess a certain 'worldly sophistication and toughness'. He indicated that Noor was 'too innocent, too emotional, and too impulsive ... too vulnerable'. Furthermore, he felt she was 'too highly strung and too nervous' to be of much use in the field. Given how matters turned out he was probably correct, but that wasn't really the point. From Buckmaster's perspective any W/T operator was better than no W/T operator. Source: http://home.earthlink.net/~mrstephenson_umsl/noor/training.html

10. Marks, *Between Silk and Cyanide*, pp. 308, 310.

11. Park interview with Martyn Cox.

12. Colby, *Honourable Men*, p. 35.

13. Author interview with Steven Kippax and with a close friend of Daphne Park.

14. Park to Steven Kippax, as recounted to the author.

15. Author interview with Steven Kippax.

16. http://desertwar.net/operation-jedburgh.html.

17. Park interview with Martyn Cox.

18. Ibid.

19. Roderick Bailey, *Forgotten Voices of the Secret War: An Inside History of Special Operations in the Second World War* (Ebury Press in association with the Imperial War Museum, 2008), interview with Marian Gamwell.

20. Park interview with Martyn Cox.

21. Warner, Memorial Address, Daphne Park Memorial Tributes, p. 22.

22. Warner, Memorial Address, Daphne Park Memorial Tributes, p. 22, and Park interview with Martyn Cox.

23. Park interview with Martyn Cox.

24. Park obituary, *The Times*, 26 March 2010, and Park interview with Martyn Cox.

Chapter 5

1. According to the 'History of Jedburghs in Europe' (UK National Archives), a further ten Jedburgh teams were dispatched to Algeria on 27 June 1944, making a total of twenty-five Jedburgh teams sent to Algeria for dispatch into France.

2. Park was issued with a gratis passport by the Passport Control Office (part of SIS and responsible for the issue of passports to SOE and SIS at that time). The passport was first used on 7 August 1944 (source: UK National Archives *per* author Phil Tomaselli).

3. Park interview with Martyn Cox.

4. Ethnic Algerian soldiers serving in the French Army.

5. As an aid to security the word 'Joe' was used to describe any agent who was waiting or transiting in any SOE base. It was more secure than using even a code name. Eventually it became slang for 'agent'.

6. Sergeant Ron Brierley, MC, OBE.

7. USAAF 885 Operations.

8. Properly called the Westwall but usually referred to as the Siegfried Line, it was a six hundred kilometre long line of fortifications, built between 1938 and 1940 with the avowed aim of defending Germany from any attack on its borders from France.

9. Park interview with Martyn Cox.

10. Ibid.

11. Ibid.

12. Ibid.

13. Ibid.

14. Bazata's first marriage to Diana Chirieleison didn't last. In 1948, after the war had ended, he divorced and married a Penelope Grant. That marriage too was later dissolved. He married for the final time in 1970.

Chapter 6

1. When Dorothy Wicken was hired by SOE to work in Beaulieu her employer was given as S.T.S. Headquarters with an address at 98 Horse Guards, Pall Mall, Whitehall (UK National Archives).

2. Helen McCarthy, *Women of the World: The Rise of the Female Diplomat* (Bloomsbury 2014), p. 115.

3. Ibid., p. 259.

4. Park obituary, *Daily Telegraph*, 25 March 2010.

5. Approximately seventy-five members of SOE transferred to SIS immediately after the war but substantially more than that number are estimated to have served in SIS in some capacity, according to the historian Steven Kippax.

6. Park interview with Martyn Cox.

7. Ibid.

8. Ibid.

9. Ibid.

10. This negative attitude towards industry was to change quickly: very soon the military (in the US at least) realised they had common cause with the industrialists (and vice versa) and so between them created the giant US military-industrial complex which influences so much international policy of the US government to this day. In his farewell speech as the outgoing US President in January 1961, President Eisenhower warned about the growing influence of that complex and the danger it represented to America.

11. See Paul Weindling, *John W. Thompson: Psychiatrist in the Shadow of the Holocaust* (University of Rochester Press, 2010), p. 119, for a description of FIAT's involvement in coordinating the hunt for the Nazi war criminals guilty of conducting medical 'experiments' in concentration camps. The official British view was that prosecutions should be limited to the very worst cases, 'otherwise practically the entire German medical establishment would have had to be put on trial'. Park was not involved in that aspect of FIAT's work.

12. Charles R. Ahern, 'The YO-YO Story: An Electronics Analysis Case History', *Studies in Intelligence* 5/4 Winter 1961.

13. Objective List of German and Austrian Scientists to be interrogated (1,600 'Scientists'), Joint Intelligence Objectives Agency, 2 January 1947.

14. *Who's Who in Nazi Germany*, Box No 2, West Central District Office, New Oxford Street, WC1.

15. Frederick I. Ordway III and Mitchell R. Sharpe, *The Rocket Team* (Apogee Books Space Series 36. Thomas Y. Crowell, 1979) (courtesy of Wikipedia).

16. Gordon Corera, *The Art of Betrayal: The Secret History of MI6: Life and Death in the British Secret Service* (Pegasus, 2011), p. 34.

17. Paul McMahon, *British Spies and Irish Rebels: British Intelligence and Ireland, 1916-1945* (Boydell Press, 2008), p. 347 and Christopher Andrew, *The Defence of the Realm* (Allen Lane, 2009), p. 220.

18. Jane Archer was MI5's main Soviet expert and the person most likely to have spotted that Philby was a Soviet infiltrator. Following her dismissal she was offered a position in SIS where she was responsible for wartime operations in the Irish Free State. After the war she moved back into SovBloc. She then transferred back to MI5 (possibly on secondment) to take part in the investigation of Philby.

19. Corera, *The Art of Betrayal*, p. 36.

20. George Kennedy Young, 'The Final Testimony of George Kennedy Young' (published in *Lobster* 19, May 1990, and attributed to Young), pp. 35-45.

21. Geoffrey Moorhouse, *The Diplomats* (Jonathan Cape, 1977), p. 63.

Chapter 7

1. Author interview with former SIS officer.

2. Renaming itself Her Majesty's Government Communications Centre (HMGCC), the transmitters for the Lincolnshire Poacher were moved to Cyprus where they remain.

3. See http://www.alancordwell.co.uk/hfradio/dwsint.html.

4. Hugh Trevor-Roper, *The Secret World* (I.B. Tauris & Co, 2014), pp. 35, 90.

5. Between 1950 and 1954 there were 119 Administrative Entrants (officer class) to the Foreign Office (which would have included SIS). 106 of the 119 were Oxbridge graduates and just two were women (Geoffrey Moorhouse, *The Diplomats*).

6. Other intelligence services envied this aspect of SIS; Markus Wolf, the legendary East German spymaster, used to invite the betrayer George Blake to address recruits in the Stasi's foreign intelligence service (HVS) in an effort to inculcate a 'sense of belonging and tradition within the Communist espionage community' (Roger Hermiston, *Greatest Betrayer* (Aurum Press, 2013), p. 329.

7. Author interview with former SIS officer.

8. Kim Philby, *My Silent War* (Grove Press, 1968).

9. Park interview with Martyn Cox.

10. In the General Election of 1945, twenty-four (4%) MPs were female. Women were excluded from membership of the House of Lords until 1958.

11. J.P. Waterfield, *Memories of 1945-50*. www.tamburlane.co.uk/resources/jpw.html.

12. Author interview with former SIS officer.

13. The SIS hostel was on the corner of Gloucester Road (No 68) and Cromwell Road and today is a hotel.

14. Author interview with former SIS officer (as recounted).

15. Author interview with lifelong friend of Daphne Park.

16. Author interview with Mrs Ann O'Regan, widow of the late Patrick O'Regan who served with Park in Moscow in the mid 1950s and who passed away in 1961.

Chapter 8

1. Roger Hermiston, *The Greatest Betrayer* (Aurum Press, 2013), p. 50 (original source not cited).

2. Trevor-Roper, *The Secret World*, p. 42.

3. Keith Jeffery, *MI6: The History of the Secret Intelligence Service 1909-1949* (Bloomsbury, 2010), p. 154.

4. Author interview with former SIS officer.

5. Author interview with Daphne Park.

6. Anthony Cave Brown, *'C': The Secret Life of Sir Stewart Graham Menzies, Spymaster to Winston Churchill* (Macmillan, 1987), p. 689.

7. Ibid., p. 684.

8. Warner, Memorial Address, Daphne Park Memorial Tributes, p. 23.

9. Ibid.

10. Corera, *The Art of Betrayal*, p. 36.

11. Cave Brown, *'C'*, p. 687.

12. In his book *Secret Wars* (Thomas Dunne Books, 2009) author Gordon Thomas describes Harold Caccia as a 'veteran MI6 officer' (p. 148). This author has not been able to establish that independently.

13. Richard J. Aldrich, Gary D. Rawnsley and Ming-Yeh Rawnsley, *The Clandestine Cold War in Asia 1945-65* (Frank Cass, 2000); Nigel West, *The Friends* (Weidenfeld & Nicolson, 1988), pp. 13-14.

14. Jed teams were comprised of three heavily armed paratroopers sent in to organise members of the resistance, SUSSEX teams consisted of two unarmed (other than with personal weapons) intelligence officers whose role was to collect intelligence and report it back to Allied HQ.

15. Address by Park to the Royal Society of Literature, May 2008.

16. Author interview with former SIS officer.

17. Evan Thomas, *The Very Best Men* (Touchstone Books, 1995), p. 66.

18. Young, 'The Final Testimony of George Kennedy Young'.

19. US Atomic Energy Commission, 'An Interim Report of British Work on Joe', 22 September 1949, Top Secret. Source: Harry S. Truman Library, President's Secretary's Files, box 199, NSC-Atomic.

20. David Holloway, *Stalin and the Bomb* (Yale University Press, 1996), p. 222.

21. The betrayer is likely to have been William Marshall, a member of the Diplomatic Wireless Service (DWS) who was posted to Moscow around that time. In 1952 Marshall was jailed for passing secret information to the Soviets after he had returned to Britain.

22. Anthony Glees, *The Secrets of the Service* (Jonathan Cape, 1987), p. 218; the newly formed (1948) Russian Committee in the Foreign Office spoke of doing everything 'by any means short of war' to uncouple the Soviet satellites.

23. Jeffery, *MI6*, p. 679 (Gallienne is referred to by position rather than by name in this reference).

24. Ibid.

25. Author interview with Stephen Dorril, intelligence author.

26. Author interview with Jean Sackur.

Chapter 9

1. Author interview with former 'deep-cover' SIS officer.

2. Jill Sheppard resigned from SIS shortly after Moscow and went to live and work in Barbados where she published *The Redlegs of Barbados* (KTO Press, 1977). Nothing more is known about her SIS career. While she is listed in the Foreign Office directory as being attached to the embassy in Moscow, her name does not appear in the biographical section for those or any other years.

3. Source: French intelligence-reporting website, http://lemondedurenseignement.hautetfort.com/archive/2008/08/26/les-officiers-du-mi6-en-poste-a-moscou.html.

4. Ibid.

5. Address by Park to the Royal Society of Literature, May 2008.
6. Ibid.
7. Ibid.
8. Ibid.
9. Warner, Memorial Address, Daphne Park Memorial Tributes, p. 23.
10. Philip H. J. Davies, *MI6 and the Machinery of Spying* (Frank Cass, 2004), p. 207.
11. CIA report 15 November 1951 (www.maryferrell.org).
12. Author interview with Dr John Lehman.
13. According to author Frank Close (*Half Life: The Divided Life of Bruno Pontecorvo*, Oneworld Publications, 2015) it was Philby who tipped off the scientist that the FBI were harbouring suspicions about where his true loyalties lay and so enabled him to escape to Moscow.
14. The phrase *la douceur de vivre* was used by Harold Macmillan to describe the undergraduate life experienced by him in Oxford University, but was more generally used to describe the gilded lives of the wealthy country-house set in Britain.
15. Caroline Alexander, p. 63.
16. Jeffery, *MI6*, p. 749.
17. Ibid.
18. Letter from Sir John Sinclair (Chief of SIS) to Foreign Secretary Harold Macmillan (1955), released in January 2014 (source: UK National Archives).
19. Murphy, Kondrashev and Bailey, *Battleground Berlin* (Yale University Press, 1977) , p. 219.
20. Changed in 1964 to the Chief of the Defence Staff (CDS).

Chapter 10

1. Author interview with Mrs Ann O'Regan.
2. Author interview with former SIS officer.
3. William Hayter, *The Kremlin and the Embassy* (Hodder & Stoughton, 1966), p. 37.
4. Ibid., p. 40.
5. John Gunther, *Inside Russia Today* (Hamish Hamilton, 1962), p. 72.
6. Ibid.
7. Hayter, *The Kremlin and the Embassy*, p. 46.
8. J.P. Waterfield, *Memories of 1945-50* (www.tamburlane.co.uk/resources/jpw.html).
9. Hayter, *The Kremlin and the Embassy*, p. 49.
10. Daphne Park, 'The Freedom to Intervene – Freedom Lost', *The Economist Intelligent Life Magazine*, Autumn 2008.
11. 'Either silence or prison', quoted in I.F. Stone, *The Haunted Fifties* (Vintage Books, 1969), p. 128.
12. SIS stations were called CXs, the digraph 'CX' preceding the host city, e.g. CX/MOSCOW. A CX was also a report from an agent or other source; the term 'serial' was also used for this.
13. The Russian Secretariat in the Moscow embassy consisted of a group of three or four expert linguists who became the first 'Kremlinologists', each spending a couple of years in the Moscow embassy. Tommy Brimelow (Lord Brimelow), a future permanent undersecretary (PUS) in the Foreign Office (and a great supporter of Park's), headed that section during one of his stints there.
14. Author interview with former CIA translator who worked in Caversham.
15. Hayter, *The Kremlin and the Embassy*, p. 33.
16. Quoted in John Gunther, *Inside Russia Today*, p. 365.
17. The First Department of the KGB (2A) was responsible for the United States and the Third (2C) was responsible for West Germany.
18. Victor Cherkashin and Gregory Feifer, *Spy Handler* (Basic Books, 2005), p. 47.
19. During Park's time in Moscow the Canadian ambassador (John Watkins) succumbed to a homosexual honey-trap, as did the assistant to the British naval attaché (John Vassall), while her opposite number in the US embassy (Edward Ellis-Smith) fell victim to a more traditional 'Valya the maid' honey-trap. All three entrapments (and many more) were initiated by Oleg Gribanov.

Chapter 11

1. Author interview with former SIS officer.

2. Caroline Alexander, p. 62.

3. Ibid.

4. There are no details available about how Park actually obtained the Soviet rail timetable. We do know, from her obituary in *The Times* (26 March 2010), that she did obtain one. Most obituaries of former SIS officers which appeared in *The Times* (and other major national newspapers) were written by former colleagues and can be considered to be reliable if incomplete. A number are quoted in this work.

5. Timetables are valuable documents. In the 1960s an Irish economist, Dr Garret FitzGerald (later to become Irish Prime Minister) used the just-published Aeroflot timetable to calculate the size of the airline's fleet. Aeroflot withdrew the timetable at once.

6. Park obituary, *The Times*, 26 March 2010.

7. Author interview with former SIS officer.

8. Ibid.

9. Account based on Wing Commander John Deverill, letter to *The Times* (2 April 2010). Deverill provides a fuller account of his service in Moscow in Volume 2 of his autobiography, *Ad Ultimo: A Memoir of International Relations in War and Peace* (Gilgamesh Publishing, 2014).

10. Between 1957 and 1960 the Legal-Traveller program 'provided useful information on Soviet offensive and defensive missile programs, strategic bombers and submarines, nuclear propulsion systems, manned space programs and bacteriological warfare capabilities' (Jeffrey Richelson, *American Espionage and the Soviet Target*, Quill, New York, 1987.

11. Ahern, 'The YO-YO Story'.

12. Ibid.

13. Soviet Bloc electronic projects of intelligence interest were assigned nicknames rather than codenames or cover names. The nicknames were agreed on a tripartite basis by a committee representing US, Canadian and British electronic intelligence specialists (Charles R. Ahern, 'The Yo-Yo Story').

14. Ibid.

15. Christopher Andrew, *For the President's Eyes Only* (Harper Collins, 1995), p. 213.

16. Clarence Ashley, *CIA Spymaster* (Pelican Publishing Company, 2004), p. 109.

17. Ahern, 'The Yo-Yo Story'.

18. The CIA approved-for-release document on Yo-Yo does not state where the packet of photographs originated from. Earlier the document refers to assistance from British sources in Moscow and actions by US military attachés. Given the photographs were taken in daylight and from 'several angles', it is unlikely that a service attaché shimmied in and took them under the noses of the Russians. The sketch map (see p. 107) may have been assembled from the surreptitious inspections possibly assisted by a source inside the Soviet system.

19. The spy flight over Kapustin Yar has never been confirmed by the British government. It was conducted by RAF 540 Squadron in the summer of 1953 using a Canberra B2 bomber equipped for photo reconnaissance (see http://www.spyflight.co.uk/robin.htm).

20. TROJAN was the codename for the USAF plan to nuclear bomb fifty named cities in the Soviet Union in the event of an outbreak of war between Russia and America. The plan was leaked to the KGB by Philby; the Soviet leadership was appalled when it saw the extent of US plans. It is probable that this contributed significantly to Stalin's decision to ring Moscow with anti-missile batteries. Some writers have since claimed that the plan really existed only on paper and that the USAF did not at that time possess the capability to implement more that a fraction of it. That is something the Soviets could have not verified, even if it was true.

Chapter 12

1. George Blake, *No Other Choice* (Jonathan Cape, 1990), p. 167.

2. Looking out for signs that an enemy is actively engaged in war preparations is one of the

oldest forms of intelligence. Signs will include call-up of reservists, increased security on public buildings and key infrastructural targets, large-scale troop movements and 'manoeuvres', particularly close to border areas, alterations in military codes and substantial increases in radio traffic.

3. Author interview with former SIS officer, Hugh Bicheno.

4. 'In the press, in Parliament, in the United Nations, from the pulpit, there is a ceaseless talk about the rule of law, civilised relations between nations, the spread of democratic processes, self-determination and national sovereignty, respect for the rights of man and human dignity.

'The reality, we all know perfectly well, is quite the opposite and consists of an ever-increasing spread of lawlessness, disregard of human contract, cruelty and corruption. The nuclear stalemate is matched by the moral stalemate.

'It is the spy who has been called on to remedy the situation created by the deficiencies of ministers, diplomats, generals and priests.

'Men's minds are shaped of course by their environments and we spies, although we have our professional mystique, do perhaps live closer the realities and hard facts of international relations than other practitioners of government. We are relatively free of the problems of status, of precedence, departmental attitudes and evasions of personal responsibility, which create the official cast of mind. We do not have to develop, like Parliamentarians conditioned by a lifetime, the ability to produce the ready phrase, the smart reply and the flashing smile. And so it is not surprising these days that the spy finds himself the main guardian of intellectual integrity.' (quoted in George Blake, *No Other Choice*, p. 168).

5. Address by Park to the Royal Society of Literature, May 2008.

6. Ibid.

7. In the days before the proliferation of live computer databases all intelligence services made use of 'live-doubles' (and still do to an extent though it is more difficult). In Brik's case his controllers arranged for him to meet a legitimate Canadian traveller/ Communist sympathiser in Vienna. The sympathiser handed over his passport. Brik substituted the original photograph for one of himself and used the altered document to gain entry into Canada. The original owner reported it stolen after Brik had used it to gain entry and disappear. Once in Canada Brik assumed the identity of a Canadian, David Soboloff, who had left Canada for Russia with his young son and was living there. The photographic studio was called the Zoboloff Studio and was based, as stated in the main text, in the suburb of Verdun in Montreal. Brik installed a shortwave radio in a bedroom over the studio to send and receive messages from Moscow Centre.

8. One reason why intelligence services are so paranoid about revealing their operational methods is that they remain in use for many years. For example, thirty years later in 1985, when SIS needed to arrange the escape of another KGB source (Oleg Gordievsky) from Moscow, the method they used bore remarkable similarities to the plans for Brik. SIS provided Gordievsky with the means to make his way to the Finnish-Soviet border where arrangements were made to smuggle him across it in the boot of a car driven by the SIS deputy head of station in Moscow accompanied by his wife. Brik was given the means to make his way to the town of Pechenga on the Norwegian-Soviet border and a map showing him where to cross (source: the Mitrokhin Archive).

9. Daphne Park tended to be quite caustic about the chauvinistic attitude of Russian Intelligence and it is true that they were quite backward even for those conservative (from today's perspective) times. She can forget though how backward her own Service was. Women were not routinely admitted to the ranks of intelligence officers until the very late 1970s, and while overseas stations made use of their station secretaries in operational roles, once back in London the women had to revert to their traditional roles. And there were petty (and some not so petty) restrictions on women, such as the bar on women intelligence officers marrying.

10. Some sources claim that the recognition signal was a shopping bag he was to carry in his left hand. Dan Mulvenna (former RCMP security service officer), who spoke to Park about the incident later in her life, claims that was incorrect.

11. KGB Major Vasili Mitrokhin was an archivist in the KGB's First Chief Directorate/FCD (foreign intelligence arm) for thirty years. However, early on in his career, Mitrokhin was barred from overseas service due to some relatively minor infringement. When the FCD archive was

being moved from the Lubyanka to its new location in Yesnevo on the south-west outskirts of Moscow, a process that took some years, Mitrokhin exacted his revenge. While supervising the move he made detailed notes, an extraordinary 25,000 pages of them, of the archive's contents. For operation after operation going back to Cheka times, he copied names, dates, places, anything he could. He smuggled the notes out each day, later hiding them under the floorboards in his dacha. In 1992, following the collapse of the Soviet Union, he made contact with the CIA. The Agency turned down his approach (to its lasting regret), the über-cautious Americans fearing a provocation or a fraud. Mitrokhin then turned to SIS which had no such qualms. The Service extracted him and his archive out of Russia. The hoard enabled SIS to identify scores of agents, some still active, others retired, uncover secret arms caches, and unravel quite a few mysteries left over from the Cold War, including that of Brik. Mitrokhin's KGB archive was published in book form (with some redactions) in 1999 (Christopher Andrew and Vasili Mitrokhin, *The Sword and the Shield: The Mitrokhin Archive and the Secret History of the KGB*). The publication outraged the KGB who considered that it broke another of the unwritten rules, i.e. 'intelligence agencies do not needlessly embarrass their opponents by publicising the names of opposing officers'.

12. Author interview with former RCMP security officer Dan Mulvenna.

13. Ibid.

Chapter 13

1. In September 1955, Henry Jones Fairlie devoted his column in *The Spectator* to how the friends and acquaintances of Guy Burgess and Donald Maclean tried to deflect press scrutiny from the men's families. He defined that network of prominent, well-connected people as the 'Establishment', explaining: 'By the "Establishment", I do not only mean the centres of official power—though they are certainly part of it—but rather the whole matrix of official and social relations within which power is exercised. The exercise of power in Britain (more specifically, in England) cannot be understood unless it is recognised that it is exercised socially.'

2. The then headquarters of the KGB was in the Lubyanka, in Dzerzhinsky Square in Moscow. The building remains occupied by the FSB, successor to the original KGB's 2nd Chief Directorate, then as now responsible for internal security.

3. Tom Bower, *The Perfect English Spy* (Heinemann, 1995), p. 204.

4. Ibid.

5. Khrushchev's suite in Claridge's was bugged by MI5 but the Soviet leader confined his remarks to discussions about his appearance and what clothes he should wear.

6. When, fourteen months after the event, Crabb's body was recovered, his head and hands were missing. Experts said that could be explained as resulting from being buffeted against rocks (there are other explanations that could fit equally well).

7. Mystery still surrounds aspects of the Crabb affair. The British government papers relating to it have been re-classified and will remain unpublished until 2056 at the earliest. The SIS papers remain sealed, probably forever. At the time DNA testing did not exist so it was not possible to prove conclusively that the recovered body was really that of Crabb. There was also the issue of where the remains had been in the fourteen months between his disappearance and the recovery. Was it possible that he had in fact been captured, taken to Russia as a prisoner, interrogated and killed? While that theory might stand up it would hardly have made sense for the Russians to go to the trouble of returning the dead man's remains, minus head and hands in some form of gesture.

8. Bower, *The Perfect English Spy*, p. 160.

9. The insiders' favourite for the post was Park's former boss Kenneth Cohen. However, according to an unnamed former SIS officer quoted in Tom Bower's *The Perfect English Spy* (p. 171), Cohen 'was a Jew just when oil mattered'.

10. Gregory W. Pedlow and Donald E. Welzenbach, *The Central Intelligence Agency and Overhead Reconnaissance: The U-2 and Oxcart Program* (History Staff, Central Intelligence Agency, 1992), p. 94.

11. Author interview with former SIS officer.

12. Peter Hennessy, *The Prime Minister* (Penguin, 2000), pp. 215-16.

13. In response to Radio Moscow and other Soviet broadcasters, the United States also stepped up broadcasting to Eastern Europe and the Soviet Union. By 1956, the Voice of America was broadcasting more than three hundred hours per week to the Soviet Union. Radio Liberation (changed in 1963 to Radio Liberty) was established in 1951 by the United States to broadcast to the Soviet Union in Russian and other Soviet languages. It began with a twenty-minute Russian programme repeated for twelve hours a day. By 1957, it had increased to speaking seventeen Soviet languages from eleven transmitters. At the same time, Radio Free Europe began speaking to Eastern Europe. By 1954, it was broadcasting 124¾ hours a week to Poland alone. Original source: Bernard Bumpus and Barbara Skelt, 'Seventy Years of International Broadcasting', *Communication and Society* 14 (UNESCO, 1983), p. 49, quoted in Mark D. Winek, 'Radio as a Tool of the State: Radio Moscow and the Early Cold War', *Comparative Humanities Review* (2009) vol. 3, Article 9. Available at http://digitalcommons.bucknell.edu/chr/vol3/iss1/9

14. Bower, *The Perfect English Spy*, p. 202.

15. Hayter, *The Kremlin and the Embassy*, p. 144.

16. Ashley, *CIA Spymaster*, p. 109.

17. Andrew, *For the President's Eyes Only*, p. 213.

18. Peter Wright, *Spycatcher* (Viking-Penguin, 1987), pp. 83-6.

19. Memorial Address (26 October 2010) by Sir Mark Allen, Daphne Park Memorial Tributes, p. 27.

20. Stephen Dorril, *MI6: Fifty Years of Special Operations* (4th Estate, 2000), p. 645.

21. Author interview with Stephen Dorril.

22. Hennessy, *The Prime Minister*, p. 226.

23. Author interview with Wing Commander (retd) John Deverill.

24. Author interview with former SIS officer.

25. Bower, *The Perfect English Spy*, p. 200.

26. In 1966 William Hayter published *The Kremlin and the Embassy*, an account of his time in Moscow. The publication drew sharp disapproval from the Kremlin on the grounds that the publication 'so soon after the event' of confidential discussions between the Soviet government and HMG's representative was a 'departure from the normal standards of diplomacy'. The Foreign Office rejected the complaint.

27. Author interview with former SIS officer.

Chapter 14

1. Mohammad Mossadeqh was the elected Prime Minister of Persia (Iran) until 1953 when his government was overthrown in a coup orchestrated by SIS and the CIA. Britain, determined to protect its oil exploration and production rights, was the prime mover behind the action.

2. Bower, *The Perfect English Spy*, p. 209.

3. Author interview with former SIS officer.

4. Bower, *The Perfect English Spy*, p. 173.

5. Author interview with former SIS officer.

6. Ibid.

7. Ibid.

8. Ibid.

9. Ibid.

10. Ibid.

11. Ibid.

12. Ibid.

13. Ibid.

14. Report by former SIS officer John Bruce Lockhart on visit to 'Black Africa', 16 December 1959, PREM 11/2585, p. 1 (UK National Archives). John Bruce Lockhart's name does not appear

on the document, but according to Tom Bower (in *The Perfect English Spy*) Lockhart did make a visit to Africa at this time and so his authorship is assumed.

15. Corera, *The Art of Betrayal*, p. 95.
16. McCarthy, *Women of the World*, p. 277.

Chapter 15

1. Lawrence Devlin, *Chief of Station, Congo: Fighting the Cold War in a Hot Zone* (Public Affairs Press, 2007), p. xiii.
2. 'We can deal with the blacks; we know them. Brussels can only theorize,' was the attitude of the whites. Ruth Slade, *The Belgian Congo* (Oxford University Press, 1960), p. 9.
3. Ibid., p. 3, referring to O. Mannoni, *Prospero and Caliban: The Psychology of Colonisation*, tr. Pamela Powesland (Praeger, 1956), 105-6, 2: '[T]he savage ... is identified in the unconscious with a certain image of the instincts – of the *id*, in analytical terminology. And civilized man is painfully divided between the desire to "correct" the errors of the savages and the desire to identify himself with them in his search for some lost paradise (a desire which at once casts doubt upon the merit of the very civilization he is trying to transmit to them).'
4. A.A.J. van Bilsen, *Un plan de trente ans pour l'emancipation politique de l'Afrique Belge* (Les dossiers de l'Action sociale catholique, Brussels, 1956), quoted in Ruth Slade's *The Belgian Congo* (Oxford University Press, 1960), p. 17.
5. The Congo Crisis, 1960-1961: A Critical Oral History Conference Organized by the Woodrow Wilson International Center for Scholars' Cold War International History Project and Africa Program (2004), p. 63.
6. Author interview with Jean Sackur.

Chapter 16

1. Address by Park to the Royal Society of Literature, May 2008.
2. McCarthy, *Women of the World*, p. 140.
3. Caroline Alexander, 'A Profile of Daphne Park', p. 64.
4. Author interview with former FCO official, Roger James.
5. 'The wind of change is blowing through this continent. Whether we like it or not, this growth of national consciousness is a political fact' (Harold Macmillan, January 1960).
6. Report on visit to 'Black Africa' by John Bruce Lockhart (1959), PREM CCCC, Para 4 (UK National Archives).
7. Matthew Hughes, 'Fighting for White Rule in Africa: The Central African Federation, Katanga, and the Congo Crisis', *International History Review*, September 2003, p. 597.
8. Ibid., p. 595.
9. Susan Williams, *Who Killed Hammarskjold?* (Hurst & Co, 2011), p. 149, and Andrew, *The Defence of the Realm*, p. 444.
10. Sayaka Funada-Classen, *The Origins of War in Mozambique: A History of Unity and Division*, tr. Masako Osada (Ochanomizu Shobo Co, 2012), p. 233.
11. Report by Former SIS officer John Bruce Lockhart on visit to 'Black Africa', 16 December 1959, PREM 11/2585, p. 4 (UK National Archives).
12. Park obituary, *Daily Telegraph*, 25 March 2010.
13. Address by Park to the Royal Society of Literature, May 2008.
14. Park obituary, *Daily Telegraph*, 25 March 2010.
15. Warner, Memorial Address, Daphne Park Memorial Tributes, p. 23.
16. Park obituary, *The Times*, 26 March 2010.
17. Elizabeth Davies, 'A Chargé Recharged: A Profile of Miss Daphne Park CMG', *Diplomatic Service Wives Association Magazine*, Autumn 1983, p. 65.
18. Park obituary, *Guardian*, March 2010.

19. Author interview with Jean Sackur.
20. Address by Park to the Royal Society of Literature, May 2008.
21. Author interview with John de St Jorre.
22. Ibid.
23. Samuel Tilman, 'Le scoutisme au Congo belge (1922-1960): une école de l'élite pour les jeunes indigènes' ['Scouting in the Belgian Congo (1922-1960): A School of the Elite for Indigenous Youth'], *Revue belge d'histoire contemporaine* (Brussels), vol. 28, 1998, p. 366.
24. Ibid., p. 372.
25. Ibid., p. 377.
26. Author interview with former SIS colleague of Park's, Hugo Herbert-Jones.
27. Caroline Alexander, 'A Profile of Daphne Park', p 64.
28. Corera, *The Art of Betrayal*, p. 119.
29. http://historyofafricaotherwise.blogspot.ie/2011/08/andree-blouin-word-of-congo-or-black.html
30. Daphne Park quoted by Corera in *The Art of Betrayal*, p. 117.
31. Ibid., p. 122; according to Corera the news of Blouin's neutralisation was conveyed by the director of the CIA, Allan Dulles, personally to a meeting of the US National Security Council. It is an indication of the importance in which Blouin was held.
32. http://historyofafricaotherwise.blogspot.ie/2011/08/andree-blouin-word-of-congo-or-black.html
33. Author interview with John de St Jorre.
34. Ibid.
35. Ibid.
36. Ibid.
37. Ibid.
38. Author interview with former SIS officer
39. Ibid.
40. Report by John Bruce Lockhart on visit to 'Black Africa', 16 December 1959, PREM 11/2585, p. 2 (UK National Archives).
41. Report by John Bruce Lockhart on visit to 'Black Africa', 16 December 1959, PREM 11/2585, p. 1 (UK National Archives).
42. Report by John Bruce Lockhart on visit to 'Black Africa', 16 December 1959, PREM 11/2585, p. 2 (UK National Archives).
43. Gordon Corera, *The Art of Betrayal*, pp. 103-4.

Chapter 17

1. *Foreign Relations of the United States 1964–1968, Vol. XXIII Congo, 1960–1968*, Department of State, Washington, p. 1.
2. The Congo Crisis, 1960-1961: A Critical Oral History Conference (2004), p. 39.
3. Ian Scott, *Tumbled House* (Oxford University Press, 1969), p. 45.
4. Ibid., p. 45.
5. Ibid., p. 47.
6. Ibid.
7. Telegram No 331 Scott to FO London, 21 July 1960 (UK National Archives).
8. Caroline Alexander, 'A Profile of Daphne Park', p. 64.
9. The founder of Fodor's travel guides, Eugene Fodor, admitted in later life to having been a CIA agent and employing other Agency officers as cover for their intelligence activities. In 1974 the *New York Times* revealed his spy secret.
10. Lawrence R. Devlin is listed as joint writer on Fodor guides to France, Italy and Austria, Finland and Switzerland and the Benelux countries, published in 1951, 1952 and 1953; in the 'game' it is called 'living your cover'.
11. Devlin, *Chief of Station*, p. 6.

12. Telegram No 347 Scott to FO London, 23 July 1960 (UK National Archives).

13. United States Senate Select Committee to Study Governmental Operations with Respect to Intelligence Activities, III. Assassination Planning and the Plots, 'A' Congo (Church Committee Hearings), p. 14.

14. Church Committee, p. 15.

15. Ibid., p. 46.

16. Devlin, *Chief of Station*, p. 66.

17. Bower, *The Perfect English Spy.*

18. Ludo De Witte, *The Assassination of Lumumba* (Verso, 2001), p. 27.

19. Ibid., p. 25.

20. Church Committee, p. 46.

21. Park rescued Kandolo from a life-threatening situation and later described him as being one of her most effective ever agents (multiple sources including Gordon Corera, *The Art of Betrayal*, p. 119).

22. Daphne Park quoted in Corera, *The Art of Betrayal*, p. 129.

23. '*Lawrence Devlin*: He [Mobutu] was never recruited, and I certainly would have known. *Herbert Weiss*: But he was given a stipend. I am almost sure of that. *Lawrence Devlin*: You don't have to be an agent to receive a stipend. An agent is a person to whom we'd say: "we expect you to do this and do that." Mobutu was never a person to whom we could say "do this and this and this." *Unidentified male*: And he would jump. *Lawrence Devlin*: He would never ask how high.' (The Congo Crisis, 1960-1961: A Critical Oral History Conference (2004), p. 41).

24. Matthew Hughes, *Fighting for White Rule in Africa*, pp. 609-10.

25. Howard Imbrey interviewed by Charles Stuart Kennedy, Association for Diplomatic Studies and Training Foreign Affairs Oral History Project. Initial interview date: 21 June 2001.

26. Church Committee, p. 17.

27. Church Committee, p. 503.

28. Telegram No 762 Scott to FO London, 27 September 1960 (UK National Archives).

29. Christopher Andrew and Vasili Mitrokhin, *The Mitrokhin Archive II*, p. 432.

30. Scott, *Tumbled House*, p. 82.

31. Author interview with John de St Jorre.

32. Daphne Park invited former ambassador, Ian Scott and his wife Drusilla to attend her investiture as her personal guests in the House of Lords (Barbara Harvey to author).

33. British Foreign Office, Africa Department, National Archives FO 371/146650.

34. British Foreign Office, Africa Department, National Archives FO 371/146650.

35. 'The [Church] committee also revealed that the CIA had a unit called Executive Action, which was in charge of planning to bump off foreign leaders, and something called the "Health Alteration Committee," the purpose of which was exactly what its name stated' (David Wise, 'No License To Kill', *New York Newsday*, 22 October 1989).

36. Church Committee, p. 19.

37. Howard Imbrey interviewed by Charles Stuart Kennedy.

38. BBC Monitoring Report to the FO London, 5 October 1960 (UK National Archives).

39. Daphne Park speaking on BBC Television's *Panorama*, 1994.

40. 'There was absolutely no effort of coordination. I was aware from various conversations, from various reports coming from Belgium, of what the objective was. For example, André Lahaye and I had never met until I went to the Congo ... Later we met when I went in to see Nendaka when he took up his position of chief of security, and it was Andre who said to me "you have so many things to do, don't worry about what's happening here, I'll keep you advised. You don't need to establish direct contact with Nendaka, I'll keep you advised." I thanked him, but I didn't put myself in the position of having a filter' (Larry Devlin, The Congo Crisis, 1960-1961: A Critical Oral History Conference (2004), pp. 154-5).

41. 'We certainly knew a number of the Belgians and cooperated with them although our programs were different' (Howard Imbrey interviewed by Charles Stuart Kennedy).

42. De Witte, *The Assassination of Lumumba*, p. 25.

43. Telegram No 1009 Scott to FO London, 5 November 1960 (UK National Archives).

44. Church Committee, p. 48.

45. Scott, *Tumbled House*, p. 104.

46. Ibid., pp. 99-100.

47. Victor Nendaka was certainly in the pay of the CIA. It is probable he was also in receipt of SIS largesse. In 1962 Hilary la Fontaine was flown to Kinshasa (formerly Léopoldville) to join her sister Jean and her husband John Sackur (SIS) to help with a research project. Some months later La Fontaine found herself on the same aircraft, but this time chartered for the use of Nendaka, then director-general of the Congolese Sûreté. It was, she discovered, being used to ferry some crates of gold bars. Later she was invited to apply for entry to SIS and enjoyed a very successful career in the Service both as an operational intelligence officer and as a senior manager.

48. De Witte, *The Assassination of Lumumba*, pp. 97-124.

49. Jean Omasombo, Professor at UNIKIN [Kinshasa University], then residing in Brussels as full time researcher at the Royal Museum for Central Africa in Tervuren, extract from The Congo Crisis, 1960-1961: A Critical Oral History Conference (2004), p. 152.

50. De Witte, *The Assassination of Lumumba*, p. 159.

51. Devlin, *Chief of Station*, p. 132.

Chapter 18

1. 'World Briefing Europe: Belgium: Apology for Lumumba Killing', *New York Times*, 6 February 2002: 'The [Belgian] government expressed "its profound and sincere regrets and its apologies" yesterday for Belgium's role in the assassination of Patrice Lumumba, the first Prime Minister of its former colony Congo, in 1961. "Some members of the government, and some Belgian actors at the time, bear an irrefutable part of the responsibility for the events that led to Patrice Lumumba's death," Foreign Minister Louis Michel told Parliament. He announced the creation of a $3.25 million fund in Mr. Lumumba's name to promote democracy in Congo, where the slain leader's son, François, leads an opposition party. Mr. Lumumba, a socialist who was a major figure in Congo's liberation from 75 years of Belgian rule, was overthrown after just a few months in office. He was killed, at the age of 35, while in detention. A Belgian commission that finished a two-year inquiry last year heard testimony that the assassination could not have been carried out without the complicity of Belgian officers backed by the C.I.A., and it concluded that Belgium had a moral responsibility for the killing. The C.I.A. has consistently denied responsibility.'

2. Bower, *The Perfect English Spy*, p. 223.

3. Report by John Bruce Lockhart on visit to 'Black Africa', 16 December 1959, PREM 11/2585, p. 3 (UK National Archives).

4. Author interview with John de St Jorre.

5. Bower, *The Perfect English Spy*, p. 223.

6. Ibid., p. 224.

7. Report by John Bruce Lockhart on visit to 'Black Africa', 16 December 1959, PREM 11/2585, p. 3 (UK National Archives).

8. Bower, *The Perfect English Spy*, p. 222.

9. Church Committee, p. 43.

10. O'Donnell had form in this regard. In the 1950s while he was COS/THE HAGUE he tangled with James Angleton over Angleton's refusal to use Station communications for reporting back on a secret assignment to the Netherlands, insisting on using his own personal code, a one-time pad secreted in his belt. O'Donnell won that battle, forcing Angleton to use the Station for his signals. O'Donnell was booted out of the Agency by Bissell in 1962 after the Bay of Pigs when he suggested at a CIA staff briefing that the architects of the fiasco should be 'thrown overboard' by the Agency. He ended his career in the Department of Defence.

11. Following convention, communications between the intelligence services of the US and those of other governments were not disclosed at the Church Committee hearings or subsequently.

Thus no direct information is available about contacts between the CIA and Belgian intelligence services in connection with the death of Lumumba.

12. Howard Imbrey interviewed by Charles Stuart Kennedy.
13. Church Committee, p. 39.
14. Ibid., p. 44.
15. Church Committee, p. 48.
16. Devlin, *Chief of Station, Congo*, p. 115.
17. Scott, *Tumbled House*, p. 100.
18. Ibid., p. 104.
19. Church Committee, p. 44.
20. In *Chief of Station, Congo* Devlin speaks of remaining on friendly terms with Nendaka up to his death in 2002.
21. Larry Devlin quoted in The Congo Crisis, 1960-1961: A Critical Oral History Conference (2004), p. 152.
22. Devlin, *Chief of Station, Congo*, p. 132.
23. Author interview with former SIS officer.
24. Ibid.
25. *London Review of Books,* vol. 35, no. 7, 11 April 2013, Letters.
26. Author interview with Jean Sackur.
27. *London Review of Books*, vol. 35, no. 11, 6 June 2013, Letters.
28. In *Tumbled House* Ian Scott maintains that his transfer was 'a routine matter' unconnected with any behind-the-scenes deal, while Devlin in *Chief of Station, Congo* claims the transfers were the results of a deal.
29. Author interview with John de St Jorre.
30. Author interview with Barbara Harvey, Vice-Principal emeritus, Somerville College, Oxford.
31. Author interview with Jean Sackur.
32. Corera, *The Art of Betrayal*, p. 3.

Chapter 19

1. John Griffith-Jones, prosecuting counsel at the *Lady Chatterley's Lover* trial in 1960 (1909-79).
2. In the British honours system OBEs are awarded for 'operational achievement', unlike many other decorations which tend to be awarded on achieving a specific rank, the 'ribbon going with the rations' so to speak. George Kennedy Young spoke of his MBE being the award 'he really sweated for' compared to the 'departmental handouts' of his later career.
3. Author interview with former SIS officer.
4. Author interview with Jean Sackur.
5. Author interview with former SIS officer.
6. Bower, *The Perfect English Spy*, p. 342.
7. Author interview with former SIS officer.
8. Bower, *The Perfect English Spy*, p. 343.
9. The Berlin Tunnel was a secret tunnel that crossed under the border between East and West Berlin where it tapped into hundreds of Soviet communication cables carrying messages between Soviet military and intelligence services in East Germany and Moscow. It was the ultimate irony that even though the KGB had learned of its existence they could not risk warning all of the Soviet units for fear of betraying the fact that Blake had turned. The KGB's own traffic was largely protected but overall the SIS/CIA intelligence take was of huge significance and justified the effort.
10. Author interview with former SIS officer.
11. Ibid.
12. Author interview with Jean Sackur.
13. Author interview with former SIS officer.
14. Nicholas Elliott in conversation with John Le Carré in Ben Macintyre's *A Spy Among Friends* (Bloomsbury, 2014), p. 293.

15. Author interview with former SIS officer.

16. Bower, *The Perfect English Spy*.

17. Trevor-Roper, *The Secret World*, pp. 206-7.

18. Andrew, *The Defence of the Realm*, p. 436. In an interview with the *Daily Telegraph* on 25 April 2014 Andrew told *Telegraph* journalist Neil Tweedie that the letter was signed by both White and Hollis.

19. Guy Liddell Diaries. In his diaries Liddell (post-war Deputy Director of MI5) refers to Hoover as 'a cross between a political gangster and a prima donna' (UK National Archives).

20. Tom Mangold, *Cold Warrior* (Touchstone, 1991), p. 245.

21. The treachery angle was not without its advocates and has its attractions; for a start it allows the blame for all mishaps to be laid on the 'traitors' and not where it probably belongs, on internal bungling or mishaps. Once the traitors are eradicated, the theory goes; everything in the garden will once again be rosy.

22. Bower, *The Perfect English Spy*, p. 339.

23. Author interview with former SIS officer.

24. Author interview with former SIS officer. In Christopher Andrew's *The Defence of the Realm* (Allen Lane, 2009) reference is made to a 'specially recruited surveillance team' (p. 507) but not to its composition.

25. Andrew, *The Defence of the Realm*, p. 504.

26. Peter Wright, *Spycatcher*, p. 170.

27. Bower, *The Perfect English Spy*, p. 328; according to Bower the MI5 members of FLUENCY were Patrick Stewart, Arthur Martin, Anne Orr-Ewing and Evelyn McBarnett. SIS was represented by Terence Lecky and Geoffrey Hinton, with others joining later.

28. Nigel West, *The Friends* (Weidenfeld & Nicolson, 1988), p. 152

29. Andrew, *The Defence of the Realm*, pp. 266-7.

30. Andrew, *The Defence of the Realm*, p. 265.

31. Wright, *Spycatcher*, p. 330.

32. Ibid., pp. 299-317.

33. Geoffrey Elliott and Harold Shukman, *Secret Classrooms* (St Ermin's Press, 2003), p. 3.

34. Macintyre, *A Spy Among Friends*, p. 268.

35. Wright, *Spycatcher*, p. 325.

36. Macintyre, *A Spy Among Friends*, p. 264.

37. Author interview with former SIS officer.

38. Ibid.

39. Ibid.

40. Author interview with former SIS officer.

41. Ibid.

42. Statement of Service in the British Foreign Office Diplomatic Directory.

43. Author interview with former SIS officer.

44. Author interview with former SIS officer, Julian Harston.

45. Author interview with former SIS officer.

Chapter 20

1. Author interview with Jean Sackur.

2. Calder Walton, *Empire of Secrets* (William Collins, 2014), p. 267.

3. John Sackur resigned from SIS in 1969. He was approached by the *Sunday Times* 'Insight' team and reportedly offered a job by them if he would cooperate in a series about Kim Philby which they were researching. SIS refused permission and Sackur instead became a successful management consultant. He and Jean Sackur later divorced.

4. Colonel Oleg Penkovsky was a senior officer in the Soviet's military intelligence service, the GRU, specialising in rocketry. In 1960 he approached first the CIA, then SIS, and offered to spy for them. His Moscow handlers were a visiting British businessman, Greville Wynne, and Janet

Chisholm, the wife of the SIS station head. Chisholm, as the wife of a known SIS officer, came under occasional surveillance by KGB counterintelligence officers. The surveillance team saw her making suspicious contact with an unknown Soviet 'citizen'. The citizen was eventually identified as Penkovsky. He was arrested, tried and executed. Wynne was on a trade mission to Budapest when Penkovsky was arrested. He too was taken into custody, transferred to Moscow, tried and sentenced to a term of imprisonment in the gulag, being swapped after six years for a Russian spy imprisoned in Britain. Penkovsky's material proved of inestimable value to the West particularly during the Cuban missile crisis of 1962.

5. Author interview with former SIS officer.

6. Warner, Memorial Address, Daphne Park Memorial Tributes, p. 23.

7. Bower, *The Perfect English Spy*, p. 346.

8. UK National Archives DO 183/480s18, quoted in Calder Walton, *Empire of Secrets*, p. 283.

9. Leon Comber, *Malaya's Secret Police 1945-60: The Role of the Special Branch* (Institute of South East Asian Studies, 2008), p. 203.

10. Author interview with former SIS officer.

11. Warner, Memorial Address, Daphne Park Memorial Tributes, p. 24.

12. Bower, *The Perfect English Spy*, p. 342.

13. Jonathan Bloch and Patrick Fitzgerald, *British Intelligence & Covert Action* (Brandon, Ireland/Junction, London, 1983), p. 151.

14. Ibid.

15. Simon Kear, 'The British Consulate-General in Hanoi, 1954-73', *Diplomacy & Statecraft* 10:1 (1999), 215-39 at p. 223.

16. Warner, Memorial Address, Daphne Park Memorial Tributes, p. 23.

17. Author interview with David Owen (Lord Owen), former Foreign Secretary.

18. Author interview with Daphne Park.

19. Address by Park to the Royal Society of Literature, May 2008.

20. There were two main externally-based nationalist/guerrilla forces, nominally united under the banner of the Patriotic Front opposing the Rhodesian UDI regime. The larger, the party of the Shona 85% majority of the population, was led by Robert Mugabe, widely considered to be Marxist in his orientation. This was the Zimbabwe African National Union (ZANU), with a military wing, the Zimbabwe African National Liberation Army (ZANLA). The second group was the Zimbabwe African Peoples Union (ZAPU), led by Joshua Nkomo, the party of the 15% Ndebele population. Its military wing was the Zimbabwe People's Revolutionary Army (ZPRA). It was ZPRA which began the liberation war in earnest in 1972. Britain did not recognise this guerrilla war as legitimate.

21. Address by Park to the Royal Society of Literature, May 2008.

Chapter 21

1. Defections from the US by alleged homosexuals were not unknown: two National Security Agency (NSA) cryptologists, William Martin and Bernon Mitchell, defected to the Soviet Union in 1960. A secret 1963 NSA study later said that 'Beyond any doubt, no other event has had, or is likely to have in the future, a greater impact on the Agency's security program.' Edward Snowden turned that forecast on its head.

2. Author interview with friend of Corbally.

3. Archie Roosevelt, *For Lust of Knowing: Memoirs of an Intelligence Officer* (Weidenfeld & Nicolson, 1988), pp. 469-70.

4. At one point the US ambassador, Bruce, was questioned as to whether he had any involvement with the Profumo set. He denied it indignantly but later shamefacedly admitted that Ward had indeed called at his home to draw a sketch of him (Archie Roosevelt, *For Lust of Knowing*, p. 470).

5. Author interview with friend of Corbally.

6. Attributed to Peter Wright.

7. Some writers claim that the device used to secure the retirements of the robber barons was reducing the retirement age in SIS to fifty-five (*The Perfect English Spy*, p. 347). This author's sources indicate that that retirement age had already been introduced, for new entrants certainly, by the late 1950s.

8. Davies, *MI6 and the Machinery of Spying*, p. 270.

9. Ibid., p. 275.

10. Author interview with former SIS officer.

11. Ibid.

12. Ibid.

13. McCarthy, *Women of the World*, p. 239.

14. Author interview with Jean Sackur.

15. Author interview with former security official. However, as with many aspects of SIS, where it suited the Service the rule was waived. In his book *The Greatest Betrayer* (Aurum Press, 2013) Roger Hermiston refers to a married couple serving in SIS at the time of George Blake's arrest in 1961. Of the two the woman was the more senior. He identifies them only as Mr & Mrs B.

16. Davies, 'A Chargé Recharged: A Profile of Miss Daphne Park CMG', p. 66.

17. Author conversation with Robin Dixon (Lord Glentoran).

Chapter 22

1. In evidence given to the Schuster Committee the work of a consul included ejecting inebriated British sailors from brothels and bars and adjudicating on homosexual 'incidents' at sea. These were tasks that made the positions 'unsuitable for women' (Helen McCarthy, *Women of the World*, p. 140). Whether Park was asked to do any such work during her consulships in Hanoi and Léopoldville is not recorded, but is unlikely to have fazed her in any event.

2. Kear, 'The British Consulate-General in Hanoi, 1954-73', p. 220.

3. Thomas J. Corcoran, political officer Saigon (1950-53) consul Hanoi (1954-55), interviewed for the Association for Diplomatic Studies and Training oral history project.

4. Ibid.

5. Kear, 'The British Consulate-General in Hanoi, 1954-73', p. 219.

6. Author interview with former foreign service officer.

7. SIS heads of station in Hanoi (H/HANOI) included: 1957 K.J. Simpson, CMG; 1960-62 J.F. Ford, CMG, OBE; 1964-65 Myles Ponsonby, CBE; 1966-67 John Colvin, CMG; 1967-68 Brian Stewart, CMG; 1969-70 Gordon Philo, CMG; 1969-70 Baroness Daphne Park, CMG, OBE; 1970-71 John Liudzius, OBE; 1971-72 Alan Prosser, MBE; 1973 Julian Harston.

8. Kear, 'The British Consulate-General in Hanoi, 1954-73', p. 224.

9. John Liudzius (consul-general and SIS station commander Hanoi) to Donald McD. Gordon (FCO), 28 August 1971 (UK National Archives).

10. The phrase is associated with the Christmas bombings of Hanoi in 1972. Called Operation LINEBACKER II, the bombing was of the same intensity as the bombing of the German cities in the Second World War, with fifteen thousand tons of ordnance dropped on Hanoi and the nearby port of Haiphong over the eleven-day Christmas period. The North was told it would be either 'bombed back to the negotiating table or into the Stone Age'. Negotiations resumed and led to the January 1973 'peace' agreement.

11. John Colvin (consul-general and SIS station commander Hanoi), *Twice Around the World* (Leo Cooper, 1991), p. 14.

12. The Tet (Vietnamese New Year) Offensive of 1968 caught both the American forces and the South Vietnamese napping and was a classic failure of intelligence. At one stage the US embassy in Saigon was overrun by Viet Cong guerrillas. While the offensive was defeated, its impact on the domestic US audience was enormous and it effectively signalled the beginning of the end for US involvement in Vietnam.

13. In 1966, John McNaughton, US Secretary of Defence for International Security Affairs, proposed the destruction of the thousands of miles of dikes, levees, dams and sluices that made up the Red River Valley system in order to flood rice paddies, disrupt the North Vietnamese food supply, and leverage Hanoi during negotiations. The then Secretary of Defence Robert McNamara, however, rejected the idea. President Richard Nixon (in favour) and Secretary of State Henry Kissinger (against) discussed bombing the dike network in a 1972 conversation on Operation LINEBACKER II (later leaked by Daniel Ellsberg). Had the dams been attacked the death toll would have been in excess of two hundred thousand (Kissinger estimated).

14. Colvin, *Twice Around the World*, p. 23.

15. William M. Leary, *CIA Air Operations in Laos, 1955-1974* (CIA Centre for the Study of Intelligence, Winter 1999/2000).

16. Ibid.

17. Author interview with former SIS officer.

18. Colvin, *Twice Around the World*, pp. 30-1.

19. Daphne Park, Valedictory Dispatch, 25 October 1970 (UK National Archives).

20. Author interview with former SIS officer, the late Hugo Herbert-Jones.

21. Daphne Park, Valedictory Dispatch.

Chapter 23

1. John Liudzius (consul-general and SIS station commander Hanoi) to Donald McD. Gordon (Saigon embassy), 28 August 1971 (UK National Archives). It is of note that the above dispatch was classified as 'CONFIDENTIAL & ECLIPSE'. Eclipse was the Foreign Office (and SIS) classification for material which is not to be disclosed to the United States (attributed to Richard Tomlinson).

2. Warner, Memorial Address, Daphne Park Memorial Tributes, p. 25.

3. Author interview with Julian Harston.

4. Author interview with former SIS officer.

5. John Liudzius (consul-general and SIS station commander Hanoi) to Donald McD. Gordon (Saigon embassy), 28 August 1971 (UK National Archives).

6. J.B. Wright (consul-general Hanoi) to W.R. Shakespeare (FCO), 11 October 1972 (UK National Archives).

7. Author interview with Julian Harston.

8. Daphne Park, Valedictory Dispatch.

9. Daphne Park to Donald McD. Gordon (FCO), 26 June 1970 (UK National Archives).

10. Daphne Park to Donald McD. Gordon (FCO) 26 June 1970 (UK National Archives).

11. Author interview with former SIS officer.

12. Note for file prepared by Mr Everard (Foreign Office), October 1972 (UK National Archives).

13. Author interview with former SIS officer.

14. John Liudzius to Donald McD. Gordon (FCO) 28 August 1971 (UK National Archives).

15. Colvin, *Twice Around the World*, p. 15.

16. John Liudzius to Donald McD. Gordon (FCO) 28 August 1971 (UK National Archives).

17. Ibid.

18. Warner, Memorial Address, Daphne Park Memorial Tributes, p. 25.

19. Ibid.

20. Author interview with Julian Harston.

21. Daphne Park, Valedictory Dispatch.

22. Author interview with Julian Harston.

23. Rachel Sylvester, 'A licence to kill? Oh heavens no', *Daily Telegraph*, 24 April 2003.

24. Kear, 'The British Consulate-General in Hanoi, 1954-73', p. 234.

25. John Liudzius to Donald McD. Gordon (FCO), 28 August 1971 (UK National Archives).

26. J.B. Wright to C.W. Squire (FCO London), 21 September 1972 (UK National Archives).

27. Rachel Sylvester and Alice Thomson, 'More Miss Marple than 007: the true face of British espionage', *Daily Telegraph*, 16 August 2008. Ms Sylvester had interviewed Park previously for the *Daily Telegraph* in 2003.

28. Confirmed by Rachel Sylvester, 1 May 2014.

29. Author interview with Julian Harston.

30. Ibid.

31. Ted Shackley (with Richard A. Finney), *Spymaster: My Life in the CIA* (Potomac Books, 2005), p. 9.

32. Park interview with Martyn Cox.

33. Golf was indirectly responsible for Andrew Fulton joining SIS. He had graduated in Law from Glasgow University and was set on a career in the profession when one afternoon he was approached by an acquaintance of his father in the club bar after a round of golf. The acquaintance asked Fulton about his career plans. Fulton replied that he was considering going the route towards becoming a QC. 'Have you ever thought about the foreign service?' the acquaintance asked. Fulton replied that he hadn't but that it sounded interesting. 'Leave it with me,' the man replied. Nine months later (after due process) Fulton was on his way to Saigon to commence his first posting as a junior SIS officer.

34. Author interview with SIS officer.

35. Daphne Park to Donald McD. Gordon (FCO) 26 June 1970 (UK National Archives).

36. Author interview with former SIS officer.

37. Park obituary, *Guardian*, 28 March 2010.

38. Park obituary, *Daily Telegraph*, 25 March 2010.

39. J.B. Wright to C.W. Squire (FCO London), 21 September 1972 (UK National Archives).

40. Former consul-general quoted by Simon Kear in 'The British Consulate-General in Hanoi, 1954-73', p. 221.

41. Daphne Park, Valedictory Dispatch.

42. Daphne Park, Valedictory Dispatch.

43. Commentary by D. McD. Gordon (FCO) on D. Park's Valedictory Dispatch, 10 December 1970 (UK National Archives).

44. Observation by Sir S. Tomlinson (FCO) on D. Park's Valedictory Dispatch, 14 December 1970 (UK National Archives).

Chapter 24

1. *Times* obituary, 26 March 2010.

2. The John Addis story about Park is contained in the *Guardian*'s obituary of Daphne Park.

3. John Colvin to Richard Evans (FCO London), 5 July 1972 (FCO 21/1078, UK National Archives).

4. Author interview with former official.

5. Address by Park to the Royal Society of Literature, May 2008, in answer to a question from a member of the audience

6. Caroline Alexander, 'A Profile of Daphne Park', p. 68.

7. Daphne Park to Richard Evans (FCO London) 11 May 1972 (FCO 21/1079, UK National Archives).

8. Daphne Park to Richard Evans (FCO London), 11 May 1972 (FCO 21/1079, UK National Archives)

9. Author interview with former SIS officer.

10. The Hoover Institution, based on the campus of Stanford University in California, has been used as cover for recruitment pitches directed at 'interesting' students attending programs in Stanford, particularly those in the 'executive education' category (source: recipient of such an approach).

11. Author interview with former FCO head of personnel.

Chapter 25

1. Author interview with former SIS officer.
2. Philip H.J. Davies, *MI6 and the Machinery of Spying*, p. 289.
3. Author interview with Hugh Bicheno.
4. Warner, Memorial Address, Daphne Park Memorial Tributes, p. 25.
5. Author interview with former SIS officer.
6. Ibid.
7. The Americas (including South and Central America) is now a core operating region for SIS and it has stations in the following locations: Argentina – Buenos Aires; Bolivia – La Paz; Brazil – Brasilia, Rio de Janeiro; Canada – Ottawa (SIS area coordination office); Chile – Santiago; Colombia – Bogota; Costa Rica – San Jose; Cuba – Havana; El Salvador – San Salvador; Falkland Islands – Stanley; Guatemala – Guatemala City; Guyana – Georgetown; Jamaica – Kingston; Mexico – Mexico City; Peru – Lima; Uruguay – Montevideo; US – Washington DC (SIS area coordination office), New York (UN); Venezuela – Caracas.
8. Author interview with Hugh Bicheno.
9. Davies, *MI6 and the Machinery of Spying*, p. 282.
10. Author interview with Hugh Bicheno.
11. Author interview with former SIS officer.
12. Author interview with Hugh Bicheno.
13. Shackley, *Spymaster*, p. 274.
14. Andrew and Mitrokhin, *The Mitrokhin Archive II*, p. 518 n. 8.
15. Ibid., p. 49.
16. David Leigh, 'The spy who loved me', interview with Anthea Temple (pseudonym), *Guardian*, 2 October 2002.
17. Andrew and Mitrokhin, *The Mitrokhin Archive II*, p. 91.
18. Ibid.
19. Ibid.
20. Colvin, *Twice Around the World* , p. 57.
21. Author interview with Julian Harston.
22. Author interview with former SIS officer.
23. David Owen, *Time to Declare* (Michael Joseph, 1991), p. 349.
24. Author interview with Peter Jay, former British ambassador to Washington.
25. Owen, *Time to Declare*, p. 350.
26. Hugh Bicheno, *Razor's Edge* (Orion/Phoenix, 2007), p. 25.
27. Author interview with Hugh Bicheno.
28. Author interview with former SIS officer.
29. Ibid.
30. Owen, *Time to Declare*, p. 350.
31. Warner, Memorial Address, Daphne Park Memorial Tributes, p. 25.
32. Author interview with former SIS officer.
33. Ibid.
34. Ibid.
35. Ibid.
36. Kevin Kelly, *The Longest War, Northern Ireland and the IRA* (Bandon Ireland, 1982), p. 277.
37. Author interview with former SIS officer.
38. An admission made by a senior (named) CIA officer to his opposite number in SIS on the occasion of his retirement (source: former SIS officer).
39. Author interview with former SIS officer.
40. Philip Agee and Louis Wolf (eds), *Dirty Work: The CIA in Western Europe* (Zed Press, 1981), p. 109.

41. Ibid., p. 112.
42. Author interview with former SIS officer.
43. Andrew and Mitrokhin, *The Sword and the Shield*, p. 369.
44. Ibid., p. 369.
45. Agee and Wolf, *Dirty Work*, p. 73.
46. Interview with Italian journalist Oriana Fallacci in 1975, quoted in *The Mitrokhin Archive*, p. 284.
47. Author interview with former Foreign Office official, Sir Stephen Wall.
48. In 1985 James Callaghan, the former Prime Minister, came to Dublin at the invitation of the Digital Equipment Corporation (DEC) to address a conference hosted by the company. The author organised the visit and 'minded' Mr Callaghan for the duration of his overnight stay. The author spent a number of hours in Mr Callaghan's company during which he volunteered the story about Portugal's communist inspired revolution and his part in countering it.
49. PREM 16/1053/1 Prime Minister's Office; PORTUGAL; Security Situation in Portugal, September 1975; Closed for forty years. PREM 16/1158 Dr Henry Kissinger's letter of January 1976 is 'missing' (UK National Archives).
50. Author interview with James Callaghan.

Chapter 26

1. Warner, Memorial Address, Daphne Park Memorial Tributes, p. 24.
2. PREM 19/111 31 August-11 September 1979 Part 6 (Thatcher Foundation).
3. Ibid.
4. Author interview with Julian Harston.
5. Author interview with Stephen Wall.
6. Stephan Wall interviewed by Thomas Raineau (Université de Paris-Sorbonne) as part of the British Diplomatic Oral History Programme (BDOHP), December 2010 and February 2012.
7. Author interview with Julian Harston.
8. Author interview with David Owen.
9. Author interview with David Owen.
10. Author interview with Julian Harston.
11. Ibid.
12. Owen, *Time to Declare*, p. 314.
13. Author interview with David Owen.
14. Author interview with Stephen Wall.
15. Author interview with Julian Harston.
16. Ibid.
17. Author interview with David Owen.
18. Ibid.
19. Author interview with Stephen Wall.
20. Author interview with Julian Harston.
21. RMJ Lynne (private secretary to foreign secretary Lord Peter Carrington) to Margaret Thatcher, 5 September 1979 PREM19/111 f.109 (Thatcher Foundation).
22. Secret CX from Daphne Park on her meeting with Kenneth Kaunda of the 27 August 1979. PREM19/110 f32 (Thatcher Foundation).
23. Ibid.
24. Ibid.
25. R.M.J. Lynne to Margaret Thatcher, 5 September 1979. PREM19/111 f.109 (Thatcher Foundation).

Chapter 27

1. Author interview with Jean Sackur.
2. Harvey, Funeral Address, Daphne Park Memrial Tributes, p. 8.
3. Author interview with Barbara Harvey.
4. Davies, 'A Chargé Recharged: A Profile of Miss Daphne Park CMG', p. 67.
5. Ibid.
6. Author interview with Dr Alice Prochaska.
7. Author interview with Barbara Harvey.
8. Ibid.
9. Author interview with Dr Mai Yamani.
10. Author interview with Dr Mai Yamani.
11. Author interview with Dr Alice Prochaska.
12. Bloch and Fitzgerald, *British Intelligence & Covert Action*, p. 270. This is the first published reference to Park's role as a spy of which this author is aware, though the book does not cite its source other than listing Park under the heading of 'controversial'.
13. Author interview with Barbara Harvey.
14. Thatcher to Park, 14 February 1983 (Thatcher Archive).
15. Professor Anna Morpurgo Davies, Daphne Park Memorial Tributes, p. 44.
16. Ibid., p. 43.
17. Ibid., pp. 41-2.
18. Author interview with Dr Mai Yamani.
19. Author interview with Barbara Harvey.

Chapter 28

1. Alasdair Milne, *DG: the Memoirs of a British Broadcaster* (Hodder & Stoughton, 1989). p. 143.
2. Ibid., p. 148.
3. Ibid., p. 202.
4. Ibid., p. 186.
5. Ibid., pp. 194, 201.
6. Nick Davies, *Observer*, 25 August 1987.
7. David Leigh and Paul Lashmar, *Observer*, 18 August 1987.
8. Nick Davies, *Observer*, 25 August 1987.
9. BBC Radio 4, *Document,* 4 March 2013; in a comment (*The Times*, 5 March 2013), Jean Seaton, the BBC's official historian, said the decision to assist SIS was 'certainly plausible BBC style'.
10. Harvey, Funeral Address, Daphne Park Memorial Tributes, p. 9.
11. Author interview with Barbara Harvey.
12. Ibid.
13. Author interview with historian Steven Kippax.
14. Author interview with Dr John Lehman.
15. Ibid.
16. Author interview with Dr Paul Bew.
17. Daphne Park to Lord Geoffrey Tordoff (recounted to the author).
18. Author interview with former SIS officer.
19. Author interview with Barbara Harvey.
20. Daphne Park to former SIS officer (recounted to author).
21. Park obituary, *Guardian*, March 2010.
22. Corera, *The Art of Betrayal*, p. 100.
23. Author interview with former SIS officer.
24. Author interview with John de St Jorre.
25. Allen, Memorial Address, Daphne Park Memorial Tributes, p. 28.
26. Author interview with Dr Mai Yamani.
27. Author interview with former RUC Detective Superintendent Bill Duff.

28. Caroline Alexander, 'A Profile of Daphne Park', p. 63.
29. Author interview with Jean Sackur.
30. Caroline Alexander, 'A Profile of Daphne Park', p. 71.
31. Author interview with Jean Sackur.
32. Warner, Memorial Address, Daphne Park Memorial Tributes, p. 26.

Select Bibliography

Aburish, Saïd K., *Beirut Spy* (Bloomsbury, 1989).

Agee, Philip and Louis Wolf (eds), *Dirty Work: The CIA in Western Europe* (Zed Press, 1981).

Charles R. Ahern, 'The YO-YO Story: An Electronics Analysis Case History', *Studies in Intelligence* 5/4 (Winter 1961).

Alcorn, Robert Hayden, *No Bugles for Spies* (David McKay Co, 1962).

Aldrich, Richard J., Gary D. Rawnsley and Ming-Yeh Rawnsley, *The Clandestine Cold War in Asia 1945-65* (Frank Cass, 2000).

Altavila, Enrico, *The Art of Spying* (Robert Hale, 1968).

Andrew, Christopher, *Secret Service: The Making of the British Intelligence Community* (Heinemann, 1985).

Andrew, Christopher and Oleg Gordievsky, *KGB: The Inside Story of its Foreign Operations from Lenin to Gorbachev* (Hodder & Stoughton, 1990).

Andrew, Christopher and Oleg Gordievsky, *Instructions from the Centre* (Hodder & Stoughton, 1991).

Andrew, Christopher, *For the President's Eyes Only* (Harper Collins, 1995).

Andrew, Christopher and Vasili Mitrokhin, *The Sword and the Shield: The Mitrokhin Archive and the Secret History of the KGB* (Allen Lane, 1999).

Andrew, Christopher and Vasili Mitrokhin, *The Mitrokhin Archive II* (Allen Lane, 2005).

Andrew, Christopher, *The Defence of the Realm* (Allen Lane, 2009).

Ashley, Clarence, *CIA Spymaster* (Pelican Publishing Company, 2004).

Aubrey, Crispin, *Who's Watching You?* (Pelican/Penguin Books 1981).

Bagley, Tennent H., *Spy Wars* (Yale University Press, 2007).

Bailey, Roderick, *Forgotten Voices of the Secret War: An Inside History of Special Operations in the Second World War* (Ebury Press in association with the Imperial War Museum, 2008).

Bank, Aaron, *From OSS to Green Berets: The Birth of Special Forces* (Presidio Press, 1986).

Bearden, Milt and James Risen, *The Main Enemy: The CIA's Battle with the Soviet Union* (Century, 2003).

Bennett, Richard M., *Espionage: An Encyclopaedia of Spies and Secrets* (Virgin Books, 2002)

Bethell, Nicholas, *Spies and Other Secrets* (Viking, 1994).

Bicheno, Hugh, *Razor's Edge: The Unofficial History of the Falklands War* (Orion/Phoenix 2006).

Blake, George, *No Other Choice* (Jonathan Cape, 1990).

Bloch, Jonathan and Patrick Fitzgerald, *British Intelligence and Covert Action* (Brandon, Ireland/Junction, London, 1983).

Borovik, Genrikh, *The Philby Files* (Warner Books, 1995).

Bower, Tom, *The Perfect English Spy* (Heinemann, 1995).

Boyle, Andrew, *Climate of Treason: Five who Spied for Russia* (Hutchinson, 1979).

Brook-Shepherd, Gordon, *The Storm Birds: Soviet Post-War Defectors* (Weidenfeld & Nicolson, 1988).

Brown, Anthony Cave, *'C': The Secret Life of Sir Stewart Graham Menzies, Spymaster to Winston Churchill* (Macmillan, 1987).

Brown, Anthony Cave, *Treason in the Blood* (Houghton Mifflin, 1994).

Carl, Leo D., *The CIA Insider's Dictionary* (NIBC Press, 1996).

Cannicott, Capt. Stanley, *Journey of a Jed* (Special Forces Club/Imperial War Museum, undated).

Cavendish, Anthony, *Inside Intelligence* (Collins, 1990).

Cherkashin, Victor and Gregory Feifer, *Spy Handler* (Basic Books, 2005).

Cowley, Chris, *Guns, Lies and Spies* (Hamish Hamilton, 1992).

Clarridge, Duane R. (with Digby Diehl), *A Spy for All Seasons* (Scribner, 1997).

Colby, William, *Honourable Men: My Life in the CIA* (Hutchinson, 1978).

Collins, Tony, *Open Verdict* (Sphere, 1990).

Colvin, John, *Twice Around the World* (Leo Cooper, 1991).

Comber, Leon, *Malaya's Secret Police 1945-60: The Role of the Special Branch* (Institute of South East Asian Studies, 2008).

Copeland, Miles, *The Real Spy World* (Weidenfeld & Nicolson, 1974).

Corera, Gordon, *The Art of Betrayal* (Weidenfeld & Nicolson, 2011).

Crosby, Col. M.G.M. (Bing), *Irregular Soldier* (XB Publications, 1993).

Crozier, Brian (ed.), *The Grenada Documents* (Sherwood Press, 1987).

Crozier, Brian, *Free Agent* (Harper Collins, 1994).

Cunningham, Cyril, *Beaulieu: The Finishing School for Secret Agents* (Pen & Sword, 1998).

Davenport-Hines, Richard, *An English Affair: Sex, Class and Power in the Age of Profumo* (Harper Press, 2013).

Davies, Philip H.J., *MI6 and the Machinery of Spying* (Frank Cass, 2004).

de Marenches, Count and Christine Ockrent, *The Evil Empire* (Sidgwick & Jackson, 1988).

De Witte, Ludo, *The Assassination of Lumumba* (Verso, 2001).

Deriabin, Peter and Frank Gibney, *The Secret World* (Doubleday, 1959).

Deriabin, Peter and T.H. Bagley, *The KGB: Masters of the Soviet Union* (Robson Books, 1990).

Devlin, Larry, *Chief of Station, Congo: Fighting the Cold War in a Hot Zone* (Public Affairs Press, 2007).

Dorril, Stephen, *The Silent Conspiracy: Inside the Intelligence Services in the 1990s* (Heinemann, 1993).

Dorril, Stephen, *MI6: Fifty Years of Special Operations* (4th Estate, 2000).

Earley, Pete, *Confessions of a Spy: The Real Story of Aldrich Ames* (Hodder & Stoughton, 1997).

Elliott, Geoffrey, *I Spy: The Secret Life of a British Agent* (St Ermin's Press, 1998).

Elliott, Geoffrey and Harold Shukman, *Secret Classrooms* (St Ermin's Press, 2003).

Evans, Harold, *My Paper Chase* (Little Brown, 2009).

Funada-Classen, Sayaka, *The Origins of the War in Mozambique: A History of Unity and Division*, tr. Masako Osada (Ochanomizu Shobo Co, 2012). R

Farago, Ladislas, *The Game of the Foxes* (Pan Books, 1972).

Felix, Christopher, *The Spy and His Masters* (Secker & Warburg, 1963).

Ferreira, Hugo Gil, *Portugal's Revolution Ten Years On* (Cambridge University Press, 1986).

Foot, M.R.D., *SOE: The Special Operations Executive 1940-46* (BBC Books, 1984).

Gates, Robert M., *From the Shadows* (Simon & Schuster, 1996).

Garbler, Florence Fitzsimons, *CIA Wife* (Fithian Press, 1994).

Glees, Anthony, *The Secrets of the Service* (Jonathan Cape, 1987).

Goldsmith, John, *Accidental Agent* (Charles Scribner's Sons, 1971).

Gordievsky, Oleg, *Next Stop Execution* (Macmillan, 1995).

Graham, Bill, *Break-In: Inside the Soviet Trade Delegation* (The Bodley Head, 1987).

Grose, Peter, *Operation Rollback: America's Secret War Behind the Iron Curtain* (Houghton Mifflin, 2000).

Grose, Peter, *Gentleman Spy: The Life of Allen Dulles* (Houghton Mifflin, 1995).

Gubbins, Major-General Sir Colin McVean (reputed author), *SOE Secret Operations Manual* (c. 1940).

Gudgin, Peter, *Military Intelligence: The British Story* (Arms & Armour Press, 1989).

Gunther, John, *Inside Russia Today* (Hamish Hamilton, 1962).

Gup, Ted, *The Book of Honor: Covert Lives and Classified Deaths at the CIA* (Doubleday, 2000).

Havill, Adrian, *The Spy Who Stayed out in the Cold* (St Martin's Press, 2001).

Hayter, William, *The Kremlin and the Embassy* (Hodder & Stoughton, 1966).

Henderson, Simon, *Instant Empire* (Mercury House, 1991).

Hennessy, Peter, *Whitehall* (Free Press, 1989).

Hennessy, Peter, *The Prime Minister* (Penguin, 2000).

Hennessy, Peter, *The Secret State* (Allen Lane, 2002).

Hermiston, Roger, *The Greatest Betrayer* (Aurum Press, 2013).

Holloway, David, *Stalin and the Bomb* (Yale University Press, 1996).

Hollingsworth, Mark and Nick Fielding, *Defending the Realm: MI5 and the Shayler Affair* (Andre Deutsch, 1999).

Hughes, Matthew, *Fighting for White Rule in Africa: The Central African Federation, Katanga, and the Congo Crisis* (Hurst & Co, 2003).

Irwin, Lt Col. Will, *The Jedburghs* (Public Affairs, 2005).

Jeffery, Keith, *MI6: The History of the Secret Intelligence Service 1909-1949* (Bloomsbury, 2010).

Joffrin, Laurent, *All that I Have* (Arrow Books, 2005).

Johansson, G.D., *Spy Talk: The Language of Terror* (St Ambrose Press, 2002).

Kalugin, Oleg, *Spymaster: My Thirty-Two Years in Intelligence and Espionage against the West* (Smyth Gryphon, 1994; Basic Books 2009).

Kear, Simon, 'The British Consulate-general in Hanoi, 1954-73', *Diplomacy & Statecraft* 10:1 (1999).

King, Stella, *Jacqueline: Pioneer Heroine of the Resistance* (Arms & Armour Press, 1989).

Kiyonaga, Bina Cady, *My Spy: Memoir of a CIA Wife* (Perennial, 2000).

Knightly, Philip, *The Second Oldest Profession* (Andre Deutsch, 1986).

La Fontaine, J.S., *City Politics: A Study of Léopoldville 1962-63* (Cambridge University Press, 1970).

Leary, William M., *CIA Air Operations in Laos, 1955-1974* (Central Intelligence Agency, 1999/2000).

Leigh, David (with Richard Norton-Taylor), *Betrayed: The Real Story of the Matrix Churchill Trial* (Bloomsbury, 1993).

Leigh, David, *The Wilson Plot* (Pantheon Books, 1988).

Lotz, Wolfgang, *A Handbook for Spies* (Harper & Row, 1980).

Mangold, Tom, *Cold Warrior: James Jesus Angleton, the CIA's Master Spy Hunter* (Touchstone, 1991).

Marchetti, Victor and John D. Marks, *The CIA and the Cult of Intelligence* (Jonathan Cape, 1974).

Mannoni, O., *Prospero and Caliban: The Psychology of Colonisation* (Praeger, 1956).

Marks, Leo, *Between Silk and Cyanide* (Harper Collins, 1999).

Masters, Anthony, *The Man who was M* (Basil Blackwell, 1984).

McCarthy, Helen, *Women of the World: The Rise of the Female Diplomat* (Bloomsbury, 2014).

McGehee, Ralph W., *Deadly Deceits: My 25 Years in the CIA* (Sheridan Square Publications, 1983).

McMahon, Paul, *British Spies and Irish Rebels: British Intelligence and Ireland, 1916-1945* (Boydell Press, 2008).

Mbogoni, Lawrence E.Y., *Aspects of Colonial Tanzania History* (Mkuki na Nyota, 2013).

Meehan, Patrick, *Framed by MI5* (Badger Moon, 1989).

Mendez, Antonio and Jonna, *Spy Dust* (Atria Books, 2002).

Mendez, Antonio J., *The Master of Disguise: My Secret Life in the CIA* (William Morrow & Co., 1999).

Miller, David, *The Cold War: A Military History* (Pimlico, 2001).

Miller, Joan, *One Girl's War: Personal Exploits in MI5's Most Secret Station* (Brandon, 1986).

Milne, Alasdair, *DG: The Memoirs of a British Broadcaster* (Hodder & Stoughton, 1989).

Milne, Tim, *Kim Philby: The Unknown Story of the KGB's Master Spy* (Biteback Publishing, 2014).

Minnery, John, *CIA: Catalog of Clandestine Weapons, Tools and Gadgets* (Paladin Press, 1990).

Mitrokhin, Vasily, *KGB Lexicon: The Soviet Intelligence Officer's Handbook* (Frank Cass, 2002).

Modin, Yuri, *My Five Cambridge Friends* (Headline, 1994).

Moorhouse, Geoffrey, *The Diplomats* (Jonathan Cape, 1977).

Morgan, Dr. William J., *Spies and Saboteurs* (Victor Gollancz, 1955).

Mulley, Clare, *The Spy Who Loved: The Secrets and Lives of Christine Granville* (Macmillan, 2012).

Murray, Gary, *Enemies of the State* (Simon & Schuster, 1993).

Murphy, D.E., S.A. Kondrashev and G. Bailey, *Battleground Berlin* (Yale University Press, 1999).

Ordway, Frederick I. and Mitchell R. Sharpe, *The Rocket Team* (Thomas Y. Crowell, 1979).

Ottaway, Susan, *Sisters, Secrets and Sacrifice* (Harper, 2013).

Owen, David, *Time to Declare* (Michael Joseph, 1991).

Parish, Daphne (with Pat Lancaster, Michelle de Vries), *Prisoner in Baghdad* (Chapmans, 1992).

Pedlow, Gregory W. and Donald E. Welzenbach, *The Central Intelligence Agency and Overhead Reconnaissance: The U-2 and Oxcart Programs* (Central Intelligence Agency, 1992).

Eleanor Philby, *Kim Philby: The Spy I Loved* (Pan Books, 1968).

Kim Philby, *My Silent War* (Grove Press, 1968).

Philby, Rufina (with Hayden Peake, Mikhail Lyubimov), *The Private Life of Kim Philby* (St Ermin's Press, 1999).

Pincher, Chapman, *Too Secret too Long* (Sidgwick & Jackson, 1984).

Pincher, Chapman, *Traitors: The Labyrinths of Treason* (Sidgwick & Jackson, 1987).

Porch, Douglas, *The French Secret Services: From the Dreyfuss Affair to the Gulf War* (Macmillan, 1996).

Ranelagh, John, *The Agency: The Rise and Decline of the CIA* (Weidenfeld & Nicolson, 1986).

Ranelagh, John, *CIA: A History* (BBC Books, 1992).

Read, Anthony and David Fisher, *Colonel Z: The Secret Life of a Master of Spies* (Hodder & Stoughton, 1984).

Richelson, Jeffrey T., *The US Intelligence Community* (Ballinger Publishing Co., 1985).

Richelson, Jeffrey T., *American Espionage and the Soviet Target* (Quill, 1987).

Richelson, Jeffrey T., *A Century of Spies* (Oxford University Press, 1995).

Rimington, Stella, *Open Secret* (Hutchinson, 2001).

Riols, Noreen, *The Secret Ministry of Ag. & Fish* (Macmillan, 2013).

Rosner, Maj. Elliot J., *The Jedburghs: Combat Operations Conducted in the Finistere Region of Brittany, France from July-September 1944* (US Army, 1976).

Roosevelt, Archie, *For Lust of Knowing: Memoirs of an Intelligence Officer* (Weidenfeld & Nicolson, 1988).

Rowan, Richard Wilmer, *The Story of Secret Service* (John Miles, 1938).

Sawatsky, John, *For Services Rendered: Leslie James Bennett and the RCMP Security Service* (Doubleday, 1982).

Seaman, Mark, *Bravest of the Brave* (Michael O'Mara Books, 1997).

Scott, Ian, *Tumbled House: The Congo at Independence* (Oxford University Press, 1969).N

Shackley, Ted (with Richard A. Finney), *Spymaster: My Life in the CIA* (Potomac Books, 2005).

Smith, Michael, *The Spying Game* (Politico's, 2004).

Slade, Ruth, *The Belgian Congo* (Oxford University Press, 1960).

Stafford, David, *Secret Agent: The True Story of the Special Operations Executive* (BBC Books, 2000).

Stone, I.F., *The Haunted Fifties* (Vintage Books, 1969).

Summers, Anthony and Stephen Dorril, *Honeytrap: The Secret Worlds of Stephen Ward* (Coronet Books, 1987).

Thomas, Evan, *The Very Best Men* (Touchstone Books, 1995).

Thomas, Gordon, *Secret Wars* (Thomas Dunne Books, 2009).

Samuel Tilman, 'Le scoutisme au Congo belge (1922-1960): une école de l'élite pour les jeunes indigènes' ['Scouting in the Belgian Congo (1922-1960): A School of the Elite for Indigenous Youth'], *Revue belge d'histoire contemporaine* (Brussels), vol. 28 (1998).

Tomlinson, Richard, *The Big Breach: From Top Secret to Maximum Security* (Cutting Edge Press, 2001).

Trevor-Roper, Hugh, *The Secret World: Behind the Curtain of British Intelligence in World War II and the Cold War* (I.B. Tauris, 2014).

Tully, Andrew, *Central Intelligence Agency* (Arthur Barker, 1962).

Turner, Stansfield, *Secrecy and Democracy: The CIA in Transition* (Sidgwick & Jackson 1986).

Urban, Mark, *UK Eyes Alpha: Inside British Intelligence* (Faber & Faber, 1996).

van Bilsen, A.A.J., *Un plan de trente ans pour l'emancipation politique de l'Afrique Belge* (extrait des Dossiers de l'Action Sociale Catholique, 1956).

Verrier, Anthony, *Through the Looking Glass* (Jonathan Cape, 1983).

Wallace, Robert and H. Keith Melton, *Spycraft* (Dutton, 2008).

Walton, Calder, *Empire of Secrets* (William Collins, 2014).

Weber, Ralph E. (ed.), *Spymasters: Ten CIA Officers in their Own Words* (Scholarly Resources, 1999).

Weindling, Paul, *John W. Thompson: Psychiatrist in the Shadow of the Holocaust* (University of Rochester Press, 2010).

West, Nigel, *A Matter of Trust: MI5 1945-72* (Weidenfeld & Nicolson, 1982).

West, Nigel, *MI5: British Security Service Operations, 1909-45* (Bodley Head, 1982).

West, Nigel, *MI6: British Secret Intelligence Service Operations, 1909-45* (Weidenfeld & Nicolson, 1983).

West, Nigel, *Unreliable Witness: Espionage Myths of the Second World War* (Weidenfeld & Nicolson, 1984).

West, Nigel, *The Friends: Britain's Post-War Secret Intelligence Operations* (Weidenfeld & Nicolson, 1988).

West, Nigel, *Games of Intelligence* (Weidenfeld & Nicolson, 1989).

West, Nigel, *The A to Z of British Intelligence* (Scarecrow Press, 2005).

Westerfield, H. Bradford (ed.), *Inside CIA's Private World* (Yale University Press, 1995).

Whittell, Giles, *Bridge of Spies* (Simon & Schuster, 2011).

Wilcox, Robert K., *Target Patton* (Regnery Publishing, 2008).

Williams, Susan, *Who Killed Hammarskjold?* (C. Hurst & Co., 2011).

Winek, Mark D., 'Radio as a Tool of the State: Radio Moscow and the Early Cold War', *Comparative Humanities Review*, vol. 3, article 9 (2009).

Wise, David and Thomas B. Ross, *The Invisible Government* (Random House, 1964).

Wise, David and Thomas B. Ross, *The Espionage Establishment* (Jonathan Cape,1968).

Wise, David, *The Spy Who Got Away* (Collins, 1988).

Wise, David, *Nightmover: How Aldrich Ames sold the CIA to the KGB for $4.6 million* (Harper Collins, 1995).

Wise, David, *The Bureau and the Mole: The Unmasking of Robert Hanssen* (Atlantic Books, 2002).

Womack, Helen, *Undercover Lives: Soviet Spies in the Cities of the World* (Weidenfeld & Nicolson, 1998).

Wright, Peter, *Spycatcher: The Candid Autobiography of a Senior Intelligence Officer* (Viking, 1987).

Wynne, Greville, *The Man from Moscow* (Arrow Books, 1981).

Wynne, Greville, *The Man from Odessa* (Granada, 1983).

Index